THE CIVIL WAR BATTLEFIELD GUIDE

THE CIVIL WAR
BATTLEFIELD
GUIDE

The Conservation Fund

Edited by Frances H. Kennedy

HOUGHTON MIFFLIN COMPANY

Boston

For information about permission to reproduce selections
from this book, write to Permissions, Houghton Mifflin Company,
215 Park Avenue South, New York, New York 10003.

Library of Congress Cataloging-in-Publication Data

The Civil War battlefield guide / edited by Frances H. Kennedy.
p.   cm.
"The Conservation Fund."
ISBN 0-395-52282-X
1. United States — History — Civil War, 1861–1865 — Battlefields —
Guide-books.   2. United States — History — Civil War, 1861–1865 —
Campaigns.   I. Kennedy, Frances H.   II. Conservation Fund
(Arlington, Va.)
E641.C58   1990   89-29619
973.7′3′025 — dc20   CIP

Printed in the United States of America

RNI 14 13 12 11 10 9 8 7 6 5

This book has been supported by a grant from
the National Endowment for the Humanities,
an independent federal agency.

Picture credits: *Harper's Pictorial History of the Civil War,* by Alfred H.
Guernsey and Henry M. Alden (Fairfax Press): pp. 19, 46, 96, 116, 135,
148, 156, 191, 195, 206, 214, 234, and 285; Museum of New Mexico
(negative no. 15782): p. 29; *The American Heritage Century Collection
of Civil War Art,* edited by Stephen W. Sears (New York: American Heritage, 1974): pp. 52, 145, 172, and 225; Library of Congress: pp. 69, 85,
102, and 263; Library of Congress Manuscript Division, Christian Fleetwood Papers: pp. 267 and 280; D. Coiner Rosen: p. 228; Virginia Military
Institute: p. 229; National Park Service: p. 297; maps on pp. xvi–xvii by
Jacques Chazaud.

Book typography by David Ford

THE CONSERVATION FUND

dedicates this book and its proceeds
to the protection of Civil War battlefields

The Conservation Fund requests your support
of its Civil War Battlefield Campaign.

The staff of The Conservation Fund will provide information,
in addition to that in this book,
about the status of Civil War battlefields
and significant historic areas, and welcomes the partnership
of citizen groups and public agencies in battlefield protection.

The Conservation Fund   1800 North Kent Street, Suite 1120   Arlington, Virginia 22209

CONTENTS

FOREWORD

The causes were complex — and distressingly simple — and the outcome was decisive. More than any other event in our nation's history, the Civil War set the direction for America's future. During the war, almost three million Americans fought across battlefields that had been quiet farms, dusty roads, and country crossroads. In the four years of courage and despair, these battlefields earned somber distinction as hallowed ground.

For over a hundred years, most of this hallowed ground was protected not by government but by private owners — often local farm families whose grandparents had seen the armies fight across their land for a few yards of stone fence, a vaulted bridge, or a wooded ridge line; families in which brothers and fathers had died at Manassas, Antietam, and Shiloh, in which uncles and cousins had manned both sides of the entrenchments at Atlanta, Richmond, and Petersburg.

But our nation is changing. What were once cornfields and woodlands have become shopping centers; the country lanes are crowded highways. After a century and a quarter, our hallowed ground is threatened with desecration. In many places farmers are being forced to sell their property for development. Generations of stewardship are in peril.

Of the fifty-eight battlefields included in this guide, more than half lack adequate protec-tion by public or private agencies. They are vulnerable in whole or in part to the pressures of commercial development. Research indi-cates that unless something is done within the next five years, most unprotected sites will be lost — a heritage gone forever.

The Conservation Fund was established to work with public and private partners to save land — open space, parkland, wildlife and waterfowl habitat, and important historic areas. Consequently, to protect our ties to the history of our nation, The Conservation Fund launched the Civil War Battlefield Campaign, a multiyear project aimed at protecting key Civil War sites. We have been successful in acquiring property at a number of critical areas, and by the time this guide is published we hope to have been able to protect additional land. But as a nonprofit organization, our re-sources are limited.

To enable us to increase our efforts before it is too late, The Conservation Fund is actively seeking donations from individuals, corpora-tions, and foundations for the Battlefield Campaign, to allow us to acquire and protect critical properties. I believe future generations will praise our foresight or curse our blind-ness.

Today you can stand at Antietam, at the edge of what is still a farm field, and visualize the waves of infantry, feel the urgency, capture for a moment the meaning of how that day changed our nation's history. The land is there as it was, and for a few minutes you are part of that terrible day, part of history. It is an unforgettable experience. In the years to come, generations of Americans will be able to share that experience. At the request of the National Park Service, The Conservation Fund purchased the cornfield at Antietam, site of the most intense fighting at that tragic battleground, as a gift to the nation to be added to the National Battlefield.

Through the Battlefield Campaign, we hope to help preserve that unique opportunity to be part of history, not just at Antietam but on land from Gettysburg to the Gulf, Glorieta to the Atlantic. Protecting these special places is not just our choice. It is our duty as a nation to the next generation. We feel that *The Civil War Battlefield Guide* will help increase public awareness of the need to safeguard our hallowed ground. We urge local governments and historic preservation and conservation orga-

nizations to join in the effort by working in partnership with each other, private landowners, the National Park Service, and The Conservation Fund to protect Civil War battlefields.

It has been said that the United States as we know it today began not with the Revolution of 1776 but rather in the new nation that emerged from the Civil War. That turbulent beginning happened in places that have since become names in history but then were fields of battle for thousands of Americans. Our goal is to continue the tradition of protection that private ownership established. Our legacy will be to do so in a way that will ensure that Americans of the coming century will know and understand the reasons for the Civil War. Our commitment must be to honor the unmatched valor of Americans of the past century, whose sacrifices built a new and stronger nation.

PATRICK F. NOONAN
President, The Conservation Fund

PREFACE

In our Civil War, we Americans failed to resolve our differences in accordance with the democratic processes established by the Founding Fathers. We made our basic decisions about the kind of nation we wanted to be, not through ballot boxes but on battlefields. Henry Adams wrote during the war, "The truth is, all depends on the progress of our armies." James M. McPherson writes in his essay in this book:

> Most of the things that we consider important in that era of American history — the fate of slavery, the structure of society in both North and South, the direction of the American economy, the destiny of competing nationalisms in North and South, the definition of freedom, the very survival of the United States — rested on the shoulders of those weary men in blue and gray who fought it out during four years of ferocity unmatched in the Western world between the Napoleonic wars and World War I.

This book urges you to go to the battlefields, to follow "the progress of our armies" as "those weary men in blue and gray" fought it out. On these battlefields we can come close to the fundamental truths for which they fought — fundamental to us as well as to them. President Abraham Lincoln, in dedicating the cemetery on the battlefield of Gettysburg four and a half months after the firing there had stopped, re-

called those dead soldiers. He challenged their survivors, who now include us, to go beyond a mere reverence for their sacrifice:

> It is for us, the living, rather to be dedicated here to the unfinished work which they who fought here have thus far so nobly advanced. It is rather for us to be here dedicated to the great task remaining before us — that from these honored dead we take increased devotion to that cause for which they gave the last full measure of devotion; that we here highly resolve that these dead shall not have died in vain; that this nation, under God, shall have a new birth of freedom; and that government of the people, by the people, for the people, shall not perish from the earth.

The very least we can do, together, is to dedicate ourselves through our private and public efforts to protect and preserve our Civil War battlefields. In these places we and those who come after us can be reminded of those who lived and died so that a "nation, conceived in liberty and dedicated to the proposition that all men are created equal," could endure.

This guidebook was written to increase visitors' understanding and to enhance the lessons the battlefields teach. It does not include all of the Civil War battlefields (see the list on pp. 291–294). Some are lost forever, covered with roads and buildings (see the list of lost battlefields on p. 295); since this is primarily a guide to battlefields rather than battles, the stories of those soldiers who fought and died on the lost battlefields go untold in these pages.

Moreover, since a guidebook that is intended to be portable and useful cannot be too large, we have had to omit some battlefields that are still in need of protection. They may be important to readers of this book, as some were to our advisers, but our choices have been made according to the consensus of those advisers. The reasons for some inclusions, perhaps surprising at first glance, will, we trust, emerge in the battle narratives.

The battles are presented in chronological order, with some adjustments for the simultaneity of actions taking place in different areas. Narratives of seven Civil War campaigns provide a context for the individual battles. Following each battle narrative are details of the battlefield's location and information on how much, if any, of it is protected by public agencies or nonprofit organizations. (When touring battlefields, please do not trespass on privately owned land. Even battlefields within the National Park System may include areas within the authorized boundaries that are privately owned and therefore not open to the public.) The number of acres of private and public land within the boundaries (as of 1989) are also given. The battlefield maps show the outer boundaries of publicly owned parks, but to avoid trespassing, consult the park authorities about the precise location of publicly owned land.

The maps for the seven campaigns are reproduced from those drawn during the war, now in the collections of the Library of Congress. The individual battlefield maps show the battle action on today's U.S. Geological Survey topographical maps. The scale and the orientation of the maps vary, depending on the size and shape of the battlefield, and are shown on each map. The battle action and the names of the officers are shown in blue for the United States and in red for the Confederacy.

The information in black includes historic as well as modern names and numbers of roads, highways, and railroads. The battle lines, as well as the advance and withdrawal arrows, show the general areas of the action, but they do not represent the exact numbers of soldiers in each unit engaged (such as a corps or a division). The combat strength and the battle casualties (the total number of soldiers killed, wounded, missing, and taken prisoner) are given on each map.

The most pleasant aspect of editing a book is recalling the kindness of those who helped make it a reality. The Conservation Fund is grateful to the authors who generously contributed their essays to this book and to Lawrence L. Sutphin, master cartographer, who drew the maps. We are grateful as well to the many Americans who gave their time and energy to help us produce this book. We intend it to be at once a guidebook that helps visitors learn what happened and where and a reference book that makes available the research of leading Civil War historians of our time. It is also a source of cartographic documentation of the crucial historic areas of significant Civil War battlefields, so that protection efforts can move ahead.

My personal thanks go, first of all, to my colleagues at The Conservation Fund, particularly the president, Patrick F. Noonan. The idea for this book was his. My thanks also go to Jack Lynn and Shannon Spencer for their generous help. I am grateful to the adviser to the Civil War Battlefield Campaign, T. Destry Jarvis; to the advisers to the book, Edwin C. Bearss, Edward C. Ezell, Gary W. Gallagher, Herbert M. Hart, James S. Hutchins, Jay Luvaas, Robert W. Meinhard, Michael Musick, and Joseph W. A. Whitehorne; to the historians whose careful reading of the manuscript made it more accurate and more interesting, particularly Edwin C. Bearss, Gary W. Gallagher, Richard M. McMurry, James I. Robertson, Jr., Richard J. Sommers, and Noah Andre Trudeau; to the historians at the Library of Congress, the National Archives, and the National Museum of American History for their encouragement and for their assistance in our research; and to Brian C. Pohanka for his help in photographic research and caption writing. I would also like to thank the editors at Houghton Mifflin, particularly Harry Foster, Liz Duvall, and Peg Anderson, whose wisdom and professional skill made this a much better book.

In addition, I express my boundless gratitude to the National Park Service. Director William Penn Mott, Jr., and his successor, Director James M. Ridenour, encouraged our research. The regional offices as well as the superintendents, rangers, and historians in the parks generously provided ideas and shared their research. The chief historian, Edwin C. Bearss, never hesitated to lengthen his working day to give us the benefit of his extraordinary knowledge of the Civil War. The National Park Service is a national treasure, to be honored by all Americans who care about our history as well as our natural areas. And very special thanks go to my husband, Roger Kennedy, who read and listened and was always interested. To the authors, whose essays will help us to learn about the past so that we can learn from it, I express my appreciation. In providing the details of battle tactics and strategy in their narratives, they have given life to those military terms while expanding our understanding of the Civil War and its meaning for us. Especially, I want to celebrate the union of our states and the abolition of slavery and to acknowledge with deep gratitude the men and women who fought and died during the Civil War.

FRANCES H. KENNEDY
Director, Civil War Battlefield Campaign
The Conservation Fund
July 1989

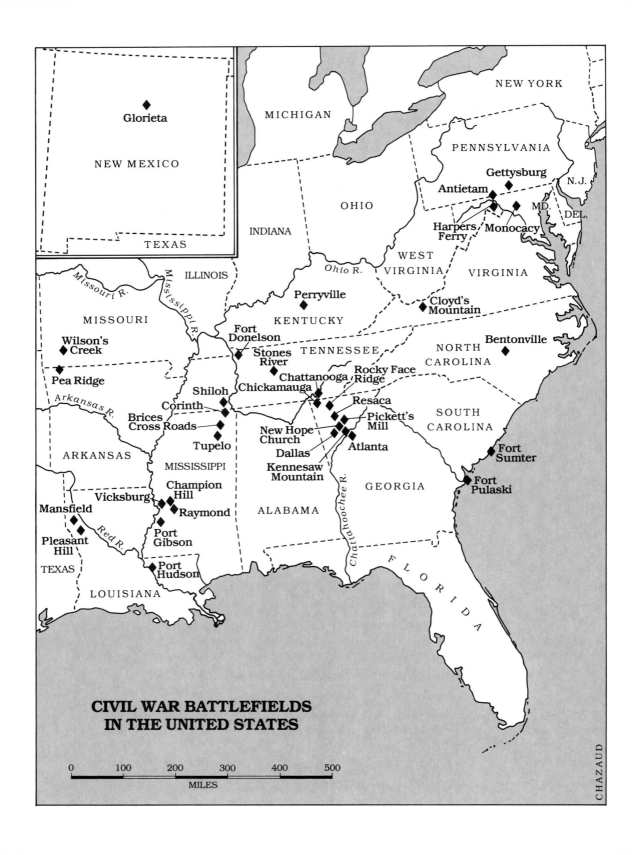

CIVIL WAR BATTLEFIELDS
IN THE UNITED STATES

NEW YORK

MICHIGAN

PENNSYLVANIA

Gettysburg

Antietam

N.J.

MD.

OHIO

Harpers
Ferry

Monocacy

DEL.

INDIANA

WEST
VIRGINIA

VIRGINIA

Ohio R.

ILLINOIS

Missouri R.

Mississippi R.

Perryville

Cloyd's
Mountain

MISSOURI

KENTUCKY

Wilson's
Creek

Fort
Donelson

TENNESSEE

NORTH
CAROLINA

Bentonville

Stones
River

Pea Ridge

Rocky Face
Ridge

Arkansas R.

Chattanooga

Chickamauga

Shiloh

Corinth

Resaca

SOUTH
CAROLINA

Brices
Cross Roads

Pickett's
Mill

Tupelo

New Hope
Church

Fort
Sumter

ARKANSAS

MISSISSIPPI

Dallas

Atlanta

Champion
Hill

Kennesaw
Mountain

Fort
Pulaski

Mansfield

Vicksburg

Raymond

ALABAMA

GEORGIA

Port
Gibson

Pleasant
Hill

Red R.

Chattahoochee R.

TEXAS

Port
Hudson

LOUISIANA

F L O R I D A

NEW MEXICO

Glorieta

TEXAS

0   100   200   300   400   500

MILES

CHAZAUD

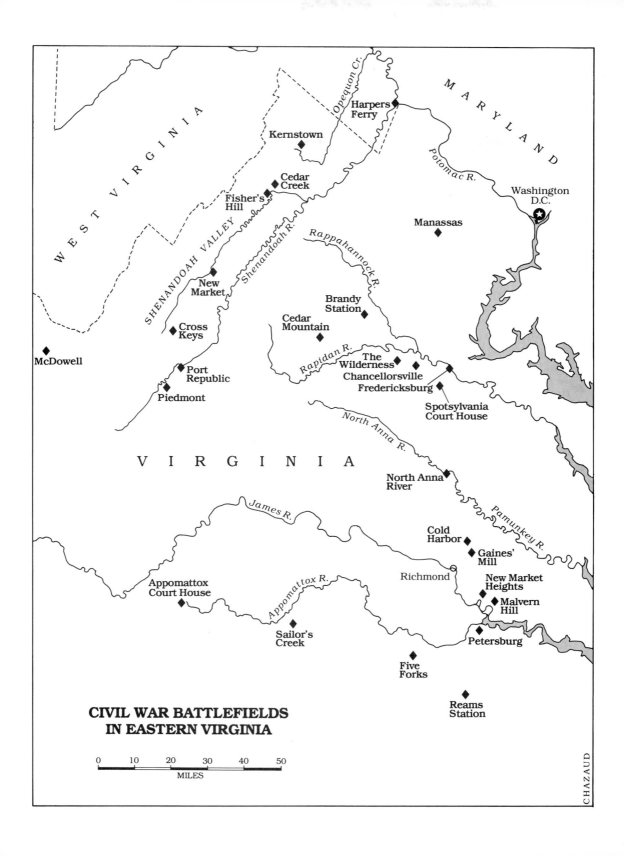

**CIVIL WAR BATTLEFIELDS
IN EASTERN VIRGINIA**

MILES

0   10   20   30   40   50

CHAZAUD

FORT SUMTER

12–14 April 1861

James M. McPherson

Built to protect Charleston from foreign invasion, Fort Sumter fired its guns only against Americans. This was just one of several ironies associated with this state-of-the-art masonry fort, which, as the Civil War with its rifled artillery was to demonstrate, was already obsolete when it was completed.

However, Sumter's most important role in the Civil War was not as a fort but as a symbol. By the time of Abraham Lincoln's inauguration as president on March 4, 1861, it was the most important piece of government property still held by United States forces in the seven states that had seceded to form the Confederate States of America. (The others were Fort Pickens, guarding the entrance to Pensacola harbor in Florida, and two minor forts on the Florida Keys.) For months national attention had centered on this huge pentagonal fortress controlling the entrance to Charleston's harbor. On the day after Christmas 1860, Major Robert Anderson had stealthily moved his garrison of 84 U.S. soldiers from ancient Fort Moultrie, adjacent to the mainland, to the five-foot-thick walls of Sumter, built on an artificial island in the middle of the channel entering Charleston Bay. He had done so to reduce his men's vulnerability to attack by the South Carolina militia, which was swarming around them in the wake of the state's secession six days earlier. A Kentuckian who was married

to a Georgian, Anderson deplored the possibility of war between North and South. Sympathetic to his region but loyal to the United States, he hoped that moving the garrison to Sumter would reduce tensions by lowering the possibility of attack. Instead, this action lit a slow fuse that exploded into war on April 12, 1861.

Southerners denounced Anderson's move as a violation of a presumed pledge by President James Buchanan not to violate the status quo in Charleston harbor. But northerners hailed Anderson as a hero. This stiffened the sagging determination of the Buchanan administration to maintain this symbol of national sovereignty in a "seceded" state, which the government and the northern people insisted had no constitutional right to secede. Maintaining that it *did* have such a right, South Carolina established artillery batteries around the harbor, pointing at Sumter. The national government decided to resupply and reinforce Anderson with 200 additional soldiers, to bring the garrison up to half the strength for which Fort Sumter had been designed. To minimize provocation, it chartered a civilian ship, *Star of the West*, instead of sending in a warship with the supplies and reinforcements. But the hotheaded Carolinians fired on *Star of the West* when it entered the harbor on January 9, 1861, forcing it to

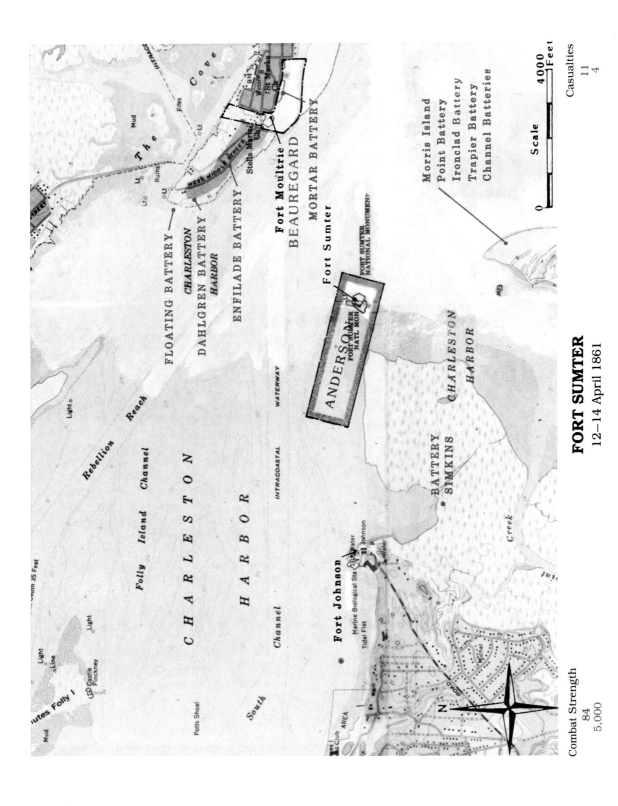

FORT SUMTER
12–14 April 1861

Morris Island
Point Battery
Ironclad Battery
Trapier Battery
Channel Batteries

Scale

0   4000
Feet

Casualties
11
4

Combat Strength
84
5,000

turn back and scurry out to sea. Lacking orders and loath to take responsibility for starting a war, Anderson did not return the fire. The guns of Sumter remained silent, and the United States remained at peace.

But this peace grew increasingly tense and fragile over the next three months. During that time six more southern states declared themselves out of the Union. As they seceded, they seized all federal property within their borders — arsenals, customhouses, mints, post offices, and forts — except Fort Sumter and the three other, less important forts. Delegates from the seven states met in Montgomery, Alabama, in February to adopt a constitution and create a government. Elected president of the new Confederate States of America, Jefferson Davis commissioned Pierre G. T. Beauregard as brigadier general and sent him to take command of the troops besieging the Union garrison at Fort Sumter. Meanwhile, all attempts by Congress and by a "peace convention" in Washington failed to come up with a compromise to restore the Union.

This was the situation that confronted Abraham Lincoln when he took the oath of office as the sixteenth — and, some speculated, the last — president of the United States. In the first draft of his inaugural address, he expressed an intention to use "all the powers at my disposal" to "reclaim the public property and places which have fallen: to hold, occupy, and possess these, and all other property and places belonging to the government." Some of Lincoln's associates regarded the threat to reclaim federal property as too belligerent; they persuaded him to modify the address to state an intention only to "hold, occupy, and possess" government property. This meant primarily Fort Sumter. All eyes now focused on that single acre of federal real estate in Charleston harbor. Both sides saw it as a powerful emblem of sovereignty. As long as the American flag flew over Sumter, the United States could maintain its claim to be the legal government of South Carolina and the other seceded states. From the southern viewpoint, the Confederacy could not be considered a viable nation as long as a "foreign" power held a fort in one of its principal harbors.

Lincoln had balanced his inaugural vow to "hold, occupy, and possess" this symbol with expressions of peaceful intent in other respects. The peroration appealed to southerners as Americans sharing four score and five years of national history. "We are not enemies, but friends," said Lincoln. "Though passion may have strained, it must not break, our bonds of affection. The mystic chords of memory, stretching from every battlefield and patriot grave to every living heart and hearthstone all over this broad land, will yet swell the chorus of the Union when again touched, as surely they will be, by the better angels of our nature."

Lincoln hoped to buy time with his inaugural address — time for southern passions to cool; time for Unionists in the upper southern states that had not seceded to consolidate their control; time for the Unionists presumed to be in the majority even in seceded states to gain the upper hand. For all of this to happen, though, the status quo at Fort Sumter had to be preserved. If either side moved to change that status quo by force, it would start a war and probably provoke at least four more states into secession.

The day after his inauguration, Lincoln learned that time was running out. Major Anderson warned that his supplies could not last more than six weeks. By then the garrison would have to be resupplied or evacuated. The first option would be viewed by most southerners as provocation; the second would be viewed by the North as surrender.

Lincoln thus faced the most crucial decision of his career at the very beginning of his presidency. General-in-Chief Winfield Scott advised him that it would take more military and naval power than the government then possessed to shoot its way into the harbor and reinforce Fort Sumter. Besides, this would put the onus of starting a war on the U.S. government. Secretary of State William H. Seward and a majority of the cabinet advised Lincoln to give up the fort in order to preserve the peace and prevent states in the upper South from joining their sister states in the Confederacy. But Montgomery Blair, Lincoln's postmaster general and a member of a powerful political family, insisted that this would be ruinous. It would constitute formal recognition of the Confederacy. It would mean the downfall of the Union, the end of a U.S. government with any claim of sovereignty over its constituent parts. Lincoln was inclined to agree. But what could he do about it? The press, political leaders of all factions, and the public showered reams of contradictory advice on the president. The pressure grew excruciating. Lincoln suffered sleepless nights and severe headaches; one morning he arose from bed and keeled over in a dead faint.

But amid the cacophony and the agony, Lincoln evolved a policy and made a decision. The key provision of his policy was to separate the question of reinforcement from that of resupply. The president decided to send in supplies but to hold troops and warships outside the harbor and authorize them to go into action only if the Confederates acted to stop the supply ships. And he would notify southern officials of his intentions. If Confederate artillery fired on the unarmed supply ships, the South would stand convicted of attacking "a mission of humanity," bringing "food for hungry men."

Lincoln's solution was a stroke of genius. It put the burden of deciding for peace or war on Jefferson Davis's shoulders. In effect, Lincoln flipped a coin and told Davis, "Heads I win; tails you lose." If Davis permitted the supplies to go in peacefully, the American flag would continue to fly over Fort Sumter. If he ordered Beauregard to stop them, the onus of starting a war would fall on the South.

Lincoln notified Governor Francis Pickens

Fort Sumter National Monument
© David Muench, 1990

of South Carolina on April 6, 1861, that "an attempt will be made to supply Fort Sumter with provisions only, and that if such attempt be not resisted, no effort to throw in men, arms, or ammunition will be made without further notice, [except] in case of an attack on the fort." In response, the Confederate cabinet decided at a fateful meeting in Montgomery to open fire on Fort Sumter and force its surrender before the relief fleet arrived, if possible. Only Secretary of State Robert Toombs opposed this decision. He reportedly told Davis that it "will lose us every friend at the North. You will wantonly strike a hornets' nest. . . . Legions now quiet will swarm out and sting us to death. It is unnecessary. It puts us in the wrong. It is fatal."

Toombs was right. At 4:30 A.M. on April 12, the batteries around Charleston harbor opened fire. After thirty-three hours in which five thousand rounds were fired (only one thousand by the undermanned fort), the American flag was lowered in surrender on April 14. The news outraged and galvanized the northern people in the same way in which the Japanese attack on Pearl Harbor eighty years later galvanized the American people. On April 15 Lincoln called out the militia to suppress "insurrection." Northern men flocked to the recruiting offices; southern men did the same, and four more states joined the Confederacy.

By the time the United States flag rose again over the rubble that had been Fort Sumter, on April 14, 1865, three million men had fought in the armies and navies of the Union and Confederacy. At least 620,000 of them had died — nearly as many as in all the other wars fought by this country combined. Most of the things that we consider important in that era of American history — the fate of slavery, the structure of society in both North and South, the direction of the American economy, the destiny of competing nationalisms in North and South, the definition of freedom, the very survival of the United States — rested on the shoulders of those weary men in blue and gray who fought it out during four years of ferocity unmatched in the Western world between the Napoleonic wars and World War I.

Fort Sumter National Monument is in Charleston harbor near Charleston, South Carolina. There are 197 acres within the authorized boundaries of this National Monument.

FIRST MANASSAS

21 July 1861

William Glenn Robertson

When the Civil War began in April 1861, most Americans expected the conflict to be brief, with one titanic battle deciding the outcome. The placement of the Confederate capital at Richmond, Virginia, a hundred miles from Washington, D.C., virtually guaranteed a clash somewhere between the two cities before the end of summer. Needing a buffer zone around Washington, Federal units in late May crossed the Potomac River and secured the heights of Arlington and the town of Alexandria. Engineers immediately began construction of an extensive line of fortifications to protect the capital. Equally important, the works would provide a secure base for offensive operations against Richmond. Since General-in-Chief Winfield Scott was too infirm to take the field in person, command of the army gathering behind the rising fortifications went to Brigadier General Irvin McDowell. Upstream, a smaller Federal force under Brigadier General Robert Patterson threatened Harpers Ferry.

South of Washington, Confederate troops withdrew to the line of Bull Run, where they shielded the important railroad center of Manassas Junction. In June, Brigadier General P. G. T. Beauregard, victor of Fort Sumter, took command of the Bull Run line, while a smaller force under Brigadier General Joseph E. Johnston guarded Harpers Ferry. Analyzing the terrain and the troop dispositions of both sides, Beauregard concluded that an advance against Manassas Junction was imminent. He also believed that the widely scattered Confederate units would be defeated unless he and Johnston consolidated their forces before the Federals could strike. Since he could get no assurance that Johnston would be ordered to Manassas, he began to strengthen his line. The Confederacy did not expect to mount an offensive, only to repulse any Federal thrust against Manassas Junction.

Beauregard's analysis of Federal intentions was essentially correct. McDowell was under pressure from the politicians, the press, and the public to begin an advance. Unsure of himself and his green troops, he begged unsuccessfully for more time to prepare his army. Ordered to advance before the end of July, he planned a three-pronged movement against the Confederates defending Manassas Junction. The plan required Patterson to prevent Johnston's units from joining Beauregard at Bull Run. By early July, Patterson's 18,000 troops had crossed the Potomac, seized Harpers Ferry, and pushed Johnston's 11,000 Confederates back to Winchester, Virginia. If Patterson could maintain the pressure on Johnston, McDowell's 39,000 troops would have a very good chance of defeating Beauregard's 21,000 men at Manassas Junction.

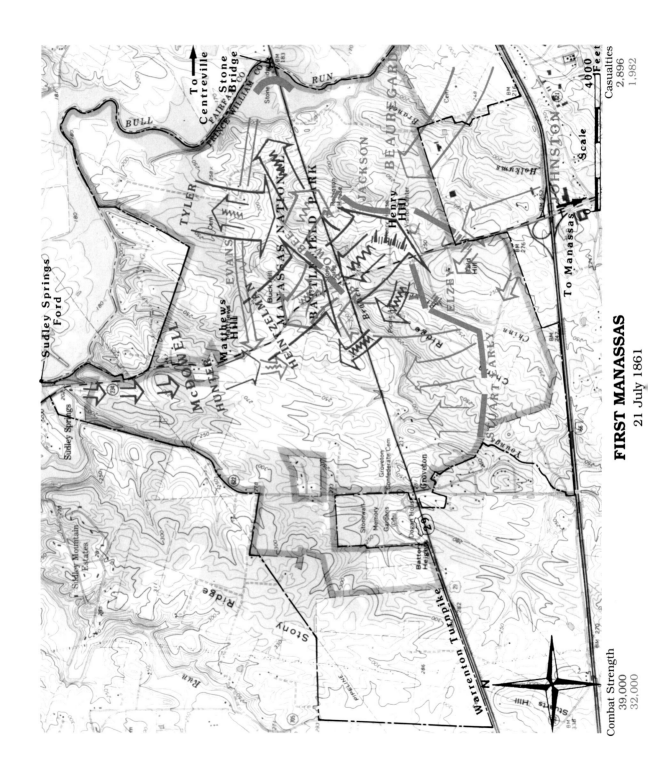

FIRST MANASSAS

21 July 1861

Combat Strength
39,000
32,000

Casualties
2,896
1,982

Scale
4000 Feet

Everything therefore depended on the two Federal armies acting in concert.

Although he was attempting to create and lead into battle the largest field army yet seen in North America, McDowell was not permitted to delay his advance beyond July 16. The populace demanded an "On to Richmond" movement, and it was McDowell's task to provide it. Consequently, in mid-July he organized his sixty separate regiments and batteries into brigades and divisions to facilitate their command and control. All of his five division commanders — brigadier generals Daniel Tyler and Theodore Runyon and colonels David Hunter, Samuel Heintzelman, and Dixon Miles — were older than McDowell, and several had more experience, but none had ever seen, much less commanded, the numbers that would be following them to Bull Run.

Around Manassas Junction, Beauregard also struggled to equip and train enthusiastic but raw recruits. To accomplish that task, he divided his army into seven infantry brigades. All of his brigade commanders — brigadier generals Richard Ewell, James Longstreet, David Jones, and Milledge Bonham and colonels Nathan Evans, Philip Cocke, and Jubal Early — were either West Point graduates or veterans of previous wars, or both. Deploying his troops on a six-mile front along the south bank of Bull Run, Beauregard concentrated the bulk of his infantry on his right center, where the Centreville–Manassas Junction road entered his lines. Bull Run itself was a substantial defensive barrier, but there were far more crossing points than Beauregard could guard effectively.

Because of the heat and the lack of troop discipline, the Federal advance was glacially slow. Reaching Fairfax Court House at noon on July 17, McDowell rested his men while he looked for routes around the Confederate eastern flank. Meanwhile he sent Tyler to seize Centreville and probe carefully beyond it. Unfortunately, the road network was inadequate for a flanking move, and Tyler blundered into an unproductive fight with the Confederates

at Blackburn's Ford. Disconcerted by these setbacks, McDowell spent the next two days at Centreville, perfecting his organization and devising a new plan of attack. The new formulation envisioned a one-division feint at Stone Bridge on the Warrenton Turnpike while two divisions marched northwest to Sudley Springs Ford, crossed Bull Run, and swept down on Beauregard's left. The attack was set for dawn on July 21.

McDowell's delay at Centreville gave Beauregard time to gather his scattered units. More important, on July 18 the Confederate government reluctantly permitted Johnston to evacuate Winchester and join Beauregard at Manassas Junction. Leaving a cavalry screen to deceive Patterson, Johnston marched toward the village of Piedmont, where trains of the Manassas Gap Railroad awaited him. His leading brigade, led by Brigadier General Thomas Jackson, reached Beauregard on July 19; Johnston and parts of two other brigades arrived at Manassas Junction the next day. This exertion overtaxed the capacity of the railroad, however, so that three fifths of Johnston's army was left at Piedmont. Nevertheless, by virtue of his superior rank, Johnston assumed command of the united Confederate forces.

Unaware that Patterson had failed to keep Johnston occupied, McDowell ordered his army forward early on July 21. As before, things went wrong quickly. Tyler's men initially blocked the road to be used by the flanking divisions of Hunter and Heintzelman. When Tyler finally began his demonstration, his performance was so unconvincing that the opposing commander, Colonel Nathan Evans, began to suspect a ruse. When he learned from both pickets and signalmen that a Federal column was moving beyond his flank, Evans left a few men to deceive Tyler and took the remainder of his small brigade toward Sudley Springs Ford. Arriving on Matthews Hill with little more than 1,000 men, Evans was just in time to block the advance of Hunter's 6,000 troops. He held his position alone until reinforced by the brigades of Brigadier General Bernard Bee and Colonel Francis Bartow, both from Johnston's army.

Eventually, sheer weight of numbers pushed Evans, Bee, and Bartow off Matthews Hill and into full retreat. Unfortunately, McDowell's green troops were slow to exploit their advantage. Beyond them the three shattered Confederate brigades climbed to the cleared plateau of Henry House Hill. There they found Jackson's brigade, which was waiting patiently in line. Uttering the immortal remark "There is Jackson standing like a stone wall," Bee rallied his remnants on Jackson's line. Others did likewise, and by early afternoon Beauregard and Johnston had gathered approximately 7,000 men along the rear edge of Henry House Hill. Still, McDowell retained a significant strength advantage. In preparation for a final effort, he advanced two artillery batteries to suppress the defenders' fire. The batteries were destroyed by a Confederate counterattack, but the infantry fight continued around the abandoned guns.

Early in the battle Beauregard and Johnston had agreed that the former would direct the battle line while the latter dispatched reinforcements from the rear. During the afternoon Johnston's efforts led to the arrival on the Confederate left of several fresh brigades. Under the pressure of these units, in late afternoon the Federal right began to crumble. At that moment Beauregard ordered a general advance, and the Confederate line swept forward. The Federal brigades gave way in confusion and could not be rallied, despite the best efforts of McDowell and other officers. Believing that the day was lost, thousands of Fed-

eral soldiers made their way to the rear as best they could. A few Confederate units followed a short distance toward Centreville, but Johnston's and Beauregard's men were in no condition to conduct a meaningful pursuit, and none was attempted.

Considering how many troops were engaged, the losses were not excessive on either side. McDowell had lost 2,896 (killed, wounded, or missing) from his army of approximately 39,000. He had also left behind twenty-seven cannon, nearly a hundred vehicles, several thousand shoulder arms, and great quantities of equipment. The Confederate victory cost Johnston and Beauregard 1,982 casualties from their combined forces of 32,000 officers and men. Both sides lost heavily in senior officers because of the need to lead the inexperienced troops by example.

Although Johnston had done more to achieve the Confederate victory, Beauregard received most of the adulation. In defeat, McDowell became the scapegoat for the mistakes of many besides himself. As for the men of both sides, most had acquitted themselves as well as could have been expected, given their inexperience.

The battle showed that those who expected a short war were utterly mistaken. It took four long years and a great many battles far more horrible than First Manassas to bring an end to the American Civil War.

Manassas National Battlefield Park is on U.S. Route 29 and Interstate 66 near Manassas, Virginia, 26 miles southwest of Washington, D.C. There are 5,083 acres of the historic battlefield within its authorized boundaries; 738 of these are privately owned.

WILSON'S CREEK

10 August 1861

Richard W. Hatcher III

The day after the Union defeat in the war's first big battle, at Manassas, Virginia, President Abraham Lincoln named Major General George B. McClellan to command the Army of the Potomac and then signed legislation for the enlistment of one million men. The president's strategy included having the Union armies in the west go on the offensive, "giving rather special attention to Missouri." This state was strategically important to the western half of the nation because the major trails to the West Coast — the California, Oregon, Santa Fe, and Pony Express trails — all began on its western edge. In addition, the three major shipping rivers of the United States — the Mississippi, the Missouri, and the Ohio — went through or next to Missouri.

On August 6, 1861, Confederate Brigadier General Benjamin McCulloch looked for a good spot to camp his 12,000- to 13,000-man army while he gathered information on the enemy, twelve miles away in Springfield, Missouri. He found a favorable location where Telegraph Road crossed Wilson Creek. Major General Sterling Price, commander of the pro-Confederate Missouri State Guard, convinced McCulloch to attack the Union army by moving up Telegraph Road to Springfield on the night of August 9, for a dawn attaek on the tenth. On the evening of August 9, as the army prepared to move on Springfield, light rain began

to fall. McCulloch canceled his attack orders, fearing that the rain would become a downpour and soak the cartridges his men carried in their pockets or in cloth bags, effectively disarming them. The regular Confederate troops under General McCulloch were somewhat better equipped than Price's militia, but many who had firearms had only short-range 1812-style flintlocks and muzzle-loading fowling pieces. The troops settled back into camp, but the pickets did not return to their guard posts.

The Union soldiers in Springfield, commanded by Brigadier General Nathaniel Lyon, were in a precarious situation. Denied reinforcements by Major General John C. Frémont in St. Louis, Lyon faced the possibility of abandoning southwestern Missouri to the Confederates. However, if he fell back to the northeast, the Confederates might send their cavalry racing ahead to block Telegraph Road, which would enable their infantry to attack the rear of the Union column. If the Union army was caught between the two enemy forces, it could be destroyed. Lyon had other concerns. Many of his men had not been paid; others were poorly clothed and fed. In addition, a large proportion of his force was ninety-day enlistees whose term of service would soon end.

Lyon decided to attack and divided his army

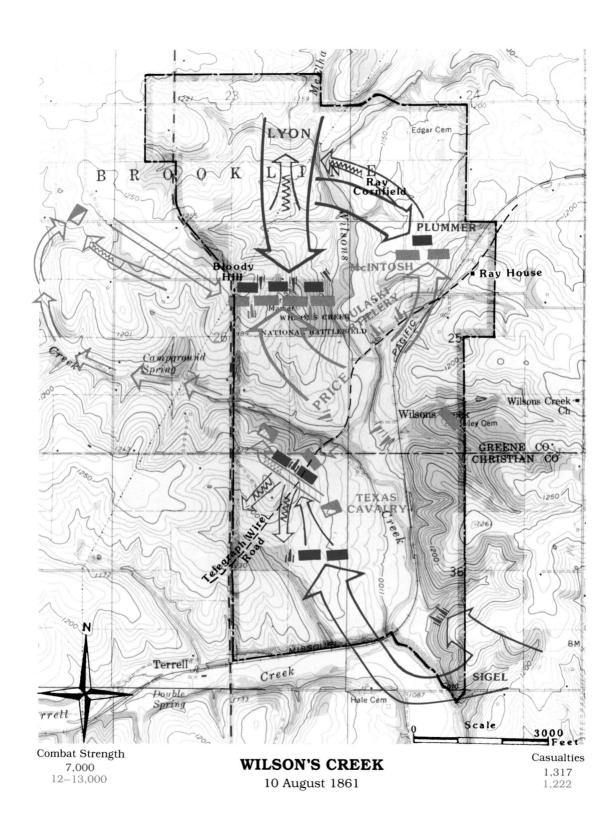

LYON

BROOKLINE

Ray Cornfield

PLUMMER

McINTOSH

Ray House

Bloody Hill

PULASKI BATTERY

WILSON'S CREEK NATIONAL BATTLEFIELD

PACIFIC

Campground Spring

PRICE

Wilsons Creek Ch

Wilsons Creek

GREENE CO.
CHRISTIAN CO.

TEXAS CAVALRY

Telegraph (Wire) Road

Terrell

Double Spring

MISSOURI Creek

Hale Cem

SIGEL

N

Scale

0   3000
Feet

Combat Strength
7,000
12–13,000

WILSON'S CREEK
10 August 1861

Casualties
1,317
1,222

into three units. One stayed in Springfield to guard the city and the army's supply wagons. The other two moved out on the night of August 9 for a dawn attack. Colonel Franz Sigel led one column of 1,200 men, and Lyon led the other with 4,200 men. At 5:00 A.M. on August 10, Lyon's column launched its surprise attack down the west side of Wilson Creek, driving a small Confederate cavalry force back onto "Bloody Hill" and into a retreat down the hill's south slope. By 6:00 A.M. the Federals had reached the crest of the hill. As they moved across its north face, Captain William E. Woodruff's Confederate Pulaski Artillery, located on a ridge on the east side of the creek, roared into action. It enfiladed Lyon's line, slowing the Union advance and giving General Price the time he needed to form his infantry into a battle line to counterattack.

On hearing Lyon's attack, Sigel, positioned on a ridge east of Wilson Creek and about two miles south of the Confederate cavalry camps, opened fire on the main camp with four of his six cannon. Taken completely by surprise, the Confederates abandoned their camp and fled to the north and west. Sigel crossed the creek, turned north, and moved into position on a knoll, blocking Telegraph Road.

By 6:30 A.M. the battle lines on Bloody Hill had been established, and the level of fighting had increased dramatically. To guard the Union left flank, Lyon sent Captain Joseph B. Plummer's infantry column to the east side of Wilson Creek. This force witnessed the effect of the Pulaski Artillery on the main column and advanced toward the battery. McCulloch countered this attack by sending Colonel James McIntosh with two infantry regiments against the Federals. After a brief fight in John Ray's cornfield, the Union column was defeated and retreated back across Wilson Creek. This action secured the east side of the battlefield for the Confederates and permitted them to concentrate their forces against Lyon and Sigel.

McCulloch sent elements of three regiments to drive Sigel off the field. As the Confederates advanced in line of battle, Sigel, assuming that the advancing Third Louisiana troops were the gray-clad First Iowa Infantry sent by Lyon as reinforcements, ordered his men to hold their fire. At forty yards the Confederates stopped and fired a massed volley into the Union position. Unprepared for this attack by what they thought were friendly forces, the Union column broke into a rout and lost five of their six cannon. By 9:00 A.M. the southern end of the battlefield had been secured, and the southerners began concentrating all their efforts on Bloody Hill.

At 7:30 A.M., 600 Missouri State Guardsmen launched an attack on Lyon's right flank — the first of three Confederate counterattacks on Bloody Hill. This assault was beaten off after a half hour of fighting. At 9:00 General Price launched his second attack. The Union line was hard pressed, but held. An hour later Colonel Elkanah Greer's Texas Cavalry Regiment, attempting to go around the Union right flank and rear, launched the only mounted assault of the battle. This action diverted the Federals' attention, which gave Price time to disengage his men and regroup for another attack. Union artillery and musketry fire broke up the mounted assault, effectively ending the Confederates' second attack. During the fighting Lyon was slightly wounded by artillery. Later, while rallying his troops, he became the first Union general to die during combat, killed by a musket ball.

During a short lull the Confederates readied an estimated 6,000 men in a line of battle a thousand yards long for the third and largest attack of the battle. As they began their advance, the Federals placed every available Union soldier, except a small reserve force, in the front line. The determined Confederates pressed their advance in spite of concentrated artillery and small-arms fire. In some areas they moved to within twenty feet of the Union line. The smoke of battle from both lines combined into one huge cloud that blanketed the south slope of Bloody Hill. The Confederates were unable to break the Union line and were soon forced back at all points.

At 11:00 A.M. the Confederates disengaged and regrouped down the hill. The Federals were exhausted and low on ammunition, their general was dead, and Sigel had been defeated. Bloody Hill had earned its name. They retreated to Springfield and then to Rolla, the nearest railhead. The Confederates were not able to follow up their victory. The battle of Wilson's Creek, the first major battle of the war west of the Mississippi River, was over. After six hours of fighting on a hot and humid August day in Missouri, 1,317 Union and 1,222 Confederate soldiers were killed, wounded, or missing.

The battle of Wilson's Creek began a chain of events that determined the fate of Missouri. After it, the Union army fell back about a hundred miles to the northeast, toward St. Louis, and General McCulloch returned to Arkansas with his troops. General Price led his Missourians north, where in September they captured the Federal garrison at Lexington, on the Missouri River.

Owing in part to the military success of the southerners, Missouri's pro-Confederate politicians, led by Governor Claiborne Fox Jackson, met in a special legislative session in Neosho and passed an ordinance of secession. During this same period pro-Federal politicians met in the state capitol at Jefferson City and declared that Missouri would remain a Union state. As a result of these separate actions, Missouri had two governments and representation in both the United States Congress and the Confederate Congress. Fortunately for the Union cause, the state's importance was recognized early in the war. As a result, reinforcements were committed to Missouri, and early Union losses were countered.

Wilson's Creek National Battlefield is near U.S. Route 60 near Republic, Missouri. There are 1,750 acres of the historic battlefield within its authorized boundaries.

Wilson's Creek National Battlefield
Bloody Hill. © David Muench, 1990

FORT DONELSON

12–16 February 1862

John Y. Simon

Fort Donelson, Tennessee, guarding the Cumberland River, became the site of the first major Confederate defeat in the Civil War. Victory at Donelson started Brigadier General Ulysses S. Grant on his road to Appomattox and the White House. His cool judgment under pressure saved the day after the Confederates threatened to break his lines, yet errors by his opponents handed him a victory that he did not fully earn.

Possession of the better part of two states vital to the South depended on the outcome of the battle at Fort Donelson. When war began in April 1861, Kentucky declared its neutrality, in response to deep cleavages of opinion among its citizens. Considering neutrality impossible to maintain, North and South maneuvered for position once Kentucky was opened to military operations. The Confederates constructed fortifications on both the Tennessee and Cumberland rivers just south of the Kentucky line. They built Fort Henry on the Tennessee River, on ground susceptible to flooding, but chose higher ground for Fort Donelson on the Cumberland.

Both sides coveted Kentucky but recognized that the first to cross its borders risked losing popular support. Confederate Brigadier General Gideon J. Pillow rashly seized Columbus, Kentucky, on the Mississippi River bluffs, a move that appalled President Jefferson Davis,

who first ordered Pillow to withdraw, then allowed him to stay when he realized that the deed could not be undone. Grant, commanding at Cairo, Illinois, then occupied Paducah at the mouth of the Tennessee and Smithland at the mouth of the Cumberland, strategic points neglected by Pillow.

In November Grant tested Confederate strength at Columbus by landing troops across the Mississippi River at Belmont, Missouri. The drawn battle that followed sent him back to Cairo still eager to advance, but not necessarily along the Mississippi. Knowing of the poor location of Fort Henry, he wanted to use Union gunboats to advantage, and foresaw that the fall of Henry would open the Tennessee River as far as northern Alabama. Winning reluctant permission from his superior, Major General Henry W. Halleck, Grant moved south in early February. The flooded Fort Henry fell to the gunboats on February 6, and most of the garrison fled to Fort Donelson, eleven miles away. Grant followed, after sending the gunboats back down the Tennessee and over to the Cumberland. In St. Louis, Halleck, a military bureaucrat par excellence, took no official cognizance of Grant's plans. If Grant captured Fort Donelson, Halleck would assume credit; if Grant failed, he would avoid responsibility.

Confederate General Albert Sidney John-

FORT DONELSON
14–15 February 1862

Combat Strength		Casualties	
27,000		2,832	
21,000		17,000	

ston, overall commander in the west, concentrated his troops at Fort Donelson, anticipating the loss of Nashville if Donelson fell. Torn between defending and abandoning the fort, Johnston took a middle course that led to disaster. He was criticized later for sending so many troops to Donelson without sending his whole force and taking command himself. By the time Grant arrived, with approximately 15,000 men, Donelson held nearly 21,000, including at least two generals too many. Brigadier General John B. Floyd, who was commanding Donelson, had been a former secretary of war in the cabinet of President James Buchanan and was widely suspected by northerners of transferring arms and munitions southward before the rebellion broke out. Pillow, the second-in-command, had little respect from his own men and contempt from Grant. Third in line but first in ability was Brigadier General Simon B. Buckner, the only professional soldier of the three.

Fort Donelson consisted of earthworks surrounding about fifteen acres, where the garrison lived in huts. Two batteries outside the fort commanded the river, and about two miles of fortifications, protecting both the artillery encampment and the nearby hamlet of Dover, stretched from Hickman Creek on the right to Lick Creek on the left. The creeks, flooded in February, protected both flanks. Confederate officers and engineers had complained continuously of shortages of men and supplies to complete the fortifications, but Federal forces encountered formidable earthworks fronted by trees felled, tangled, and sharpened to impede attack.

Grant advanced on February 12 and began to encircle Fort Donelson the next day, ordering Brigadier General Charles F. Smith's division to probe the Confederate right, commanded by Buckner, and Brigadier General John A. McClernand's division to probe the Confederate left, under Brigadier General Bushrod R. Johnson. Grant found the Confederate lines too strong and well positioned for assault. Relying on this strength, however, the Confederates permitted Union troops to

complete a virtual encirclement, leaving only a small gap on their right, and to select high ground for their base. If Grant's boldness had been matched by his opponents, they might have struck Union troops as they marched on two separate roads to Donelson, or the Confederates might have counterattacked at Donelson while they had superior numbers and Grant lacked naval support. However, they did not. Flag Officer Andrew H. Foote's gunboat fleet arrived late at night, carrying fresh troops, and a division commanded by Brigadier General Lewis Wallace marched from Fort Henry. Ultimately, Grant's army numbered 27,000.

Both armies froze when overnight temperatures unexpectedly fell to twelve degrees. On February 14 Foote tested the water batteries with six warships, four of them ironclads, and the batteries prevailed, inflicting heavy damage on the flotilla. Although heavily outgunned, artillerists found the range when the gunboats came too close, and the fleet suffered too much to resume the assault.

The next morning Grant consulted Foote on his flagship, where he lay immobilized by a wound inflicted by the Confederate batteries. While they discussed their next move, Pillow struck the Union right with devastating force. Buckner's line was denuded as the Confederates massed troops to break free of encirclement. McClernand's right began to roll back on the center, until reinforcements from Wallace halted the victorious Confederates. When the fighting slackened, Pillow held the Forge Road, leading to Nashville.

Pillow had two sound choices: to press the attack to consolidate victory or to break free of Grant's grip by evacuating Fort Donelson. Inexplicably, he rejected both and withdrew to his original line. Stung by the morning offensive, the Union troops were confused and demoralized until Grant returned. Inspecting the haversacks of fallen Confederates, which contained rations for three days, Grant concluded that the assault represented a desperate effort to escape and ordered his troops to press the enemy. Smith's division was successful against Buckner's weakened line, which put U.S. troops inside the Confederate fortifications and threatened the redoubt.

Otherwise, the three days of fighting had left the armies close to their initial positions. Grant's reinforcements, however, were much exaggerated in the Confederate imagination, and Floyd and Pillow had squandered their only opportunity to evacuate. During the evening of February 15, the Confederate commanders planned the surrender. Floyd relinquished command to Pillow and Pillow to Buckner. The top brass slipped away by water with about 2,000 men. Colonel Nathan Bedford Forrest led his cavalry and a few infantry safely by land to Nashville.

When Buckner asked Grant to appoint commissioners to negotiate the terms of capitulation, Grant responded succinctly that "no terms except an unconditional and immediate surrender can be accepted." Denouncing this response as "ungenerous and unchivalrous," Buckner surrendered anyway. Meeting later at the Dover Hotel, Buckner told his old friend and military academy schoolmate that if he had held command, Union forces would not have encircled Donelson so easily. Grant answered that if Buckner had been in command, he (Grant) would have chosen different tactics.

Grant lost 2,832 killed or wounded, Floyd about 2,000, but Grant took about 15,000 prisoners, 48 artillery pieces, and other war matériel the South could not afford to lose. The Confederates fell back from Kentucky and from much of middle Tennessee, abandoning Nashville. Grant won fame and promotion, while both Floyd and Pillow lost command. Robert E. Lee's later successes in Virginia obscured the significance of Fort Donelson as the first step toward the Confederate loss of the west, which spelled doom for the new nation.

Fort Donelson National Battlefield is on U.S. Route 79 at Dover, Tennessee, 28 miles west of Clarksville. There are 537 acres of the historic battlefield within its authorized boundaries; 12 of these are privately owned.

Fort Donelson

PEA RIDGE

7–8 March 1862

William L. Shea and Earl J. Hess

The battle of Pea Ridge resulted from Federal efforts to secure control of the border state of Missouri. Union Brigadier General Nathaniel Lyon had seized control of St. Louis and the Missouri River, but was killed at Wilson's Creek in his unsuccessful effort to eliminate Major General Sterling Price's pro-Confederate State Guard. In September 1861, Price pushed north, captured Lexington on the Missouri River, and then retired in the face of converging Union forces. He took refuge in the southwestern corner of the state, where he menaced Federal control of Missouri and threatened to disrupt the logistical support for a planned Federal invasion of the Confederacy down the Mississippi River.

In late December, Brigadier General Samuel Ryan Curtis was appointed commander of the Union Army of the Southwest and was instructed to drive Price out of Missouri. Curtis launched his campaign on February 11, 1862, chasing Price down Telegraph Road into northwestern Arkansas. Price joined Confederate troops under Brigadier General Benjamin McCulloch in the rugged Boston Mountains. Curtis halted near Pea Ridge, forty miles north of these mountains, and assumed a defensive position to shield Missouri.

On March 2, Major General Earl Van Dorn, newly appointed commander of Confederate troops west of the Mississippi, joined Price

and McCulloch. He named their combined force the Army of the West and immediately began preparations for an invasion of Missouri. His offensive began on March 4 in the midst of a blizzard.

Learning of Van Dorn's approach, Curtis consolidated his 10,250 troops where the Telegraph Road crossed Little Sugar Creek, three miles south of Pea Ridge and the nearby hostelry called Elkhorn Tavern. The Federals fortified their naturally strong position along the creek. On March 6 Van Dorn managed to move fast enough to catch a small rear guard, led by Curtis's second-in-command, Brigadier General Franz Sigel, as it retreated from Bentonville toward the creek position. Sigel escaped from the pursuing Confederates with minor casualties.

That evening Van Dorn's army of 16,500 men, divided into two divisions led by Price and McCulloch, reached Little Sugar Creek. Rather than attack Curtis in his fortifications, Van Dorn decided to envelop the Federals by moving his army around to their rear. During the night of March 6–7, the weary Confederates marched along the Bentonville Detour, a local road that passed around the right flank of the Federal position. Price's division reached the Telegraph Road by midmorning on March 7 and turned south toward Elkhorn Tavern, but McCulloch's division fell so far be-

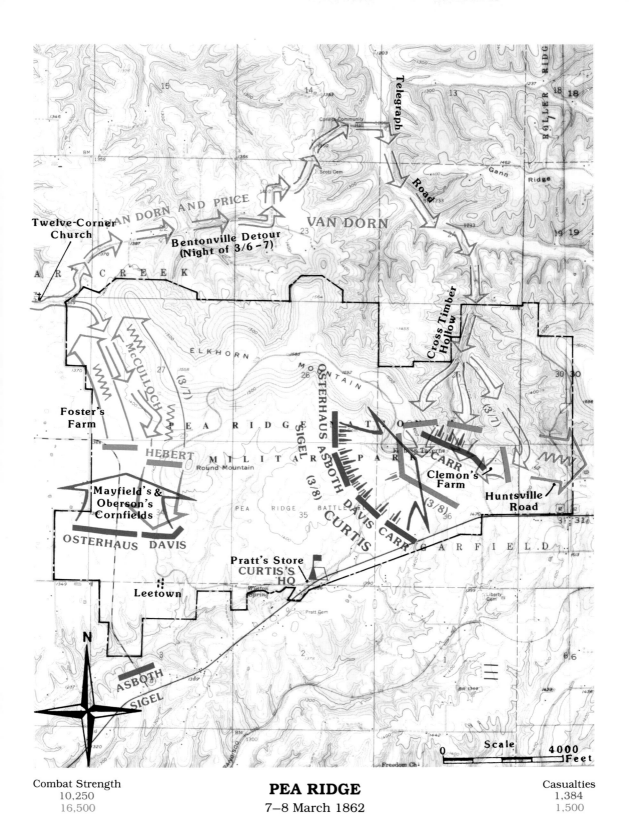

PEA RIDGE

7–8 March 1862

Combat Strength
10,250
16,500

Casualties
1,384
1,500

hind that Van Dorn ordered it to leave the detour and strike the enemy several miles west
of Elkhorn Tavern. This decision divided the
Confederate army and meant that the battle
of Pea Ridge actually involved two separate engagements, at Leetown and Elkhorn Tavern.

Curtis, who learned of the Confederate maneuver on the morning of March 7, was ready.
He turned much of his army to the rear, so
that his troops were facing north instead
of south — one of the most extraordinary
changes of front in the Civil War. He then
launched sharp attacks against both Confederate divisions. McCulloch's division was in-
tercepted a mile north of the hamlet of
Leetown by the First and Third divisions, commanded by colonels Peter J. Osterhaus and
Jefferson C. Davis. Price's troops were blocked
by Colonel Eugene A. Carr's Fourth Division.
Curtis held the remaining troops in reserve.

The fighting at Leetown was divided into
three sectors by the vegetation, cultivated
fields, and road system. The first sector was
Foster's farm, where McCulloch first encountered the enemy. The farm was a partially
cleared swale from which a Federal battery,
supported by a small cavalry force, fired on his
division. McCulloch's cavalry, supported by
two regiments of Cherokee Indians, easily captured the battery and scattered the cavalry.

The second sector was the cornfields of Ob-
erson's and Mayfield's farms. Osterhaus and
Davis established a solid line of infantry and
artillery in these fields, which were separated
from Foster's farm by a belt of timber. As
McCulloch led the advance, he was killed by a
volley from two companies of Federal skirmishers posted in the woods. His successor,
Brigadier General James McIntosh, ordered a
general infantry attack. He personally led one
regiment through the timber, and he too was
killed by the Federal skirmishers. McIntosh's
death ended the fighting in the Oberson-May-

Pea Ridge National Military Park
© David Muench, 1990

field fields as fighting began in the third sector.

This was an area of thick scrub timber and densely tangled brush east of the cornfields, separated from them by the road that ran north from Leetown. Colonel Louis Hébert led 2,000 Confederate infantry troops through this thicket. They were opposed by half as many Federals in two regiments of Davis's Third Division in an hour-long fight, in which the brush reduced visibility to seventy-five yards. Hébert's men pushed these regiments back toward Leetown and captured two Federal cannon in the southeast corner of the cornfield.

This Confederate advance was repulsed as two Indiana regiments of Davis's other brigade outflanked Hébert's left and Osterhaus's division struck his right. Exhausted and unsupported, the remnants of Hébert's command retreated to the Bentonville Detour in mid-afternoon, along with the rest of McCulloch's division. Hébert was captured by the Federals. Just then Sigel arrived at Leetown with heavy reinforcements, helped to secure the battlefield, and then marched toward the ongoing fight at Elkhorn Tavern.

Price's division, with Van Dorn at its head, had encountered Carr's Fourth Division at the tavern. The Confederates were at the bottom of a deep canyon known as Cross Timber Hollow; the Federals occupied a superb defensive position on top of the Pea Ridge plateau. For several hours Van Dorn engaged the Federals with artillery before ordering Price to attack. The Confederates ascended the steep hill, pushed back both of Carr's flanks, and gained a foothold on the plateau. The most intense fighting of the entire battle of Pea Ridge occurred around Elkhorn Tavern and just to the east, at Clemon's farm. Carr's men were forced back nearly a mile before reinforcements arrived. Darkness halted the fighting.

During the night of March 7–8, Curtis concentrated his remaining 9,500 troops on the Telegraph Road in order to drive the Confederates away from Elkhorn Tavern in the morning. Van Dorn ordered the remnants of McCulloch's division to the tavern. With only about half of his 12,000 troops in any condition to fight, because of exhaustion and lack of food, Van Dorn formed his men into a V-shaped defensive line running along the edge of the woods south and west of the tavern.

At dawn on March 8 Curtis deployed the First, Second, Third, and Fourth divisions in numerical order from left to right, facing north. It was one of the few times in the war that an entire army from flank to flank was out in the open for all to see. Sigel directed the First and Second divisions west of the Telegraph Road, while Curtis directed the Third and Fourth divisions east of the road and retained overall command. During the next two hours Sigel gradually advanced and wheeled his troops around until they faced northeast. In this fashion the Federal line soon roughly corresponded to the V-shaped Confederate line.

To cover this movement the Federals hammered the rebels with twenty-one cannon, most of them directed personally by Sigel. This unusually well-coordinated fire compelled the Confederates to fall back to safer positions. Van Dorn's ordnance trains had been separated from the army as a result of negligent staff work, so the Confederates did not have enough ammunition for their artillery. The Federal army then advanced. After a brief fight the Confederate rear guard disengaged and the rout began. Van Dorn retreated southeast, leading the main body of his battered army entirely around the enemy army, a maneuver unique in the Civil War. Other Confederate units scattered north and west via their approach route, rejoining Van Dorn several days later in Van Buren. However, hundreds of Confederate soldiers left the colors to return home. Curtis did not know until the next day which route Van Dorn and the main column had taken, and by that time pursuit was futile.

The Confederates began the campaign with approximately 16,500 soldiers, including 800 Native Americans, but because the advance was so rapid, about 15,000 were present at Pea Ridge and even fewer were actually engaged. About 1,500 Confederates were lost in the battle. The Federals had 10,250 soldiers at Pea Ridge and suffered 1,384 casualties. Half of the Federal losses were incurred by Carr's Fourth Division during the fighting at Elkhorn Tavern on March 7.

Despite being outnumbered three to two, the Federals achieved a decisive tactical and strategic victory at Pea Ridge. The outcome of the battle ended any serious Confederate threat to Missouri and led to the conquest of Arkansas. Van Dorn's impulsiveness, his obsession with speed and surprise, and his unconcern for logistics and staff work gravely weakened the Confederate effort. Conversely, Curtis's coolness and tactical boldness were major factors in the Federal victory.

Pea Ridge National Military Park is on State Route 71 near Pea Ridge, Arkansas, 20 miles northeast of Fayetteville. There are 4,300 acres of the historic battlefield within its authorized boundaries.

GLORIETA

26–28 March 1862

Don E. Alberts

During March 1862, Union and Confederate troops fought the key battle of the Civil War in the Far West, the battle of Glorieta, in the Territory of New Mexico. The Confederates were Texans of Brigadier General Henry Hopkins Sibley's Army of New Mexico. After an advance party took the southernmost Federal post in the territory, Fort Fillmore near Mesilla, Sibley's brigade moved northward, fighting and winning the battle of Valverde on February 21. Leaving the defeated but intact Union forces behind in nearby Fort Craig, the Texans continued northward along the Rio Grande, occupying the towns of Albuquerque and Santa Fe during early March. There they delayed to gather provisions for a further advance on Sibley's primary objective, Fort Union, the Federal supply center about a hundred miles northeast of Santa Fe on the Santa Fe Trail and on the route to the gold mines around Denver City, Colorado Territory.

The Union force was a regiment of frontiersmen from the mining districts around Denver City, the First Colorado Volunteers, commanded by Colonel John P. Slough, a Denver lawyer. These "Pikes Peakers" were augmented by detachments of cavalry and infantry from the regular garrison of Fort Union. On March 22, Slough led his field column of 1,340 men out of Fort Union toward the Texans in the vicinity of Santa Fe.

General Sibley remained at his headquarters and supply depot in Albuquerque and sent his main field column through the mountains toward Fort Union. A smaller vanguard, under Major Charles L. Pyron, Second Texas Mounted Rifles, occupied Santa Fe. On March 25 Pyron led his troops eastward along the Santa Fe Trail to find the enemy. His 400-man force included his own battalion, four companies of the Fifth Texas Mounted Volunteers, several locally recruited units, including the "Company of Santa Fe Gamblers," artillerymen, and two cannon.

On the morning of March 26, Pyron's Texans left their camp at Cañoncito and again rode eastward along the Santa Fe Trail. Slough's advance guard, approximately 420 men under the command of Major John M. Chivington, First Colorado Volunteers, marched westward toward them on the same road. The Union troops surprised and captured Pyron's advance party, then attacked his main body of troops. Forming in line of battle across the road approximately a mile west of Glorieta Pass, the Texans unlimbered their artillery and opened fire. The Union forces outflanked Pyron's line by climbing the hillsides bordering the Santa Fe Trail. The Confederates then withdrew westward toward Apache Canyon, a small valley of cultivated fields, and established a second battle line and probably a third. Chivington repeated his outflanking

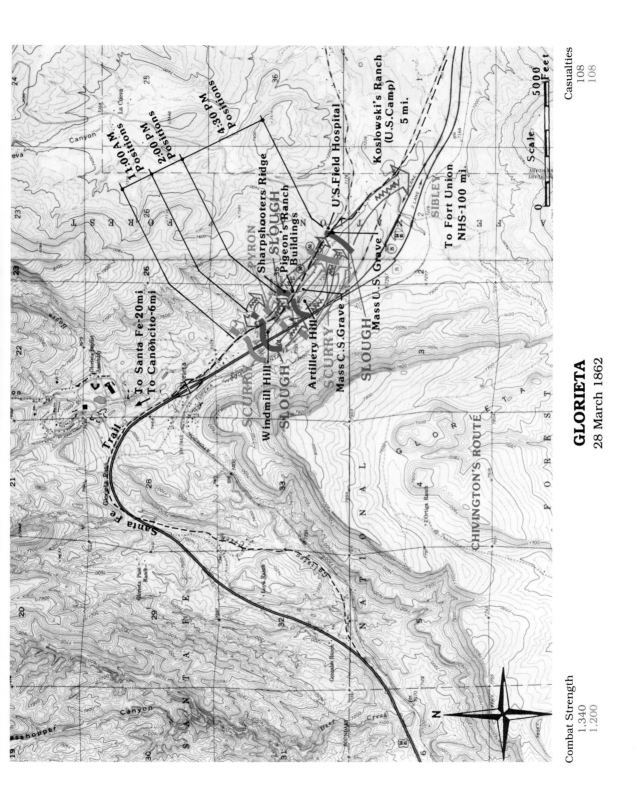

GLORIETA
28 March 1862

Combat Strength
1,340
1,200

Casualties
108
108

tactic, and in addition sent a furious cavalry charge against the Texans' positions. Pyron managed to extract his two cannon, but the Union horsemen were among his infantry just as Chivington's flanking parties reached his rear. Seventy Confederates were captured during the battle of Apache Canyon, and 4 Texans died and 20 were wounded. Pyron retreated to his camp at nearby Cañoncito and sent an urgent request for assistance to the main Texas column, camped fifteen miles away.

Major Chivington, with 5 men killed and 14 wounded, broke off the action and retired to the Union camp at Koslowski's Ranch, a Santa Fe Trail station twelve miles away from the Texans. The following day both Chivington and Pyron awaited attacks that never came.

Leaving their supply wagon train behind at Cañoncito, guarded by a handful of noncombatants with a single cannon, the Confederates again marched eastward on the morning of March 28, seeking the enemy, who barred their way to Fort Union and its necessary supplies. Lieutenant Colonel William R. Scurry of the Fourth Texas Mounted Volunteers commanded approximately 1,200 men with three cannon. The forces advanced toward one another along the same road. The Texans encountered Colonel Slough's main Union force resting and filling canteens at Pigeon's Ranch, a hostelry one mile east of Glorieta Pass. At about 11:00 A.M., scattered shots opened the battle of Glorieta. Slough had approximately 850 men available, supported by two artillery companies of four guns each. The balance of Slough's troops, approximately 490 men led by Chivington, had left the main force earlier to act as a flanking force in attacking the Texan camp at Cañoncito. As the battle opened, Chivington was pushing his men across a heavily wooded mesa south of the trail, unaware that the main columns had already met near Glorieta.

Both forces unlimbered their artillery and formed battle lines across the Santa Fe Trail a half mile west of Pigeon's Ranch. They exchanged fire until about 2:00 P.M., when,

slightly outnumbering the foe, Scurry's troops outflanked the Union line, forcing Slough to withdraw to a second defensive line near the ranch buildings and corrals. Scurry then attempted a three-pronged attack, which failed on the right and center but was successful north of the road. Gaining the heights above the Union troops, the Texans forced Slough to withdraw to a third position another half mile east of Pigeon's Ranch. The Confederates followed, and both sides exchanged desultory cannon and small-arms fire. This effort died out in mutual exhaustion at dusk, and Slough decided to withdraw to his camp at Koslowski's Ranch, about five miles to the rear. Scurry was left in possession of the battlefield. His feeling of triumph was immediately dashed, however, by word of disaster in his rear.

As the battle raged around Pigeon's Ranch, Chivington's party reached a point two hundred feet directly above the Texans' wagon park and camp at Cañoncito. They drove off the weak guard, descended the steep slopes, disabled the cannon left at the site, and burned and destroyed the eighty-wagon supply train. It contained virtually everything Scurry's force owned — reserve ammunition, baggage, food, forage, and medicines. The Union soldiers retraced their route and rejoined Slough's main force at Koslowski's Ranch after dark. That phase of the battle of Glorieta, more successful than could have been expected, sealed the fate of the Confederate invasion of New Mexico.

The key battle ended in the darkness around Pigeon's Ranch. The Texans had 48 killed and 60 wounded, and the Union forces took almost identical casualties. Both sides felt they were victorious, the Confederates since they remained on the field of battle and the Federals since they believed they had been unjustly kept from renewing the battle. The fight around the ranch saw neither side defeated, so it was considered a drawn battle, especially since the foe still stood between the Texans and their objective, Fort Union. When the undoubted Union victory at Cañoncito is considered, however, the battle of Glorieta becomes a significant Federal victory, since it turned back the Confederate thrust into New Mexico and saved the Far West for the Union.

Slough's men returned to Fort Union after the battle, but Scurry remained at Pigeon's Ranch for another day, treating his wounded in the main building and burying his dead in a mass grave across the Santa Fe Trail from the hospital. The Texans returned to Santa Fe in an unsuccessful attempt to recoup their fortunes and continue the campaign northward. Forced to evacuate the territorial capital, they joined Sibley's final retreat southward and out of New Mexico. They had fought bravely and well at Glorieta, but had been turned back by chance and a determined enemy.

After Glorieta, Slough resigned as commander of the First Colorado in favor of Chivington. He returned to New Mexico after the Civil War as the territory's chief justice. There he was shot to death in Santa Fe's La Fonda Hotel by a political rival. Chivington subsequently led the First Colorado, then commanded the Second Colorado in the infamous Sand Creek Massacre during 1864, for which he was ultimately cashiered. Sibley met a similar fate: he was court-martialed for drunkenness and cowardice following the 1863 battle of Franklin, Louisiana, and although he was acquitted, he never again held a command during the Civil War. After the war he was dismissed from the khedive of Egypt's army for similar offenses. Lieutenant Colonel Scurry became a brigadier general and led Texas troops at Galveston and in the Louisiana Red River campaigns during 1863 and 1864. He was killed on April 30, 1864, at the battle of Jenkins' Ferry, Arkansas.

Glorieta battlefield is on U.S. Route 85 near Glorieta, New Mexico, 18 miles east of Santa Fe. The entire battlefield is privately owned.

Pigeon's Ranch in 1880. Photo by Ben Wittick

SHILOH

6–7 April 1862

George A. Reaves III

The Union victories at Fort Henry and Fort Donelson in February 1862 opened the Tennessee and Cumberland rivers to Union gunboats. Major General Ulysses S. Grant's army thrust south up the Tennessee River to the Pittsburg Landing area on the west bank, about twenty-two miles northwest of Corinth, Mississippi, arriving in mid-March. This was the closest all-weather landing to the railroad intersection at Corinth. To prevent the loss of this vital junction, the Confederates concentrated their forces for an attack on Grant.

At the battle of Shiloh, which began on April 6, 1862, the Confederate Army of the Mississippi was commanded by General Albert Sidney Johnston. The Union Army of the Tennessee was commanded by General Grant, and its Army of the Ohio by Brigadier General Don Carlos Buell. The Confederates planned to attack Grant's army, which was camped around Shiloh Methodist Church, cut it off from Pittsburg Landing, and force it into the swamps north and west of the landing before Buell arrived from Nashville with reinforcements.

General P. G. T. Beauregard, second-in-command of the Confederate army, planned the Confederate attack. Major General William Hardee's corps would lead with his troops in one long line stretching between Snake Creek and Owl Creek. Behind him would come Major

General Braxton Bragg's corps, also in line. The reserves were under Major General Leonidas Polk and Brigadier General John C. Breckinridge.

The Confederates were able to camp and deploy within a mile of the Union army, because Grant thought he would have to march to Corinth to fight the Confederates and did not issue orders for adequate patrolling and picketing. The Confederate attack on the morning of April 6 came as a tactical surprise. The initial attack rolled over the divisions commanded by brigadier generals Benjamin M. Prentiss and William T. Sherman.

In spite of the Confederate surprise, most of the Union soldiers did not panic. During the day they succeeded in taking up a series of defensive lines which slowed the Confederate attacks and absorbed the shock of their charges. The first of these lines was south of the Hamburg-Purdy Road, extending from Owl Creek on the right to the Tennessee River on the left. There were several gaps in this line, however, and the Confederates found them and forced the Federals back to the road, where they made another stand, only to be routed again.

By late morning the Union troops had taken a position running from the bluffs near the Tennessee River on the left, along an abandoned farm road through a place called the

Hornets' Nest, to the high ground overlooking Owl Creek on the right. This line was several miles long and there were thin spots, but it was continuous. The major disadvantage was the lack of an overall commander.

On the Confederate left, Johnston directed a series of attacks against the northern troops holding the area around a peach orchard. At about 2:30, while trying to locate and turn the Union left, Johnston was killed, and Beauregard assumed command of the Confederate army.

Savage southern attacks were also directed against the Federals holding the Hornets' Nest, at the center of the line. Here eleven separate assaults were made against the position held by 6,000 Federals, the remnants of Prentiss's Sixth Division and two brigades of W. H. L. Wallace's Second Division. In directing most of these attacks, General Bragg did not commit enough of his 20,000 to 25,000 troops for an overwhelming attack or probe for a Federal weak spot. Instead he attacked piecemeal and expended men who would have been more effectively deployed on other parts of the field.

Grant had ordered Wallace and Prentiss to hold this sector of the line at all costs. This they did from 10:00 A.M. until 5:30 P.M., when their flanks were exposed and the Confederates partially encircled them. Pinned down by the fire of sixty-two cannon, the two Union divisions broke for the rear. Many made it, but Wallace was killed, and Prentiss, along with 2,100 men of the Second and Sixth divisions, was forced to surrender.

The Union stronghold was finally overwhelmed by the Confederates, but by then Grant had established a final defense line — its left posted behind Dill Branch, its right behind Tilghman Branch, and its center on the Corinth Road, strengthened by artillery massed on both sides. This protected both Pittsburg Landing, where Buell's men were arriving, and the Hamburg-Savannah Road — the route followed by Brigadier General Lewis Wallace's division on a roundabout march from Crumps Landing by way of Adamsville to reinforce Grant. To attack this final line, the Confederates were forced to descend a sixty-foot-high bluff, cross the marshy bottom of the ravine formed by Dill Branch, and climb the bank on the far side — a terrible challenge after thirteen hours of fighting and marching. They faced the fire of fifty-three Union cannon supported by some 20,000 troops. In spite of the odds, two Confederate brigades succeeded in gaining a toehold on the northern bank of Dill Branch ravine. They could not hold on, however, and were compelled to withdraw to the far side of the hollow.

By nightfall on April 6, the Confederates had forced the Army of the Tennessee to retreat three miles. Of the five Union divisions on the field at the start of the day, one had been destroyed and four had suffered heavy losses. The camps of four divisions had been captured by the Confederates, along with reserve ammunition and supplies. The Union army had reinforcements: Buell's Army of the Ohio, arriving at Pittsburg Landing from downriver, and Lewis Wallace's division, arriving by way of the Hamburg-Savannah Road. The Confederates received no additional men.

On the second day the Union troops advanced on a broad front, using their superior numbers to force the Confederates back. The southerners retreated slowly, making local counterattacks in an unsuccessful attempt to regain the initiative. After one last thrust at about 2:00 P.M. at Water Oaks Pond, Beauregard decided to withdraw his army to Corinth. The Federals occupied the area around Shiloh Church and used the Pittsburg and Hamburg landings as staging areas for a massive buildup for their pending advance on Corinth.

The battle of Shiloh was decisive. Though Grant was later criticized for not being prepared for the Confederate attack, the Confederate effort to crush his army and recover the initiative in western and middle Tennessee was checkmated. Any Confederate hope of regaining control of Nashville and the iron-

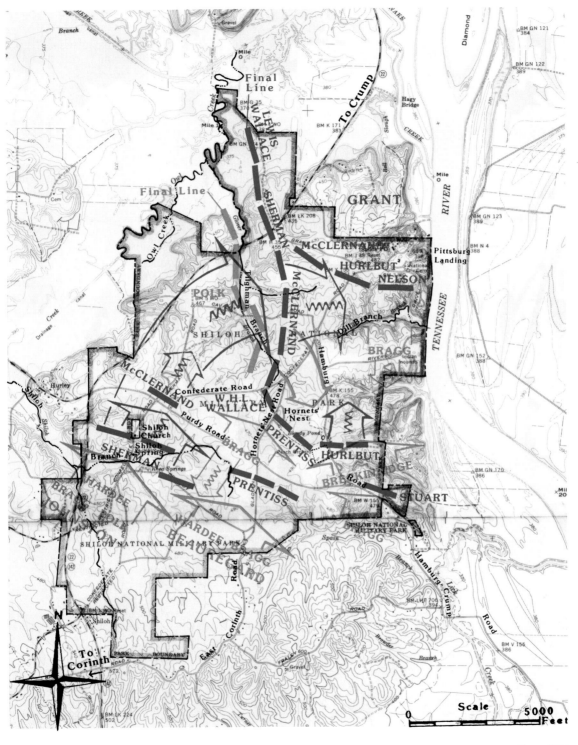

Combat Strength
62,000
44,000

SHILOH

6 April 1862

Casualties
13,047
11,694

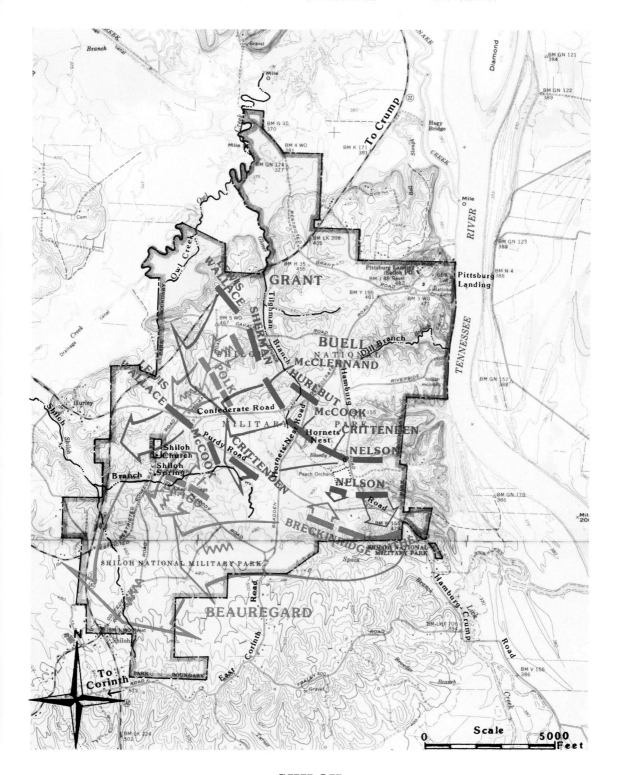

SHILOH

7 April 1862

producing areas of western Tennessee was, for the time being, abandoned.

Shiloh was the largest battle America had known. The Union army of 62,000 had 13,047 killed, wounded, or missing; the Confederate army lost 11,694 of its 44,000 men. Corinth, a key intersection on the only direct rail link between the Confederate capital at Richmond and the Mississippi River and the north-south Mobile and Ohio Railroad, was doomed. The evacuation of Corinth on May 29 and 30 cost the Confederacy Memphis, with its boatyards, industrial production, and population.

Shiloh National Military Park is on State Route 22 in Shiloh, Tennessee, 25 miles northeast of Corinth, Mississippi. There are 3,838 acres of the historic battlefield within its authorized boundaries; 4 of these are privately owned.

Shiloh National Military Park
Final Union line, April 6, 1862. © David Muench, 1990

FORT PULASKI

10–11 April 1862

Daniel A. Brown

Cockspur Island is typical of the low marshy islands along the Georgia coast. It sits at the mouth of the Savannah River, astride the two navigable channels, washed by the Atlantic Ocean on the east. It is approximately eighteen miles from Savannah, in a natural defensive position for guarding the seaward approaches to the port city. The tiny island's strategic advantages were evident to the early settlers of the Georgia Colony. The British constructed Fort George there in 1761 and abandoned it in 1776.

After the War of 1812, Congress authorized the army to improve the coastal defenses of the nation. In 1816 General Simon Bernard, a distinguished French military engineer, was engaged. The fortifications devised by the Bernard Commission are known as the third-system forts. Twenty-six of these were constructed along the American coastline.

The fort constructed on Cockspur Island was named after Count Casimir Pulaski, the hero of the Revolution who was mortally wounded during the siege of Savannah in 1779. A young engineering officer who had graduated second in his class at West Point, Second Lieutenant Robert E. Lee, surveyed the fort site in 1829 and designed the dike system necessary for draining and protecting the construction area. Lee left Savannah in 1830, and construction began in 1831, when a more ex-

perienced engineer, First Lieutenant Joseph K. F. Mansfield, was assigned to the fort.

By 1847 the basic structure of Fort Pulaski was completed. The fort enclosed approximately five acres and was capable of mounting 146 guns. The brick walls were built seven and a half feet thick and thirty-five feet high, and were surrounded by a moat seven feet deep and thirty-five feet wide. The landward (west) side was protected by a triangular "demilune," or earthwork, also surrounded by a moat twenty-five feet wide. During the crisis with Great Britain in 1839, twenty 32-pounder cannon were mounted in the casemates. The rest of the armament was never completed.

On the eve of the Civil War, the fort was under the care of an ordnance sergeant and a caretaker, posted there to maintain the guns and other minimal military stores. On January 3, 1861, volunteer militia from Savannah, acting under orders from Governor Joseph E. Brown, landed on Cockspur Island and raised the flag of the State of Georgia over Fort Pulaski. State and Confederate forces began repairs on the fort and upgraded the armament.

Fort Pulaski National Monument
View from the fort across the Savannah River toward Tybee Island, site of the Federal siege batteries. © David Muench, 1990

Twenty-eight guns were added, including several 8-inch and 10-inch Columbiads manufactured at Tredegar Iron Works in Richmond, Virginia. The Confederates got two 24-pounder Blakely rifled cannon through the Federal blockade from Britain.

On November 7, 1861, Union naval and land forces bombarded and captured Hilton Head Island, north of Cockspur Island. Brigadier General Thomas W. Sherman, commander of the South Carolina Expeditionary Corps, and his naval counterpart, Captain Samuel F. du Pont, laid out the plans for the siege and capture of Fort Pulaski. On November 10 the Confederates retreated from Tybee Island, to the south. Union troops moved in under the command of Engineer Captain Quincy Adams Gillmore.

Gillmore was an outstanding engineering officer and a staunch proponent of the power and accuracy of rifled cannon, but rifled cannon had never been used successfully beyond six hundred yards, and it was more than a mile from Tybee Island to Fort Pulaski. The history of fortification supported the opinion of Robert E. Lee, who told Colonel Charles H. Olmstead, the Confederate commander at the fort, that Union guns on Tybee Island could "make it pretty warm for you here with shells, but they cannot breach your walls at that distance." Military history had demonstrated that cannon and mortar could not break through heavy masonry walls at ranges beyond a thousand yards.

Sherman was committed to a siege operation and requested the heavy ordnance. By February 21, when the cannon began to ar-

---

The map of the siege of Fort Pulaski, Georgia, by Union forces on April 10 and 11, 1862, prepared to accompany the report of the event by Brigadier General Quincy A. Gillmore. This copy is from *The Atlas to Accompany the Official Records of the Union and Confederate Armies*, the most detailed atlas of the Civil War, published by the Government Printing Office in thirty-seven parts between 1891 and 1895. (Civil War map no. 99, Geography and Map Division, Library of Congress)

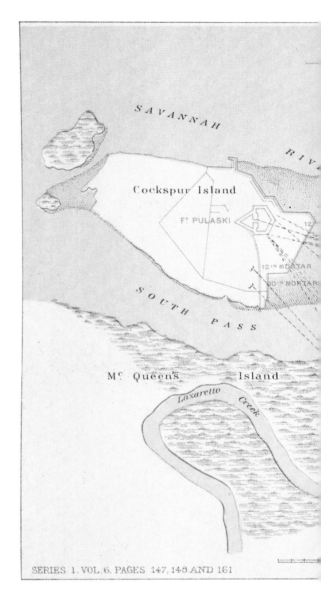

SERIES 1. VOL. 6. PAGES 147, 148 AND 161.

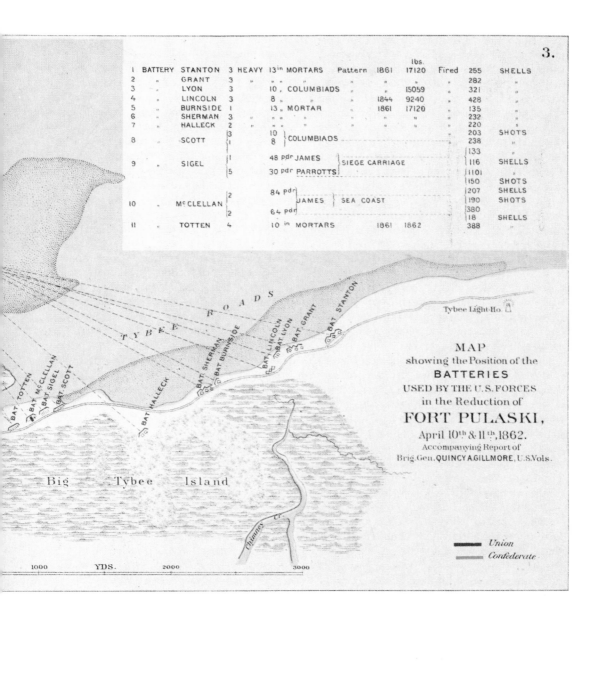

	BATTERY					Pattern		lbs.	Fired		
1	BATTERY STANTON	3	HEAVY	13 in MORTARS		Pattern	1861	17120	Fired	255	SHELLS
2	" GRANT	3	"	"	"	"	"	17120	"	282	"
3	" LYON	3		10 " COLUMBIADS	"	"		15059		321	"
4	" LINCOLN	3		8 " "	"		1844	9240	"	428	"
5	" BURNSIDE	1		13 " MORTAR	"		1861	17120	"	135	"
6	" SHERMAN	3	"	"	"	"	"	"	"	232	"
7	" HALLECK	2	"	"	"	"	"	"	"	220	"
8	" SCOTT	3 / 1		10 / 8 COLUMBIADS						203 / 238	SHOTS / "
9	" SIGEL	1 / 5		48 pdr JAMES / 30 pdr PARROTTS	SIEGE CARRIAGE					133 / 116 / 1101 / 150	SHELLS / " / SHOTS
10	" McCLELLAN	2 / 2		84 pdr / 64 pdr JAMES	SEA COAST					207 / 190 / 380	SHELLS / SHOTS /
11	" TOTTEN	4		10 in MORTARS			1861	1862		18 / 388	SHELLS

MAP
showing the Position of the
BATTERIES
USED BY THE U.S. FORCES
in the Reduction of
FORT PULASKI,
April 10th & 11th, 1862.
Accompanying Report of
Brig. Gen. QUINCY A. GILLMORE, U.S. Vols.

Tybee Light-Ho.

ROADS

TYBEE

BAT STANTON
BAT GRANT
BAT LYON
BAT LINCOLN
BAT BURNSIDE
BAT SHERMAN
BAT HALLECK
BAT SCOTT
BAT SIGEL
BAT McCLELLAN
BAT TOTTEN

Big Tybee Island

Chimney Cr.

Union
Confederate

1000   YDS.   2000   3000

rive, Gillmore had decided to locate the batteries on the northwestern tip of Tybee Island. Union forces began the backbreaking task of moving the heavy guns. Working parties landed thirty-six smoothbores, mortars, and rifled guns in a heavy surf and built a two-and-a-half-mile road, firm enough to support the weight of the artillery, across the sand and marsh. To avoid detection by the Confederates at Fort Pulaski, Gillmore's men had to work on the last mile at night and in virtual silence. Within the month eleven siege batteries, mounting thirty-six pieces, were in place less than two miles from the fort. Included in this formidable array were nine rifled cannon in batteries Sigel and McClellan, about one mile from the fort and bearing on its southeast angle. Unlike smoothbore cannon, rifled guns have spiraled grooves inside the barrel, which cause the projectile to spin as it emerges, making it more accurate and giving it increased range and penetration power.

The Confederate garrison under Colonel Olmstead consisted of five Georgia infantry companies, totaling 385 men. It had forty-eight guns, twenty of which could be brought to bear on Gillmore's siege batteries: six 8-inch Columbiads, four 10-inch Columbiads, four 32-pounder guns, three 10-inch seacoast mortars, two 12-inch seacoast mortars, and one 24-pounder Blakely rifle. One 10-inch and the two 12-inch mortars were located in advance batteries outside the fort but were abandoned.

At 8:10 A.M. on April 10, 1862, a single 13-inch mortar in Battery Halleck lofted its 197-pound shell in a graceful arc over Fort Pulaski. The fire of the Union Columbiads and rifled cannon concentrated on the southeast angle of the fort. The rifles aimed first at the guns on the parapet, then shifted to the walls, literally picking away at the brickwork. The great Columbiads shattered the brick loosened by the rifled projectiles. Confederate fire, at first brisk, diminished as gun after gun was dismounted or rendered unserviceable by the accurate fire of the Union artillerymen. By nightfall Olmstead's position was precarious. An inspection of the southeast angle revealed the enormous destruction wrought by the rifled cannon. Two embrasures had been enlarged and the surface of the wall had been reduced to half its thickness.

On April 11 Gillmore's gunners commenced firing at daylight. Confederate guns remounted during the night were quickly put out of action. The Union bombardment concentrated on enlarging the breech. By twelve o'clock shells were passing through the opening and exploding against the northwest powder magazine, which housed forty thousand pounds of powder. Olmstead knew the situation was hopeless. At 2:30 P.M. a white sheet replaced the Stars and Bars on the rampart wall. Fort Pulaski had fallen.

The cost in life and matériel was minor: the Union lost one man; one Confederate man was mortally wounded; all other wounds were not serious. The Union army expended 5,275 rounds from the thirty-six pieces in the thirty-hour bombardment. The rifled guns had done the real work while firing fewer than half the total rounds. The victory was as stunning as it was complete. An entire defense system, which had taken nearly fifty years to perfect, was made obsolete in less than two days. Today the fort serves not only as a memorial to the valor and dedication of those connected with its construction, bombardment, and defense but, in a larger sense, as a history lesson on the elusiveness of invincibility.

Fort Pulaski National Monument is on Cockspur Island, across from Tybee Island, near Savannah, Georgia. There are 5,623 acres of the historic battlefield within its authorized boundaries.

MAPPING THE CIVIL WAR

Richard W. Stephenson

On the eve of the Civil War, few detailed maps existed of areas in which fighting was likely to occur. Uniform, large-scale topographic maps, such as those produced today by the United States Geological Survey, did not exist and would not become a reality for another generation.

The most detailed maps available in the 1850s were of selected counties. Published at about the scale of one inch to a mile or larger, these commercially produced wall maps showed roads, railroads, towns and villages, rivers and streams, mills, forges, taverns, dwellings, and the names of residents. The few maps of counties in Virginia, Maryland, and southern Pennsylvania that were available were eagerly sought by military commanders on both sides.

Federal military authorities were keenly aware that any significant campaign into the seceding states could be carried out successfully only after good maps, based on reliable data from the field, had been prepared. Existing Federal mapping units, such as the Army's Corps of Topographical Engineers, the Treasury Department's Coast Survey, and the Navy's Hydrographic Office, were considered of immense importance to the war effort. In this the Union had one great advantage over the Confederacy: it was able to build on existing organizational structure, equipment, and trained personnel.

Federal authorities used every means at their disposal to gather accurate information on the location, number, movement, and intent of Confederate armed forces. Army cavalry patrols were constantly probing the countryside in search of the enemy's picket lines; travelers and peddlers were interrogated; southerners sympathetic to the Union were contacted and questioned; and spies were dispatched to the interior. The army also turned to a new device for gathering information, the stationary observation balloon. Early in the war a balloon corps was established under the direction of Thaddeus S. C. Lowe and was attached to the Army of the Potomac. Although used chiefly for observing the enemy's position in the field, balloons were also successfully employed in making maps and sketches.

Field and harbor surveys, topographic and hydrographic surveys, reconnaissances, and road traverses by Federal mappers led to the preparation of countless thousands of manuscript maps and their publication in unprecedented numbers. The superintendent of the Coast Survey in his annual report for 1862 noted that "upwards of forty-four thousand copies of printed maps, charts and sketches have been sent from the office since the date of my last report — a number more than double the distribution in the year 1861, and upwards of five times the average annual distribution of former years." Large numbers of maps were also compiled and printed by the Army Corps of Engineers. The chief engineer reported that in 1865, 24,591 map sheets were furnished to the armies in the field.

The development and growing sophistication of the Union mapping effort was apparent in 1864, when it became possible for Coast Survey officials to compile a uniform, ten-mile-to-the-inch base map described by the superintendent as "the area of all the states in rebellion east of the Mississippi River, excepting the back districts of North and South Carolina, and the neutral part of Tennessee and to southern Florida, in which no military movements have taken place." Moreover, as the superintendent noted, the map was placed on lithographic stones so that "any limits for a special map may be chosen at pleasure, and a sheet issued promptly when needed in prospective military movements."

Armies in the field also found it useful to have printing and mapmaking facilities so that multiple copies of maps could be produced quickly. On the eve of the Atlanta campaign, for example, the Army of the Cumberland's Topographical Department included draftsmen and assistants and was equipped with a printing press and two lithographic presses; it could also photograph and mount maps. To prepare for the campaign, the department worked night and day to compile, draw, edit, and lithograph an accurate campaign map of northern Georgia. "Before the commanding generals left Chattanooga," one participant wrote, "each had received a bound copy of the map, and before we struck the enemy, every brigade, division, and corps commander in the three armies had a copy." In addition to producing a standard edition of the campaign map lithographed on paper, the department printed it directly on muslin and issued it in three parts, mainly for the convenience of the cavalry, who needed a map that was sturdy, of a manageable size, and washable.

The Confederacy had difficulty throughout the war in supplying its field officers with adequate maps, because of the lack of estab-lished government mapping agencies and the inadequacy of printing facilities. The situation was further complicated by the almost total absence of surveying and drafting equipment and the lack of trained military engineers and mapmakers to use the equipment that was available.

In early June 1861, shortly after Robert E. Lee was made head of the army in Virginia, he took prompt action to improve the Confederate mapping situation. He assigned Captain Albert H. Campbell to head the Topographical Department. Survey parties were organized and dispatched into the countryside around Richmond and into other Virginia counties in which fighting was likely to occur to collect the data for accurate maps. Based on the new information, Confederate engineers under the direction of Campbell and Major General Jeremy F. Gilmer, chief of engineers, prepared detailed maps of most counties in eastern and central Virginia. These were drawn in ink on tracing linen and filed in the Topographical Department in Richmond. Prepared most often on a scale of 1:80,000, with a few at 1:40,000, each county map generally indicated boundaries, villages, roads, railroads, relief (by hachures), mountain passes, woodland, drainage, fords, ferries, bridges, mills, houses, and names of residents.

Initially, when the Topographical Department received a request for maps of a particular area, a draftsman was assigned to make a tracing of the file copy. But "so great was the demand for maps occasioned by frequent changes in the situation of the armies," Campbell noted,

that it became impossible by the usual method of tracings to supply them. I conceived the plan of doing this work by photography, though expert photographers pronounced it impracticable, in fact impossible. . . . Traced copies were prepared on common tracing-paper in very black India ink, and from these sharp negatives by sun-printing were obtained, and from these negatives copies were multiplied by exposure to the sun in frames made for the purpose. The several sections, properly toned, were pasted together in their order, and formed the general map, or such portions of it as were desired; it being the policy as a matter of prudence against capture to furnish no one but the commanding general and corps commanders with the entire map of a given region.

Perhaps the finest topographical engineer to serve during the Civil War was Jedediah Hotchkiss, a schoolmaster from Staunton, Virginia. He began his military service on July 2, 1861, when he joined the Confederate forces at Rich Mountain, where he made his first official maps. Because of his demonstrated skill in mapmaking, he was assigned to General Thomas J. "Stonewall" Jackson as topographical engineer of the Valley District, Department of Virginia. Shortly after his arrival, Hotchkiss was called before the great commander and told "to make me a map of the valley, from Harpers Ferry to Lexington, showing all the points of offense and defense in those places." The resulting comprehensive map, drawn on tracing linen and measuring seven and a half by three feet, was of significant value to Jackson and his staff in planning and executing the Valley campaign in May and June 1862. Hotchkiss went on to prepare hundreds of sketch maps, reconnaissance maps, battle maps, and reports, many of which are now preserved in the Library of Congress.

Throughout the Civil War, commercial publishers in the North and to a lesser extent in the South produced countless maps for a public in need of up-to-date geographical information. Maps of places in the news, particularly those perceived to be the sites of victories, guaranteed the publisher a quick profit. To give authenticity to their products, publishers based their maps on "reliable" eyewitness accounts, including those of active participants. Compared to publishers in the North, those in the South produced few maps for the general public, issuing those that did appear in small numbers. Printing presses and paper, as well as lithographers and wood engravers, were in short supply in the Confederacy. The few maps published for sale to the public were invariably simple in construction, relatively small, and usually devoid of color.

Cartography changed during the Civil War. Field survey methods were improved; the gathering of data became more sophisticated; faster, more adaptable printing techniques were developed; and photoreproduction processes became an important means of duplicating maps. The result was that thousands of manuscript, printed, and photoreproduced maps of unprecedented quality were prepared of areas where fighting erupted or was likely to occur.

It was not until 1879 that Congress created the U.S. Geological Survey, establishing the beginnings of a national topographic mapping program. Many years passed, therefore, before modern topographic maps became available to replace those created by war's necessity. The maps of the Civil War are splendid testimony to the skill and resourcefulness of Union and Confederate mapmakers and commercial publishers in fulfilling their responsibilities.

THE 1862 SHENANDOAH VALLEY CAMPAIGN

23 February–9 June 1862

James I. Robertson, Jr.

One of the most famous military campaigns of all time occurred in the spring of 1862 in the Shenandoah Valley of Virginia. The general whose brilliance in those three months of marching and fighting made him a living legend was Thomas J. "Stonewall" Jackson.

A former professor at the Virginia Military Institute in the upper (southern) end of the Valley, Major General Jackson was a God-fearing, humorless, close-mouthed commander who believed in secret marches and unexpected attacks. "Old Jack," as his troops affectionately called him, was aware of the importance of the Shenandoah to the Confederate war effort. The region lying between the two easternmost ranges of the Allegheny Mountains was a bountiful source of grain, fruit, and livestock. Since the Valley ran from southwest to northeast, it was a natural avenue of invasion into the heart of the North. Whoever controlled the Valley also controlled the key to military operations in Virginia.

The Civil War was entering its second spring when a Union force of 38,000 men under Major General Nathaniel P. Banks began inching into the Valley at Winchester. Jackson had barely 6,000 ill-equipped soldiers to defend the Shenandoah. The Confederates fell back to Mount Jackson, thirty-five miles south of Winchester, where Jackson learned that part of Banks's army was preparing to head east to reinforce Major General George B. McClellan's army as it advanced on Richmond. The reinforcements had to be stopped.

On March 23 Jackson attacked part of Banks's force at Kernstown, just south of Winchester. The Confederates suffered a tactical defeat, and Jackson lost 718 men, to 568 Union casualties. Yet the battle of Kernstown was a strategic success, because it convinced Union authorities to keep Banks's army intact at the northern end of the Valley. By April the lower Shenandoah swarmed with Union soldiers. Jackson received help with the arrival of an 8,500-man division under crusty Major General Richard S. Ewell. The stage was now set for Jackson to pin down the Union forces in his front and then attack each segment individually and unexpectedly.

Late in April Jackson left Ewell's division to face Banks's army and disappeared with the rest of his command. Banks became convinced that Jackson was going to Richmond. Yet on the morning of May 8, Jackson's 9,000 troops suddenly appeared at McDowell, across the mountains to the west of Staunton, and confronted 6,000 Federals. An all-day fight brought Jackson a victory, even though his

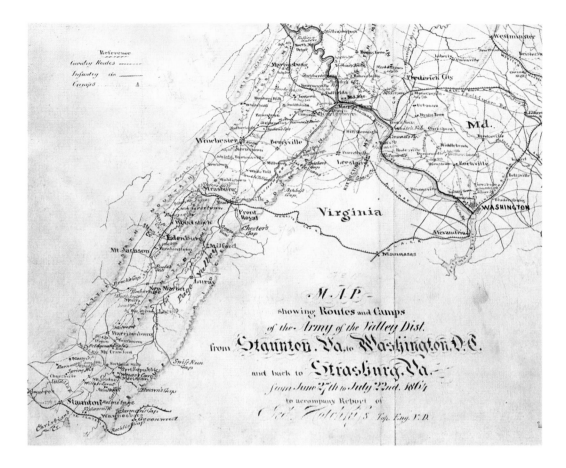

MAP
showing Routes and Camps
of the Army of the Valley Dist.
from Staunton, Va. to Washington, D.C.
and back to Strasburg, Va.
from June 27th to July 22nd 1864
to accompany Report of
Capt. Jed. Hotchkiss S. Top. Eng. V.D.

Jedediah Hotchkiss, one of the outstanding topographical engineers and mapmakers of the war, began mapping the Valley with General Jackson in 1862. This map is included in the "maps & sketches" prepared to accompany the unpublished *Report of the Camps, Marches & Engagements, of the Second Corps, A.N.V. . . . during the Campaign of 1864*. (Hotchkiss map collection no. 8, Geography and Map Division, Library of Congress)

losses (498) were twice those of the Federals. With the McDowell area secured and his left flank thus protected, he marched hastily back into the Valley and rejoined Ewell for a concentrated offensive against Banks.

In mid-May part of Banks's force began preparing to depart for the Richmond front. Jackson advanced with his entire army. Between New Market and Front Royal, a long, high ridge known as Massanutten Mountain divides the Shenandoah into two valleys. Jackson slipped through the pass at New Market and, using the lesser-known part of the Valley, rapidly marched northward toward Banks's unsuspecting command.

The men at the Union outpost at Front Royal were concerned only about the unusually hot weather when Jackson's Confederates rushed screaming from the woods on May 23. Beginning near noon, the fight lasted as long as it took the Confederates to dash through Front Royal. Banks's men in the

Shenandoah Valley proper and Jackson's troops in the Luray Valley now began the race to Winchester. On May 25 the two forces fought for control of the town. The Union army disintegrated and fled north toward the Potomac River.

A week later three different Union forces began moving on Jackson's small command from the west, north, and east. By means of a march of fifty miles in two days — a march that earned Jackson's infantry the title "foot cavalry" — the Confederates escaped the closing vise. Jackson and Ewell together fell back to Harrisonburg, with Union columns under Major General John C. Frémont and Brigadier General James Shields in steady pursuit.

Jackson knew that the parallel roads on which Frémont and Shields were advancing eventually converged at the hamlet of Port Republic. He quickly posted Ewell's men four miles to the northwest of the village to confront Frémont, while his own men took positions on the rolling ground at Port Republic.

On June 8 Frémont sent a small portion of his command in a weak and dispirited assault against Ewell at Cross Keys. The most vicious fighting of the campaign was at Port Republic, along the banks of the South Fork of the Shenandoah River. There, on June 9, Jackson defeated Shields and sent the Federals reeling back down the Valley.

Cross Keys and Port Republic ended the fight for the Shenandoah Valley. Jackson had won the most spectacular victory of the war to date. A quiet, demanding general who sucked lemons and spoke little, he had saved Richmond and preserved his beloved Valley through a series of extraordinary military movements. His accomplishments altered the course of the Civil War. With no more than 16,000 men, Jackson had frustrated the designs of 64,000 Union troops. In the process he had inflicted 7,000 casualties, at a cost of 2,500 of his troops. Jackson's success brought new hope to the Confederacy and created a legend that still lives.

Front Royal

MCDOWELL

8 May 1862

Robert G. Tanner

On May 8, 1862, a small Confederate army under Major General Thomas J. "Stonewall" Jackson fought a battle in the mountains of western Virginia near the village of McDowell, thirty-two miles west of Staunton. A year later, on May 10, 1863, when Stonewall Jackson died of wounds received at Chancellorsville, he was a legend to his countrymen. His "foot cavalry" had become one of the finest fighting forces in the history of war. The year that spanned those two May days was one of triumph, a success that began with the battle of McDowell.

Yet at the beginning of May 1862, there seemed scant hope for the Confederacy. The war had not gone well for its troops for many months. They had been defeated at Pea Ridge and Shiloh. A huge Union army was advancing on Richmond, and Federal armies were on the attack across the South. The great port of New Orleans had recently fallen to the Union navy. Jackson, who led the small Confederate army defending the Shenandoah Valley of Virginia, had been badly beaten in March at Kernstown in his first battle as an independent commander. He had rebuilt his army over the next two months but had had to surrender most of the Valley to Union Major General Nathaniel P. Banks. Another Union army, under Major General John C. Frémont (the famous "Pathfinder of the West" in the 1840s), was closing

in on Jackson from the Alleghenies, west of the Shenandoah. By early May Jackson knew that Frémont's 3,500-man advance guard under Brigadier General Robert H. Milroy was in the area of McDowell. On May 8 Milroy was reinforced by Brigadier General Robert C. Schenck's brigade of 2,500 men.

Jackson accepted the challenge and began moving his 9,000 soldiers into the Alleghenies. These were tough marches, the first of many that the foot cavalry would endure. They hustled through the windy passes and gorges west of Staunton, and by the morning of May 8 they were within sight of McDowell. There were 6,000 Federals around the village. Although heavily outnumbered, the Union forces took the offensive, led by Colonel Nathaniel McLean's Ohio regiments.

The battle that erupted was influenced by features of the terrain that can still be seen today, because the battlefield is largely undisturbed. The jagged high ground surrounding McDowell was so rough that it was almost impossible to bring cannon to the summits. Cannon situated on the lower ground were unable to reach the heights. McDowell was destined to be an infantryman's fight.

The battle occurred on a ridge running generally north and south along the eastern side of the Bull Pasture River, five hundred feet below. The flat area in the center of that ridge,

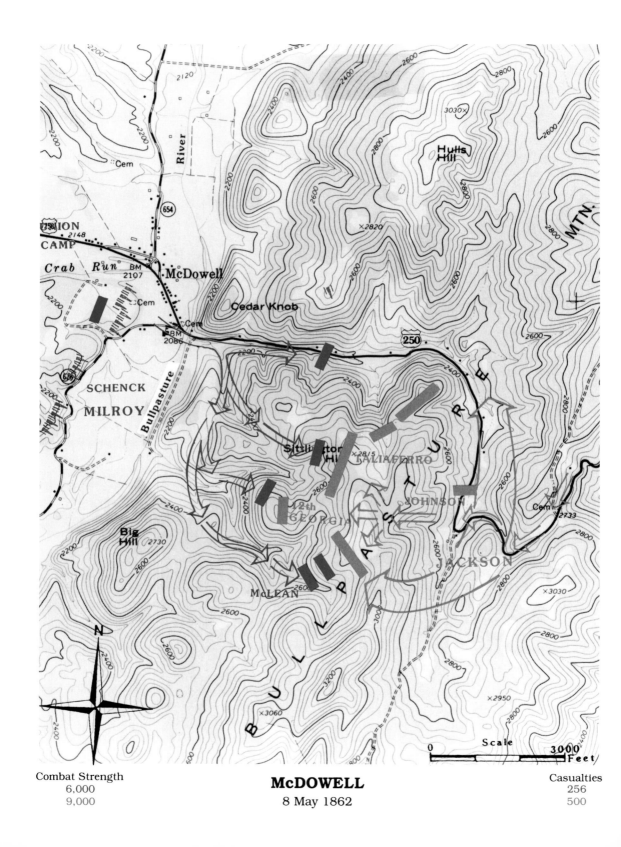

Combat Strength
6,000
9,000

McDOWELL

8 May 1862

Casualties
256
500

Sitlington's Hill, is topped by an open field perhaps a mile in length surrounded by precipitous and densely forested slopes. Jackson moved quickly by way of a ravine that left the main turnpike about a mile and a half east of McDowell, and seized Sitlington's Hill. From its top he surveyed the terrain to find a way to outflank the Union forces on the far side of the river. He was joined by his second-in-command, Brigadier General Edward "Allegheny" Johnson.

Before Confederate plans could unfold, however, General Milroy launched his assault. Fighting their way up through tangled forest, the Union columns became ragged and somewhat disordered; nonetheless, they attacked with courage, taking advantage of depressions in the ground to find cover. With the sun to their backs, they were hidden by the ground and the shadows of the surrounding trees. The Confederates at the top of the hill were silhouetted against the brighter sky, making them easy targets. They suffered alarming casualties, including General Johnson, who was severely wounded.

General Jackson rode his lines. The Union firing was so intense that he ordered reinforcements — Brigadier General William B. Taliaferro's men — to the Confederate right. Moving down the ridge into the woods along the right side of the hill, Taliaferro's troops stopped the Union thrust up the slope.

The fighting was increasingly intense, and heavy casualties were inflicted on Confederate troops in the center of Sitlington's Hill. That post was held by the Twelfth Georgia, which had entered the fray with 540 men. By the end of the day, 40 had been killed and 140 wounded, losses three times greater than those of any other regiment engaged. Nonetheless, the regimental commander was unable to make his men move back even a short distance to a better-protected position. Refusing such a retreat, one Georgia private blurted out: "We did not come all this way to Virginia to run before Yankees."

Finally, no Federal attack made significant progress, given the number of Confederates and their firepower. By nightfall Milroy withdrew his troops across the Bull Pasture River and retreated to Monterey. He could have the satisfaction of knowing that his casualties, 256 men, were about half those of the Confederates, 500 men. An army attacking uphill against heavy odds could not expect to maintain a battle for this length of time, much less inflict greater casualties. The ratio of losses reflected shrewd use of the terrain by Union forces.

The next day, May 9, Jackson's foot cavalry entered McDowell and found that the enemy had withdrawn. The battle had been so rough that even Jackson did not launch an immediate pursuit. He spent the day resting and refitting his forces, and then paused briefly to write a famous message. Ever laconic, he gave his superiors in Richmond a one-sentence report: "God blessed our arms with victory at McDowell yesterday." Jackson began his pursuit of Milroy the following day, continuing his great Valley campaign.

McDowell battlefield is on U.S. Route 250 at McDowell, Virginia, 35 miles west of Staunton. One hundred and forty acres of the historic battlefield are owned by the Lee Jackson Foundation and are open to the public with prior permission (P.O. Box 8121, Charlottesville, VA 22906).

CROSS KEYS

8 June 1862

Donald C. Pfanz

The battle of Cross Keys is perhaps the least famous of the many battles fought by Major General Thomas J. "Stonewall" Jackson's troops in the 1862 Shenandoah Valley campaign. However, the victory secured by Confederate troops there on June 8 was important, because it set the stage for Jackson's victory at Port Republic one day later. Taken together, Cross Keys and Port Republic marked the climax of a campaign that is still considered a military masterpiece.

Cross Keys was among the last of a series of victories won by Jackson in the Valley that spring. With an army of just 17,000 men he had defeated Union detachments at McDowell, Front Royal, and Winchester and pushed his confounded opponents back to the Potomac River. Though substantially outnumbered by the Union armies that all but surrounded him, Jackson skillfully utilized the Valley's terrain to keep his opponents apart and struck the scattered components of the Union army before they could unite against him.

Such was the strategy he used at Cross Keys. After Jackson's victory at Winchester on May 25, Federal troops led by Major General John C. Frémont and Brigadier General James Shields converged on the town of Strasburg in an attempt to cut Jackson off and destroy his small army. Jackson eluded their trap, however, and retreated up the Shenandoah Valley toward Harrisonburg, pursued by Frémont, while Shields moved by a parallel route up the Luray Valley, which lies a few miles to the east.

Jackson ordered Major General Richard S. Ewell to hold back Frémont. His plan was to defeat Shields quickly and then turn on Frémont before the Union general could react to Shields's defeat by retreating down the Valley. Ewell was a career soldier who had previously served at posts on the Plains and in the Southwest desert, where, he claimed, he "had learned all about commanding fifty United States dragoons and forgotten everything else." The Virginian proved he could handle a division as well as he did a company. On the day of the battle he had about 5,000 men, divided into three infantry brigades commanded by brigadier generals Arnold Elzey, George H. Steuart, and Isaac R. Trimble, and four batteries of artillery.

Ewell decided to block Frémont's progress at Cross Keys, a rural tavern located seven miles southeast of Harrisonburg. He placed his division in line of battle astride the Port Republic Road on a high, wooded ridge one mile south of the tavern. A shallow stream rippled across his front. In the center of the line, facing open fields, he massed his artillery, supported by Elzey's brigade. He posted Steuart's and Trimble's brigades in the woods to his left

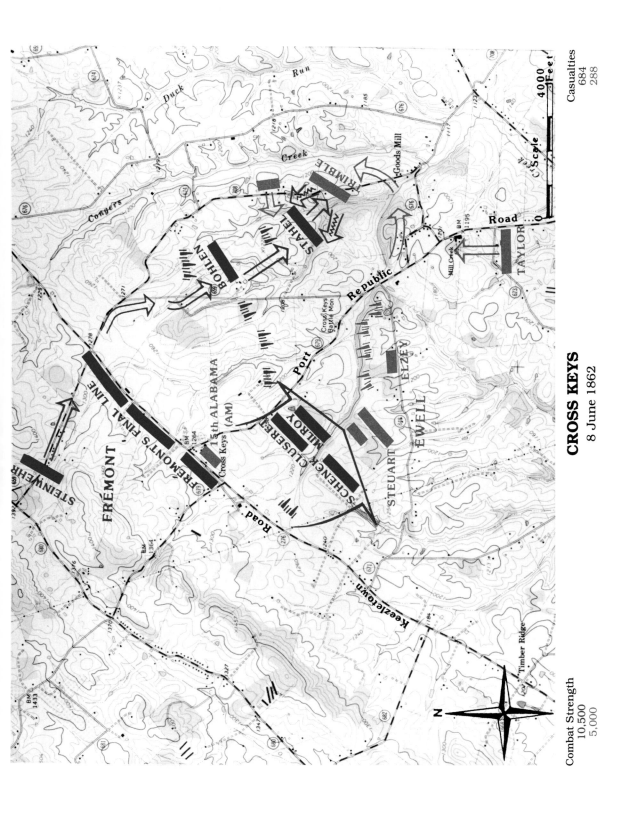

CROSS KEYS
8 June 1862

Combat Strength
10,500
5,000

Casualties
684
288

and right, with Trimble's brigade, on the right, slightly advanced.

The battle opened at 9:00 A.M., when Frémont, pushing down the Port Republic Road, collided with Confederate pickets at Union Church, near the tavern. The skirmishers fell back stubbornly, allowing Ewell time to complete his defensive arrangements. Finding the Confederates in force, Frémont brought forward his artillery to the hills opposite Ewell's position and engaged the Confederates in an artillery duel, at the same time deploying his infantry in line of battle around the village. Altogether he had about 10,500 men, divided into six brigades of infantry, one brigade of cavalry, and ten batteries of artillery. Commanding his infantry brigades were brigadier generals Julius Stahel, Henry Bohlen, Robert H. Milroy, Robert C. Schenck and colonels John A. Koltes and Gustave P. Cluseret.

Frémont made a cursory reconnaissance of the battlefield and judged Ewell's right to be the strategic flank. If he could successfully assail that flank, he could block Ewell's line of retreat and perhaps destroy the Confederate force. He accordingly ordered Stahel's brigade forward into the woods east of the Port Republic Road at 11:00 A.M., supported by Bohlen. Stahel soon encountered a line of Confederate skirmishers, which he pursued through the woods and across a wheatfield toward the main Confederate line. Trimble's brigade lay concealed behind a fence at the far edge of that field. Trimble allowed Stahel's men to approach within fifty yards of his line, then unleashed a savage volley.

Stahel's men fell back across the field in confusion. When they failed to renew the advance, Trimble seized the initiative and ordered his troops forward. Leaving two regi-

The battle of Cross Keys. Drawing by Edwin Forbes

ments in line behind the fence to hold the Union soldiers' attention, he led the Fifteenth Alabama Volunteers up a nearby ravine to a position opposite Stahel's left flank. At Trimble's command, the Alabamians fell upon their unsuspecting foes and forced them back on Bohlen's brigade, which was advancing to their relief. Reinforced by two regiments from Elzey's brigade, Trimble continued the attack, driving the Union troops back toward the Keezletown Road.

While Stahel and Bohlen were giving ground in the face of Trimble's spirited attacks on the left, Union brigades on the center and right moved forward to the attack. Cluseret and Milroy advanced through the woods west of the Port Republic Road, but finding the center of Ewell's line too strong to attack, they simply held their ground. Schenck's brigade meanwhile moved up on Milroy's right in an attempt to turn the left end of the Confederate line. Ewell perceived this threat to his flank and took steps to meet it. Early in the afternoon Jackson had reinforced him with the brigades of Colonel John M. Patton and Brigadier General Richard Taylor, and Ewell now hurried portions of these commands to support Steuart's brigade on his left. They were not needed. Before Schenck could launch his attack, Frémont, shaken by Stahel's repulse, ordered the entire Union army to withdraw to a new defensive line along the Keezletown Road. Ewell then advanced the wings of his army to occupy the ground held by Frémont during the battle. Trimble, feisty as ever, implored Ewell to attack the new Union position, but his commander, in accordance with Jackson's instructions, chose instead to break off the action.

Casualties on both sides had been light: the Union army lost 684 men in the contest, the Confederates 288. That night Ewell quietly withdrew most of his men from Frémont's front and marched to Port Republic, where he arrived in time to turn the tide of battle in Jackson's favor the next day. Frémont took up the pursuit early the next morning, marching over the ridge held by Ewell during the previous day's fight. As his troops tramped over the crest and down the opposite slope, they passed a Confederate field hospital located in a white frame church. By then Jackson and Ewell were engaged in battle with Shields at Port Republic. The sound of the fighting swelled on the wind as Frémont's men passed the church, and in the distance they saw a column of black smoke, where Ewell's rear guard had set the South River bridge aflame. Unable to cross the river, Frémont's men looked on helplessly as Jackson and Ewell overwhelmed Shields's force and drove it from the field.

Cross Keys battlefield is southeast of Harrisonburg, Virginia, on State Route 276, 2.5 miles south of U.S. Route 33. Seventy acres of the historic battlefield are owned by the Lee Jackson Foundation and are open to the public with prior permission (P.O. Box 8121, Charlottesville, VA 22906).

PORT REPUBLIC

9 June 1862

Donald C. Pfanz

Port Republic was the final, climactic battle of Major General Thomas J. "Stonewall" Jackson's 1862 Shenandoah Valley campaign. In early June 1862, Jackson retreated up the Valley, pursued by two Union forces commanded by Major General John C. Frémont and Brigadier General James Shields. Frémont followed Jackson directly up the main valley, while Shields paralleled the Confederate march on the east, up the Luray Valley. By dividing their forces, the Union commanders gave Jackson the offensive opportunity he sought.

The Massanutten range separates the Shenandoah and Luray valleys. Through the Luray Valley, running between the Blue Ridge Mountains on the east and the Massanutten on the west, runs the South Fork of the Shenandoah River, which in 1862 was spanned by four bridges upstream from Front Royal: three near Luray and one at Conrad's Store (now Elkton). Jackson's cavalry destroyed each of these bridges and kept Frémont's and Shields's forces separated. The next closest point of crossing was at Port Republic, where the North and South rivers meet to form the South Fork. Two fords crossed the South River there, and a bridge arched the rain-swollen North River at the northern end of town.

Jackson marched his 6,000-man army to Port Republic and confidently turned to meet his pursuers. He adopted a simple yet ambitious plan: attack Shields east of the South Fork, overwhelm his small force, then cross the river and defeat Frémont before he could retreat down the Valley. In one day Jackson might achieve a double victory. The success of his plan depended on having Shields and Frémont approach him at the same time, separated from each other by the river. This did not happen. Frémont, marching on the Valley Turnpike, was one day ahead of Shields, whose troops had to march along the unimproved roads of the Luray Valley. In order to hold back Frémont until Shields arrived, Jackson left Major General Richard S. Ewell with one division at Cross Keys, four miles up the road. On June 8 Frémont attacked Ewell's force and was repulsed.

While Ewell battled Frémont at Cross Keys, Jackson waited for Shields at Port Republic. His army was camped on a bluff overlooking the North River. Suddenly a small Union cavalry force appeared. The troopers charged across the lower ford of the South River and through the main street of town, firing their revolvers. Jackson and his staff were staying at the home of Dr. George Kemper in town and were nearly captured in the sudden assault. Jackson eluded capture, however, and galloped to his camp across the river.

Meanwhile, Union cavalrymen unlimbered a

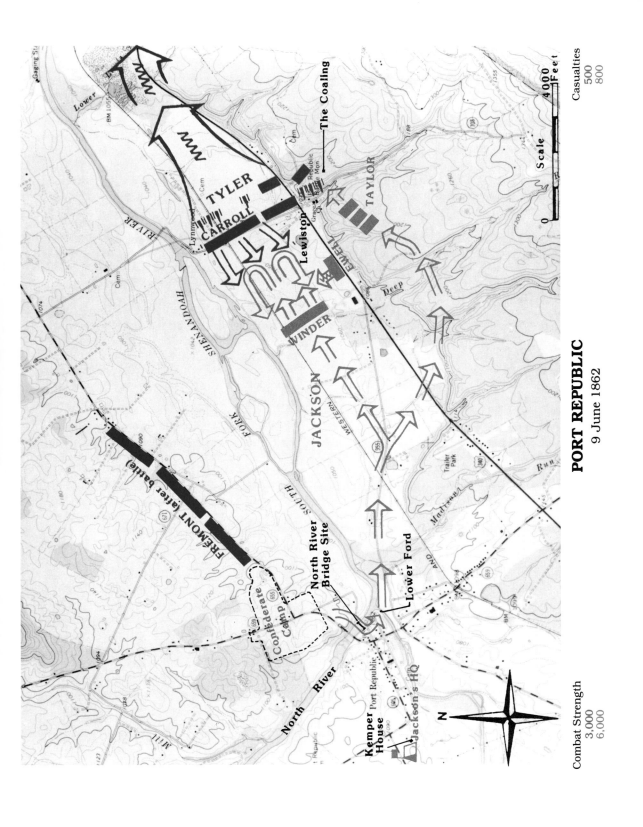

PORT REPUBLIC

9 June 1862

Combat Strength
3,000
6,000

Casualties
500
800

0   Scale   4000
Feet

gun in town and began shelling the Confederate position. Jackson engaged the hostile guns with batteries of his own, then sent Colonel Samuel Fulkerson's Virginia regiment charging across the bridge. The Union cavalry scattered in the face of Fulkerson's determined attack, abandoned their cannon, and escaped by way of the South River's lower ford. The cavalry belonged to the vanguard of Shields's division, commanded by Brigadier General Erastus B. Tyler, which reached the Port Republic area that day.

With both Tyler and Frémont within easy striking distance, Jackson sprang his trap on June 9. Before dawn he ordered Brigadier General Charles Winder's brigade across the South River to attack Tyler — a prelude to an assault on Frémont's larger force later in the day. To reach Tyler's position, Winder had to cross a wide, open plain bordered by the South Fork on his left and the Blue Ridge on his right.

Tyler had chosen his position well. His two brigades of 3,000 infantrymen occupied a line a half mile long. Their right flank was on the river, and their left flank was anchored on a commanding knoll known as the Lewiston Coaling, where a local family had recently produced charcoal. Tyler posted seven guns on the knoll, and as Winder's brigade approached they ripped into its right flank. At the same time Tyler's infantry opened a withering fire from their position below. The Confederate advance slowed, then came to a halt altogether, as Winder's dazed men sought some form of shelter on the exposed plain.

Because of a snarl at the South River crossing, Winder's brigade initially found itself without support. When Brigadier General Richard Taylor's Louisiana brigade finally reached the field, Jackson sent one regiment to Winder's relief, while Taylor led the rest of the brigade through the tangled woods on the right to attack the smoking guns at the coaling. Winder resumed his stalled offensive. Finding himself outnumbered and pinned down both in front and on his flank, the Virginian ordered his men forward in a desperate attempt to forestall a Union attack on his position — an attack that he had every reason to believe would succeed. Supported by Confederate artillery, he charged to within two hundred yards of the enemy line before being halted by hostile fire. For an hour his men held on, taking heavy losses in an effort to buy Jackson time. Finally, their ammunition nearly exhausted, the Confederates gave way and rushed in panic to the rear, chased by their opponents. But once again Confederate reinforcements saved the day. As the Federals streamed forward across the plain in pursuit of Winder, General Ewell arrived and struck the Union left flank with two regiments of infantry.

At about the same time, the guns located at the coaling above fell silent. Taylor had successfully stormed the position by struggling through a jungle of thick mountain laurel for more than an hour. Without pausing to form a proper line, the impetuous Louisianian had charged the guns. He was thrown back, but twice more he led his men forward, and in bloody hand-to-hand fighting they finally captured the guns. Tyler, seeing that the battery had been captured, wheeled his line to the left to charge the hill. To Taylor, his advancing blue masses seemed like a solid wall. "There seemed nothing left but to set our backs to the mountain and die hard," he later recalled. Just when all seemed lost, the sounds of artillery and musketry erupted once more on the plain below. Jackson had rallied Winder's men and, with the help of reinforcements, once more moved out to attack the foe.

For the Federals it was too much. Like Winder's men an hour before, they found themselves outnumbered and attacked on two sides. When the Confederate troops at the coaling added their fire to the melee, the Union line lost all cohesion, and its men broke for the rear. The Confederates pursued for five miles.

For Jackson, the hard-fought battle was won. In the four-hour fight he had lost 800

Port Republic battlefield
© David E. Roth, *Blue & Gray Magazine*,
Columbus, Ohio.

men while inflicting 500 casualties on the Union army and capturing as many more. Because of the length and severity of the battle, he was unable to recross the river and attack Frémont. His troops were in no condition to fight another battle that day. Realizing this, Jackson burned the North River bridge to prevent its capture by Frémont and withdrew his army to Brown's Gap, a short distance south, to rest and refit his men for future battles.

Jackson's victory at Port Republic capped a campaign in which he had defeated portions of four Union armies, totaling over 60,000 men. His success in the Valley changed the military outlook in Virginia and gave the struggling Confederacy new life.

Port Republic battlefield is located on U.S. Route 340 near Port Republic, Virginia, 15 miles north of Waynesboro. Nine acres of the historic battlefield are owned by the Association for the Preservation of Civil War Sites and are open to the public with prior permission (P.O. Box 1862, Fredericksburg, VA 22402).

THE SEVEN DAYS CAMPAIGN

25 June–1 July 1862

Herman Hattaway

The Seven Days campaign, fought from June 25 to July 1, 1862, was a singular episode of the Civil War. At the culmination of the Peninsula campaign, which had begun in March, Union forces had pushed to within seven miles of the Confederate capital at Richmond. In this week-long, fluid, and ongoing battle, which scholars have likened to those in World War II, the Confederates attacked time after time. The result was costly in Confederate casualties, but the Union army was forced to maneuver backward, yielding previously won territory, until it was about thirty miles from the capital.

On June 1, 1862, General Robert E. Lee assumed command and named his force the Army of Northern Virginia. He had about 72,000 men to grapple with Major General George B. McClellan's 100,000-man Army of the Potomac. Before the campaign began, Lee's men labored hard, strengthening the field fortifications near Richmond, while McClellan ordered heavy artillery to be dragged toward the lines. Lee decided to snatch the initiative before McClellan's ordnance was fully in place. The Union army's potentially vulnerable position gave Lee the opening he needed. McClellan had about 70,000 men south of the Chickahominy River and on the north side only 30,000, Brigadier General Fitz-John Porter's reinforced Fifth Corps. Porter was there to protect the Federal supply base and connect with Major General Irvin McDowell's troops, expected to arrive from the north.

On June 12 Lee dispatched his brilliant and flamboyant cavalry chief, Brigadier General J. E. B. Stuart, to determine McClellan's precise position. In a bold four-day ride, led by a then unknown lieutenant named John Singleton Mosby, Stuart's cavalry rode completely around McClellan's army. Most significant, Stuart captured prisoners and learned that the Federal army's right flank (northern side) lay unanchored.

Lee acted daringly. He gambled by leaving only the 25,000 men in the divisions of major generals Benjamin Huger and "Prince John" Magruder, already known for his ability to practice deception, on the south side of the

During and after the Civil War, commercial publishers, especially in the North, printed for the general public maps showing the theaters of war, major campaigns, and battles. This is a portion of "Johnson's Map of the Vicinity of Richmond, and Peninsular Campaign in Virginia," published in 1863 in Richard S. Fisher's *A Chronological History of the Civil War in America* and in editions of *Johnson's New Illustrated Family Atlas of the World*. It is from the 1870 edition of the *Family Atlas*. (Civil War map no. 602.65, Geography and Map Division, Library of Congress)

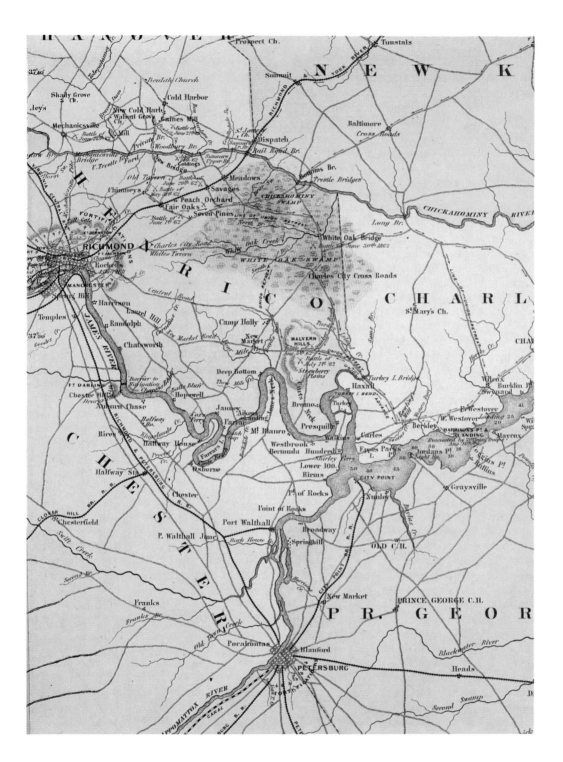

Chickahominy. They were all that remained between Richmond and McClellan's 70,000-man assault force. Lee hoped to deploy his other 47,000 men so they could destroy Porter's corps. To deceive the Federals, he sent one division west toward the Shenandoah Valley but recalled Major General Thomas J. "Stonewall" Jackson's 18,000 men from the Valley. Jackson was to attack Porter's unsupported north flank. Lee's plan was to threaten the Federals into leaving their position and fighting at a disadvantage.

Meanwhile, McClellan was nearly ready for his assault on Richmond, but he remained cautious, believing his faulty intelligence reports that the Confederates outnumbered him two to one. Lee's scanty 25,000-man security guard became 50,000 in McClellan's mind. "I am in no way responsible . . . ," McClellan asserted in a complaining dispatch he sent to Washington. "I have not failed to represent repeatedly the necessity for reinforcements. . . . If the result . . . is a disaster, the responsibility cannot be thrown on my shoulders." On June 25 his reconnaissance troops south of the Chickahominy clashed with Confederates at Oak Grove (King's Schoolhouse), in a brief but spirited engagement that marked the opening of the Seven Days campaign.

The next day Lee's men splashed across the Chickahominy. Three Confederate divisions, those of major generals Ambrose P. Hill, Daniel H. Hill, and James Longstreet, held back, waiting for Jackson. Jackson failed to appear. Indeed, throughout this campaign Jackson's men were uncharacteristically sluggish in all their maneuvers. (Soon Jackson's critics would suggest that the famous nickname "Stonewall," which had been bestowed on him during the battle of Manassas nearly a year earlier, was in fact a derisive suggestion that Jackson would not move.) Jackson and his men were exhausted from their celebrated Shenandoah Valley campaign, which had concluded on June 9, and Jackson recently had endured several sleepless nights. But his slow-

ness stymied the Confederate plan, and the ensuing campaign turned into a fruitless series of frontal assaults.

The impetuous A. P. Hill waited for Jackson until midafternoon and then decided to cross the river at Meadow Bridge and assault Porter's troops. The Federals were well placed and strongly entrenched behind Beaver Dam Creek, and they wrecked Hill's charging brigades. The Federals' rifle, musket, and artillery fire inflicted a terrible toll while they remained secure in their prepared works. D. H. Hill brought up reinforcements, but they encountered a similar fate. The hottest fighting took place around and past a little structure called Ellerson's Mill, located on a lightly wooded, gently sloping expanse of terrain. This battle of Mechanicsville cost the southerners 1,484 casualties, compared with only 361 sustained by Porter's force.

After dark Porter withdrew about five miles to a new position, behind Boatswain's Swamp southeast of Gaines' Mill, a complex of brick buildings surrounded by rough and undulating ground. The bulk of the Confederate army was dangerously far from Richmond, so to protect the capital, Lee struck Porter again on June 27 at Gaines' Mill. The terrain provided the Federals with a defensive advantage, and McClellan ordered the position held. A series of vicious Confederate assaults began in midafternoon and continued for five hours, but the Federals stood stalwart in a strong semicircular emplacement. Two Confederate brigades pierced the Union center and forced a retreat in confusion across the Chickahominy. Both sides suffered heavily — 8,750 Confederate casualties and 6,837 Union losses — but the action constituted Lee's first clear victory.

On June 28 McClellan began to move his base to Harrison's Landing, on the James River. Though this move enabled the Union navy to provide better support, it was also a retreat from Richmond. It was not until nearly three years later, when Lieutenant General Ulysses S. Grant at last succeeded in taking

Richmond, that any sizable body of Union troops would get as close as McClellan's advance had been. McClellan referred to his move as a strategic withdrawal, but his critics called it a "great skedaddle." He decided to withdraw even though brigadier generals Joseph Hooker and Philip Kearny informed him that the Confederate defense immediately before Richmond was weak.

For the next four days, June 28 to July 1, Lee tried in vain to destroy portions of McClellan's force, especially its huge wagon train, and to take its cattle herd. His plans were too complicated, and his staff bungled them so that the Confederate movements were awkward and uncoordinated. Inadequate maps and local traditions that twisted names and pronunciations plagued both sides. Several Confederate divisions attacked in piecemeal fashion at Savage Station on the Richmond and York River Railroad on June 29. Fierce fighting continued the next day in a disjointed and diffuse battle at White Oak Swamp — a "nightmarish morass" — and at Glendale. The Union line gave ground at Glendale but rallied and held firm.

On July 1 McClellan concentrated his forces in a strong position on Malvern Hill and brought Union artillery into effective play. Lee's men thrust haplessly forward, but fal-

tered in the face of heavy cannonading. This bloody southern defeat, resulting in more than 5,000 Confederate and 3,000 Union casualties, ended the campaign.

In one week Lee sustained a staggering casualty total of 20,141; the more numerous Federals lost 15,849. In this campaign, combined with the related battle of Seven Pines, the Confederates lost nearly 30 percent of their available force. The Federals, fighting on the more advantageous defensive, had lost only about 20 percent of their engaged forces.

The threat to the Confederate capital was diminished, and the war's future course in Virginia was permanently altered. General Lee and President Jefferson Davis were both educated by the Seven Days experience: victories could be purchased at too great a cost. The Confederates afterward eschewed purely offensive battle tactics.

As for McClellan, he lost rather little militarily, but he suffered much loss of esteem. There was little doubt in the minds of the northern populace as to who had won, and President Abraham Lincoln termed McClellan's campaign a "half defeat," which seriously depressed popular morale. The Seven Days campaign set the stage for the second Manassas campaign and for Lee's subsequent invasion of Maryland.

GAINES' MILL

27 June 1862

Michael J. Andrus

The Seven Days campaign, beginning on June 25, 1862, ended a three-month Union effort to capture Richmond. For a week the armies of General Robert E. Lee and Major General George B. McClellan fought, marched, and maneuvered from the Chickahominy swamps to the James River. These battles engaged more men and produced more casualties than any previous campaign in American military history. Gaines' Mill was that week's largest and most costly engagement.

Although Lee had been in command of the newly organized Army of Northern Virginia for less than a month, he had clearly seized the initiative from his adversary. While McClellan pouted about lack of support from Washington, Lee quickly consolidated his forces for the relief of Richmond. He had six Confederate divisions to confront Brigadier General Fitz-John Porter's huge Fifth Corps — 30,000 men, who were separated from the other four corps of the Union Army of the Potomac by the swollen Chickahominy River.

On June 26 an impetuous assault failed to drive Porter from his entrenched position along Beaver Dam Creek. With Major General Thomas J. "Stonewall" Jackson's command pressing his right flank, Porter withdrew closer to the military bridges over the Chickahominy. That night and the following day, both army commanders were busy planning the fate of the Union army; McClellan wanted to preserve his command, while Lee hoped to destroy it. On June 27 Lee's plans were continually frustrated by inaccurate maps, poor staff work, and piecemeal attacks. Even Lee's assumption that McClellan would move to protect his supply base on the Pamunkey River proved wrong. Most threatening of all, a nearly impregnable Union position loomed before any Confederate advance.

Union engineers had chosen Porter's defensive line carefully. It lay atop a partially wooded plateau just beyond a marshy creek known locally as Boatswain's Swamp. Brigadier General George W. Morell's three brigades secured the left, their line running north, then swinging east along the creek's wooded slope. Brigadier General George Sykes's division extended Morell's right across the plateau. Artillery batteries unlimbered opposite the openings in the woods. Brigadier General George McCall's Pennsylvania division plus two regiments of cavalry acted as a reserve. The front stretched for two miles, with the left anchored on the Chickahominy and the right protecting the main road to Grapevine Bridge. If disaster struck, three military bridges linked Porter to McClellan's main force and headquarters south of the Chickahominy.

"The morning of Friday, the 27th day of June, 1862," recalled one Federal veteran,

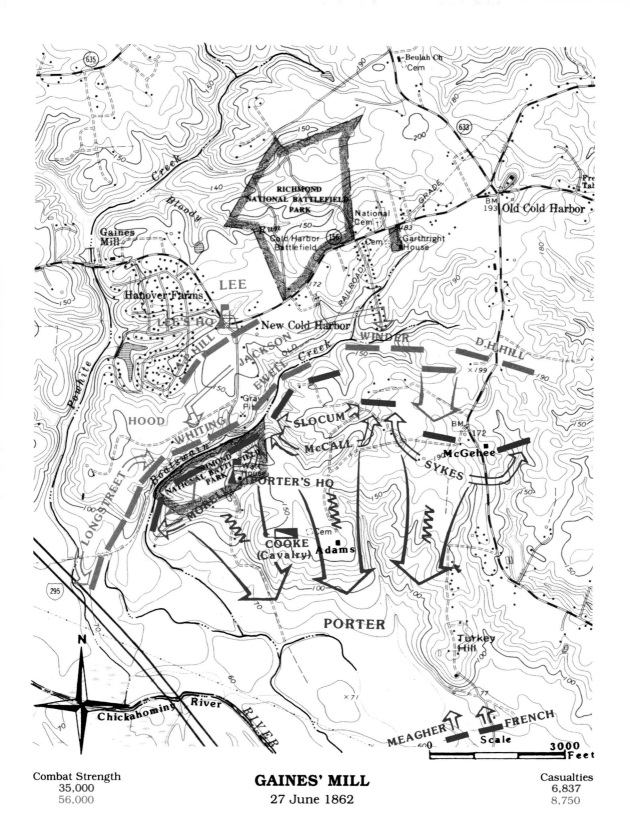

GAINES' MILL

27 June 1862

Combat Strength
35,000
56,000

Casualties
6,837
8,750

"broke hot and sultry." On a day more suited for napping than fighting, the Union infantry hastily prepared for the anticipated attacks. Just beyond the Watt house, Porter's headquarters, Morell's front line formed along the swamp's brush-tangled bottom. A second line hugged the ravine's crest. Breastworks of knapsacks, logs, and dirt were quickly thrown up. Artillery commanders positioned their guns to contest any enemy advance across the open fields beyond the ravine. And it was here that Lee opened the battle.

Brigadier General Maxcy Gregg's South Carolina brigade, part of Major General A. P. Hill's division, led the first assaults. Just after 2:30 P.M. his men sprang with a roar from the pine woods surrounding New Cold Harbor. The advance led across several hundred yards of cultivated fields and immediately caught the attention of the Union artillerists. The shelling, said one observer, turned the field into "one living sheet of flame." Once across, the Confederates swept down the wooded slopes before struggling through Boatswain's Swamp. When they reached the top of the opposite crest, they received orders to lie down and rest.

Gregg's attack came against the very center of the Union line, held by Colonel Gouverneur K. Warren's brigade. One of his two regiments, the Fifth New York, was dressed in the gaudy but somewhat tattered Zouave uniform of crimson breeches, short blue jacket, and red fez with a yellow tassel. The men had a fighting spirit to match. As Gregg's troops appeared against the distant woodline, the Zouaves steadied themselves.

"Charge bayonets!" screamed Colonel J. Foster Marshall, of the First South Carolina Rifles. And with that 500 men surged from the woods, aiming straight for the Union artillery. Spotting the advance, the Zouaves launched an attack of their own. They stormed into the First Rifles' flank. For a few minutes it was a hand-to-hand struggle with rifle butt and bayonet. Nearly half the thousand men engaged were killed or wounded before the Confederates fell back into the woods.

Gregg's attack typified the Confederate effort that afternoon. Porter's artillery devastated A. P. Hill's movements across open ground, while his infantry denied every attempt to break the line. On the Confederate left, near Old Cold Harbor, Major General D. H. Hill focused on three of General Sykes's batteries. A spirited charge by the Twentieth North Carolina succeeded in capturing several guns, but a counterattack led by the Sixteenth New York recaptured the pieces. On the right, Lee held Major General James Longstreet's division in reserve while he awaited the arrival of Stonewall Jackson.

For the second day in a row Jackson was late reaching the field. A civilian guide, misunderstanding the general's destination, led the command down a wrong road. Felled trees blocked the route, causing further delay. It was 5:00 P.M. before Jackson's three divisions arrived, commanded by Brigadier General Charles S. Winder, Major General Richard S. Ewell, and Brigadier General W. H. C. Whiting. Lee finally had his entire command of 56,000 men on the battlefield.

After four hours of what many felt had been the heaviest fighting of the war, both sides paused. Exhausted men collapsed from the oppressive heat and humidity. Rifles, fouled by constant use, were cleaned or discarded. Cartridges were gathered from the dead and wounded. Counting the 5,000 reinforcements sent to Porter from the commands of brigadier generals Henry W. Slocum, William Henry French, and Thomas F. Meagher, 90,000 soldiers now faced each other across Boatswain's Swamp.

The "ominous silence" Porter remembered finally broke at around 7:00 P.M. Lee, hoping to end matters decisively, ordered an all-out assault to break the Union defense. The main effort focused against Morell's division, over the same ground A. P. Hill's six brigades had failed to carry. This time the brigades of Brigadier General John Bell Hood and Colonel Evander Law spearheaded the attack. As the Confederate columns formed, Lee stopped Hood for a last word. "Can you break his line?"

Lee asked. "I will try," Hood replied, and started forward.

Advancing on Law's left, Hood soon noticed a gap in the Confederate line. He personally led the Fourth Texas and Eighteenth Georgia behind Law and into the opening. Both the dead and the living of A. P. Hill's division covered the ground. Survivors grabbed at the legs of the assaulting soldiers to prevent what they considered a suicidal act. All the while Union artillery tore through the ranks. But on the Confederates went, screaming the Rebel yell, under orders not to fire until they reached the enemy line. The wave never faltered, streaming down the wooded slope and across the shallow creek.

Elements of Morell's division, reinforced by Brigadier General Henry Slocum's division, met the attack but could not check its concentrated fury. For the first time Confederate soldiers pierced the Union lines. Broken regiments scrambled up the slope, preventing a return fire and carrying away a second line. The sudden breach forced a general retreat along the entire front.

With darkness rapidly approaching, Porter's reinforced corps began its withdrawal toward the Chickahominy. One last incident caused years of controversy. Hoping to stem the enemy's pursuit, Brigadier General Philip St. George Cooke ordered a desperate charge by the Fifth and Second U.S. Cavalry. The charge soon turned into a rout as Confederate musketry fire killed or wounded many of the cavalry. In the resulting confusion, Hood and others captured fourteen guns. Porter never forgave Cooke for the loss.

Nightfall brought an end to the fighting. Lee's exhausted soldiers dropped to the ground atop the plateau, and many fell instantly asleep. Many others, however, took up the task of searching the battlefield for friends. In one day Lee's army had suffered nearly 9,000 casualties. Porter's command took more than 6,800 casualties. Although several battles remained, Fitz-John Porter's masterful defense behind Boatswain's Swamp allowed McClellan to continue his change of base to Harrison's Landing on the James River. Nonetheless, Gaines' Mill was the first major victory of Lee's celebrated career. Two years later, his last major victory came on the same ground — at the battle of Cold Harbor.

Gaines' Mill Battlefield, a unit of Richmond National Battlefield Park, is northeast of Richmond, Virginia, off State Route 156. There are 60 acres of the historic battlefield within the authorized boundaries of this unit.

MALVERN HILL

1 July 1862

Michael D. Litterst

On July 1, 1862, fifteen miles southeast of Richmond, two mighty armies numbering 160,000 men prepared to do battle for the sixth time in a week. In those seven days the Union Army of the Potomac, commanded by Major General George B. McClellan, had been driven from the gates of Richmond by General Robert E. Lee and the Confederate Army of Northern Virginia. At Malvern Hill, a sharp rise seven miles from their base at Harrison's Landing, McClellan's forces made a final stand before reaching safety under cover of the U.S. Navy's guns on the James River.

The Union position was a formidable one. Malvern Hill — more a plateau than a hill — rises about a hundred feet at its crest and forms a mile-and-a-half-long crescent, bordered on the east by Western Run and on the west by Crewes Run. The creeks and high ground formed a natural defensive position that made a flank attack difficult. Beyond the crest an open, gently falling slope dotted with shocks of wheat stretched north for a quarter of a mile. The Union had massed 80,000 infantry, consisting of Brigadier General Edwin Sumner's Second Corps, Brigadier General Samuel Heintzelman's Third Corps, and Brigadier General Fitz-John Porter's Fifth Corps. In addition, more than 100 pieces of artillery rimmed the slope, and 150 more were in reserve near the Malvern house. Despite a warn-

ing by Confederate Major General Daniel Harvey Hill against attacking this strong position, Lee continued to bring his troops up and prepare for battle.

Throughout the Seven Days campaign, Lee had been plagued by costly troop movement delays, and Malvern Hill was no exception. It was noon on July 1 before the bulk of his army, 80,000 troops, began forming along a mile-long front at the base of the hill. Still missing, however, was Major General John B. Magruder, whose six brigades had mistakenly been sent down a road that led *away* from the gathering Confederate army. His arrival hours late hurt the Confederates in the battle.

During a reconnaissance of the area, Major General James Longstreet found a plateau on the Confederate right that was suitable for massing artillery against the Union line. Longstreet felt that with sixty guns on this plateau and an accompanying fire from Major General Thomas J. "Stonewall" Jackson's cannon on the left, Union troops would be caught in a crossfire that would allow Lee's infantry to assault their lines. D. H. Hill's and Magruder's commands were to spearhead the attack. Two of Jackson's divisions, under Major General Richard S. Ewell and Brigadier General W. H. C. Whiting, were in reserve. Longstreet's and Major General A. P. Hill's forces were to be held from the action because they had been

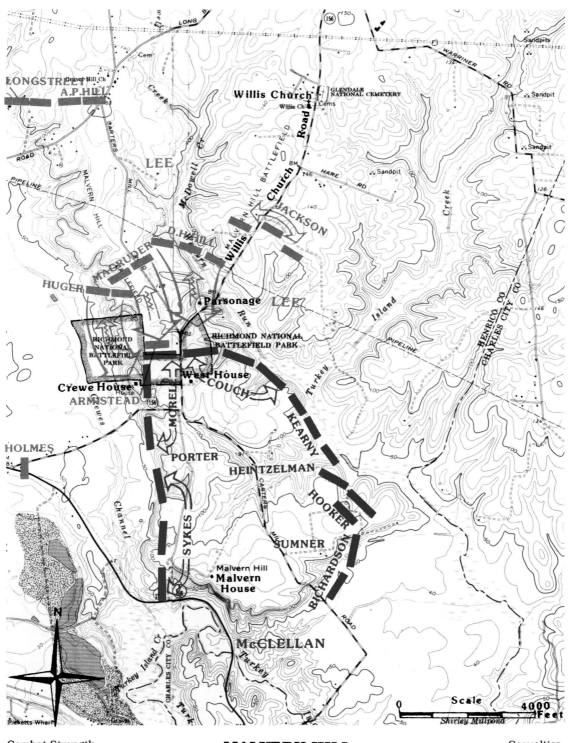

LONGSTREET
A.P. HILL

Willis Church

GLENDALE NATIONAL CEMETERY

Willis Ch

LEE

Church Road

HARE RD

JACKSON

D.H. HILL
MAGRUDER

Willis

HUGER

Parsonage

LEE

RICHMOND NATIONAL BATTLEFIELD PARK

RICHMOND NATIONAL BATTLEFIELD PARK

Crewe House
ARMISTEAD
West House
COUCH

MOREL

KEARNY

HOLMES

PORTER

HEINTZELMAN

HOOKER

SYKES

SUMNER

RICHARDSON

Malvern Hill
Malvern House

N

McCLELLAN

Scale
4000 Feet

Shirley Millpond

Picketts Wharf

Combat Strength
80,000
80,000

MALVERN HILL
1 July 1862

Casualties
3,000
5,355

severely engaged the day before at the battle of Glendale.

Lee thought that this plan had the greatest chance of success, and at about 1:30 P.M. he told his commanders: "Batteries have been established to rake the enemies' line. If broken, as is probable, [Brigadier General Lewis A.] Armistead, who can witness the effect of the fire, has been ordered to charge with a yell. Do the same." It soon became apparent, though, that it was far from "probable" that the Confederate artillery would succeed. Swampy ground and heavily wooded terrain blocked access to Longstreet's firing positions. The Confederate reserve artillery was not brought up, so only 20 guns out of Longstreet's planned 140 were deployed. Those that did manage to get in position were quickly silenced by the massed Union artillery. Lee soon realized that his plan would not succeed, and he began looking for another avenue of attack. Unfortunately, he failed to notify his commanders of the change in plans, and they continued operating on the assumption that the original order was still in effect.

While the Confederate artillery tried unsuccessfully to get into position, Armistead's men began coming under heavy fire from Union skirmishers. In an effort to protect themselves, they charged forward to drive back the enemy. Magruder finally appeared, arriving just in time to hear Armistead's troops rush onto the field. Remembering Lee's orders that "Armistead will charge with a yell," Magruder excitedly sent word to Lee that the Confederate attack was under way.

Hoping that the attack could succeed after all and not realizing that Armistead's men had not launched a full-scale assault, Lee sent Magruder orders to "advance rapidly . . . and follow up Armistead's success." Perhaps because of a rebuke by Lee a few days earlier, Magruder felt determined not to give his commander any opportunity for criticism. Though his troops had not yet arrived, he was so determined to follow orders that he ordered the advance of two brigades not under his command. At 4:45

P.M. troops of Major General Benjamin Huger pressed forward through the hail of Union shot and shell and soon were joined by Armistead's men, who had been pinned down between the lines.

To the left of this attack, D. H. Hill heard the commotion. Believing that this was the signal referred to in Lee's orders, he quickly ordered his five brigades to enter battle, shortly before 6:00 P.M. When Hill's half-mile-wide battle line reached the base of Malvern Hill, four hundred yards from the Union line, the Union artillery switched from solid shot to canister, turning the cannon into giant shotguns. At this point Hill's advance across the wheatfield began to sputter, as the men desperately tried to find cover. The Third Alabama Infantry advanced to within two hundred yards of the Union line manned by Brigadier General Darius Couch's division, only to find they were now within range of the infantry's muskets. The pressure eventually became too much for Hill's men, and at about 7:00 P.M. they began to fall back.

To Hill's right, the brigades originally sent in by Magruder had battled to within seventy-five yards of the Union line held by Brigadier General George W. Morell, where they remained, hugging the ground, unable to advance any farther. At the right of the Confederate line, Brigadier General Robert Ransom's brigade managed to reach a point only twenty yards from the Union position before being driven off by "a fire the intensity of which is beyond description."

All along the battle line the situation was the same. The Union artillery and infantry prevented the Confederates from mounting a serious threat. A Union soldier wrote home after the battle that an artillerist told him "it made him heartsick to see how [firing the guns] cut roads through [the Confederates], some places ten feet wide." The infantry was firing so rapidly that their gun barrels overheated and "the men held their guns by the sling strap."

Despite their rapidly mounting casualties, the Confederates kept coming. Magruder's lagging command finally arrived, and he committed them to the battle. But with 7,000 Union troops in reserve and darkness rapidly falling, there would be no last-minute victory for the Confederates, as there had been at Gaines' Mill a few days earlier. Their failure to organize their forces and coordinate their attacks had doomed any chance of success. In a letter to James Longstreet after the war, D. H. Hill recognized these critical mistakes: "We attacked," he aptly summed up, "in the most desultory, harum-scarum way."

As the rattle of musketry died away and the booming of the Union artillery ceased, the terrifying sights and sounds of battle slowly gave way to war's horrifying aftermath. The next day a summer storm added to the grisly scene of dead and wounded: "The howling of the storm, the cry of the wounded and groans of the dying . . . the ground slippery with a mixture of mud and blood, all in the dark, hopeless, starless night; surely it was a picture of war in its most horrid shape."

The following day the Army of the Potomac completed its withdrawal to Harrison's Landing. It had suffered more than 3,000 casualties at Malvern Hill. For the Confederacy, the threat to Richmond had been relieved, but the cost had been very high indeed. In the course of the Seven Days campaign Lee's Army of Northern Virginia had suffered more than 20,000 casualties. Of that total, 5,355 fell in the bloody attack up the slopes of Malvern Hill. As D. H. Hill, who had seen his division cut to pieces there in a few short hours, wrote afterward, "It was not war, it was murder."

Malvern Hill Battlefield, a unit of the Richmond National Battlefield Park, is on State Route 156 near the intersection of State Route 5 southeast of Richmond, Virginia. There are 131 acres of the historic battlefield within the authorized boundaries of this unit.

The battle of Malvern Hill. Drawing by Alfred Waud

CEDAR MOUNTAIN

9 August 1862

Robert K. Krick

On August 9, 1862, Major General Thomas J. "Stonewall" Jackson came close to suffering a thorough trouncing at the hands of a much smaller Union force that surprised him with a sharp attack launched across rolling farmland below the shoulder of Cedar Mountain in Culpeper County. He salvaged an important victory by personally rallying his men under intense hostile fire. The fight at Cedar Mountain — where Jackson drew his sword for the only time during the war — was his last independent battle. He won further fame as General Robert E. Lee's strong right arm, but he never again led a campaign as an independent commander.

Jackson's dazzling success in the Shenandoah Valley during the spring of 1862 had made his name a household word in both the North and the South. In late June he hurried to Richmond to help Lee drive Union troops away from the Confederacy's capital. Jackson fumbled in the unfamiliar swampy country below Richmond during the costly but successful campaign there. When a new Union threat loomed in northern Virginia, Lee sent Jackson with three divisions to suppress it.

The Union army operating west of Fredericksburg in the vicinity of Culpeper was commanded by Major General John Pope, who had achieved some success in the West. More important, he was allied with the radical politicians then holding sway in Washington. Pope,

who issued bombastic orders that his troops laughed at, announced draconian measures against southern civilians, adding an ugly new aspect to the conflict. In response the Confederate government declared him, and by extension his officers, outlaws whose demeanor put them outside the boundaries of civilized warfare.

Jackson faced Pope across the Rapidan River in early August, from encampments around Gordonsville and Orange Court House. On August 7 he thought he saw an opportunity to assail part of Pope's army near Culpeper Court House without having to face the rest of the Union strength. The effort to hurl his divisions, totaling 22,000 troops, at the 12,000 Union soldiers sputtered badly because of dreadful weather and poor country roads, combined with confused marching orders that resulted from Jackson's habitual reticence to share his plans with his principal subordinates. Troops who had won fame as Jackson's "foot cavalry" because of their hardy marching stood in the dust for hours without moving. Many units covered less than a mile. The Confederates crossed the Rapidan on August 8 and pushed into Culpeper County, but without engaging the enemy force or advancing with any real vigor. Early on August 9, a disgruntled Jackson wired Lee: "I am not making much progress."

By the time he sent that message, though,

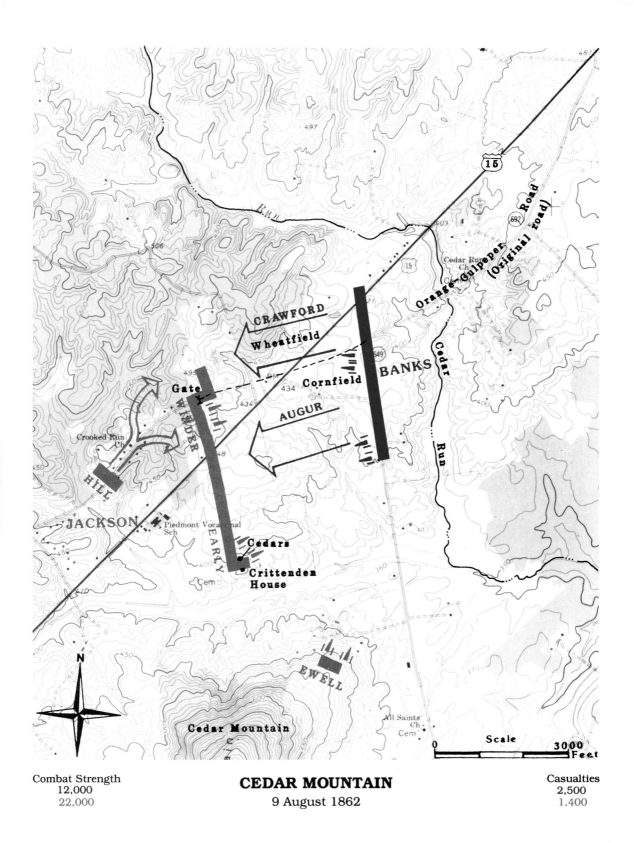

CEDAR MOUNTAIN
9 August 1862

Combat Strength
12,000
22,000

Casualties
2,500
1,400

his forward elements were approaching a Union position near the northwest corner of Cedar Mountain. Men of both armies fell out of ranks because of the high temperature, some of them suffering fatal heat stroke. Brigadier General Jubal A. Early, commanding the first Confederate brigade on the field, found Union cavalry spread across the farmland just above Cedar Run. He could see hostile artillery positioned behind them, and assumed that infantry supported the guns. Confederate artillery was moved to the front into strong positions all across a line perpendicular to the main road. Some of Jackson's cannon clustered under the protection of a wooded knoll that came to be known as the Cedars; more struggled up the steep slope of Cedar Mountain and found an artillery aerie on the mountain's shoulder, elevated above the infantry

arena. During the fighting that ensued, that rock-solid position on the mountainside anchored the Confederate right.

A third cluster of Confederate guns gathered around a bottleneck where the main road emerged from woods at the gate to a long lane leading to the Crittenden house. While artillery dueled all across the front, Confederate infantry maneuvered into position along a woodline facing a wheatfield and along the thousand-yard-long Crittenden Lane.

During the inconclusive artillery duel, the Union commander on the field, Major General Nathaniel P. Banks, launched some of his force against the Confederate guns near the Crittenden gate and the rest of his men through a cornfield toward Crittenden Lane. Brigadier General Samuel W. Crawford's brigade of men from Connecticut, Maine, Wisconsin, Pennsylvania, and New York moved into the wheatfield and headed for the Con-

Cedar Mountain battlefield
© Clark B. Hall

federate woodline without knowing that they faced an enemy who heavily outnumbered them, but fortune smiled on the brave Union soldiers. Jackson concentrated his attention on the artillery duel, perhaps because of the interest he had developed during his Mexican War service. The Confederate infantry line was therefore poorly situated. Brigadier General Charles S. Winder of Maryland, commanding Jackson's old division, also focused on artillery matters, but a Union round shattered his side, mortally wounding him, just as the Union onslaught crashed through the wheatfield.

Crawford's men fell on a seam between Jackson's units and unraveled the entire left of his army, shattering brigade after brigade in the process. At the same time, Brigadier General Christopher C. Augur's division boiled out of the rows of a cornfield and up against the Confederates near Crittenden Lane. Confederate artillery at the Cedars and the Crittenden gate limbered up and dashed away just in time.

At the crisis Jackson waded into the melee, waving his sheathed sword in one hand and a battle flag in the other while Union bullets flew past from three directions. The fleeing troops rallied at the sight of their fabled leader, but they probably could not have held on without Major General A. P. Hill's substantial reinforcements. As darkness fell, fresh brigades cleared the field and forced the Federals back toward Culpeper. The 22,000 Confederates defeated 12,000 Federals, at a cost of about 2,500 casualties for the Federals and 1,400 for the Confederates.

Jackson subsequently declared that Cedar Mountain was "the most successful of his exploits," a judgment surely based on the excitement of an adrenaline-laced personal involvement rather than any sense of tactical or strategic prowess. Two days later Jackson fell back south of the Rapidan to await Lee's arrival from Richmond with the rest of the Army of Northern Virginia, to begin a campaign that ended three weeks later in the battle of Second Manassas.

Cedar Mountain battlefield is on U.S. Route 15 between Orange and Culpeper, Virginia, 70 miles southwest of Washington, D.C., on U.S. Route 29. The entire battlefield is privately owned.

SECOND MANASSAS

28–30 August 1862

John Hennessy

The warm winds of the late summer of 1862 blew across a hopeful and ambitious Confederacy. Union offensives of the spring and summer were, as one southerner joyously described it, "played out," and victory-starved northerners were grumbling with discontent. European recognition of the nascent Confederacy seemed a real possibility; so did independence. Confederate forces from Richmond to the Mississippi wanted to strike the blow that would bring the war to a triumphant close.

In Virginia, on which the eyes of most observers were firmly fixed, the job of striking such a blow fell to General Robert E. Lee. After dispatching Union Major General George B. McClellan's Army of the Potomac during the Seven Days campaign, Lee turned his eyes northward to a second Union threat: Major General John Pope's new Army of Virginia. Lee knew that if he allowed McClellan's 120,000 men, now on the move northward, to join Pope's 63,000 in northern Virginia, the Confederates would be outnumbered more than two to one. No strategic or tactical magic could overcome those numbers. Lee knew he must beat Pope before McClellan joined him.

In late July Lee ordered Major General Thomas J. "Stonewall" Jackson away from Richmond to confront Pope with 24,000 men. After Jackson's mismanaged and dearly

bought victory over part of Pope's army at the battle of Cedar Mountain, Lee marched with the rest of his army — Major General James Longstreet's wing (31,000 men) — to join Jackson and defeat Pope's entire force. Pope and Lee sparred inconclusively for two weeks, first along the Rapidan River and then along the Rappahannock.

Finally, on August 25, Lee found his opening. Jackson and his "foot cavalry" marched fifty-four miles in thirty-six hours around Pope's right flank to cut the Federal army's supply line to Washington at Manassas Junction. Pope groped for Jackson, boasting he would "bag" the famous Confederate, only to have Jackson elude him. Jackson torched the Federal supplies at Manassas Junction and marched five miles north to familiar ground near the scene of the war's opening battle. There he secreted his men behind woods and ridges along an old unfinished railroad bed, north of the Warrenton Turnpike (now Route 29). He waited not just for Lee and the rest of the Confederate army (marching about thirty-six hours behind) but for Pope as well.

At 6:00 P.M. on August 28, one of Pope's columns appeared in Jackson's front, tramping unwarily eastward along the Warrenton Turnpike. Jackson quickly roused himself from a nap and rode out alone to watch the Union troops. On the ridge not far from farmer John

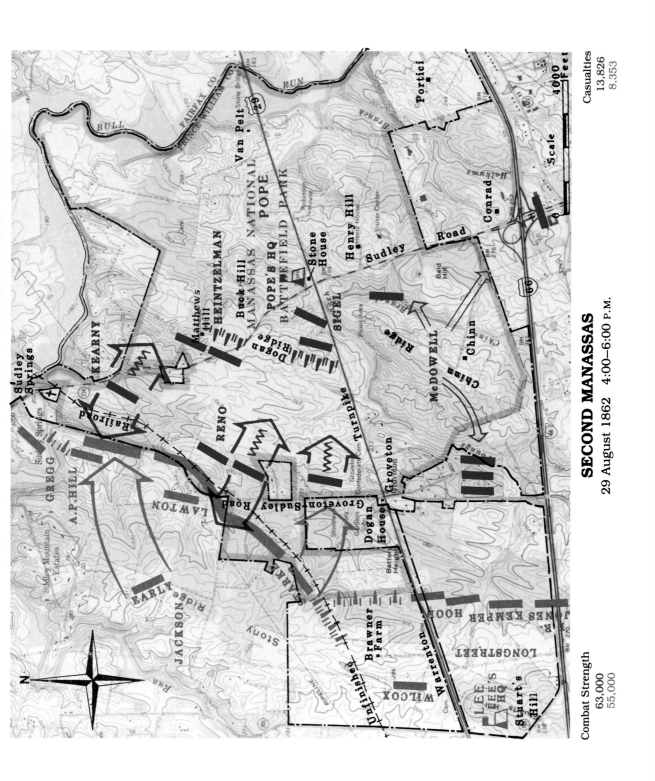

SECOND MANASSAS

29 August 1862   4:00–6:00 P.M.

Combat Strength
63,000
55,000

Casualties
13,826
8,353

Brawner's house, within easy musket shot of the Federal column, Jackson paced his horse nervously, watching the Federals for perhaps three minutes. Suddenly he wheeled his horse and galloped toward his men in the distant woods. "Here he comes, by God," exclaimed one of his officers. Jackson neared and reined his horse to a stop. As if conversing with a next-door neighbor, he said quietly, "Gentlemen, bring up your men." The second battle of Manassas was about to begin.

Within minutes Jackson's artillery appeared and shells began screaming over and through the Union column, sending the men scrambling for roadside cover. These men from Wisconsin and Indiana, later to be known as the Iron Brigade, formed expertly into lines of battle and swept across the fields and woods toward the Confederates. Near the Brawner house the two lines collided in a tumult of smoke and death. At a range of less than a hundred yards, with little cover other than splintered rail fences, Jackson's men and the Union forces battered each other. After two hours of bloody stalemate, darkness brought an end to the day's fighting. Thirty-three percent of those engaged were casualties.

Believing that he did indeed have Jackson "bagged," Pope ordered his army to converge on the Confederates. The next morning Jackson's men awoke to the distant boom of Union artillery as the Federals prepared to attack. Jackson hastily deployed his troops along the cuts and fills of the unfinished railroad at the base of Stony Ridge. His left rested near the hamlet of Sudley Springs on Bull Run, and his right amid the wreckage at the Brawner farm. Stony Ridge rose behind Jackson's line, its lower reaches studded with his artillery. The ground undulated gently, marked here and there with woods, cornfields, and small farms as it sloped toward the Warrenton Turnpike.

Despite his loud proclamations that he would dispose of Jackson, Pope launched only a series of small, disjointed attacks against the Confederates on August 29. He struck Jackson's center with two regiments, then his left

with five, and at about 4:00 P.M. the center again, with three regiments. Each of these attacks briefly broke Jackson's line, but each time Pope gave Jackson the opportunity to patch the breech and drive the unsupported Federals back. Only late in the day did he seriously threaten Jackson.

At 5:00 P.M. Major General Philip Kearny, the pugnacious one-armed Mexican War veteran, led his division against Jackson's left. (Kearny died three days later at the battle of Chantilly.) His men crossed the unfinished railroad and drove Major General A. P. Hill's men beyond the Groveton-Sudley Road (now Route 622) to the lower slopes of Stony Ridge. There the Confederates stiffened. Once again Pope failed to send reinforcements, and for the fourth time that day Union success turned into inglorious retreat.

While Pope focused single-mindedly on Jackson, Lee and Longstreet arrived on the field to complete the Confederate assemblage. Unknown to Pope, Lee placed Longstreet on Jackson's right, extending the Confederate line more than a mile southward and wrapping it around Pope's exposed left. Shaped like a huge pair of gaping jaws with Pope between them, Lee's line was ready to snap shut.

Pope's mild successes on August 29 were enough to encourage him to resume the attacks on August 30. After a morning of light skirmishing and cannon fire, Pope massed 10,000 men to attack Jackson's line at what was later called the Deep Cut. At 3:00 P.M. these troops swept forward. Jackson's men, protected by the unfinished railroad, cut them down in huge numbers. "What a slaughter! What a slaughter of men that was!" remembered one Georgian. "They were so thick it was just impossible to miss them." After thirty minutes of the battle's most intense fighting, the Federals, lashed also by Confederate artillery to their left, broke and fell back. Pope's biggest attack of the battle had failed.

At his headquarters on what came to be known as Stuart's Hill, Lee saw his opportunity and ordered Longstreet forward in a massive counterattack against the exposed Union left. Thirty thousand Confederates surged ahead, barreling over all Union opposition until they reached Chinn Ridge. Pope, facing disaster, patched together a makeshift defense, trying to buy enough time to get his army safely off the field. For more than an hour the fighting raged on the ridge, each side throwing in regiments and brigades as fast as they arrived. Finally, at about 6:00 P.M., the Federals gave way, but Pope had gained enough time to put together another line on Henry Hill (where thirteen months before the first battle of Manassas had come to a climax). Longstreet hurled his men against this line, but darkness brought an end to the fighting. That night Pope led his badly beaten men back toward Washington. On their retreat they met troops from McClellan's army marching to assist them.

Lee did not let Pope go easily. The next day he sent Jackson on a march around Pope's right. This time, however, Pope was warier. He met Jackson's column near the crossroads of Chantilly on September 1 and in a driving thunderstorm battled the Confederates to a halt. Seeing little more to be gained in pur-suing Pope farther, Lee allowed the Federal retreat to Washington to continue. In less than a week Pope, who had come to symbolize the ills that affected the Union war effort during 1862, was ordered to Minnesota to fight Indians.

The second battle of Manassas brought Robert E. Lee and the Confederacy to the height of their power and opened the way for Lee's first invasion of the North. But his victory came with horrid losses to both sides: 3,300 dead and 15,000 wounded (Union, 9,931; Confederate, 8,353; the Union listed another 3,895 as missing). For years the land bore the scars: mangled trees, rows of depressions from disinterred graves, the bleached bones of dead horses. As one of the soldiers at Manassas said, "War has been designated as Hell, and I assure you that this was the very vortex of Hell."

Manassas National Battlefield Park is on U.S. Route 29 and Interstate 66 near Manassas, Virginia, 26 miles southwest of Washington, D.C. There are 5,083 acres of the historic battlefield within its authorized boundaries; 738 of these are privately owned.

HARPERS FERRY

13–15 September 1862

Dennis E. Frye

In the Blue Ridge Mountains, at the confluence of the Potomac and Shenandoah rivers, lies West Virginia's most historic town, Harpers Ferry. Just before the battle of Antietam, Major General Thomas J. "Stonewall" Jackson, a native of Clarksburg (now in West Virginia), encircled and captured the United States Army garrison there.

In September 1862 General Robert E. Lee marched his Army of Northern Virginia into Maryland, expecting the 14,000 Union troops at Harpers Ferry and Martinsburg to be withdrawn north of the Potomac. Instead the Federal high command instructed the garrison commander, Colonel Dixon S. Miles, "to hold Harpers Ferry to the last extremity." With Union troops firmly planted south of the Potomac, Lee faced a serious problem: these troops prevented him from establishing essential supply and communication lines through the Shenandoah Valley and threatened his invasion of the North.

Lee's solution was to divide his army into four parts and send three to Harpers Ferry to eliminate the problem. The fourth column would march to Boonsboro, fifteen miles north of Harpers Ferry, and await the return of the campaigners. Because Jackson had been commander of the Confederate units at Harpers Ferry in the spring of 1861 and knew the topography of the region, Lee placed him in command. Jackson responded favorably to the task, observing that he had lately neglected his "friends" in the Valley.

At sunrise on September 10, three converging columns of Confederates methodically began driving toward Harpers Ferry. Major General John G. Walker's division of 2,000 swung south across the Potomac River and then east toward Loudoun Heights. The 8,000 men of Major General Lafayette McLaws veered west and south toward Maryland Heights. Jackson, with three divisions — 14,000 veterans — raced west toward Martinsburg and then east toward Bolivar Heights.

Miles knew the Confederates were coming. Outnumbered almost two to one and further handicapped by his inexperienced troops — more than two thirds of them had been in the army for less than three weeks — he weakened his overall defense by dividing his forces to cover Maryland and Bolivar Heights. On September 13 the Confederates took up their positions near his garrison. Loudoun Heights fell quickly to Walker's men, and after a six-hour battle McLaws seized Maryland Heights. Jackson then drove in from the west, deploying his forces along School House Ridge, one half mile west of Bolivar Heights.

Later that night Confederate cannoneers dragged artillery to the ridgetops. At about 2:00 P.M. on September 14, the hills erupted

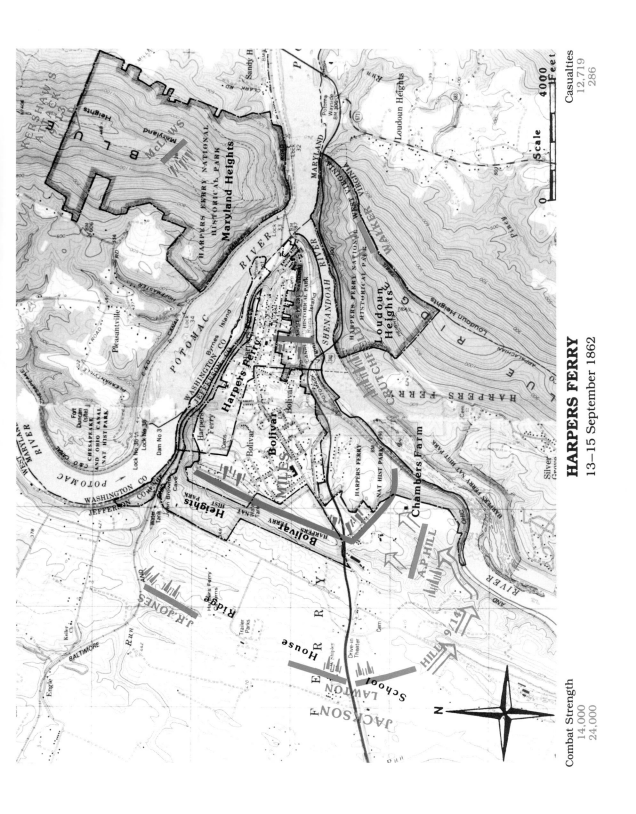

HARPERS FERRY

13–15 September 1862

Combat Strength
14,000
24,000

Casualties
12,719
286

Scale

0   4000
        Feet

in smoke and flame, and the bombardment continued until dark. Jackson's gunners zeroed in on Bolivar Heights, the main position of the trapped Federals. One Union lieutenant recalled the horror of the bombardment: "The infernal screech owls came hissing and singing, then bursting, plowing great holes in the earth, filling our eyes with dust, and tearing many giant trees to atoms." Darkness finally ended the firestorm, with the Stars and Stripes still flying over Harpers Ferry.

Jackson was becoming impatient. Word had arrived from Lee that the situation in Maryland had deteriorated. The Union army had advanced unexpectedly, aided by the discovery of Lee's original orders, and the Confederates had been forced to abandon South Mountain. Lee informed Jackson that he would have to cancel the invasion of the North if Harpers Ferry did not fall in the morning.

To ensure success, Jackson ordered Major General A. P. Hill to take his 3,000 men from the south end of School House Ridge and flank the Union left on Bolivar Heights. Jackson felt certain that this move, in conjunction with additional artillery on Loudoun Heights, would end the Union resistance. During the night of September 14, Hill's Confederates quietly snaked along the banks of the Shenandoah until they discovered ravines leading up to the Chambers farm. In the darkness, in open pastures behind the Union left, Hill deployed his men and artillery. The fate of Harpers Ferry was sealed.

A thick fog blanketed the valley on the morning of September 15. As the rising sun burned away the mist, Confederate shells from the mountains again filled the sky. One Vermont soldier declared, "We [were] as helpless as rats in a cage." At about 8:00 A.M., with his artillery ammunition exhausted and his troops surrounded, Miles ordered white flags raised. Jackson received the formal Union surrender on School House Ridge, where he had coordinated the siege. He captured 73 pieces of artillery, 11,000 small arms, and 200 wagons, with a loss of only 286 men. In addition to the 219 Union men killed and wounded, 12,500 Federals were taken prisoner — the largest surrender of U.S. troops during the Civil War.

Lee greeted the news with enthusiasm, as the fall of Harpers Ferry allowed him to make a stand in Maryland. However, the resulting battle of Antietam — America's bloodiest single-day battle — changed the course of the war in favor of the Union.

Harpers Ferry National Historical Park is on U.S. Route 340 at Harpers Ferry, West Virginia, at the confluence of the Potomac and Shenandoah rivers. There are 2,239 acres of the historic battlefield and town within its authorized boundaries; 37 of these are privately owned.

ANTIETAM

17 September 1862

Stephen W. Sears

General Robert E. Lee was driven by two ambitions in leading his Army of Northern Virginia across the Potomac River into Maryland early in September 1862. The first was to shift the contest from war-torn Virginia to what he called the Confederacy's northern frontier. The second was to force Major General George B. McClellan's Army of the Potomac into a showdown battle that would be decisive for the South's independence.

That battle was fought along Antietam Creek, at Sharpsburg, Maryland, but not in the setting Lee originally planned. Chance had intervened. Several days earlier a Confederate courier had lost a copy of his operational orders, which were found by a Union soldier and turned over to McClellan. Although McClellan moved too slowly on September 14 to break through the gaps in South Mountain and cut off the scattered parts of the Confederate army, he did force Lee to decide to give battle sooner than he wanted and with fewer troops than he intended. Despite the odds against him, Lee deliberately chose to stand and fight at Sharpsburg, confident that he and his soldiers would win.

His confidence stemmed in part from the good defensive position he had chosen. He drew his line of battle on some four miles of rising ground behind Antietam Creek, taking advantage of the concealment offered by the rolling terrain, rocky outcroppings, scattered woodlots, and fields of corn standing tall and ready for harvest. He would have to fight defensively, for even when all his troops finally reached Sharpsburg from Harpers Ferry, where they had successfully besieged a Union garrison, he would have hardly 38,000 men of all arms. The Union commander, massing his troops and guns along the eastern bank of Antietam Creek, could put about 75,000 men on the firing line.

The terrain influenced McClellan's battle plan as well. South of Sharpsburg, where the right of Lee's line was posted, the ground was steep, broken, and difficult for maneuvering troops. Although his plan included a threat to that flank, McClellan intended the main weight of his assault to fall on the enemy's opposite flank, north of Sharpsburg, where the ground was more open. Antietam Creek itself was a major defensive feature, like a moat protecting a castle. Union troops crossing the creek to open an attack were supported by artillery batteries and ammunition trains that had to use one of the fords or one of the three stone bridges spanning the stream in the vicinity of Sharpsburg. As the battle lines were first drawn, two of these bridges were controlled by Union troops and one by the Confederates. All along the high ground east of the creek, McClellan massed his powerful long-range artillery to support his offensive. He regarded the creek as his own first line of defense should Lee attempt a counterstroke.

The battle opened at first light on September 17 as Major General Joseph Hooker's Union First Corps struck hard against the Confederate left, under the command of Major General Thomas J. "Stonewall" Jackson. Hooker's objective was the open plateau in front of the little whitewashed Dunker church, where Confederate artillery batteries were massed. Off to the west on Nicodemus Hill, Confederate cavalryman Major General J. E. B. Stuart directed the fire of other batteries against the advancing Federals. The fighting surged back and forth through the East Woods and the West Woods and farmer David Miller's thirty-acre cornfield between them. In a series of charges and countercharges, both sides poured reinforcements into the struggle, but neither could gain a decisive advantage. In the first four hours of the battle that morning almost 13,000 men fell dead or wounded.

At midmorning, more by misdirection than by design, other Union troops ran up against the center of Lee's line, posted in a farm lane so worn down over the years by erosion and travel that on the military maps it was labeled Sunken Road. Before long it earned another name: Bloody Lane. Two Union divisions were hurled repeatedly against this strong position and were driven back. Then, through a mix-up in orders, the Confederates gave up Bloody Lane and retreated. For a critical moment it appeared that Lee's army would be cut in two. The cautious McClellan could not bring himself to renew the attack, however, and the thin Confederate line held.

One final act remained to be played in the drama. During the morning Major General Ambrose E. Burnside's corps had been ordered by McClellan to make a diversionary attack against Lee's right flank while the main

Antietam National Battlefield
Sunken Road. © David Muench, 1990

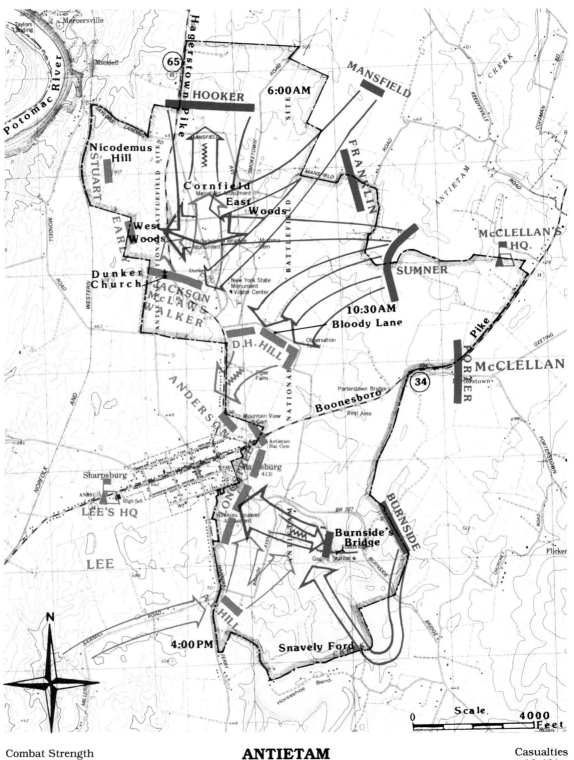

Combat Strength
75,000
38,000

ANTIETAM
17 September 1862

Casualties
12,401
10,318

blow was struck against his left. But Burnside ran into great difficulty trying to force a crossing of Antietam Creek at the bridge on his front. A flanking column sent downstream to find a fording place lost its way and was three hours locating Snavely's Ford and making a crossing. Back at the bridge, meanwhile, a storming party launched a headlong assault that finally gained the span, which from then on was called Burnside's Bridge. By afternoon Burnside had his corps across the creek and positioned to advance on Sharpsburg.

Throughout the day Lee had pulled men from this sector to reinforce the hard-pressed troops holding the rest of his line. Now the few remaining defenders were pushed back through Sharpsburg by Burnside's relentless advance. Once again the Confederate army seemed on the brink of defeat. Then, at the last possible moment, the division of Major General A. P. Hill arrived on the field, after a hard march from Harpers Ferry, and smashed

into Burnside's battle lines. The force of Hill's counterattack drove the Union forces back to the heights overlooking Burnside's Bridge as darkness ended the fighting.

September 18 found Lee holding his lines and defiantly inviting another attack, but McClellan refused the challenge. He was satisfied with the fact that his army had survived the battle, and he was unwilling to risk it further by renewing the fighting that day. During the night Lee led his army back across the Potomac into Virginia. He left behind a battlefield unique in American history. On no other field, on no other single day of battle, would so many Americans be killed, wounded, and missing: 22,719 — nearly 13,000 Federals and about 10,000 Confederates.

Antietam also proved to be one of the turning points of the Civil War. It ended Lee's invasion of the North and his hope of winning a decisive battle on northern soil in 1862. Although McClellan's cautious generalship prevented a decisive Union military victory, the battle's consequences were enough to con-

Sketch by Edwin Forbes of the Federal charge across Burnside's Bridge, September 17, 1862.

vince Abraham Lincoln to issue the preliminary Emancipation Proclamation. What before Antietam had been a war waged solely for the Union now became a war against slavery as well, and that doomed the South's hope for foreign intervention. The course of the war, and the course of the nation, were forever changed as a result.

Antietam National Battlefield is near State Route 65 at Sharpsburg, Maryland, twelve miles south of Hagerstown. There are 3,244 acres of the historic battlefield within its authorized boundaries; 981 of these are privately owned.

Antietam National Battlefield
A cornfield. © Brien Culhane

CORINTH

3–4 October 1862

George A. Reaves III

Even before their victory at Shiloh, the Union armies led by Major General U. S. Grant and Major General Don Carlos Buell were planning an advance on Corinth, Mississippi, where the east-west Memphis and Charleston Railroad and the north-south Mobile and Ohio Railroad crossed. These railroads were the means for a rapid concentration of forces from the Deep South; they linked Virginia with Memphis on the Mississippi River, with Mobile on the Gulf Coast, and with Columbus, Kentucky, on the Mississippi River, a short distance south of its confluence with the Ohio. Corinth could serve the Confederacy as an offensive springboard for advances to recover western and middle Tennessee and for thrusts deep into Kentucky and on to the Ohio River. The loss of Corinth would be a major disaster for the Confederacy, because it would force the evacuation of Memphis and much of northern Mississippi and northwestern Alabama.

In the spring of 1862 General P. G. T. Beauregard, commander of the Confederate forces west of the Tennessee River, prepared the defense of the town. In mid-April he was reinforced by Major General Earl Van Dorn with 14,000 men from the Trans-Mississippi. These made up for the losses at Shiloh, but the Confederates were still unable to match the 120,000-man army group that Major General Henry W. Halleck was assembling at Pittsburg and Hamburg landings.

Union generals Halleck and Grant recognized the importance of Corinth. When Grant's army moved to the Pittsburg Landing area, his superior, Halleck, ordered him to wait there for the arrival of Buell's Army of the Ohio from Nashville before advancing on Corinth. Halleck intended to go to Pittsburg Landing and take command of the combined armies. He also ordered his field army on the Mississippi River, commanded by Major General John Pope, to move from Plum Point Bend on the Mississippi to Hamburg Landing on the Tennessee River. Pope had occupied New Madrid in March and had captured Island No. 10 and its 7,000 defenders on April 8, 1862.

To counter the Union's numerical advantage, the Confederates improved their entrenchments covering the northern and eastern approaches to Corinth. These extended in an arc about one and one half miles from town, anchored east and west on the Memphis and Charleston Railroad. This seven-mile line included rifle pits with battery emplacements at key points.

On April 29 the Union troops marched out of their bases at Pittsburg and Hamburg landings and began the advance on Corinth. General Halleck commanded this combined force. General Grant was second-in-command, but because of Halleck's distrust and jealousy, he had no responsibility. Halleck's army group included the Army of the Tennessee, led by

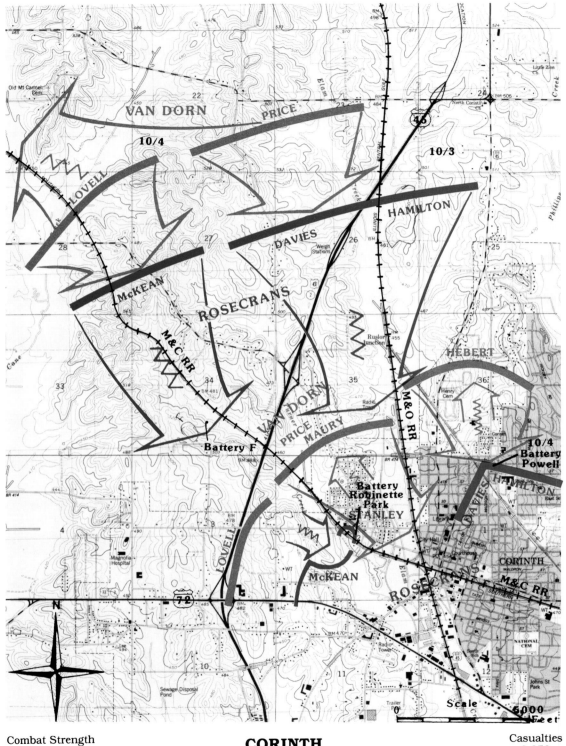

Combat Strength
23,000
22,000

CORINTH

3–4 October 1862

Casualties
2,350
4,800

Major General George H. Thomas; Buell's Army of the Ohio; and Pope's Army of the Mississippi.

The Union armies advanced on a broad front and by early May were in close contact with the Confederates in the Corinth area. The strengthened Confederate defenses compelled Halleck to begin formal siege operations against the town. Beauregard watched for a chance to cut off and destroy a portion of the Union army; his attempts were primarily to the east, near Farmington, particularly against Pope's army on May 9. By the middle of May, Beauregard decided that Corinth was untenable. The water was bad, Halleck was astride the Mobile and Ohio Railroad north of the town, and Union forces had cut the Memphis and Charleston Railroad to the east. On the night of May 29–30 the Confederates successfully withdrew to the Tupelo area, and on the morning of May 30 the Union armies occupied Corinth. The siege was over.

Beauregard had saved his 55,000 men to fight again, in spite of the overwhelming numbers that Halleck had deployed against him. Losses were not high, because after Shiloh, neither army sought combat. Casualties from sickness, however, were excessive, particularly among the Confederates.

After the occupation of Corinth, the Federal armies began to rebuild the railroads in the area. They felt their way toward Tupelo, but did not force the Confederates to retreat farther south. There were important changes in command: Halleck was called to Washington to become general-in-chief, Pope went to northern Virginia to lead the newly constituted Army of Virginia, Grant resumed command of the District of West Tennessee, and under him, Major General William S. Rosecrans took charge of Pope's Army of the Mississippi, which occupied the Corinth area. Buell's Army of the Ohio headed eastward into the Tennessee Valley, rebuilding the Memphis and Charleston Railroad as it marched.

General Beauregard went on sick leave in mid-June, and President Jefferson Davis used this as an excuse to replace him with General Braxton Bragg. In mid-July Bragg began to shift his Army of the Mississippi by rail to Chattanooga, where he intended to operate against the Union forces. He beat Buell to Chattanooga and then began a campaign in cooperation with Major General Edmund Kirby Smith, the Confederate commander in eastern Tennessee. Their armies were soon deep into Kentucky, threatening Louisville and Cincinnati. Bragg left soldiers in Mississippi, commanded by major generals Sterling Price and Earl Van Dorn; he expected these to advance into middle Tennessee to support his thrust into Kentucky. After Price's Army of the West battered Rosecrans at Iuka on September 19, Van Dorn, the senior of the two generals, decided to attack Corinth, the linchpin of Union defenses in northeastern Mississippi, and then advance into western or middle Tennessee, as circumstances dictated. Using his seniority to control Price's movements, Van Dorn ordered an advance against Corinth.

Before Halleck had left for Washington, he had ordered that a defensive line be constructed to protect Corinth against a Confederate force approaching from the west or south. Rosecrans considered these fortifications too extensive to be manned by the force available and questioned Grant about them. Grant agreed to modify the line so that it protected the vital supply magazines in and around the intersection of the two railroads. Several of the completed battery positions of the projected Halleck line, among them Battery F, lay between the Confederate entrenchments and Corinth. Thus, when Rosecrans concentrated his 23,000 troops in and around Corinth on October 2, his line was much shorter than Beauregard's Confederate line had been the spring before.

These inner defenses consisted of batteries Robinette, Williams, Phillips, Tannrath, and Lothrop, in the College Hill area. Rosecrans gave orders to connect them by breastworks and to strengthen them, where possible, by abatis — logs sharpened and arranged in front for greater defense (the Civil War fore-runner of barbed wire). The line was also extended to cover the northern approaches of the town. Battery Powell, although it was not complete when the fighting started, was laid out for this purpose.

On October 2 Rosecrans discovered Van Dorn's Confederates advancing on Corinth from the northwest, which put Van Dorn between Rosecrans and any reinforcements that he might receive from General Grant at Jackson and Bolivar, Tennessee. The Confederates deployed their army in an arc to the northwest of Corinth. Major General Mansfield Lovell's division was on the right, and Sterling Price's two-division corps was on the left.

Rosecrans planned his defense to take advantage of all of the fortifications that had been built around Corinth. His skirmish line was posted along the old Confederate entrenchments, which were the outermost works. He planned to meet the Confederate attack with his main forces along the Halleck line, which was about a mile from the center of town. His final stand would be made in the battery positions in and around College Hill. This defense enabled him to sap the Confederates' strength as they advanced and to defend the supply depots in downtown Corinth and the railroad intersection.

The attack started at about 10:00 A.M. on October 3, when three of Rosecrans's divisions advanced into old Confederate rifle pits north and northwest of town. Brigadier General Thomas A. Davies was in the center of the Federal line, with Brigadier General Thomas J. McKean on the left and Brigadier General Schuyler Hamilton on the right. A fourth division, Brigadier General David S. Stanley's,

was held in reserve south of town. The Confederates attacked and applied pressure all along the line. By evening the Union soldiers had been forced south two miles, back into the inner line of fortifications.

During the night Rosecrans positioned his troops in an arc-shaped line two miles long, with redoubts at key points. Van Dorn put Lovell's division on the right, south of the Memphis and Charleston Railroad, Brigadier General Dabney S. Maury's in the center, in front of Battery Robinette, and Brigadier General Louis Hébert's on the left. The next morning the Confederates stormed Battery Powell. Their charges were repulsed in savage fighting before Battery Robinette, where Colonel William P. Rogers, a Mexican War comrade of Jefferson Davis's, was killed as he led the Second Texas. Union counterattacks soon drove the Confederates from Battery Powell and from the town.

By noon the Confederates had withdrawn, retreating toward the northwest. They had lost 4,800 of their 22,000 men. Rosecrans attempted to follow up, but because of his losses (2,350 of his 23,000 soldiers) and the exhaustion of his troops, his units were unable to mount an effective pursuit. The battle of Corinth was over. The Union continued to hold Corinth until the winter of 1863–64, when they abandoned it as no longer having any strategic significance.

Corinth battlefield is in Corinth, Mississippi, on U.S. routes 45 and 72, eight miles south of the Tennessee border. Five acres of the historic battlefield are within the authorized boundaries of Fort Robinette, at the intersection of Wenasoga Road and Linden Street.

A CIVIL WAR LEGACY

William H. Webster

The battle that was fought outside the town of Perryville, Kentucky, on October 8, 1862, began as a squabble between Confederate and Union troops over access to the pools of water in a small creek. It ended with some question as to the victor. The North claimed that the battle kept Kentucky from joining the Confederacy. Southerners pointed to the high cost of this achievement — a loss by the Federals of more than 3,500 men. A small part of the field where this battle took place has been preserved as a state park. I attended the battlefield's dedication as the official delegate from Missouri, but I also attended to pay a personal tribute to an ancestor who gave his life in the battle.

Colonel George Penny Webster, my great-grandfather, was not a professional soldier. He was a loyal and patriotic American who left a law practice to serve his country in time of war. He had fought in the Mexican War with Zachary Taylor and volunteered again when the Civil War broke out. In the early stages of the conflict, Webster served as major of the Twenty-fifth Ohio Volunteer Infantry. The unit fought against the Confederates in western Virginia (now West Virginia) and central Virginia in late 1861 and early 1862. It performed with exceptional distinction, fighting against

Major General Thomas J. "Stonewall" Jackson during the battle of McDowell on May 8, 1862.

In late summer of that year George Webster was promoted to colonel and transferred to the western theater. He formed his own regiment and was then given command of the Thirty-fourth Brigade of the Army of the Ohio's Tenth Division. Within two months Webster led the Thirty-fourth in the battle of Perryville. In that battle the brigade lost 579 men, including Colonel Webster, who fell from his horse, mortally wounded. The men of the Thirty-fourth mourned the loss of their leader, and after the war they gathered to dedicate a monument to him.

George Webster wrote to his wife every day from the camp and the battlefield. She saved his letters, and they have been passed on through the generations of our family. I keep them now, and I value them for helping me to appreciate the sacrifices and hardship he accepted in serving his country. Visiting the battlefield at Perryville reminds me that our nation's past embraces many acts of individual sacrifice, hardship, and heroism. Together, these acts form a heritage and a history in which all Americans can share — a history that is preserved for us at our Civil War battlefields.

PERRYVILLE

8 October 1862

Paul Hawke

The importance of Kentucky in the Civil War was best stated by Abraham Lincoln: "I hope to have God on my side, but I must have Kentucky. I think to lose Kentucky is nearly the same as to lose the whole game." Perryville gave Kentucky to Lincoln. The battle that preserved the state for the Union was the largest and bloodiest fought in the state. It was tactically indecisive, but it ended the Confederate sweep across middle Tennessee and deep into Kentucky and provided a needed boost of morale in the North.

During the summer of 1862, Union forces threatened Chattanooga and held the strategic rail junction of Corinth, Mississippi, and most of western and middle Tennessee. In the east the Confederates won victories at Cedar Mountain and Second Manassas. General Braxton Bragg moved the Confederate Army of the Mississippi to operate with Major General Edmund Kirby Smith's army against Major General Don Carlos Buell. On August 30 General Smith defeated a Union force at Richmond, Kentucky. Bragg's movement was designed to force Buell to follow, thus relieving the pressure on Chattanooga and bringing Kentucky into the Confederacy.

Conditions in the state were difficult. The weather was hot and dry, and a drought had made water scarce. Bragg spread his forces over a large area to forage and to locate the Union army. He had expected to be enthusiastically welcomed as his troops moved into Kentucky, but he was not, and Bragg, who had hoped for enlistments, was disappointed.

Buell responded to the threat of southern occupation by ordering his columns to converge on Perryville or Harrodsburg, south of Frankfort and southwest of Lexington, where Confederate concentration was reported. He had an additional problem: Washington was dissatisfied with his performance, and ordered Major General George H. Thomas to take command. Thomas turned down the assignment so Buell could remain in control during the impending battle.

In 1862 Perryville had a population of several hundred residents. The softly rolling hills to the west and northwest were dotted with woods and farms, and the Chaplin River meandered northward from the center of town. The battlefield included Wilson's Creek on the northwest and Doctor's Creek in the middle. Bull Run Creek flowed south into Doctor's Creek near the Mackville Pike crossing and the H. P. Bottom house. Because of the drought, none of the creeks had much water for the thirsty soldiers.

While Bragg was in Frankfort, the state capital, installing a provisional Confederate state government, Buell's forces drew closer to Perryville. Bragg's cavalry, commanded by Colonel

Combat Strength
36,940
16,000

PERRYVILLE
8 October 1862

Casualties
3,696
3,145

Joseph Wheeler, skirmished with the advancing Union columns on October 7. Union Acting Major General Charles C. Gilbert's Third Corps troops were on the Springfield Pike, and Major General Alexander McD. McCook's First Corps were on the Mackville Pike. Confederate Major General William J. Hardee prepared a line of battle. His force consisted of Major General Simon B. Buckner's division of the brigades of brigadier generals Sterling A. M. Wood, Bushrod R. Johnson, and St. John R. Liddell. Hardee placed Wood's brigade north of town and Johnson's brigade to the right of Wood's. Both were east of the Chaplin River, near the Harrodsburg Pike. Liddell's brigade formed on the crest of a hill just east of Bull Run Creek, north of the Springfield Pike, in anticipation of the Union forces' need for water.

The first shots of the battle were fired in the early-morning darkness of October 8, when Buell ordered Gilbert to send skirmishers to find water. The scouts ran into Confederate pickets positioned by Liddell along Peter's Hill, three quarters of a mile to the front. Near the Turpin house, Colonel Daniel McCook's brigade of Brigadier General Philip H. Sheridan's division pushed the Seventh Arkansas back to Liddell's main line. The fighting along the Springfield Pike escalated as Sheridan — who had just earned his first star — pushed up the road. By daylight the battle subsided. Sheridan positioned his men and made his headquarters at the Turpin house. Buell could not hear the fighting from his headquarters at the Dorsey house and knew nothing of the action.

Bragg ordered Major General Leonidas Polk to Perryville to "attack the enemy immediately, rout him, and then move rapidly to join Major General Smith." The Confederates arrived in Perryville by 10:00 A.M., and Bragg made his headquarters at the Crawford house. Along the Springfield Pike the fighting had gradually decreased. During the lull Bragg improved Polk's position. Major General Benjamin Franklin Cheatham's division moved around

the right flank to the south of Walker's Bend. Buckner's division occupied the center, and Brigadier General James Patton Anderson's division the left. Colonel John A. Wharton's Confederate cavalry, moving across Walker's Bend onto the Benton Road, then down the Dug Road, reported that the Union left was farther north than expected. Cheatham's division moved into Walker's Bend and attacked across the Chaplin River by 2:00 P.M.

The Confederate attack did not hit the Union left flank as planned but slammed into the front of McCook's First Army Corps. The fighting increased as Buckner's and Anderson's divisions became involved. As more Confederates joined the advance and the fighting escalated, McCook's men slowly withdrew. Union brigadier generals James S. Jackson and William R. Terrill were killed in the action. Confederate General Polk narrowly averted capture when, late in the day, he rode up to troops in the fading light and ordered them to stop firing into a brigade of fellow Confederates. Then he discovered that the troops were Federals from Indiana. Their colonel was not as quick to capture Polk as the general himself had been earlier in the day when he took prisoner a Union officer who confused him with one of McCook's officers.

Some of the heaviest fighting took place near the H. P. Bottom house on Doctor's Creek. As Bushrod Johnson's Confederates advanced over the creek, they came under heavy fire and took cover behind a stone fence. Brigadier generals Patrick R. Cleburne's and Daniel W. Adams's men were able to carry the hill because a burning barn kept the Union forces, the Third Ohio and the Fifteenth Kentucky, from firing effectively. As the Confederates pushed forward along the Mackville Road, they encountered Colonel George P. Webster's brigade of Jackson's division and Colonel William H. Lytle's brigade of Brigadier General Lovell H. Rousseau's division (McCook's right) and pushed them back to the Russell house. Webster was mortally wounded while attempting to rally his men. Cleburne was also wounded, but was able to stay on the field to direct his advancing Confederate troops. Brigadier General John C. Starkweather's brigade of Rousseau's division (McCook's left) fell back in front of Cheatham's advance. Sheridan's division of Gilbert's Third Corps watched helplessly as disaster befell McCook's corps, but Sheridan was under orders not to engage. The disorganized Union forces were able to establish and hold new positions, however, as the fighting on McCook's front subsided at around 4:00 P.M. Buell, who was having dinner with Gilbert at his headquarters and heard only the sounds of sporadic cannon fire, still knew little of the battle.

At about 4:15 activity along the Springfield Pike resumed as Colonel Samuel Powell's Confederate brigade advanced west. The attack fell on Sheridan's division, which repulsed their advance and followed their retreat toward Perryville. Colonel William P. Carlin's brigade of Brigadier General Robert B. Mitchell's division also followed. Carlin attacked the Confederates on the flank and chased Powell's men into the streets of Perryville. Finding that he had put himself into an isolated pocket, he withdrew to his lines, and the last action of the day was over. Bragg decided that he was too heavily outnumbered to continue the battle. As Buell brought up the rest of his forces during the night, Bragg withdrew. He joined Kirby Smith near Harrodsburg and moved through the Cumberland Gap into eastern Tennessee.

For its size, the battle of Perryville was one of the bloodiest battles of the Civil War. Bragg lost about 20 percent of his 16,000 men: 3,145 casualties. Buell lost 3,696 of his 36,940 troops. It was a costly battle for Bragg, considering that Buell had engaged barely half of his men. The North's morale improved with Bragg's retreat from Kentucky, Lee's with-

Perryville Battlefield
© Paul Hawke

drawal from Maryland, Major General Sterling Price's defeat at Iuka, and Van Dorn's battering at Corinth. Perryville kept Kentucky in Union hands for the rest of the war.

Perryville Battlefield is in Perryville, Kentucky, near the intersection of U.S. routes 68 and 150, 35 miles southwest of Lexington. There are 196 acres of the historic battlefield within its authorized boundaries.

Perryville

FREDERICKSBURG

11–13 December 1862

A. Wilson Greene

Catharinus Putnam Buckingham knocked gently on the pole of the commanding general's tent. With him stood a tall, handsome officer known best for his genial personality and distinctive whiskers. Major General George B. McClellan welcomed his visitors to the headquarters of the Army of the Potomac and guessed the reason for their call. Buckingham carried President Abraham Lincoln's order to remove McClellan from his post and replace him with Major General Ambrose E. Burnside, who watched uncomfortably as Little Mac digested the news of his professional demise. This quiet transfer of power led to one of the great battles of the Civil War.

General Burnside's reputation later suffered because of his conduct of the Fredericksburg campaign in the autumn of 1862. However, his strategy when he assumed control of the Army of the Potomac had merit: use pontoon bridges to cross the Rappahannock River at Fredericksburg and move directly south against Richmond. To succeed, he would have to march quickly and get to Fredericksburg before Lee's two corps, led by lieutenant generals James Longstreet and Thomas J. "Stonewall" Jackson.

Burnside set his army in motion on November 15, 1862, organized into four grand divisions: the right, under Major General Edwin V. Sumner; the center, under Major General Joseph Hooker; the left, under Major General William B. Franklin; and the reserve, under Major General Franz Sigel (it did not participate in the battle). Some 120,000 Union soldiers were involved.

On November 17 Sumner's division appeared on Stafford Heights, overlooking Fredericksburg. However, because of an inefficient bureaucracy and bad roads, the vital bridging equipment had not arrived. When the pontoons did arrive, more than a week later, Lee had arrived too. By late November the basic premise of Burnside's campaign — an unopposed crossing of the Rappahannock — was no longer valid.

Lee positioned Longstreet's corps on the high ground west of Fredericksburg, occupying a line anchored at Taylor's Hill near the Rappahannock on the left and at Hamilton's Crossing near marshy Massaponax Creek on the right. Jackson's four divisions ranged twenty miles downstream, guarding against any attempt to turn the far right flank. Lee's entire army numbered 78,000 men.

At 3:00 A.M. on December 11, Union engineers slipped their pontoons into the Rappahannock's icy waters and went to work. Their bridges progressed nicely until the first rays of dawn penetrated the foggy gloom that enveloped the river valley. Then minié balls whizzed through the mist, and the defenseless

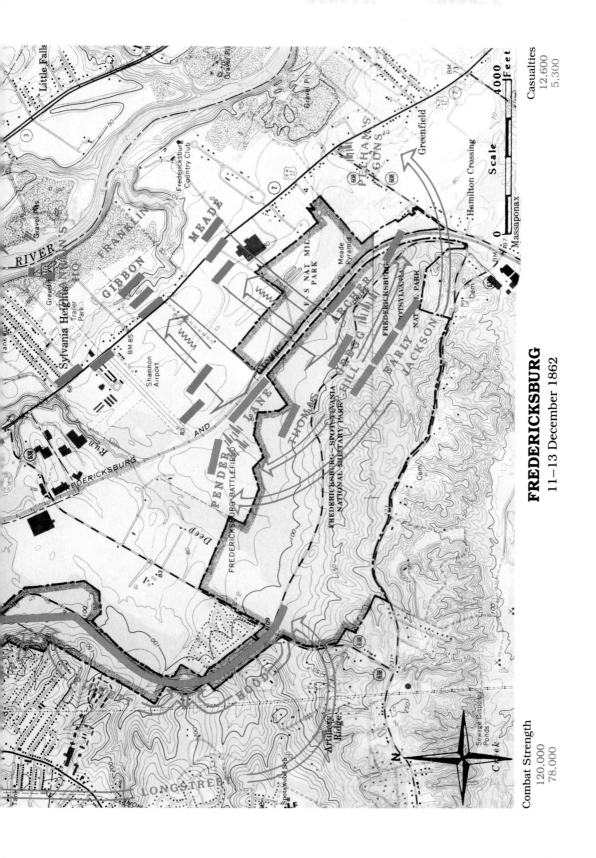

FREDERICKSBURG
11–13 December 1862

Combat Strength
120,000
78,000

Casualties
12,600
5,300

carpenters scrambled from their half-finished spans. The gunfire came from Brigadier General William Barksdale's Mississippi troops, who concealed themselves behind fences and in cellars near the water's edge. Burnside ordered a massive hour-long bombardment of Fredericksburg, in which 150 cannons rained 8,000 projectiles on the town. When the guns fell silent and the engineers warily returned to their spans, Barksdale's men met them with the familiar .58-caliber greeting.

Only one course remained. Union volunteers from Michigan, Massachusetts, and New York ferried themselves across the Rappahannock in the clumsy pontoon boats and battled the troops from Mississippi and Florida until the Confederates withdrew at darkness to their main line a mile in the rear, conceding the control of Fredericksburg to Burnside. Lee had never intended to prevent the Union forces from crossing the river; in fact he hoped Burnside would test his defenses behind the town. Barksdale's tenacity merely bought time for Lee to recall Jackson's corps from downstream and mass his army against Burnside's long-anticipated offensive.

On the following morning, December 12, the Army of the Potomac crossed the Rappahannock en masse and squandered the day by looting the empty city in a shameful display of vandalism. Burnside had based his battle plan on the assumption that he faced only a portion of Lee's army, a circumstance that ceased to exist by December 13. Using tentative, ambiguous language, he ordered assaults against Hamilton's Crossing on the Confederate right and Marye's Heights behind the town on Lee's left center.

The left grand division bore responsibility for the attack against Jackson. Even though he controlled almost 60,000 troops, Franklin placed the most literal and conservative inter-

Fredericksburg and Spotsylvania National Military Park
Fredericksburg, the stone wall. © David Muench, 1990

pretation on Burnside's orders and committed only 4,500 men to the offensive. Major General George G. Meade's division of Pennsylvania Reserves prepared to advance, supported on each flank by two other divisions.

Meade moved out at 8:30 A.M. His men, covered by a dissipating fog, crossed the Richmond Stage Road and began to march west toward Hamilton's Crossing. Suddenly Confederate artillery erupted behind them and to their left, halting the Union soldiers in their tracks. The guns belonged to a twenty-four-year-old Alabamian, Major John Pelham, commander of the Confederate horse artillery. The young officer had recklessly advanced two pieces directly on Meade's flank and rear and boldly maintained his position, despite losing one gun to counterfire. Pelham defied orders to retreat and returned to his lines only after he had exhausted his ammunition.

Pelham's heroics not only delayed the Union advance but induced Meade's supports on the left to remain east of the Richmond Stage Road to meet other such unexpected attacks. Once

Pelham withdrew, Meade's forces resumed their approach. When they were within five hundred yards of Jackson's line, Confederate artillery, masked in the woods to their front, blasted them. The Union infantry found hasty cover in the fields, where they responded to the Confederate fire. During the extended artillery duel that followed, a Federal missile exploded a southern ammunition wagon. Meade's troops then dashed toward a triangular point of woods that extended across the railroad tracks at the base of Jackson's position. To their surprise, it was unoccupied. They had accidentally found the Achilles' heel of Jackson's defense — a six-hundred-yard gap in the front lines.

The Federals quickly pressed through the woods and up to the high ground, upending a South Carolina brigade. Meade broke through, but could see Confederates gathering in his front. Jackson's response to the emergency was to organize a devastating counterattack, so Meade's soldiers and a portion of Brigadier General John Gibbon's di-

The Rappahannock River at Fredericksburg. Photo by Timothy H. O'Sullivan

vision, which had surged forward on Meade's right, withdrew across the railroad, through the open fields, and back to the Richmond Stage Road. By this time Franklin's reserves had stemmed the Confederate rush, and Jackson stubbornly resumed his original position.

In Fredericksburg, Lee brilliantly crafted his defense so that artillery swept the open ground west of the city with a chilling efficiency. "A chicken could not live on that field when we open on it," boasted one Confederate cannoneer. Confederate infantry supported the guns and occupied the base of the hills as well. Immediately below Marye's Heights, soldiers from Georgia and North Carolina crouched in a sunken road behind a stone wall and waited.

Burnside intended to begin his attack against Marye's Heights after Franklin had rolled up the Confederate right. When Meade's and Gibbon's attack bogged down in late morning, he unwisely opted to go forward with the second half of his offensive. This decision resulted in one of the great disasters of the Civil War. Wave after wave of Union troops left the cover of the town, crossed a canal ditch hidden in a small valley, and moved west toward Marye's Heights across four hundred yards of open terrain. The Federals staggered through the fire of massed artillery only to encounter a sheet of flame from the infantry 150 yards away, behind the stone wall. Men screamed as they moved forward, hunching their shoulders as if breasting a violent storm of wind and hail.

Tactics did not matter here. Lee poured reinforcements into the sunken road, where his riflemen stood six ranks deep on some portions of the line. Burnside ordered brigade after brigade — fifteen in all — to challenge the position, usually one or two at a time because the canal ditch valley could shelter only a few thousand men simultaneously. The attacks began at noon and continued until dark. When the firing ended, no Union soldier had laid a hand on the stone wall.

Burnside wanted to counter his losses by leading a new assault personally the following morning, but his lieutenants dissuaded him. The armies remained on the field for two more days. Many of the Union wounded froze to death in the no man's land between the lines. During a torrential downpour on the night of December 15–16, Burnside withdrew his men across the Rappahannock, and the battle concluded.

The battle of Fredericksburg cost Burnside 12,600 casualties, almost two thirds of which occurred on the few acres in front of the sunken road. Lee lost only 5,300. It appeared that the Army of Northern Virginia had won an overwhelming victory, but the Union army had not been destroyed, and Burnside quickly replaced his losses. Union morale dropped, but it never sagged enough to threaten the war effort. By the following spring Burnside's successor had refashioned the Army of the Potomac into a splendid fighting machine.

Lee regretted his opponent's escape across the Rappahannock, although in reality he could have done little to prevent it. His victory at Fredericksburg only postponed the next "On to Richmond" campaign by a few months.

Fredericksburg Battlefield, a unit of Fredericksburg and Spotsylvania National Military Park, is near Interstate 95 at Fredericksburg, Virginia, 45 miles south of Washington, D.C. There are 1,429 acres of the historic battlefield within the authorized boundaries of this unit; 148 of these are privately owned.

STONES RIVER

31 December 1862–2 January 1863

Grady McWhiney

Just after Christmas in 1862, Union Major General William S. Rosecrans moved the Army of the Cumberland south from Nashville toward Murfreesboro, Tennessee, to drive Confederate General Braxton Bragg's Army of Tennessee out of the state. "Press them, hard! Drive them!" Rosecrans urged his subordinates. "Make them fight or run!"

Bragg refused to run, even though an entire division had just been transferred from his army to Vicksburg by President Jefferson Davis, who advised Bragg to "fight if you can, and [then] fall back beyond the Tennessee [River]." Bragg deployed his forces on both sides of Stones River, north of Murfreesboro, in mostly open country without strong natural defenses, where trees grew in thick patches that could conceal the enemy and hamper Confederate cavalry and artillery movements. If Stones River rose — a likely event after the heavy rains earlier in December — he might be in trouble. But he disregarded these disadvantages in picking his battle line, because it was the only place he could concentrate the army and still cover the roads leading to his supply depot in Murfreesboro. He also feared that a retreat farther southward would expose east Tennessee to invasion.

Even though Bragg's defensive position was the best he could find for his purposes, he committed the serious tactical error of failing to entrench. He missed the most obvious lesson he should have learned from earlier battles: defenders in strong positions generally lose fewer men than the attackers do. Perhaps Bragg believed his men did not have time to use their spades to good advantage, but he also underestimated the value of fieldworks.

In the last days of December the two armies skirmished and groped into closer contact. As Rosecrans's forces moved toward Murfreesboro, Bragg sent Brigadier General Joseph Wheeler's cavalry around the Federal army to destroy supply trains and disrupt communications. The Confederates captured hundreds of prisoners, horses, wagons, and enough weapons to arm a brigade. But the cavalry raid was only the preliminary to what Bragg had in mind.

When Rosecrans failed to attack on December 30, Bragg decided to outflank the Federal right, cut the enemy's line of retreat, and fold Rosecrans's army back on itself like a closing jackknife. Near dawn on December 31, four fifths of the Confederate army began a wheeling movement from left to right on the west side of Stones River. Bragg's actions surprised the Federals. Rosecrans had planned to attack the Confederate right flank that same morning with the corps of Major General Thomas L. Crittenden and Major General George H. Thomas, but Bragg's men moved first, led by

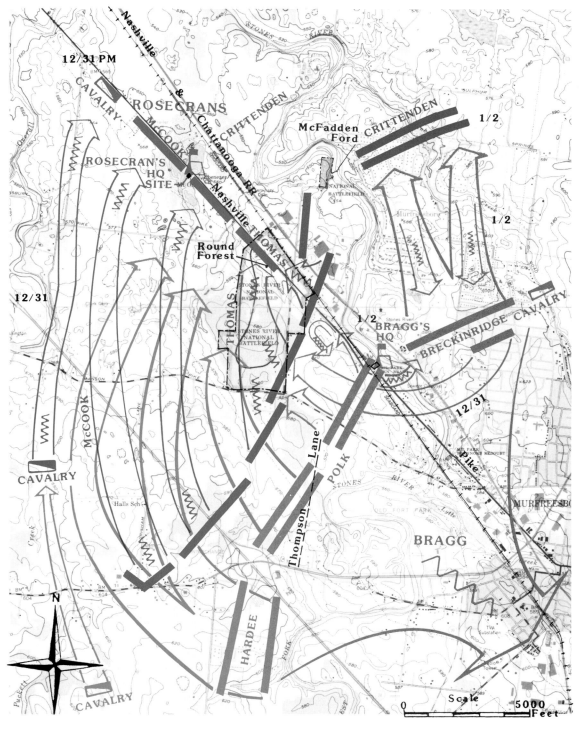

STONES RIVER

31 December 1862–2 January 1863

Combat Strength
44,000
34,000

Casualties
13,000
13,000

Lieutenant General William J. Hardee's corps and followed by Lieutenant General Leonidas Polk's corps. Their initial assault hit Major General Alexander McD. McCook's corps, whose only assignment for the day had been to protect the Federal right. The strong resistance put up by Brigadier General Philip Sheridan's men in the right center saved the Union from disaster by protecting the pike, the Federal supply line. Outflanked and overwhelmed by the Confederates, however, McCook's men retreated.

With the Federals forced back toward the Murfreesboro-Nashville Pike, Rosecrans called off his offensive and struggled to construct a defense line to save his only escape route. A Union general recalled that Rosecrans's "usually florid face had lost its ruddy color, and his anxious eyes told that the disasters of the morning were testing his powers to the very verge of endurance." Attacks against the Union right continued, but gradually the Federals rallied; their deadly rifle and artillery fire slowed and then checked the Confederate advance. The movement Bragg had expected his army to perform was more suited to an open parade field than to the rough terrain dotted with cedar thickets over which the Confederates advanced. Officers soon found it impossible to keep their lines unbroken, as Bragg's orders required, or even to maintain contact with units on their flanks. As losses multiplied, more men straggled.

By noon the sharpest action was in the Round Forest, near the Union center, where the Federal line formed an acute angle. The Confederates struck this strong natural position repeatedly but unsuccessfully; half the men in Brigadier General James R. Chalmer's Forty-fourth Mississippi Regiment charged the Federal position armed only with sticks, and most of his Ninth Mississippi attacked with their rifles too wet to fire, because of the previous night's rain. As the Mississippians faltered, Confederate Brigadier General Daniel S. Donelson's Tennessee Brigade rushed forward and was nearly destroyed: one regiment

lost half its officers and 68 percent of its men; another lost 42 percent of its officers and over half its men.

Unable to break the Federal line with Polk's troops, Bragg ordered four fresh brigades from Major General John C. Breckinridge's division on his right flank across the river. He could not have picked a worse spot to make this major attack, and Polk compounded the error by sending these reinforcements, which arrived shortly before 2:00 P.M., into battle piecemeal. They were slaughtered. "The Federals," as one general reported, "were strongly posted in two lines of battle, supported by numerous batteries. One of [the lines formed] an excellent breastwork. We had no artillery, the nature of the ground forbidding its use. It was deemed reckless to [continue the] attack."

Action continued sporadically until dark, but the Confederates could not break the Federal line, now defended by units of McCook's, Thomas's, and Crittenden's corps. To Hardee's final appeal for reinforcements sometime after 4:00 P.M., Bragg replied that he had no men to send. Hardee refused to order another assault. "The enemy," he recalled, "lay beyond the range of our guns, securely sheltered behind the strong defense of the railroad embankment, with wide open fields intervening, which were swept by their superior artillery. It would have been folly, not valor, to assail them in this position."

No further major action took place until January 2, 1863, when Bragg decided to dislodge a Union force, led by Colonel Samuel Beatty of Crittenden's Third Division, that had crossed Stones River and occupied a position on the east bank, "from which . . . Polk's line was both commanded and enfiladed." Bragg ordered Breckinridge's division, supported by artillery and cavalry, to drive the Federals back across the river. To divert attention from Breckinridge's assault, he opened an artillery barrage along Polk's front at 3:30 P.M. About thirty minutes later Breckinridge's men advanced in two lines. "The front line had bayonets fixed," reported Breckinridge, "with orders to deliver one volley, and then use the bayonet." A member of Bragg's staff left the best brief account of what happened. "The division moved beautifully across an open field," he observed. "A murderous fire was opened upon them. The enemy had concentrated a large force . . . and had combined a concentric fire from his artillery. . . . Our troops nevertheless marched up bravely and drove the enemy from the hill. The left of the division improvidently crossed the river contrary to orders: it was driven back in confusion. In [the] meantime, the enemy in large force assailed the right of the division, and it was compelled to retire. The [Confederate] cavalry[men] on the right were ordered to cooperate, but they were mere spectators. It was a terrible affair, although short." An hour and twenty minutes of combat had gained the Confederates nothing but casualties.

Bragg's position was now precarious. Soldiers who had fought and waited in the rain and cold for five days without sufficient rest were exhausted. Straggling had increased significantly. Stones River, which had risen rapidly after several more days of heavy rain, might soon become unfordable, which would isolate part of the army. Furthermore, Bragg had just seen captured documents that indicated that Rosecrans had received reinforcements.

The Confederate retreat from Murfreesboro, which began at 11:00 P.M. on January 3 in drenching rain, was made without mishap. Supply trains led the way south, followed by the infantry. A cavalry screen protected their movements. Rosecrans did not pursue, but nearly 2,000 wounded Confederates and their medical attendants were left behind.

Stones River was one of the bloodiest battles of the Civil War. Of the approximately 44,000 Federals and 34,000 Confederates engaged in action near Murfreesboro, each side lost about 13,000.

To many people the end of the war seemed no nearer after Stones River. A Confederate who admitted that he was "sick and tired" of fighting could "see no prospects of having peace for a long time to come. I don't think it ever will be stopped by fighting," he reasoned; "the Yankees can't whip us and we can never whip them, and I see no prospect of peace unless the Yankees themselves rebel and throw down their arms, and refuse to fight any longer." Northern leaders, in contrast, regarded Stones River as an important victory. It cost the Confederates not only a little more of Tennessee but a lot of what they could ill afford to lose — men. The Federals, who had more manpower, gained little additional territory, yet after the battle President Lincoln thanked Rosecrans for his "hard-earned victory" and confessed that had Stones River "been a defeat instead, the nation could scarcely have lived over [it]."

Stones River National Battlefield is on State Route 41 near Interstate 24 at Murfreesboro, Tennessee, 25 miles southeast of Nashville. There are 405 acres of the historic battlefield within its authorized boundaries.

CHANCELLORSVILLE

1–3 May 1863

Robert K. Krick

During the first week of May 1863, Confederate General Robert E. Lee and Lieutenant General Thomas J. "Stonewall" Jackson led a dramatically outnumbered Army of Northern Virginia to victory in the battle of Chancellorsville. That battle has been aptly called Lee's greatest victory and was one of the Confederacy's brightest moments.

The crushing Union defeat at the battle of Fredericksburg in December had left the Army of the Potomac in disarray during the winter of 1862–63. Officers and men alike doubted (with good cause) the capacity for command of the army's leader, Major General Ambrose E. Burnside. As the two contending armies settled into camps facing one another across the icy Rappahannock River that winter, the northern cause was apparently at its nadir. Burnside compounded his troops' unhappiness when he led them out of their wintry camps in mid-January on a disastrous venture that came to bear the derisive name "the Mud March." Almost at once he was replaced by a general known for his political machinations and aggressiveness, Major General Joseph "Fighting Joe" Hooker. Burnside slipped into relative oblivion and is best remembered today not for his military exploits but for his eponymous whiskers.

As soon as springtime made Virginia's roads passable, Hooker moved part of his army up and across the Rappahannock above Fredericksburg. His plan to fall on the rear of Lee's army was a daring one, and it was crisply executed. Placed at a disadvantage as great as any he faced during the war, Lee rushed his men west of Fredericksburg toward the tiny country crossroads of Chancellorsville, where there was only a single house. Dense, wiry underbrush covered more than half the battlefield in an area known since the earliest settlement as the Wilderness of Spotsylvania. For an outnumbered army thrown on the defensive, such terrain offered tremendous advantages. The confusing sea of impenetrable thickets served as a sort of ready-made barbed wire behind which Lee could maneuver his slender military resources.

Hooker arrived at Chancellorsville late on the last day of April. The next morning he turned east, in the direction of Fredericksburg, and moved toward the rear of the Confederate position he had so thoroughly outflanked — and toward the eastern edge of the Wilderness. During the morning his advance reached the foot of a commanding ridge on which stood the small wooden Baptist sanctuary called Zoan Church. This ridge was the highest ground for miles; equally important, it was beyond the edge of the entangling Wilderness.

Lee and Jackson meanwhile conceived a re-

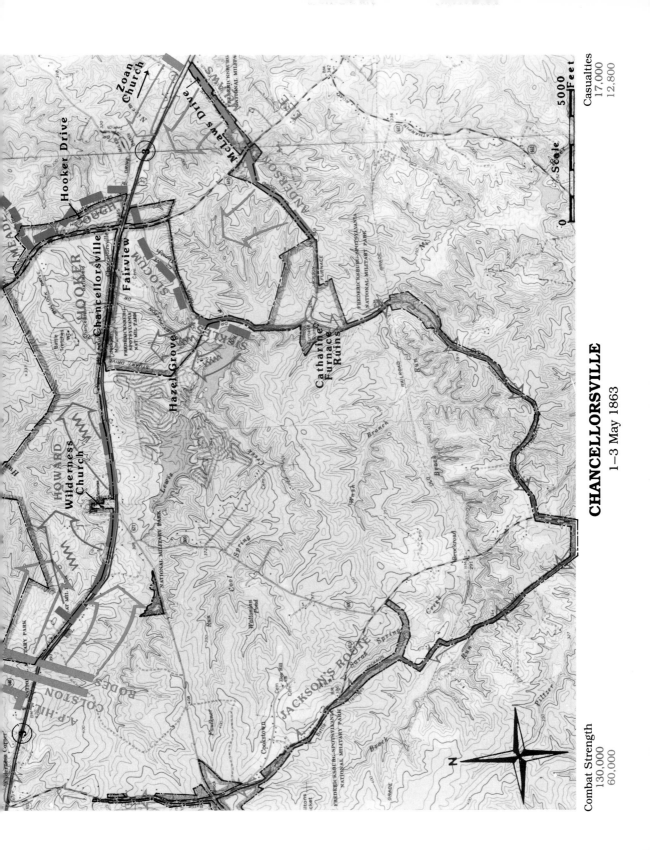

CHANCELLORSVILLE

1–3 May 1863

Combat Strength
130,000
60,000

Casualties
17,000
12,800

Scale

0   5000

Feet

markable plan for dealing with Hooker. Although the Federals outnumbered them more than two to one — about 130,000 to 60,000, the largest imbalance of any major battle in Virginia during the war — the Confederate commanders determined to divide their forces, leaving a rear guard at Fredericksburg. Jackson arrived at Zoan Church just as the Union advance was on the verge of capturing that crucial ridge. He attacked immediately and drove a suddenly pliant Hooker back toward Chancellorsville on two parallel roads. May 1 ended with the Union army digging in around and west of the crossroads, its right flank stretched somewhat aimlessly westward beyond Wilderness Church.

Through the dark hours of that night Lee and Jackson reviewed their alternatives and selected the most daring of the lot. In complete contravention of most of the established rules of warfare, they further divided their small force. Starting early on May 2, Jackson displayed the enormous energy and determination that were his dominant military traits as he hurried most of the available infantry on a twelve-mile march all the way around Hooker's army. While Jackson surged far out on a limb, Lee remained behind with a relative handful of men and did his best to bemuse Hooker into assuming that he faced dire danger in his front.

Late in the afternoon of May 2, Jackson had his 30,000 men aligned behind the unsuspecting Union troops. When the general said to Major Eugene Blackford, commanding the skirmishers, "You can go forward then," the Confederate cause was at its highest tide. The hordes of ragged Confederates who came loping out of the Wilderness, screaming their spine-chilling Rebel yell, had little difficulty rolling over their opponents and destroying half of Hooker's line.

After darkness halted the advance, Jackson rode in front of his disorganized men in quest of a route that would offer new opportunities. When he came back toward his troops, a North Carolina regiment fired blindly

at the shadowy figure and mortally wounded him. Jackson died eight days later, in the office building of the Chandler plantation, south of Fredericksburg.

The most intense fighting during the battle of Chancellorsville developed on the morning of May 3, across the densely wooded Wilderness near where Jackson had fallen. The pivotal advantage finally came from Confederate artillery crowded onto a small, high clearing known as Hazel Grove. The guns at Hazel Grove supplied momentum to weary infantrymen who surged across the fields around Chancellorsville crossroads in midmorning to seal a southern victory that cost the Union 17,000 casualties.

A separate drama unfolded on May 3 at Salem Church, on the outskirts of Fredericksburg. A Union force that had remained near the town brushed aside the Confederates there and pushed west toward the main action, threatening Lee's success at Chancellorsville. Some stray Confederates, notably Alabamians under Brigadier General Cadmus M. Wilcox, found good ground at Salem Church from which to resist this force. The little brick country church, hand-built by its constituents in 1844, served the Alabama troops as a fort during the battle and then became a charnel house in the aftermath.

The campaign wound down during the next three days, as static lines waited for Hooker's decision to admit defeat and recross the river. The battle of Chancellorsville gave the Army of Northern Virginia momentum that Lee turned into an aggressive campaign a few weeks later. That campaign led to Gettysburg. Chancellorsville cost the Confederacy 12,800 casualties, including the incomparable Stonewall Jackson.

Chancellorsville Battlefield, a unit of Fredericksburg and Spotsylvania National Military Park, is on State Route 3 west of Fredericksburg, Virginia, 45 miles south of Washington, D.C., on Interstate 95. There are 1,252 acres of the historic battlefield within the authorized boundaries of this unit; 111 of these are privately owned.

BRANDY STATION

9 June 1863

Clark B. Hall

In the early morning of June 9, 1863, a large Union cavalry column under Brigadier General John Buford positioned itself along the Rappahannock River for a peremptory rush across Beverly's Ford. Buford's horsemen, as well as a wing of equal strength headed by Brigadier General David McMurtrie Gregg six miles below at Kelly's Ford, had arrived in Culpeper County, Virginia, looking for a fight. Colonel Benjamin F. "Grimes" Davis's New York Cavalry led the Union column thundering across the ford, thus opening the battle of Brandy Station, the most hotly contested cavalry engagement of the Civil War. It was the largest single mounted battle ever fought on the American continent: of the 20,000 troops that were engaged, 17,000 were cavalrymen.

At Chancellorsville in early May, Union forces under Major General Joseph Hooker had been stunningly defeated by the skillful flanking movements of General Robert E. Lee. In early June "Fighting Joe" Hooker was informed of a growing Confederate cavalry presence near the town of Culpeper. His scouts were partially correct. Most of the Confederate cavalry were in fact in Culpeper County, but they were at Brandy Station, not Culpeper. Hooker did not know that two full corps of Confederate infantry, under lieutenant generals James Longstreet and Richard S. Ewell, were preparing for the march north that would

lead them to Gettysburg. The Confederate cavalry was positioned to screen this infantry from discovery and to protect the army's flank as it proceeded north across the Blue Ridge. The Confederates included brigadier generals Wade Hampton, W. H. F. "Rooney" Lee, and William E. "Grumble" Jones, Colonel Thomas T. Munford, Major Robert F. Beckham of the horse artillery, and 9,500 troopers, all commanded by the bold Major General J. E. B. Stuart.

In addition to Colonel Davis, the Union cavalry commanders included colonels Judson Kilpatrick and Percy Wyndham and captains Wesley Merritt, George Armstrong Custer, and Elon J. Farnsworth. Hooker ordered most of his cavalry and two brigades of infantry — about 11,000 men in all, commanded by Major General Alfred Pleasonton — to "disperse and destroy" the Confederates. When Buford stormed across Beverly's Ford, he was not expecting to find the enemy in immediate force. The Confederates were also taken by surprise: the cavalry was asleep. Buford's orders directed him to Brandy Station, four miles to the front, where he was to link up with Gregg, but his attack stalled when the gallant Colonel Davis fell to the dirt on Beverly's Ford Road, a saber in his hand and a bullet in his head.

Taking heavy losses but regrouping effec-

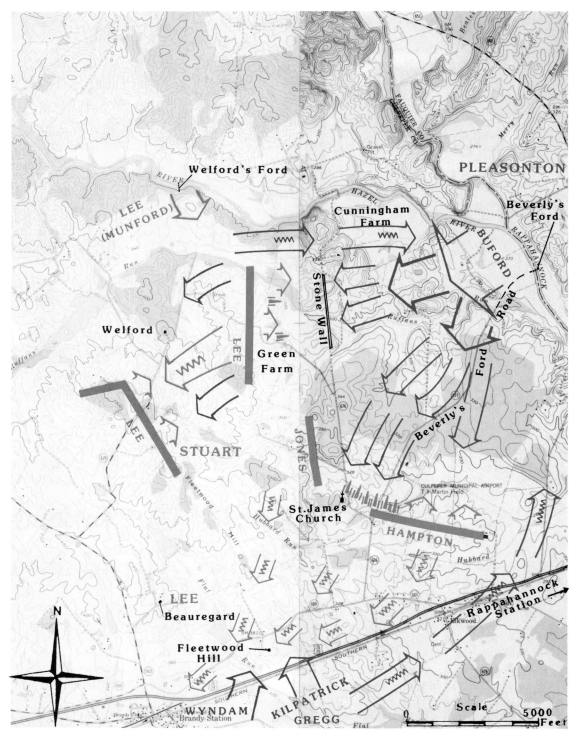

BRANDY STATION

9 June 1863

Combat Strength
11,000
9,500

Casualties
868
515

Brandy Station battlefield
© Clark B. Hall

tively, the Confederates quickly established a strong position anchored near a little brick church on a slight ridge above Beverly's Ford Road. Their horse artillery was centered at St. James Church, Hampton's brigade was east of the cannon, Jones was to the west of the church, and Rooney Lee's brigade faced east along a north-south ridge of the Yew Hills. Lee positioned artillery at Dr. Daniel Green's house and ordered dismounted troopers to a low stone wall three hundred yards beneath and east of the Green house plateau.

In hand-to-hand combat, men fought for control of the thick woods across from the church. The Sixth Pennsylvania cavalry emerged in perfect order from the woods and pounded directly for the spewing cannon at the church, sabers drawn, guidons flying high in the morning sun. Several astonished Confederates later recorded this assault as the most "brilliant and glorious" cavalry charge of

the war. In spite of such superlatives, many brave men of Pennsylvania never arose again from the broad plain beneath the church.

Continuing his attempts to turn the Confederate left, Buford shifted most of his Union cavalry to the Cunningham farm, where they stubbornly assaulted the stone wall below the Green house. Having a clear terrain advantage, Rooney Lee's line continued to hold firm. Startling developments at the Confederate rear, however, created timely opportunities for Buford and potential disaster for the Confederate cavalry.

As Buford's emphasis shifted to the Confederate left, Gregg arrived from Kelly's Ford with his 2,400-man division. They entered the village of Brandy Station from the south, near Fleetwood Hill. Whoever controlled this elevation would dominate the battlefield.

Gregg's arrival caused Stuart hurriedly to abandon his St. James line. He dispatched Jones's and Hampton's brigades to save the hill and his recent headquarters near the

Fleetwood house. Rooney Lee's right was dangerously unsupported, so he pulled back through the Yew Hills toward yet higher ground on Fleetwood. Buford followed, fighting all the way against Lee's rear guard.

On the southern flanks of the two-and-a-half-mile-long Fleetwood Hill, opposing regiments collided. As a participant wrote, "Thousands of flashing sabers steamed in the sunlight; the rattle of carbines and pistols mingled with the roar of cannon; armed men wearing the blue and the gray became mixed in promiscuous confusion; the surging ranks swayed up and down the sides of Fleetwood Hill, and dense clouds of smoke and dust rose as a curtain to cover the tumultuous and bloody scene."

Stuart later wrote: "The contest for the hill was long and spirited." General Robert E. Lee observed part of the battle from the Barbour house (now Beauregard), and later praised the gallantry on both sides. After desperate charges by Hampton, the Confederates finally won Fleetwood Hill and the ground south of the railroad and east of Brandy Station — and saved their chief's headquarters. A Union division of 1,900 men under Colonel Alfred Duffié, sent via Stevensburg, was delayed there by two Confederate regiments in a valiant stand. Duffié could have made a difference in the fight, but he arrived too late to be put into action.

Realizing an opportunity on his far left, Stuart ordered Rooney Lee to counterattack Buford's forces. In this charge, which Major Heros von Borcke later asserted "decided the fate of the day," Rooney Lee went down with a severe wound, but the Virginians and North Carolinians slammed on into Buford, who then received orders to disengage and retrograde across Beverly's Ford.

The day-long battle of Brandy Station was over, resulting in 868 Union and 515 Confederate casualties. The Union cavalry had begun its rapid rise to power over the proud but dwindling Confederate cavalry.

Brandy Station battlefield is on U.S. routes 29 and 15 at Brandy Station, near Culpeper, Virginia. The entire battlefield is privately owned.

PRESERVING CIVIL WAR BATTLEFIELDS

John Heinz

"History with its flickering lamp stumbles along the trail of the past, trying to reconstruct its scenes to revive its echoes, and kindle with pale gleams the passion of former days."
— Winston Churchill

It is often said that we learn the lessons of history so that we might not fall victim once more to the mistakes of the past. But it is more important to note that history often provides examples of virtue, discipline, courage, and honor to which we individually aspire. To study history is to understand humanity. Nonetheless, Winston Churchill was quite correct in describing the light that history sheds on the "passion of former days" as most often like a "flickering lamp."

The value of history is undisputed, but the value of historic preservation is perhaps less clear. Yet if history comes to us only through academic discourse, the light that shines on the past may indeed "flicker." Recognizing this, we can soon see the importance of historic preservation. Undisturbed pieces of the past provide the individual with an undisturbed historical perspective. To appreciate history, we must evoke our imaginations, and this is best achieved through direct contact with the things that remain from past days.

Civil War history illustrates my meaning. Fort Sumter, the Gettysburg address, Stonewall Jackson, and Robert E. Lee are standard chapters in American history classes, supplemented by Civil War photography. (My favorite is the famous picture of Abraham Lincoln, who seems to exude some tangible moral confidence, towering above his generals in conference outside an army tent.) But we have only to look at the faces of schoolchildren visiting the Gettysburg battlefield to understand how intensely the field commands their attention and imaginations.

The battlefield at Antietam offers another opportunity to honor the heroes of the Civil War. Richard Halloran wrote, "It should be said that walking the battlefield at Antietam is a somber experience. It takes but little imagination to hear the thunder of cannon and the rattle of musketry, to listen to the cries of mangled young men, to see the rows of dead and to recall the carnage of that day." There were nearly 23,000 casualties on September 17, 1862, at Antietam; more American men died there than in any one-day battle in World War II, Korea, or Vietnam. Preservation of this and other Civil War battlefields is an important part of the vital task of preserving the memory of sacrifices made to ensure the survival of this nation and of freedom and justice for all.

In this light, we must consider the practical question of responsibility for the preservation of Civil War battlefields. These are areas of national historic importance, and the duty for their preservation should and does fall primarily on the federal government. But the national effort cannot succeed without a comparable, if not greater, commitment of resources and effort by the private sector, by individual volunteers, and by state and local governments. Many states and localities are home to invaluable battlefield sites that are not likely to be incorporated into the National Park System. These governments can and should take steps to preserve these sites and to provide for their historic interpretation. Community and national organizations can help. This process has already begun as individuals organize to purchase and preserve historic property.

National efforts to protect and restore historic sites, particularly battlefields, have generated controversy and a renewed emphasis on policies that govern such sites. The efforts of private groups like The Conservation Fund are appropriate to ensure a tangible history for our own and future generations and to prevent the irreversible loss of our national heritage. The federal government cannot possibly acquire and manage every battlefield or every historical site. Given this truth, I laud the efforts of The Conservation Fund, and of all private individuals and groups involved in preservation. Without their continuing efforts, the goals of historic preservation cannot possibly succeed.

Gettysburg: the summit of Little Round Top, July 2, 1863

GETTYSBURG

1–3 July 1863

Harry W. Pfanz

The battle of Gettysburg, fought from July 1 to July 3, 1863, was the great battle of the Civil War and one of the crucial events in America's history. More than 170,000 men fought in it, and over 50,000 became casualties. Four and a half months later, on November 19, President Abraham Lincoln delivered his Gettysburg address on that battlefield at the dedication of its cemetery for the Union dead.

In 1863 Gettysburg had a population of 2,400 and was at the center of a network of some ten roads. Two led to passes in South Mountain, about ten miles to the west, and to the Cumberland Valley beyond. Others ran to Harrisburg, Baltimore, and other nearby towns in Pennsylvania and Maryland. The gently rolling terrain, dominated by low north-south ridges and scattered granite hills, provided defensive positions for the armies that would fight there. The town was surrounded by small farms with cultivated fields, orchards, and woodlots that concealed outcroppings of granite boulders.

The battle of Gettysburg was the culmination of General Robert E. Lee's Pennsylvania campaign, which he launched in June to relieve Virginia of the burden of war, to disrupt the Union's summer operations, and to win a battle in the north which, unlike his victories in Virginia, would prove decisive. His Army of Northern Virginia began to cross the Potomac in mid-June, and by the end of the month the 75,000 soldiers were spread from Chambersburg to Carlisle and York. On June 28 Lee learned to his dismay that the 95,000-man Army of the Potomac, led by its new commander, Major General George G. Meade, had crossed the Potomac and might soon strike his scattered force. Lee ordered his army to concentrate east of the mountains in the Gettysburg-Cashtown area in order to give battle.

On July 1, as the Confederate army marched east through Cashtown Pass, Lieutenant General A. P. Hill sent two divisions of his corps toward Gettysburg to test the strength of Union forces seen there the previous day. At midmorning the Confederates met cavalry pickets just west of the town. Hill's men deployed on Herr Ridge and advanced, striking Union troops on McPherson Ridge. In the sharp fight that followed, the Confederate attack was repulsed, but the Union commander on the field, Major General John F. Reynolds, was killed. Reinforcements for both sides arrived during the lull that followed the battle, until nearly 40,000 troops were on the field west and north of the town. Toward midafternoon Confederate Lieutenant General Richard S. Ewell's corps attacked the Union Eleventh Corps in the north as Hill's corps again struck the Union First Corps on Mc-Pherson Ridge. After hard fighting Lee's men drove the outnumbered Union troops to Cemetery Hill, just south of the town, where major generals Oliver O. Howard and Winfield S. Hancock rallied them and sent some units to occupy Culp's Hill, to the east.

Most of the remainder of both armies arrived during the night and morning of July 1–2 and prepared for battle. Meade's army established a fishhook-shaped line that embraced Culp's Hill on its right, Cemetery Hill, and Cemetery Ridge south two miles to two hills known as the Round Tops. The Army of Northern Virginia took positions facing its foe along Hanover Road east of the town, between the town and Cemetery Hill, and along Seminary Ridge, less than a mile west of Cemetery Ridge. At noon Major General Daniel E. Sickles, commanding the Union Third Corps, committed a dangerous blunder — he advanced his 10,000-man corps from Cemetery Ridge near Little Round Top to high ground along the Emmitsburg Road, between the ridges. His line then ran from the peach orchard that bordered the road, back by a wheatfield, to the massive boulders of Devil's Den in front of the Round Tops.

Late that afternoon Lieutenant General James Longstreet, at Lee's order, launched a delayed attack with Major General John B. Hood's and Major General Lafayette McLaws's divisions against Sickles's salient, as Major General Richard H. Anderson's division of Hill's corps assaulted the Union center. Longstreet smashed Sickles's troops, but prompt action by Meade with forces directed by Hancock and Major General George Sykes broke the Confederate attack at dusk. The Union soldiers' stout defense and the arrival of their Sixth Corps rendered them secure in their position on Cemetery Ridge.

As the firing died along the ridge, Ewell's corps opened a belated attack against the Union positions on Culp's Hill and Cemetery Hill in order to aid Longstreet's attack. A few of the Confederates who attacked the Union's

Eleventh Corps position on Cemetery Hill reached the crest of the hill, but they were driven back. Those who attacked Culp's Hill secured a precarious hold on its eastern slope in front of the breastworks of the Union Twelfth Corps, and a foothold on its lower crest in works vacated temporarily by Union soldiers sent off to the fighting on Cemetery Ridge. The firing on Culp's Hill died out before midnight, but the Confederates held their gains and were reinforced. Returning Union Twelfth Corps troops sealed off their penetration on the lower crest to keep them from the Baltimore Pike nearby and then reopened the fight at daybreak with immense and incessant rifle fire. The armies battled for six hours until late in the morning, when Ewell's men broke off their futile fight and fell back beyond Rock Creek at the base of the hill.

In spite of only minimal successes on July 2, Lee remained optimistic. Early on July 3 he ordered a major assault against the Union center on Cemetery Ridge. This was to be supported by Ewell's troops on Culp's Hill and by a thrust around the Union right by Major General J. E. B. Stuart's 10,000 cavalrymen, who had arrived late on July 2. Unfortunately, the Confederates were driven off Culp's Hill before the main assault could be launched. Stuart's tired troopers, however, began their move early in the afternoon. Three miles east of Gettysburg they collided with Union cavalry under Brigadier General David M. Gregg, posted near the Hanover Road. Stuart deployed his horsemen on a front of nearly a mile, and skirmishing began. This fighting intensified rapidly and climaxed in thundering mounted charges across the fields of the Rummel farm. Gregg's men held, and Stuart's thrust was stopped.

While Stuart's troopers rode east, Confederate batteries fired for two hours to pave the way for the assault against Cemetery Ridge. At 3:00 P.M. their firing ceased and the infantry attack, later known as Pickett's Charge, began. Twelve thousand men from the divisions of major generals George E. Pickett, Henry Heth (now led by Brigadier General

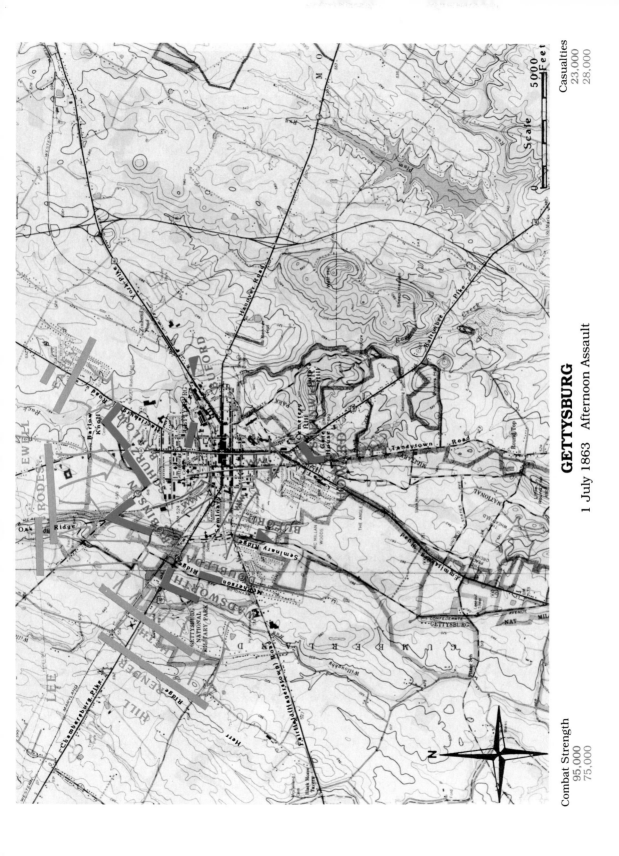

GETTYSBURG

1 July 1863   Afternoon Assault

Combat Strength
95,000
75,000

Casualties
23,000
28,000

GETTYSBURG

2 July 1863   Afternoon Assault

GETTYSBURG

3 July 1863   Afternoon Assault

Johnston Pettigrew), and William D. Pender (commanded by Major General Isaac Trimble) trudged in long lines across open, undulating fields toward Cemetery Ridge. Union shot and shell plowed gaps in their formations, but their ranks closed and pressed on. After they crossed the Emmitsburg Road, however, canister and rifle fire raked their line and decimated their formations. A mass of men surged against the Union Second Corps at a copse of trees, but their firepower and momentum failed. Those not shot or captured were driven back. The charge was over.

Lee's try for a decisive victory in Pennsylvania had failed. On the night of July 4 the Army of Northern Virginia slogged in a drenching rain from Gettysburg toward the Potomac, south of Hagerstown. It had lost 28,000 men. Lee's men found the river too swollen to cross, and they were unable to return to Virginia until the night of July 13.

There were two years of war ahead, but Meade's Army of the Potomac — despite having lost 23,000 men — had won a decisive victory at Gettysburg. After this defeat Lee was never again able to launch a major offensive. His road from Gettysburg was long and hard, and ultimately led to Appomattox Court House and surrender.

Gettysburg National Military Park is on U.S. Route 15 (business) at Gettysburg, Pennsylvania, 37 miles southwest of Harrisburg. There are 3,874 acres of the historic battlefield within its authorized boundaries; 184 of these are privately owned.

Gettysburg National Military Park
Little Round Top. © David Muench, 1990

Gettysburg National Military Park
Cemetery Hill. © David Muench, 1990

THE GETTYSBURG ADDRESS

Abraham Lincoln

Fourscore and seven years ago our fathers brought forth on this continent, a new nation, conceived in Liberty, and dedicated to the proposition that all men are created equal.

Now we are engaged in a great civil war, testing whether that nation or any nation so conceived and so dedicated can long endure. We are met on a great battlefield of that war. We have come to dedicate a portion of that field, as a final resting place for those who here gave their lives that that nation might live. It is altogether fitting and proper that we should do this.

But, in a larger sense, we cannot dedicate — we cannot consecrate — we cannot hallow — this ground. The brave men, living and dead, who struggled here, have consecrated it far above our poor power to add or detract. The world will little note nor long remember what we say here, but it can never forget what they did here. It is for us, the living, rather to be dedicated here to the unfinished work which they who fought here have thus far so nobly advanced. It is rather for us to be here dedicated to the great task remaining before us — that from these honored dead we take increased devotion to that cause for which they here gave the last full measure of devotion; that we here highly resolve that these dead shall not have died in vain; that this nation, under God, shall have a new birth of freedom; and that government of the people, by the people, for the people, shall not perish from the earth.

THE VICKSBURG CAMPAIGN AND SIEGE

29 March–4 July 1863

Edwin C. Bearss

In the final days of March 1863, Major General Ulysses S. Grant was checkmated in his campaign to capture Vicksburg and open the Mississippi River. His four attempts to bypass Vicksburg from upriver had failed. These included a bold attempt to move his forces by water by digging a canal across the De Soto Point, west of the Mississippi River and opposite Vicksburg. The winter camps in northeastern Louisiana near the Mississippi River were unhealthy, and the number of men on sick call was alarming. As Grant saw it, he had three alternatives: to launch an assault across the Mississippi at Vicksburg, to return his army to Memphis and resume his advance overland, or to move his army through the Louisiana parishes opposite Vicksburg, return to the Mississippi at New Carthage, and then cross the river to operate against Vicksburg from the south or join forces with the Army of the Gulf in an attack on Port Hudson. The first alternative he rejected as too costly. The second, although it was championed by major generals William T. Sherman and James B. McPherson — his two favorite corps commanders — he rejected because it would be interpreted in Washington and by the public as a step backward, and he might as a consequence be relieved of his command. Grant chose the third alternative and marched south.

On March 29 Major General John A. McClernand, who supported Grant's plan, moved with alacrity to open a road across Madison Parish, Louisiana, from Milliken's Bend to New Carthage. McPherson's troops, which were in Lake Providence, Louisiana, were ordered to follow McClernand's route. Meanwhile, on the nights of April 16 and 22 the Union navy ran the Vicksburg gauntlet with eight gunboats and seven transports, so that Grant would be able to move McClernand and McPherson across the Mississippi south of Vicksburg. Rear Admiral David D. Porter lost no gunboats, but the Union army lost two steamboats to Confederate fire.

Grant ordered three diversions to confuse the Confederates about his objectives. He moved Major General Frederick Steele's division down Deer Creek to destroy Confederate Lieutenant General John C. Pemberton's food sources. He ordered Colonel Benjamin H. Grierson to occupy Pemberton's attention by raiding and damaging railroads from La Grange, Tennessee, to Baton Rouge, Louisiana. To cover his crossing of the Mississippi, Grant ordered Sherman to attack Snyder's Bluff with gunboats and an infantry division.

On April 30 Grant crossed the great river, put 24,000 men and sixty cannon ashore at Bruinsburg, and quickly moved McClernand and McPherson to secure the high ground.

Brigadier General John S. Bowen, Pemberton's ablest subordinate, called for reinforcements on April 27 to oppose Grant's impending landing, but Pemberton, taking Grant's bait, had sent his strategic reserve in a futile pursuit of Grierson and was unable to help. On May 1, west of Port Gibson, Bowen was outnumbered three to one but held against 24,000 of McClernand's and McPherson's men for eighteen hours. In the afternoon, however, the Confederates were outflanked and retreated across Bayou Pierre. The next morning Grant's columns occupied Port Gibson and drove northward. The Confederates evacuated Grand Gulf and retired across the Big Black River. Having secured his beachhead with the battle of Port Gibson, Grant halted his army and awaited Sherman's corps, which was en route down the Louisiana side of the Mississippi from Milliken's Bend and Young's Point.

Grant had two options for his next move. He could move against Vicksburg from the south, using his bridgehead across the Big Black at Hankinson's Ferry. Such an advance would lead to the capture of the city, but Pemberton's army would be able to escape northeast up the Benton Road. Or he could march by way of Cayuga and Auburn and strike the Southern Railroad of Mississippi between Edwards and Bolton. Then, pivoting to the west, he could close in on Vicksburg from the east. An approach from this direction could cost Pemberton his army as well as the city. Grant, a great captain, had no trouble making his decision.

Grant put Sherman's and McPherson's corps in motion. Sherman crossed the Mississippi at Grand Gulf, and the Army of the Tennessee resumed its advance on May 8, supplied by large, heavily guarded wagon trains. Grant sent McPherson's corps, which was to constitute his right, through Utica toward Raymond. McClernand's corps, to be Grant's left, screened the Big Black crossings. Sherman's corps, to be the center, closed in on Auburn.

On May 11 Confederate Brigadier General John Gregg and his brigade of men from Texas and Tennessee arrived in Jackson from Port Hudson and marched southwest to Raymond, where they took position. At 10:00 A.M. on May 12, Gregg sighted McPherson's vanguard on the Utica road. Cannon bellowed, and the fight began. Gregg was outnumbered three to one, although he did not realize it until late in the day. His 3,000 troops held the initiative for more than four hours, while McPherson failed to use his greater numbers of men and artillery to undertake a coordinated attack. Finally Gregg disengaged and retired through Raymond toward Jackson.

The Raymond fight had important repercussions. When McPherson reported the battle, he doubled Gregg's strength. This, along with rumors that General Joseph E. Johnston was expected in Jackson, caused Grant to alter his plan. Instead of striking for Edwards and Bolton on May 13, he turned his army to the east. McPherson's and Sherman's corps were to capture Jackson, disperse the Confederates, and break up the railroads. McClernand's corps would cover this movement.

The corps marched as ordered. Sherman and McPherson had easy tasks, but McClernand did not. Pemberton, who had transferred his headquarters from Jackson to Vicksburg on May 2, ordered his army to concentrate at Big Black Bridge, where it was within easy striking distance of a Union corps. McClernand gained time by bluffing an attack on Edwards. While the Confederates called up troops and dug in on the hills south of the village, he broke contact. Stealing a march on Pemberton, he camped at Raymond on the night of the thirteenth.

General Johnston reached Jackson late that day from middle Tennessee. After conferring with Gregg, he telegraphed to Richmond, "I am too late." Preparations were made to abandon the city. To gain time and to cover the shipment of supplies to Canton, the troops were posted well in front of the Jackson earthworks.

On May 14, in a driving rain, McPherson's and Sherman's corps converged on the town. There was savage skirmishing on the Clinton and Raymond roads, then the Confederates retired into the fortifications. Before Union troops could mount an assault, word arrived that the Confederates had evacuated Jackson with their supply trains and were retiring up the Canton Road.

Since the Federals now held Jackson, the brigade en route to reinforce Johnston from Port Hudson was turned back at Crystal Springs, two brigades coming from middle Tennessee detrained at Meridian, and one coming from South Carolina was turned back at Brandon. Johnston's unfortunate decision to abandon Jackson almost without a fight had left his army scattered. Critical days passed before it was concentrated.

Johnston ordered Pemberton to march eastward and attack the Union army near Clinton. One of the Confederate couriers was a Union agent who delivered Johnston's orders to Grant on May 14. Grant ordered Sherman to destroy Jackson's railroads and industrial facilities while McPherson's and McClernand's corps marched to intercept Pemberton. Grant accompanied McPherson's column as it headed west toward Vicksburg.

On May 16 Pemberton's pickets clashed with the vanguard of Grant's columns, who were advancing via the Raymond and Middle roads.

Pages 128–133: The battles of Port Gibson and Champion Hill, Mississippi, and the siege of Vicksburg, from Lieutenant Colonel James H. Wilson's "Map of the Country between Milliken's Bend, La. and Jackson, Miss. shewing the Routes followed by the Army of the Tennessee . . . in April and May 1863," one of several battlefield maps published in the 1870s by the U.S. Army Office of the Chief of Engineers. (Civil War map no. 261, Geography and Map Division, Library of Congress)

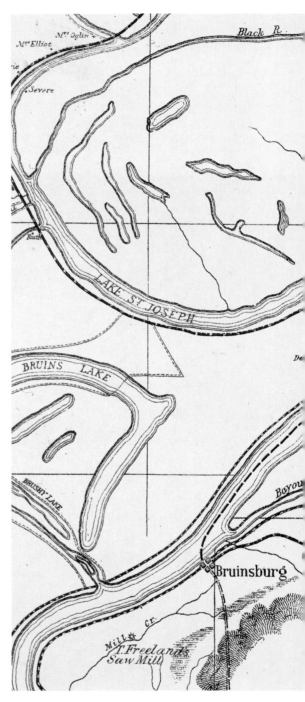

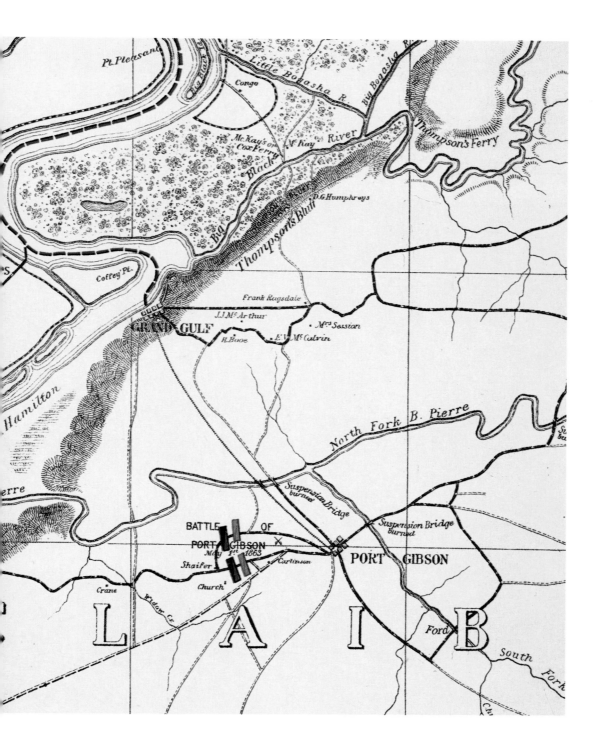

Pemberton received another dispatch from Johnston drafted after the evacuation of Jackson, repeating the order for a concentration north of the Southern Railroad of Mississippi. Although he had previously rejected this movement as "suicidal," Pemberton issued orders to countermarch through Edwards and out the Brownsville Road north of the railroad.

He was too late. McPherson had advanced on the Jackson Road from Bolton and was approaching Champion Hill, a commanding elevation. Pemberton deployed three brigades of Major General Carter L. Stevenson's division on the double to meet this threat to his left, while General Bowen's and Major General William W. Loring's divisions faced east to oppose McClernand's columns. By 10:30 A.M. Grant had launched an all-out assault on Stevenson's division. In the bitter fighting that followed, the crest of Champion Hill and the crossroads beyond changed hands three times, and Bowen's division made one of the magnificent charges of the war. By 5:00 P.M. the Confederates were outmaneuvered but not outfought. They fled across Baker's Creek, leaving twenty-seven cannon and hundreds of prisoners on the field. One of Pemberton's three divisions, Loring's, was cut off on the retreat to the Big Black but eventually joined Johnston. The victorious Union army slept on the Champion Hill battlefield.

The advance was resumed on May 17, with Grant pushing his men relentlessly. Pemberton, not knowing what had become of Loring, told Bowen to hold the line of breastworks on the east side of Big Black Bridge with three brigades and eighteen cannon. Grant's plan called for Sherman and McPherson to cross the Big Black upstream from the Confederate bridgehead, with McClernand keeping the Confederates pinned behind their fortifications east of the bridge. But before the two corps could cross the river, one of McClernand's brigades charged the breastworks. A brigade from east Tennessee panicked and fled across the river. To delay pursuit, Confederate engineers put the torch to the railroad

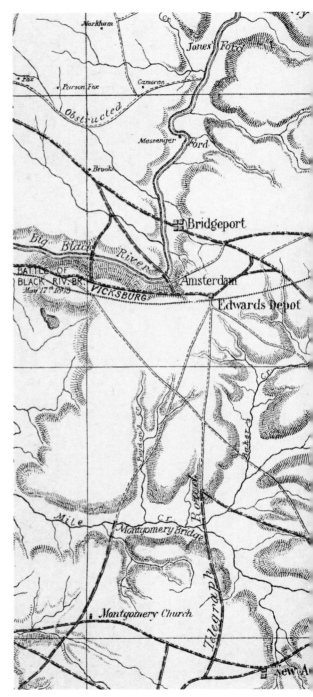

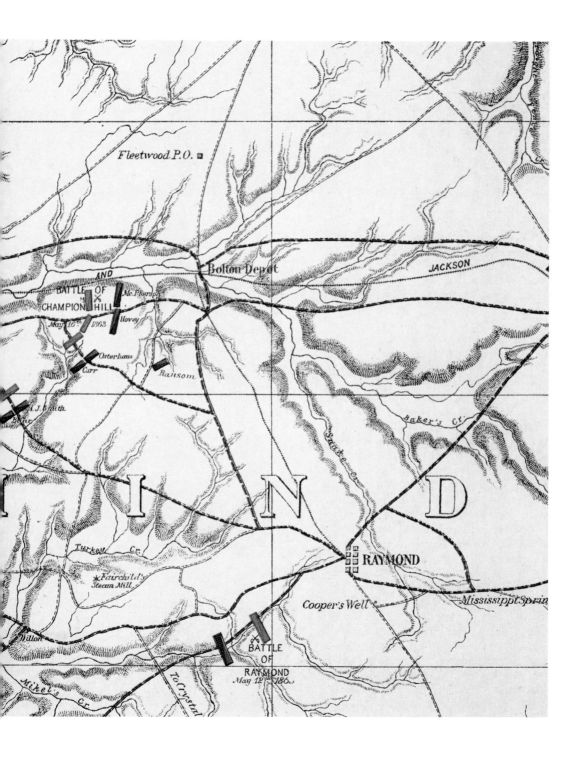

Fleetwood P.O. ▣

Bolton Depot

JACKSON

AND

BATTLE OF CHAMPION HILL
May 16th 1863

Mc.Pherson

Hovey

Osterhaus

Carr

Ransom

A.J.Smith

Baker's Cr.

Smithe Cr.

I N D

Turkey Cr.

Fairchild's Steam Mill

RAYMOND

Cooper's Well

Mississippi Spring

Dillon

Mikel's Cr.

To Crystal

BATTLE OF RAYMOND
May 12th 186

bridge and the steamer that they were using as a bridge. Pemberton retired into Vicksburg that afternoon with more of a mob than an army.

The Army of the Tennessee crossed the Big Black on the night of May 17 and closed in on Vicksburg the next day. On May 19 Grant re-established contact with Porter's fleet on the Yazoo River, above Vicksburg. Supply depots were established at Chickasaw Bayou and Snyder's Bluff, and roads were opened to supply the confident, aggressive Union army. Grant, who thought that the victory at Champion Hill and the rout at the Big Black River had shattered Pemberton's army, did not know that Pemberton had left two divisions in and around Vicksburg. These fresh units held the earthworks guarding the Graveyard, Jackson, and Baldwin's Ferry roads — the routes over which the three Union corps approached. General Stevenson's mauled divisions occupied the rifle pits extending south of the railroad to the Mississippi, while Bowen's constituted Pemberton's reserve.

At 2:00 P.M. on the nineteenth, Sherman's corps advanced against the defenses covering the Graveyard Road. Rugged terrain and felled timber threw the battle lines into disorder. Crashing volleys from Mississippi and Louisiana regiments decimated the Union ranks, and their surge was checked. However, McPherson's and McClernand's corps eventually drove in the Confederate pickets and seized ground within a quarter mile of the Vicksburg perimeter. After dark Sherman withdrew the soldiers who had been pinned down in front of Stockade Redan.

Thus Grant learned that Pemberton's army had not been shattered. He spent the next seventy-two hours regrouping his army, emplacing artillery, and preparing for an all-out attack. On the morning of May 22 massed cannon hammered the Confederate works. Porter steamed up the Mississippi with his ironclads and bombarded the river forts south of the city. At 10:00 A.M. the artillery fell silent, and massed brigades from the three corps

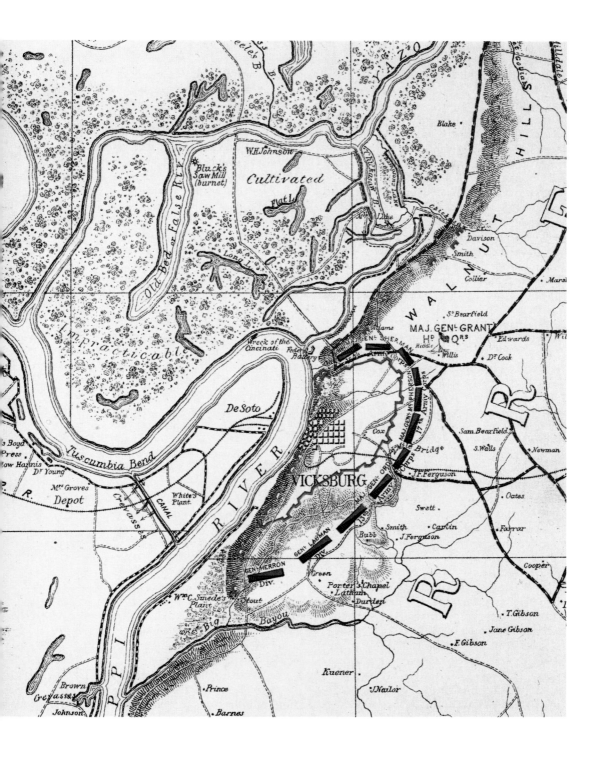

charged. Sherman's and McPherson's rushes were blunted with ease, but McClernand's troops at the Second Texas Lunette gained the ditch fronting the work as they stormed Railroad Redoubt. Lack of a ready reserve prevented McClernand from exploiting his success, but, learning of his gains, Grant ordered the assaults renewed. Sherman hammered in vain at the Mississippi, Missouri, and Louisiana units posted in the works covering Graveyard Road; McPherson made a feeble effort to storm the Third Louisiana Redan. Pemberton's reserves, counterattacking savagely, cleared the ditch at the Texas Lunette and drove the Union soldiers from Railroad Redoubt before support troops could intervene. When he was satisfied that his men could not storm the Vicksburg defenses, Grant ordered the attack suspended. In the day's fighting, the Union side had suffered 3,199 casualties and the Confederates less than 500.

On May 25 Grant issued instructions for his engineers to begin siege operations, cutting off ammunition, food, and reinforcements to the city. Porter's fleet controlled the Mississippi above and below the city, and Union soldiers occupied the Louisiana shore. Along the siege lines, Union engineers pushed thirteen approach trenches toward the Confederate defenses. Advance breeching batteries were established. To conserve ammunition, Pemberton was compelled to restrict his cannoneers, and the Union artillery quickly established its ascendancy, hurling thousands of shells into the city. To escape the horrors of the bombardment, citizens dug caves in the hillsides. On June 25 and again on July 1, mines were exploded under the Third Louisiana Redan. An attack followed the detonation of the first mine, but the defenders from Louisiana and Missouri repulsed it.

Grant called for reinforcements to ensure the siege's success. Soldiers from as far away as Kentucky and Missouri were rushed to Mississippi, and by the third week of June Grant had more than 77,000 troops. President Jefferson Davis provided Johnston with reinforcements and urged the Confederates of the Trans-Mississippi Department (west of the Mississippi) to hold Vicksburg and save Pemberton's army. Johnston, however, was overly cautious, and attacks by his troops on Union enclaves west of the river were repulsed.

Rations were in short supply by the fourth week of June, and the soldiers defending Vicksburg subsisted principally on pea bread. Mules and horses were slaughtered, and the meat was issued to the troops in lieu of beef and pork. There was no rationing or price controls. Citizens with the wherewithal were able to get plenty to eat, while those lacking the means suffered more than the soldiers. The long, hot days and nights in the rifle pits sapped the men's vigor. Morale sagged as it became clear that Johnston was not coming to their relief.

By July 2 Pemberton had only two options — to cut his way through the investing army or surrender. He argued for the first, but the majority of his generals explained that their men were in no condition to attack or make the necessary marches once the Union lines ruptured. Accordingly, Pemberton met with Grant on the afternoon of July 3 to discuss terms for the possible surrender of his army. Grant demanded unconditional surrender. Pemberton refused. That evening Grant modified his terms, after discussing the subject with his principal subordinates. The Confederates would surrender and sign paroles not to fight again until exchanged.

After some discussion with his division and brigade commanders, Pemberton accepted these terms. At 10:00 A.M. on July 4, 1863, the Confederate army, 29,500 strong, marched out in front of the works and stacked arms. Selected units from Grant's army marched in, took possession of Vicksburg, and raised the Stars and Stripes over the Warren County Courthouse.

The Vicksburg campaign and siege, culminating in the surrender of the city and its defending army, was a milestone on the road that led to the final success of the Union army and the reunification of the nation. The campaign, particularly the twenty days from April 30 to May 19, was critical to Grant's career and ensured his reputation as one of the great generals in U.S. military history. In the days following their Bruinsburg landing, his troops marched more than two hundred miles, won five battles, inflicted more than 8,000 Confederate casualties, and captured eighty-eight cannon. Although generals Pemberton and Johnston between them had more soldiers and presumably were more familiar with the area, Grant so maneuvered his columns that he had a decisive superiority in numbers and artillery at each battle. From Vicksburg, Grant's career took him to Chattanooga, then — as commander of all the Union armies — to the Wilderness, Petersburg, and Appomattox, and finally to Washington and the presidency.

On July 4, a thousand miles to the northeast of Vicksburg, General Robert E. Lee's Army of Northern Virginia was about to begin its retreat from Gettysburg. Although the war continued for another twenty months, these twin disasters blunted southern morale and hopes. News that Vicksburg had fallen caused the Confederate force invested at Port Hudson to surrender. With the capture of these two bastions, the Union regained control of the Mississippi River from Cairo to the Gulf, and President Abraham Lincoln wrote, "The Father of Waters again goes unvexed to the sea."

The Confederacy was now divided. In the weeks between March 29 and July 4, Grant had destroyed a Confederate army of 40,000 at a cost of 10,000 battle casualties. He had captured 260 cannon, 60,000 stand-of-arms, and more than two million rounds of ammunition. The Confederacy could not afford such a loss of men and matériel.

Vicksburg National Military Park is on U.S. Route 61 at Vicksburg, Mississippi. There are 1,620 acres of the historic battlefield within its authorized boundaries; 2 of these are privately owned.

Major General John A. McClernand's corps marching through the bog

PORT GIBSON

1 May 1863

Edwin C. Bearss

Four miles west of Port Gibson, Mississippi, on May 1, 1863, the first shots were fired in a bitter fight between 8,000 Confederates led by Brigadier General John S. Bowen and 24,000 Union soldiers commanded by Major General Ulysses S. Grant. The Union troops, following their march south through the Louisiana parishes from Milliken's Bend, had crossed the Mississippi River and landed at Bruinsburg on the last day of April. They quickly headed east toward the high bluffs several miles back from the river. Rapid marches were essential if they were to attack the Confederates before they could bring in reinforcements. Victory in the ensuing Port Gibson battle secured Grant's Mississippi bridgehead.

Bowen was the commander at Grand Gulf, the Confederate bastion on the Mississippi River thirty miles south of Vicksburg. He had warned Lieutenant General John C. Pemberton about the Union march south and the troops, invasion barges, and steamboats preparing to cross the Mississippi. Pemberton, however, gave higher priority to coping with Union incursions into the delta north of Vicksburg and to the threat to his railroad communications from Colonel B. H. Grierson's cavalry, which was raiding the heart of Mississippi. If Bowen had been properly reinforced by troops from Vicksburg, the battle of Port Gibson might have had a different outcome.

The battle was hard fought. The Confederates, although outnumbered more than three to one and outgunned in artillery by five to one, held their own for nearly eighteen hours. Bowen and his senior officers gave the Federals a bitter lesson in how to exploit the topography, and Bowen's application of offensive-defensive tactics kept them off balance. No one has better described the ground and the problems confronting the Federals than Grant, who wrote: "The country in this part of Mississippi stands on edge, the roads running along the ridges except when they occasionally pass from one ridge to another. Where there are no clearings the sides of the hills are covered with a very heavy growth of timber and with undergrowth, and the ravines are filled with vines and canebrakes, almost impenetrable. This makes it easy for an inferior force to delay, if not defeat, a far superior one."

The battle was a desperate struggle that focused on the ridges and the hollows crossed by the Rodney and Bruinsburg roads. East of the Shaifer farm road, connecting the Rodney and Bruinsburg roads, was the deep and forbidding Centers Creek Hollow, which separated the troops battling on the Rodney Road from those fighting for the Bruinsburg Road as effectively as if they were many miles apart rather than two. The roads converged about two miles west of Port Gibson.

Two Confederate brigades, led by brigadier

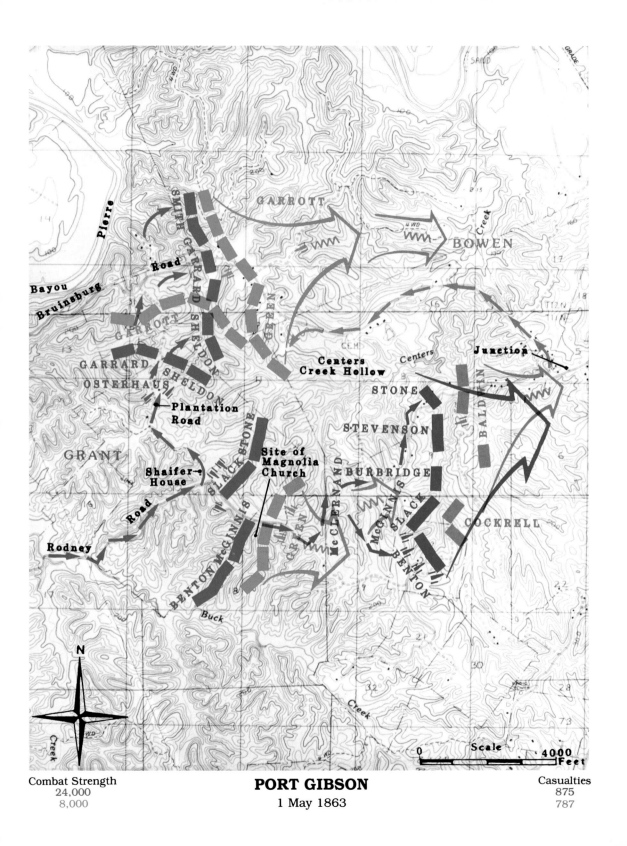

PORT GIBSON

1 May 1863

Combat Strength
24,000
8,000

Casualties
875
787

generals Edward D. Tracy and William E. Baldwin, marched forty-four miles from Vicksburg to reinforce Bowen but arrived exhausted from the twenty-seven-hour forced march. Grant had already gained his beachhead and was moving rapidly inland. Bowen posted Brigadier General Martin E. Green's brigade, which had arrived after a short march from Grand Gulf, along a north-south ridge across the road that ran from Port Gibson to Rodney by way of the A. K. Shaifer house and Magnolia Church. Tracy's brigade guarded the Bruinsburg Road approximately a thousand yards north of and parallel to the Rodney Road.

Shortly after midnight on May 1, Green rode forward from Magnolia Church to the Shaifer house to warn his pickets to be alert. He assured the women of the Shaifer household, who were hurriedly loading a wagon, that their haste was unnecessary, because the Union forces could not possibly advance to that point before daylight. As they spoke, Confederate pickets suddenly began firing. As minié balls from the Union vanguard struck the house, the Shaifer women whipped their team frantically down the road to Port Gibson.

The next several hours saw skirmishing and artillery fire as more and more Union troops arrived on the field. To delay the Union army until Major General William W. Loring's reinforcements arrived from Jackson, the Confederates set up roadblocks on the Bruinsburg and Rodney roads.

North of the Shaifer house and just south of the Bruinsburg Road, Union Brigadier General Peter J. Osterhaus's division clashed with Tracy's Alabama brigade. Tracy was killed, and Colonel Isham Garrott took command. On the Rodney Road the Federal brigades of Brigadier General William M. Stone, supported by Brigadier General Alvin P. Hovey's division, fought the determined but much weaker Confederates of Green's brigade. Green held his line until around 10 A.M., when he was forced back

across Arnolds Creek and into the Irwin Branch hollow. Baldwin took over the defense of the Irwin Branch position while Green reorganized, and Bowen then sent Green to the Bruinsburg Road to assist Garrott.

Bowen's Fourth Brigade, under Colonel Francis M. Cockrell, arrived from Grand Gulf at about noon and was placed in line behind Baldwin. Hovey's and Carr's Union troops came under Baldwin's fire in a severe ninety-minute fight, then Bowen sent two of Cockrell's regiments to turn Major General John A. McClernand's right flank as his soldiers worked their way through canebrakes near the head of White Branch. Cockrell's Missourians overran Colonel James R. Slack's brigade, but they in turn encountered a Union brigade and the fire of thirty cannon. Their ranks thinned by the savage fighting, Cockrell's men gave ground.

By now Grant was sending brigade after brigade into the Union lines. The right wing of the Confederate defenses posted on the Bruinsburg Road gave way, and Bowen, fearful that Union columns would outflank and cut off his troops, ordered retreat. The Confederates retired in good order, resisting until dark, when the pursuit ended. Accompanied by three brigades, Bowen crossed Bayou Pierre. Baldwin's brigade withdrew through Port Gibson and across Little Bayou Pierre. The Confederate rear guard burned the suspension bridges over these streams as well as the Bayou Pierre railroad bridge.

The Confederates reported their Port Gibson losses as 60 dead, 340 wounded, and 387 missing, most of whom had been captured. Grant listed his casualties as 131 dead, 719 wounded, and 25 missing.

Port Gibson battlefield is near Port Gibson, Mississippi, on U.S. Route 61, 25 miles south of Vicksburg. There are 15 acres of the historic battlefield within the authorized boundaries of Grand Gulf Military Monument.

RAYMOND

12 May 1863

Edwin C. Bearss

The battle of Raymond was Union Major General James B. McPherson's first as the commander of a major unit. It was not a success. He fought his troops piecemeal during the six-hour struggle, and he did not undertake a co-ordinated attack on the enemy, although he outnumbered them three to one and out-gunned them in artillery seven to one.

Confederate Brigadier General John Gregg's aggressive tactics, coupled with the failure of his scouts and patrols to assess the enemy's strength correctly, should have been his undoing, but against the cautious and hesitant McPherson he was successful — until there were just too many Union soldiers. His ability to put the fire of battle in his men marked Gregg as an invaluable brigade commander. In the winter of 1863–64 he was to assume command of one of the war's best-known fighting units, the Army of Northern Virginia's Texas-Arkansas Brigade.

The significance of the Raymond fight, however, has nothing to do with either the body count or the merits and demerits of McPherson and Gregg as battle commanders. The battle is important because of its effect on Major General Ulysses S. Grant's campaign plans. It forced Grant into a new estimate of the situation. First, he now knew that the Confederate forces assembling near Jackson were stronger than he had supposed. Second,

he heard reports that Confederate reinforcements were pouring into Jackson, including General Joseph E. Johnston, the Confederate commander of the Department of the West. If these reports were correct, the proposed crossing of the Big Black River near Edwards Station would be exceedingly dangerous, because it would leave a powerful army commanded by an able general in Grant's rear.

Grant changed his orders: instead of concentrating forces at Edwards Station, he ordered a march on Jackson. He realized that McPherson's corps at Raymond, which was closest to the capital city, would probably be inadequate to capture it, especially since Jackson was reported to be strongly fortified. Grant was determined to strike with his entire army, so he ordered McPherson to thrust northeast from Raymond to Clinton and then drive down the Jackson-Clinton Road to Jackson. Major General William T. Sherman's corps was ordered to march on Jackson from the southwest, via Raymond and Mississippi Springs. Major General John A. McClernand was to march three divisions of his corps along the road north of Fourteenmile Creek to Raymond. His fourth division, under Brigadier General A. J. Smith, was to march to Old Auburn and await the arrival of Major General Frank Blair's division from the Grand Gulf enclave. The corps commanders had misgivings — such

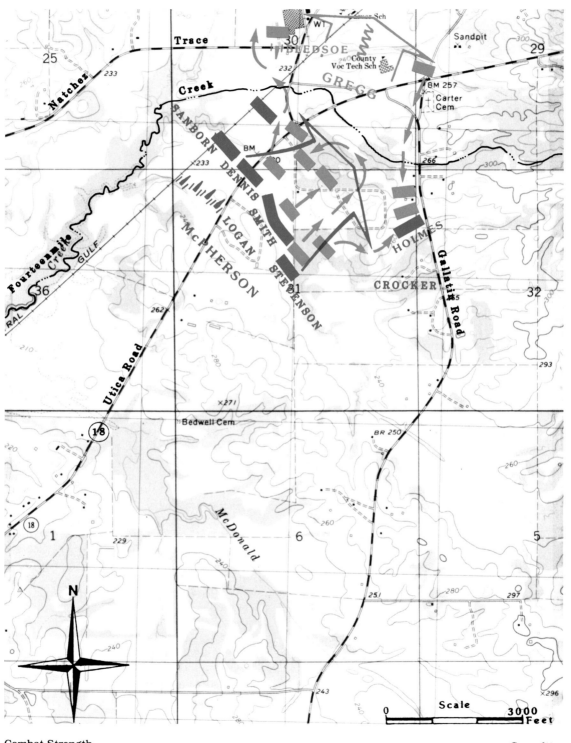

Combat Strength
12,000
4,000

RAYMOND

12 May 1863

Casualties
442
514

audacity was unheard of in modern military annals. Generals do not usually split their armies and send them into unfamiliar territory against a strong enemy who presumably knows the terrain.

On May 11 Confederate General Gregg and his brigade, having reached Jackson from Port Hudson, Louisiana, marched to Raymond. Gregg was alerted by Lieutenant General John C. Pemberton, then at Vicksburg, to look out for the advance of a Union column from the southwest up the Utica Road. This force was composed of two divisions of McPherson's corps, 12,000 strong. McPherson had his column on the road before daylight on May 12, and by 10:00 A.M. his vanguard had ascended a ridge three miles southwest of Raymond.

Alerted to the Union army's approach by scouts, Gregg posted three infantry units north of Fourteenmile Creek to dispute the nearby Utica Road crossing. Cannoneers of Captain H. M. Bledsoe's Missouri battery unlimbered their three guns while Gregg's other regiments marched out the Gallatin Road, taking a position from which they could sweep cross-country and envelop the Union army's right.

As McPherson's skirmishers came down the far slope, Bledsoe's gunners opened fire. One Union brigade, Brigadier General Elias Dennis's, followed by a second, Brigadier General John E. Smith's, deployed into line of battle, descended the grade, and entered the woods bounding the creek. Smoke and dust kept Gregg from seeing that he was outnumbered, and he hurled his troops against the Union soldiers. Some Union troops broke, but Major General John A. Logan rallied them and forced two of Gregg's regiments that had forded the creek to withdraw.

By 1:30 P.M. Colonel John Sanborn's brigade of Brigadier General Marcellus M. Crocker's division had arrived and filed into position on Logan's left. Supported by the fire of twenty-two cannon, McPherson ordered a counterattack and seized the initiative. For the next several hours McPherson's and Gregg's regiments generally acted on their own, in confused fighting in which smoke and undergrowth kept the senior officers from knowing where their units were and what they were accomplishing.

After the collapse of his right wing, Gregg ordered the fight abandoned. The Confederates disengaged, retreated through Raymond, and took the road to Jackson. They halted for the evening on a ridge a mile east of Snake Creek, where they were reinforced by 1,000 men led by Brigadier General W. H. T. Walker. On May 13 the Confederates withdrew into the Jackson defenses. The Federals occupied Raymond and camped there. Union losses in the battle were 66 killed, 339 wounded, and 37 missing. Gregg listed 72 killed, 252 wounded, and 190 missing.

Raymond battlefield is on State Route 18, 10 miles southwest of Jackson, Mississippi. The entire battlefield is privately owned.

CHAMPION HILL

16 May 1863

Edwin C. Bearss

On the evening of May 14, Major General Ulysses S. Grant and his generals met in a Jackson hotel and decided to counter the threat posed by Confederate General Joseph E. Johnston. Johnston had ordered his outnumbered troops to retreat from Jackson northward up the Canton Road. He had also commanded Lieutenant General John C. Pemberton to march east with the 22,000 soldiers he had assembled at Edwards Station and attack the Union army near Clinton. The next day Grant positioned seven divisions (about 32,000 soldiers) along a five-mile front passing through Raymond and Bolton.

Pemberton conferred with his generals at Edwards Station and concluded that Johnston's May 13 order for the converging attack was "extremely hazardous," so he marched instead to the southeast, to intercept and destroy the Union supply trains en route from Grand Gulf to Raymond. At dusk on May 15 his army bivouacked along nearly four miles of roadway, with the advance guard at Mrs. Ellison's house. His supply train brought up the rear, at the crossroads where the Jackson Road turned to the left and passed over the crest of Champion Hill, one quarter mile to the north.

The next morning, May 16, a courier reached Pemberton's command with a message from Johnston dated May 14, reiterating his May 13 orders. Although Pemberton had previously rejected them as "suicidal" and had wasted many hours marching in a different direction, he ordered the countermarch. The rear brigade with the trains became the vanguard as the Confederate army returned to Edwards via the Jackson-Vicksburg Road. To protect the army from a reported Union force approaching the crossroads, Brigadier General S. D. Lee moved up the Jackson Road to the crest of Champion Hill and deployed his Alabama brigade on the ridge overlooking the Baker's Creek bottom.

From the hill Lee spotted the Union column, which consisted of Major General James B. McPherson's corps, spearheaded by Brigadier General Hovey's Thirteenth Corps. When Hovey reached the Champion house, about a half mile northeast of the crest of Champion Hill, he sighted Lee's soldiers and deployed his division to the left and right of the Jackson-Vicksburg Road. Grant and McPherson arrived with Major General John A. Logan's division, which formed for battle on Hovey's right.

Lee realized that the two Union divisions could overwhelm his brigade, despite his commanding position on Champion Hill. His division commander, Major General Carter L. Stevenson, rushed reinforcements to him: three regiments of Georgians led by Brigadier General Alfred Cumming. One formed a sal-

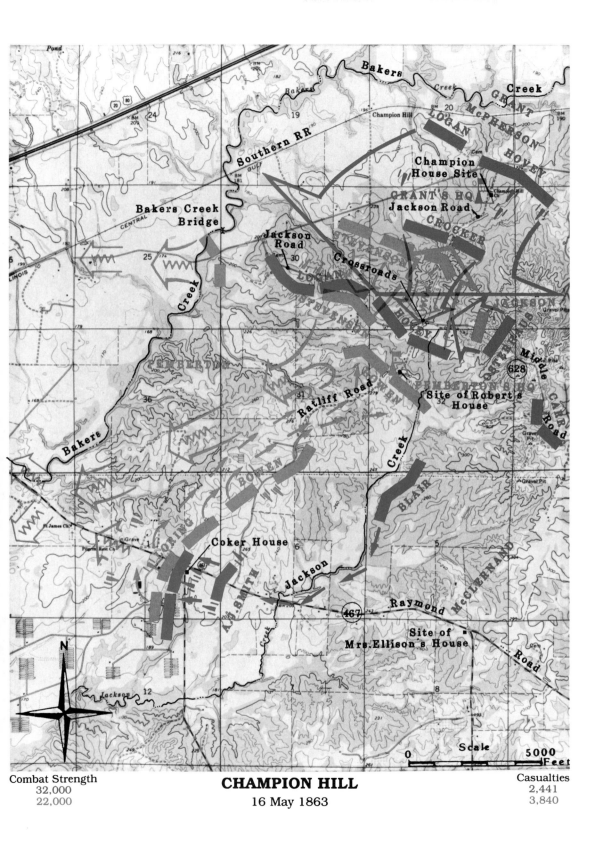

CHAMPION HILL

16 May 1863

Combat Strength
32,000
22,000

Casualties
2,441
3,840

ient angle at the crest of the hill, with Lee's soldiers in line along the ridge to the northwest. Brigadier General Seth Barton's Georgia brigade came to Lee's assistance and took up a position on the left, with its supporting batteries on the ridge on the soldiers' left.

The Confederate line thus formed nearly a right angle, with Cumming, Lee, and Barton on the left. Pemberton's right, anchored on the Raymond-Edwards Road, was held by two Confederate divisions — Brigadier General John S. Bowen's and Major General William W. Loring's — which were deployed by Pemberton on the high ground overlooking Jackson Creek. At the center were two of Cumming's regiments, positioned at the crossroads with a four-gun Alabama battery to support Colonel J. E. B. Jackson's roadblock. Their mission was to cover the Ratliff Road and maintain contact with the right. To Loring's front, Brigadier General A. J. Smith's and Major General Frank P. Blair's Union divisions cautiously felt their way forward. The divisions of brigadier generals Eugene A. Carr and Peter J. Osterhaus were on the Middle Road opposite the Confederate center.

At 11:30 A.M. Logan's and Hovey's battle lines assailed the Confederate left. They shattered Barton's brigade and then the three regiments of Cumming's brigade, on the left and right of Lee's soldiers. Large numbers of Georgians were captured, along with twelve cannon. The Confederate soldiers were outflanked and forced back to the Jackson-Vicksburg Road. Hovey's left flank brigade, under Colonel James R. Slack, drove for the crossroads, where they overpowered two Georgia regiments and the Alabama battery. From their position occupying the crossroads, the Federals could either swing to the right and crush Lee's forces or advance down the Ratliff Road to take Bowen's division in the flank. They could also destroy Jackson's men, who were blocking the Union advance on the Middle Road.

Pemberton's situation was desperate. He ordered Bowen to support Stevenson's mauled brigades. Bowen's vanguard marched up the Ratliff Road, reaching Pemberton's headquarters at the Roberts house just as Cumming's men at the crossroads were routed. The fate of Pemberton's army was in the balance, and Bowen responded with alacrity. Colonel Francis M. Cockrell's Missouri brigade deployed to the left, Brigadier General Martin E. Green's Arkansas-Missouri brigade moved to the right, and both advanced to the attack with savage vigor. Cockrell's brigade showed once again why it was one of the war's most respected combat units. Bowen's men drove Slack's from the crossroads and recovered the four guns captured by the Federals. Pressing on, the Confederates routed Hovey's other brigade, commanded by Brigadier General George F. McGinnis, from the crest of Champion Hill and captured two Union cannon.

Bowen's men continued their advance. Less than a half mile to their front was the Champion house, Grant's headquarters. Union Brigadier General Marcellus M. Crocker reached the field and deployed two brigades, sending one to reinforce Logan on the right and the other to plug the hole torn in the Union front by the defeat of Hovey's division. Cannoneers then unlimbered sixteen guns southeast of the Champion house and enfiladed the onrushing Confederate battle lines.

Pemberton lacked reserves to capitalize on Bowen's earlier success. He had called on Loring to come to the left, but Loring had refused, citing the strong Union columns to his front on the Raymond-Edwards Road. After the order was repeated, Loring marched for the battle's cockpit with two of his three brigades, leaving the third under Brigadier General Lloyd Tilghman to guard the Raymond-Edwards Road. However, Loring marched too late and by a roundabout route.

Meanwhile, Bowen engaged Colonel George B. Boomer's fresh brigade of Crocker's division. After a desperate struggle the Federals regained the upper hand. Bowen's men grudgingly gave ground until the crest of Champion Hill and the crossroads were recovered by

The battle of Champion Hill. Drawing by Theodore R. Davis

McPherson's troops. This was the third and final time that this terrain changed hands.

Loring covered the defeated Confederate army's retreat along the Raymond-Edwards Road. Carr's and Osterhaus's Union troops smashed Jackson's roadblock and reached the crossroads soon after Bowen's retreat, and Carr's division continued west along the Jackson-Vicksburg Road and secured the Baker's Creek bridge. Tilghman, whose brigade remained to guard the Raymond-Edwards road, was killed by artillery fire from the ridge near the Coker house. At about midnight Loring saw the glare of fires to the north and, realizing that Edwards had been abandoned, gave up his efforts to rejoin the army. He turned his division to the southeast and marched by way of Crystal Springs to report to Johnston at Jackson.

Grant's troops bivouacked on the field. They spent the late afternoon and evening tending the wounded, burying the dead, and counting the prisoners and spoils of war. Although Pemberton's army had escaped destruction, it was terribly mauled. Incomplete returns filed by Confederate officers listed their losses as 381 killed, 1,018 wounded, and 2,441 missing. Twenty-seven of their cannon had been left on the field. Union casualties totaled 410 killed, 1,844 wounded, and 187 missing.

The Union victory at Champion Hill was decisive. It prevented Pemberton and Johnston from uniting their armies and forced Pemberton back into Vicksburg.

Champion Hill battlefield is midway between Bolton and Edwards, Mississippi, 20 miles east of Vicksburg on Interstate 20. The Coker house and 5 acres of the historic battlefield on State Route 467 are owned by the Jackson Civil War Roundtable, Inc. (not open to the public).

PORT HUDSON

22 May–9 July 1863

Lawrence Lee Hewitt

Control of the Mississippi River was one of the key objectives of the Union strategists at the beginning of the Civil War. In August 1862 Confederate forces under Major General John C. Breckinridge, a former vice president of the United States, occupied Port Hudson and began constructing a bastion as formidable as that at Vicksburg.

The terrain immediately surrounding Port Hudson is varied. The Mississippi River, which has eroded the citadel, skirts the southwestern corner of the battlefield. A broad alluvial plain, where the river flowed in 1863, extends westward from the bluff. On the north and northeast the terrain is virtually impassable. Canyonlike ravines, sixty- to eighty-foot bluffs, and dense woods stretch to Foster Creek and beyond. The plateau on the east is grazing land. A mile and a half below Port Hudson, a massive ravine bounds the plateau on the south. This area has been drastically altered by industrial development since World War II.

In the spring of 1863 Union Rear Admiral David Glasgow Farragut attempted to force the evacuation of Port Hudson by cutting off the food supplies it received down the Mississippi River. Of his seven vessels that attempted to pass the batteries on the night of March 14, only two, including the flagship *Hartford*, succeeded. These two vessels proved insufficient to halt the flow of supplies to Port Hudson.

In late March Union Major General Nathaniel P. Banks, a former speaker of the U.S. House of Representatives and governor of Massachusetts, concentrated his troops west of the Mississippi. His Nineteenth Corps moved up Bayou Teche and seized Alexandria, on the Red River. This severed Port Hudson's supply line with the Confederate Trans-Mississippi Department west of the Mississippi, but the Confederates continued to garrison Port Hudson.

In mid-May Banks moved down the Red River to attack Port Hudson from the north. Additional Union columns marched north from Baton Rouge and New Orleans to attack from the south and east. When Banks closed the noose on Port Hudson on May 22, his 30,000 soldiers, supported by U.S. Navy vessels both upstream and downstream from the town, faced 7,500 Confederates behind four and a half miles of earthworks.

On the morning of May 27, Banks ordered a simultaneous assault all along the line, but the difficult terrain, vague orders, and uncooperative subordinates prevented a coordinated effort. The Confederates on the north side of Port Hudson, aided by reinforcements drawn from other portions of their line, managed to repulse several assaults against Commissary Hill and Fort Desperate and along the Telegraph Road. Except for scattered musketry and artillery fire, the fighting along the

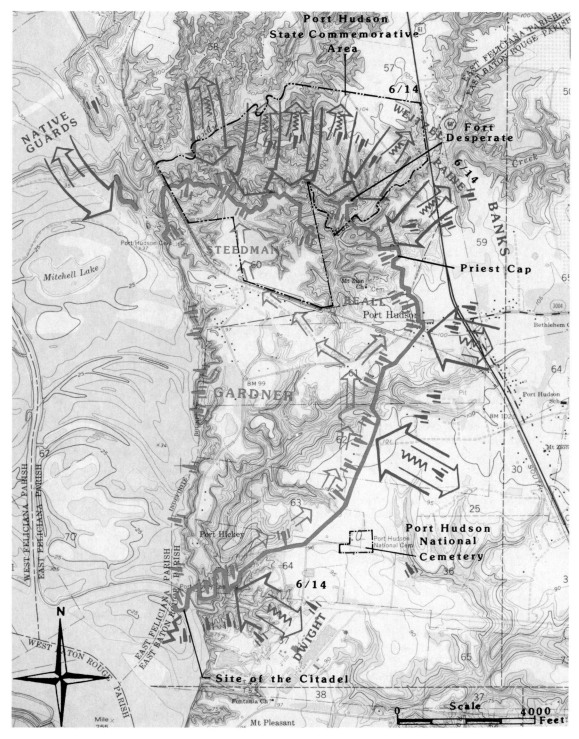

Port Hudson
State Commemorative
Area

6/14

Fort
Desperate

6/14

NATIVE
GUARDS

BANKS

STEEDMAN

Priest Cap

Mitchell Lake

BEALL
Port Hudson

GARDNER

Port Hudson
National
Cemetery

Port Hudson
National Cem

Port Hickey

6/14

DWIGHT

N

Site of the Citadel

Scale

0   4000

Feet

Combat Strength
40,000
7,500

PORT HUDSON

22 May–9 July 1863

Casualties
10,000
7,500

Port Hudson

north front ended before the remainder of Banks's army advanced from the east. The delay allowed the Confederates to redeploy men to repulse the Federal assaults across Slaughter's Field and against the Priest Cap.

That evening the Confederate lines remained unbreached. The terrain contributed to this unexpected turn of events, as the thickly wooded ravines on the Union right separated enlisted men from their regimental officers and prevented any organized Federal effort. A withering fire covered the fields in front of the Confederate center and right, so that Union soldiers were unable to reach the earthworks. On May 27, 2,000 Union soldiers were killed or wounded; Confederate casualties were less than 500.

Several hundred of the Federal casualties were black soldiers. These included men of the First and Third Louisiana Native Guards. The First Louisiana Native Guards, and a majority

of its line officers, consisted almost entirely of free blacks from New Orleans. These men, because of their education, wealth, and status in the community, were able to have an all-black unit in the antebellum Louisiana state militia. In the spring of 1862, when the Confederate government refused to arm the regiment, its members offered to fight for the United States.

During the siege of Port Hudson, the Native Guards units were redesignated. The First became the First Corps de Afrique; this designation was changed again in April 1864, when it became the Seventy-third United States Colored Troops. The Third Louisiana Native Guards, organized by the government in 1862, was composed of former slaves commanded by white officers. It too was twice redesignated during the war.

In the May 27 assault, the First and Third Louisiana Native Guards advanced across open ground against the strongly fortified position of the Thirty-ninth Mississippi. Captain André Cailloux, a free black from New Orleans, led the advance, shouting orders in both English and French until a shell struck him dead. Other black troops waded through the backwater of the Mississippi to engage the enemy. Although repulsed with heavy casualties, the soldiers demonstrated both their willingness and their ability to fight for the Union and for abolition.

Having committed himself, Banks commenced siege operations and ordered sharpshooters and round-the-clock artillery fire. On June 13, after receiving reinforcements and additional cannon, Union gunners opened a tremendous one-hour bombardment. Banks then demanded that the garrison surrender. New York–born Confederate Major General Franklin Gardner replied, "My duty requires me to defend this position, and therefore I decline to surrender." Banks resumed the bombardment and ordered a full-scale assault the next day.

An entire Union division, commanded by Brigadier General Halbert E. Paine and supported by diversionary attacks on the right by Brigadier General Godfrey Weitzel and on the left by Brigadier General William Dwight, advanced toward the Priest Cap at about 4:00 A.M. on June 14. A few of the Federals managed to enter the works, but the breach was quickly sealed. By 10:00 A.M. the assault had failed and the Union had suffered 1,805 more casualties.

Banks spent the remainder of June and early July digging approach saps (trenches) and advancing his artillery. Although reduced to eating rats and mules, the Confederates were still holding out on July 7, after forty-six days of siege. When Gardner received word that Vicksburg had surrendered on July 4, however, he negotiated surrender terms. Without its counterpart up the Mississippi, Port Hudson lacked strategic significance.

On July 9 the Confederate garrison grounded arms. The longest true siege in American military history had ended. At Port Hudson about 7,500 Confederates had tied up more than 40,000 Union soldiers for nearly two months. Confederate casualties included 750 killed and wounded and 250 dead of disease. The Federals took 6,500 prisoners, but their own losses were nearly 10,000, almost evenly divided between battle casualties and disease, including sunstroke.

Port Hudson State Commemorative Area is at Port Hudson, Louisiana, on U.S. Route 61, 15 miles north of Baton Rouge. There are 640 acres of the historic battlefield within its authorized boundaries.

CHICKAMAUGA

18–20 September 1863

William Glenn Robertson

When Union Major General William S. Rosecrans brought the Army of the Cumberland to the Tennessee River in August 1863, his goal was to capture Chattanooga, Tennessee. A city of only 2,500 people, Chattanooga was important because of its rail lines, its mineral resources, and its position astride a railroad pathway through the Appalachian Mountains into the South's heartland. Defending Chattanooga was the Confederate Army of Tennessee, commanded by General Braxton Bragg with 50,000 troops. Rosecrans's army numbered approximately 80,000 officers and men, but nearly one fifth remained in the rear, guarding middle Tennessee and the army's long line of communications.

In early September, while four Union brigades executed a masterly deception upstream from Chattanooga, the bulk of Rosecrans's army crossed the Tennessee unopposed at four sites far south of the city. Rosecrans divided his army into three columns and then began a wide-front advance on Chattanooga while Burnside took Knoxville, one hundred miles to the north. Outflanked and outnumbered, Bragg abandoned Chattanooga on September 8 without a battle. Rather than retreat toward Atlanta, however, Bragg concentrated his army near La Fayette, Georgia, and prepared for a counterstroke. When his subordinates failed in two attempts to de-

stroy isolated elements of the Army of the Cumberland, Bragg suspended operations for several days. During this period reinforcements arrived from Mississippi and Virginia, swelling his army to approximately 65,000 men.

Finally recognizing his dangerous position, Rosecrans hastily began to concentrate his scattered units and move them north toward Chattanooga. After an epic march, Major General Alexander McCook's Twentieth Corps joined Major General George Thomas's Fourteenth Corps on September 17. Together the two corps then continued northward along the west bank of Chickamauga Creek toward Major General Thomas Crittenden's Twenty-first Corps at Lee and Gordon's Mill. On September 18, fearing that Bragg would attempt to cut him off from Chattanooga, Rosecrans ordered Thomas to occupy a new position beyond Crittenden's left flank. At the same time, believing that Crittenden's corps was Rosecrans's northernmost unit, Bragg ordered most of his army to seize crossings over Chickamauga Creek downstream of the Federals, then drive Rosecrans's army south into McLemore's Cove and away from Chattanooga.

By the evening of September 18 Confederate Brigadier General Bushrod Johnson's provisional division had captured Reed's Bridge, crossed Chickamauga Creek, and advanced south toward the La Fayette Road. The corps of major generals William H. T. Walker and Simon B. Buckner had also gained the west bank of Chickamauga Creek and had bivouacked for the night in the woods east of the La Fayette Road. None of the Confederate units were aware of Thomas's Fourteenth Corps as it marched northward through the night and took position on the La Fayette Road at the Kelly farm. The only night contact occurred when a Federal brigade of Major General Gordon Granger's reserve corps, attempting to destroy Reed's Bridge, bumped into rear-echelon elements of Johnson's division at a road junction near Jay's Mill.

Believing that they had trapped a single Confederate brigade west of the creek, Granger's men withdrew to rejoin the reserve corps early on the morning of September 19. Thomas sent Brigadier General John Brannan's division east into the forest to destroy that brigade. In the forest west of Jay's Mill Brannan's men met a Confederate cavalry brigade covering Bragg's right rear, and the battle was joined. For the remainder of the day both Rosecrans and Bragg could do little more than feed reinforcements into the fight in order to stabilize the situation. Their efforts were hindered by the nature of the battlefield, which consisted of a thick forest occasionally broken by a few small farms. The woods limited maximum visibility to 150 yards, far less than rifle range, and made it almost impossible to control linear battle formations. Similarly, the terrain provided few fields of fire for the armies' artillerymen. Neither commander had wanted a battle in the thickets between Chickamauga Creek and the La Fayette Road, but the collision near Jay's Mill ensured that the battle would be fought there.

Bragg brought forward Walker's reserve corps to drive Brannan's men back. In turn, Thomas reinforced Brannan with more of the Fourteenth Corps. When Walker was supported by part of Lieutenant General Leonidas Polk's corps, Rosecrans sent divisions from both McCook and Crittenden to assist Thomas. Next a division of Buckner's corps joined the fight. In a spirited effort it shattered one of Crittenden's divisions, gained the La Fayette Road, and threatened to split the Federal army. Federal reinforcements finally forced Buckner's men to withdraw eastward into the forest. Confederate Major General John Hood's forces mounted the final threat of the day at the Viniard farm but were finally fought to a bloody standstill by elements of all three Federal corps. When darkness closed the fighting, the Federals still held the La Fayette Road, but Thomas's men had been forced back to a defensive position around the Kelly farm.

During the night Rosecrans strengthened his lines with log breastworks and prepared for a coordinated defense the following day. Meanwhile Bragg planned a coordinated attack, beginning on the Confederate right and rolling southward, which would again attempt to outflank the Federal army and drive it away from Chattanooga. The arrival during the night of Lieutenant General James Longstreet permitted Bragg to reorganize his five infantry corps into two wings, with Longstreet commanding the left wing of six divisions and Polk the right wing of five divisions. Lieutenant General Daniel Harvey Hill's corps was to begin the attack at sunrise on September 20, but because of poor staff work and lack of initiative, Hill did not learn of his critical mission until the day was well advanced.

When the Confederate attack finally began, four hours late, one of Hill's divisions actually passed beyond Thomas's flank and several hundred yards into the Federal rear before being ejected by Federal reinforcements. Elsewhere troops of the Confederate right wing futilely assaulted Thomas's unyielding defenses. One of Longstreet's divisions, attacking soon after Hill's men, also made no impression on the Federal line. Just to the south along the Brotherton Road, Hood's three divisions in column were withheld by Longstreet until just after 11:00 A.M., when they swept forward with the remainder of the left wing. Fortuitously, Hood's column

Combat Strength
62,000
65,000

CHICKAMAUGA

19 September 1863

Casualties
16,170
18,454

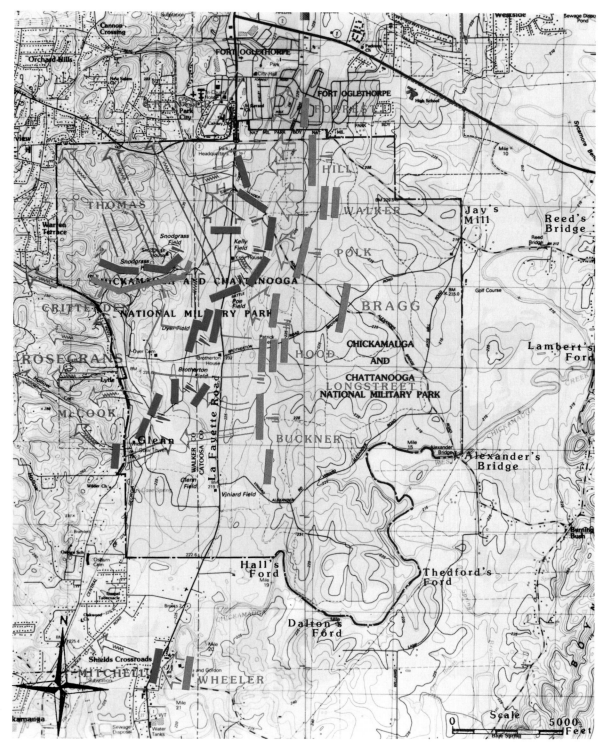

CHICKAMAUGA

20 September 1863

struck a segment of the Federal line that was momentarily devoid of troops and crashed through.

The opening in the Federal line was the result of a complicated series of events that had been developing all morning. Even before the action began on the Federal left, Thomas had been calling for reinforcements, and he continued to do so in the face of the Confederate attacks. Both Rosecrans and Thomas ordered units from the army's center and right toward the left. As a result of these movements, Rosecrans came to believe that a gap existed in the Federal right-center, and he ordered Brigadier General Thomas Wood's division, already in line, to move north to close it. In fact, there was no gap in the Federal line until Wood's departure created one. McCook agreed to occupy Wood's position, but Hood's corps crashed through before he could act, and the Federal line was irreparably split.

As Longstreet's troops swept through the gap into the Dyer field, Federal units on both sides of the break crumbled and fled to the rear. Rosecrans, McCook, and Crittenden were all swept from the field. Two intact Federal brigades and fragments of several others rallied northwest of the break on a rugged, timber-clad height known as Horseshoe Ridge or Snodgrass Hill. Just as they were about to be outflanked by Bushrod Johnson's Confederates, they were reinforced by Brigadier General James Steedman's division of Granger's reserve corps, which had just arrived from Rossville. Although Confederate units continued to attack Snodgrass Hill for the remainder of the afternoon, they were unable to drive the Federals from the commanding ridge. Finally, near sundown, Thomas received a message from Rosecrans to withdraw the surviving Federal units beyond Missionary Ridge. Although a few units were lost, Thomas suc-

Chickamauga and Chattanooga National Military Park
Chickamauga, Seventy-ninth Pennsylvania Regiment Monument. © David Muench, 1990

cessfully gathered most of the Army of the Cumberland at Rossville. One day later the Federals withdrew into Chattanooga, their original objective.

Both armies suffered heavily at Chickamauga for little tangible gain. Rosecrans lost 16,170 killed, wounded, and missing out of about 62,000 engaged, while Bragg suffered a total of 18,454 casualties out of approximately 65,000 engaged.

As the largest battle and last Confederate victory in the western theater, the battle of Chickamauga served mainly to buy a little more time for the southern cause. Federal troops in both Virginia and Mississippi were diverted from their primary missions to rescue the defeated Army of the Cumberland, thereby affecting the timetable for Federal victory in those areas. Otherwise the great expenditure of lives by both sides had little effect. Because they left the field while others stayed, Rosecrans, McCook, and Crittenden all had their military careers blighted. Nor did the victors, Bragg and Longstreet, gain much from their success. Only George Thomas, the "Rock of Chickamauga," left the dark woods bordering the "River of Death" with his reputation enhanced.

Chickamauga Battlefield, a unit of Chickamauga and Chattanooga National Military Park at Fort Oglethorpe, Georgia, is south of Chattanooga near Interstate 75. There are 5,574 acres of the historic battlefield within the authorized boundaries of this unit; 17 of these are privately owned.

Chattanooga from the north bank of the Tennessee River

CHATTANOOGA

24—25 November 1863

Charles P. Roland

The Union Army of the Cumberland, approximately 40,000 troops, which reeled back into Chattanooga after its defeat at Chickamauga on September 20, 1863, was disorganized and demoralized. The army commander, Major General William S. Rosecrans, wired his superiors in Washington, "We have met with a serious disaster. . . . The enemy overwhelmed us, drove our right, pierced our center, and scattered the troops there." The following day he ended another gloomy telegram with the alarming statement, "We have no certainty of holding our position here."

President Abraham Lincoln was keenly aware of the strategic importance of Chattanooga, the gateway to the lower South. The city is situated just above the Tennessee-Georgia line on the Moccasin Bend of the Tennessee River — a shape resembling an Indian shoe — at the point where the river's westward flow cuts through the Cumberland Plateau. The major east-west railroad of the South, the Memphis and Charleston, met the Nashville and Chattanooga, which at Chattanooga joined with lines to South Carolina and Virginia.

The Confederate commander, General Braxton Bragg, chose to conduct a siege instead of an attack, and deployed the Army of Tennessee, initially between 40,000 and 50,000 troops, in an effort to cut off Union supplies and oblige the Federals to either surrender or abandon Chattanooga. The terrain appeared to be suited to his purpose. Towering above the city on the southwest, and dominating both the river and the Nashville and Chattanooga Railroad, was the promontory of Lookout Mountain; overlooking the city on the east and extending south of it, controlling the railroads to Knoxville and Atlanta, was a rugged escarpment known as Missionary Ridge.

Bragg's main body occupied this ridge with an advance line on Orchard Knob, a foothill three quarters of a mile to the front. On the shoulder of Lookout Mountain (around the Cravens house), between the peak and the Tennessee River, Bragg located a force of approximately 2,700. Their orders were to command the river and the railroad in an attempt to sever the Union army from its railhead at Bridgeport, Alabama, and from its primary base at Nashville. At Brown's Ferry, across the bend from the city and marking the head of safe navigation on the river, Bragg stationed a detachment of about 1,000 troops to prevent supplies from arriving by that route.

Lincoln wired messages of reassurance to his shaken general and ordered heavy reinforcements to Chattanooga: 20,000 troops from Mississippi under Major General William

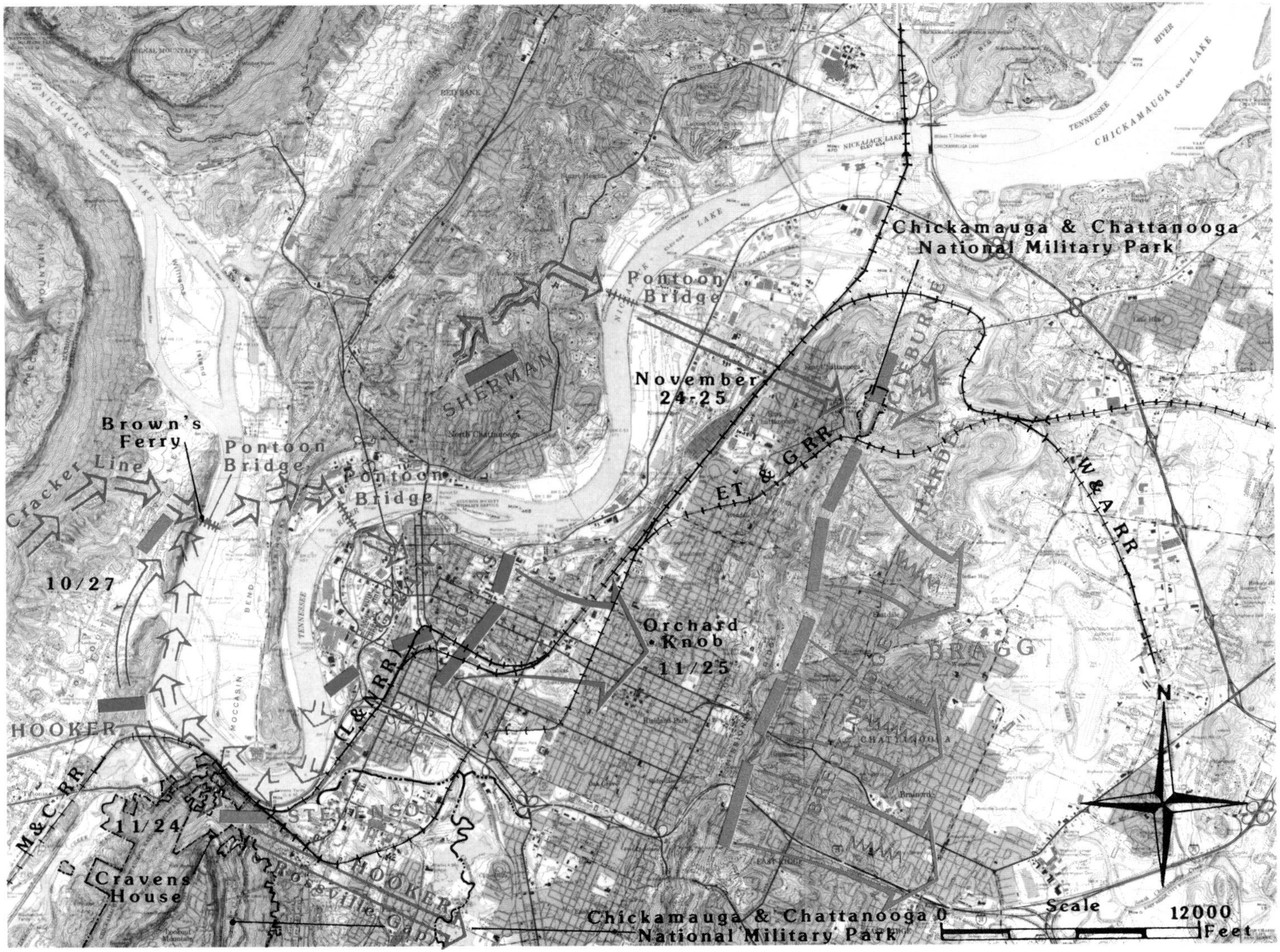

CHATTANOOGA
24–25 November 1863

Combat Strength
70,000
50,000

Casualties
5,815
6,667

Chickamauga & Chattanooga National Military Park

Chickamauga & Chattanooga National Military Park

Scale
0   12000
        Feet

N

CHICKAMAUGA LAKE

TENNESSEE RIVER

W & A RR

HARDEE

BRAGG

CLEBURN

ET & G RR

November 24-25

Pontoon Bridge

SHERMAN

Orchard Knob
11/25

Brown's Ferry Pontoon Bridge

Pontoon Bridge

Cracker Line

10/27

HOOKER

TENNESSEE

MOCCASIN BEND

M & C RR

N & C RR

Craven's House

11/24

Rossville Gap

LOOKOUT MOUNTAIN

Tecumseh Sherman and a like number from northern Virginia under Major General Joseph Hooker. Though Rosecrans gradually began to recover from the shock of Chickamauga, his messages for weeks remained vague and unpromising. He seemed unable to regain his poise and confidence; Lincoln came to the conclusion that he was acting "confused and stunned like a duck hit on the head." On October 17 the president appointed Major General Ulysses S. Grant, fresh from the victorious Vicksburg campaign, to command all Union forces between the Appalachians and the Mississippi, as well as those in Arkansas. Grant immediately sent orders dismissing Rosecrans and replacing him with Major General George H. Thomas — savior of the army at Chickamauga — with instructions to hold Chattanooga at all costs, to which the indomitable Thomas replied, "We will hold the town till we starve."

The Confederate force was insufficient to invest the city completely, and the Union army there was able to bring in a trickle of supplies from its railhead by a roundabout, sixty-mile trail through the mountains north and west of the city. But the Union situation soon became extremely desperate; the troops eventually were reduced to eating only half of the usual daily ration.

Grant reached Chattanooga on October 23 and immediately approved a plan for opening an effective supply line. Before dawn on October 27 a force was floated by pontoons downriver to a point near Brown's Ferry, and a column marched across the neck formed by the river's loop to the same place. Together these forces attacked and drove off the Confederates guarding the site. The following day a column from Hooker's command, which was at Bridgeport after an epic rail journey of more than 1,100 miles in eleven days, established contact at Brown's Ferry. Once this position was taken, pontoon bridges were laid across the river at the ankle of Moccasin Bend, creating a direct route into the city. On the night of October 28–29 one division of Confederate

Lieutenant General James Longstreet's corps attacked the town of Wauhatchie in the Lookout Valley in an effort to break Hooker's line of communications to the bridgehead, but the attack miscarried. The new Union supply route — quickly named the "cracker line" — was secure. Grant awaited Sherman's arrival, when he would be strong enough to attempt to break the siege.

The Confederate command at Chattanooga was in serious disarray. Bragg's failure to press the Union army after Chickamauga had destroyed the corps commanders' last traces of confidence in his leadership, and immediately after the battle they requested President Jefferson Davis to remove him. General Longstreet, hero of the Confederate victory at Chickamauga, put aside a previous disagreement with General Robert E. Lee at Gettysburg and wrote to the secretary of war, "I am convinced that nothing but the hand of God can save us or help as long as we have our present commander. . . . Can't you send us General Lee? The army in Virginia can operate defensively, while our operations here should be offensive — until we recover Tennessee at all events. We need some great mind as General Lee's (nothing more) to accomplish this." Of the Confederate siege of Chattanooga, Longstreet later wrote in derision, "We were trying to starve the enemy out by investing him on the only side from which he could not have gathered supplies."

Davis responded to these overtures by paying Bragg and his subordinates a visit in early October. He dealt with the criticisms by leaving Bragg in command and removing his severest critics. Davis ordered Lieutenant General Leonidas Polk to Mississippi, removed Lieutenant General Daniel Harvey Hill and left him without a command, and approved Bragg's plan to dispatch Longstreet with 15,000 troops to retake Knoxville, which had been captured earlier by a Union column marching from Kentucky under Major General Ambrose E. Burnside. This left Bragg with only about 50,000 troops available for duty at

Chattanooga to oppose a Union aggregation that would soon reach 70,000. The Union forces were being concentrated under their three most capable generals, while the Confederate forces were being dispersed and led by the weakest of their field commanders.

Sherman arrived in mid-November, and Grant completed his plans for a coordinated attack. Sherman was to lead the main effort, crossing the river above the city to strike the northern end of the Confederate line on Missionary Ridge. Hooker was to drive off the Confederate force, now commanded by Major General Carter L. Stevenson, which was holding the slope between Lookout Mountain and the river, then move to the Rossville Gap and envelop the southern flank of the Confederate line on Missionary Ridge. Thomas was to seize Orchard Knob and demonstrate against the center of the Confederate line on Missionary Ridge to prevent Bragg from reinforcing his flanks. On November 23 Thomas's troops took their objective. The following day Hooker accomplished the first part of his mission. His troops scaled the mountain, drove off the handful of Confederates there, and planted the Stars and Stripes amid the mists of Point Lookout. The entire Lookout Mountain operation soon became romanticized as "the battle above the clouds."

Sherman's repeated assaults on November 25 against the Confederate right (Major General William J. Hardee's corps) were fierce, but the line held. The troops of Confederate division commander Major General Patrick Cleburne — known by his associates as the "Stonewall Jackson of the West" — fought with particular stubbornness. Hooker was slow in crossing Chattanooga Creek and approaching the Rossville Gap; his attack became more or less a mopping-up operation. The decisive action of the day, one of the most

**Chickamauga and Chattanooga
National Military Park**
Chattanooga and Moccasin Bend from Lookout Mountain. © David Muench, 1990

remarkable actions of the war, was carried out by Thomas's troops in the center against the corps of Major General John C. Breckinridge. In the late afternoon, after advancing and seizing the line of Confederate rifle pits along the base of Missionary Ridge, the Union troops charged, without orders but with invincible spirit, up the steep slope of the ridge while Grant and Thomas watched from below in alarm. Grant said somebody would "pay for" the blunder if the assault failed.

It did not fail. The Confederate position at the center of the line was improperly located along the comb of the ridge instead of the "tactical crest," that is, the line of the forward slope allowing the longest unobstructed field of observation and fire. But perhaps most damaging was the Confederates' pervasive demoralization and lack of faith in their commanding general. In a moment of panic at the climax of the Union charge, the Confederate center broke and the soldiers fled. The siege of Chattanooga ended with the Union "Miracle of Missionary Ridge."

With Cleburne's division fighting a grim and effective rear-guard action, Bragg was able to concentrate his disorganized army in the vicinity of Dalton, Georgia, on the railroad twenty-five miles south of Chattanooga. Disheartened and disgraced, he asked to be relieved of command and confided to Davis, "The disaster [at Missionary Ridge] admits of no palliation, and is justly disparaging to me as a commander. . . . I fear we both erred in the conclusion for me to retain command here after the clamor raised against me." On Lee's advice, Davis recalled General Joseph E. Johnston from inactivity and placed him at the head of the Confederate army in Georgia.

The toll in casualties at Chattanooga was not heavy when compared with such other Civil War battles as Antietam, Gettysburg, or Chickamauga. Union losses: 5,815 overall, 752 killed, 4,713 wounded, 350 missing or captured; Confederate losses: 6,667 overall, 361 killed, 2,160 wounded, 3,146 missing or captured. But both the tactical and strategic results were immense. One of the two major Confederate armies had been utterly defeated. Southern morale, soaring after Chickamauga, now plummeted. Chattanooga was left firmly in Union hands; five months later it would be the staging point for Sherman's mission of havoc to the sea.

Chattanooga Battlefield, a unit of Chickamauga and Chattanooga National Military Park, which includes the battlefields of Lookout Mountain, Orchard Knob, Missionary Ridge, and Wauhatchie, is at the intersection of interstates 59 and 75 at Chattanooga, Tennessee. There are 2,493 acres of the historic battlefield within the authorized boundaries of this unit.

THE RED RIVER CAMPAIGN

11 March–20 May 1864

Ludwell H. Johnson

The primary military objective of the Union invasion of northwestern Louisiana (March–May 1864) was the capture of Shreveport, headquarters of the Confederate Trans-Mississippi Department, and the consequent breakup of organized resistance in that theater of operations. Major General Nathaniel Prentiss Banks, a Massachusetts politician devoid of military talent, led the main column of about 30,000 men, including 10,000 loaned to him by Major General William T. Sherman. This force was to move up the Red River accompanied by vessels from the Mississippi Squadron commanded by Rear Admiral David Dixon Porter, who was flamboyant, able, and sticky-fingered. A supporting column of 10,000 men under Major General Frederick Steele was to march on Shreveport from Little Rock, Arkansas. Confederate Lieutenant General E. Kirby Smith, commander of the semiautonomous Trans-Mississippi Department, was responsible for meeting this formidable invasion by Banks, Porter, and Steele. Smith ordered Major General Richard Taylor, District of West Louisiana, to defend the Red River. Taylor was the son of former president Zachary Taylor, a skillful amateur soldier and a veteran of General Thomas J. "Stonewall" Jackson's Shenandoah Valley campaign.

These military particulars give no hint of the real origins of the campaign. Years before the war began, some Americans, especially New Englanders and New Yorkers, had called for a migration of northerners to Texas. There Yankee civilization would replace southern barbarism, the new settlers would find rich farms, and the textile mills of the Northeast would have an alternative source of cotton. The coming of war seemed to make this dream realizable. The French invasion of Mexico and the fall of Mexico City in the summer of 1863 gave the Lincoln administration an additional reason to heed those who were lobbying for the occupation of Texas; a possible collaboration between Jefferson Davis and Napoleon III along the Rio Grande was not a comforting thought.

Furthermore, invading Texas by way of the Red River would open up more of Louisiana to the plan of political reconstruction Lincoln had set forth in his proclamation of December 8, 1863, and which he had ordered Banks to expedite. Finally, the valley of the Red River reportedly contained large quantities of baled cotton, the price of which had risen manyfold since 1861. This cotton could feed the mills of both England and New England and enrich the swarms of traders who planned to follow the armies, carrying Treasury Department or presidential permits to trade with the enemy. As for Porter and his jolly tars, they looked forward to a new opportunity for lining their pockets with the proceeds from cotton seized as "prize of war." This was the web of causality that drew the Federals up the Red River in the spring of 1864.

The campaign began on March 11 when 10,000 men under Brigadier General Andrew J. Smith, sent from Vicksburg by Sherman, landed at Simmesport, on the Red River near its juncture with the Mississippi, and proceeded to capture Fort de Russy. After brushing aside the outnumbered Confederates, Smith's soldiers and Porter's sailors went on to Alexandria, which they occupied on the fifteenth. While waiting for Banks to come up from southern Louisiana, Porter's men fanned out through the countryside, commandeering wagons and teams, collecting "prize" cotton, and stuffing it into their gunboats. Ten days later Banks arrived with 20,000 infantry, artillery, and cavalry. After elections were held in the name of the "restored" government of Louisiana, the army and navy pressed on up the river. Taylor, with no more than 7,000 troops of all arms, fell back.

On April 3 Banks reached Grand Ecore. Thus far he had been keeping close to the river and to the comforting guns of the Mississippi Squadron. After holding more elections, Banks left the river, turned west, and began to follow the crest of the watershed between the Red and Sabine rivers, where a few narrow roads ran over low hills and through dense pine woods. The road chosen led through Pleasant Hill and Mansfield and then, turning back toward the river, to Shreveport.

Taylor, still looking for a chance to turn on the enemy, fell back until he reached Mansfield, where he made a stand east of the town. At about 4:00 P.M. on April 8, as the advance

A portion of the manuscript map of the Red River Campaign, March 11–May 20, 1864, prepared under the direction of Captain Richard Venable, chief of the Topographical Bureau of the West Louisiana and Arkansas District, C.S.A. A copy of this map accompanied an 1864 report by Confederate General E. Kirby Smith. (Civil War map no. 241.2, Geography and Map Division, Library of Congress)

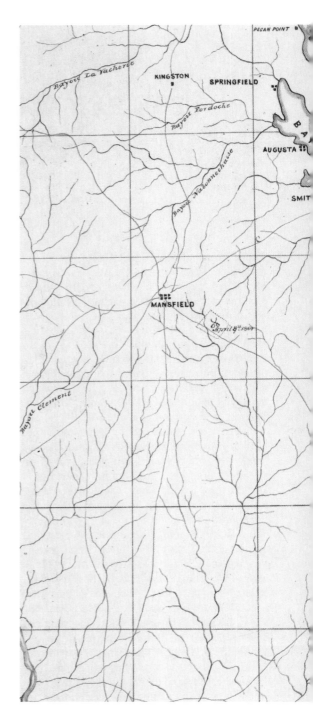

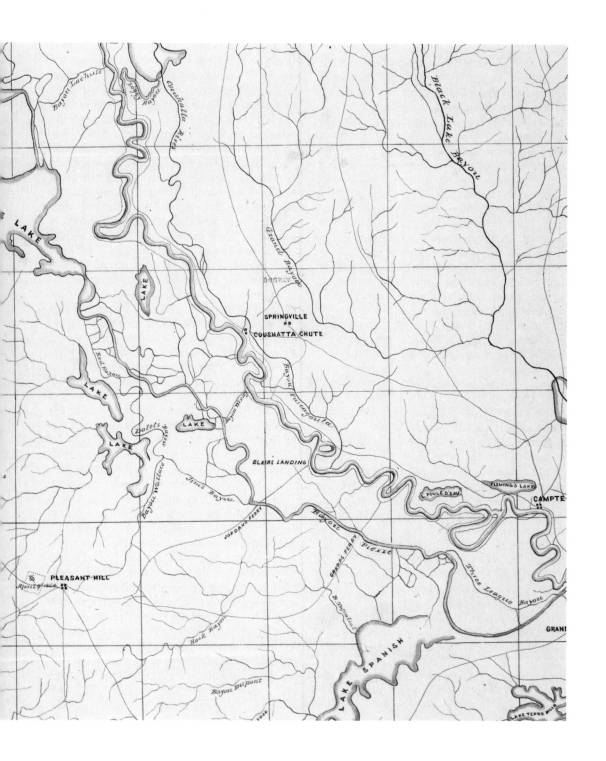

force of the Union army emerged in a clearing, Taylor attacked. Recent reinforcements allowed him to put 8,800 men into the battle against the Federal vanguard of 7,000. The result was a resounding Confederate victory. Banks's men were driven back in disorder for two miles until they met 5,000 reinforcements coming to their support. Taylor's men attacked again but could accomplish nothing before darkness put an end to the fighting. Total casualties at the battle of Mansfield (or Sabine Crossroads, as the Federals called it) came to 2,235 for Banks, of whom about 1,500 were captured, and about 1,000 for Taylor, virtually all of them killed or wounded.

Late that night Banks fell back to Pleasant Hill, concentrated his forces, and invited an attack. Taylor, reinforced by two small infantry divisions ordered down from Arkansas by E. Kirby Smith, followed Banks and attacked at 5:00 P.M. on April 9. The Confederates were partially successful on their left, but faulty deployment allowed the right to be heavily repulsed by A. J. Smith. About 12,000 troops were engaged on either side at Pleasant Hill; Union losses were 1,369, Confederate 1,626.

After the battle of Pleasant Hill, E. Kirby Smith made the grave mistake of taking most of Taylor's infantry to Arkansas to meet Steele, who, harassed by Confederate cavalry and very short of food, had already begun to retreat. Taylor was outraged, for this decision eliminated any chance that he might cut Banks off and capture Porter's gunboats, which were experiencing great difficulties because of unusually low water in the Red.

Acting on the advice of several of his generals, Banks fell back from Pleasant Hill to Grand Ecore, and by the nineteenth had resumed his retreat to Alexandria: 25,000 Federals stalked by 5,000 Confederates. Banks's men burned everything that could not be stolen, leaving behind them a smoking wasteland. Taylor tried to trap Banks between the Red and Cane rivers on April 23 and 24, but failed because the odds against him were too heavy. By the twenty-sixth, Banks was back in Alexandria, where reinforcements brought Federal strength up to 31,000. It was essential to make a stand here because the water on the falls was so shallow that Porter's flotilla was trapped. Time was needed to build a 750-foot-wide dam, which was to become famous in the history of military engineering: constructed in two weeks, it raised the water level sufficiently to allow the Mississippi Squadron to escape downstream, though not until the gunboats jettisoned their "prize of war" cotton.

Now Banks was free to conclude one of the most wretched Union failures of the war. The army moved out of Alexandria on May 13, but not before the town was fired by soldiers belonging to the command of A. J. Smith, who rode amid the flames shouting, "Hurrah, boys, this looks like war!" At Mansura and at Yellow Bayou, Taylor tried again to disrupt the enemy's retreat. There was some brisk fighting at Yellow Bayou, but as usual the disparity in numbers was too great for the Confederates to prevail. By May 20 Banks had put Atchafalaya Bayou between him and his pursuers, and the campaign was over.

The Red River expedition had important effects on the major campaigns east of the Mississippi. Sherman lost the services of A. J. Smith's 10,000 hard-fighting veterans, whom he had planned to use in his advance on Atlanta. Banks's fiasco also tied up troops intended for an attack on Mobile. That in turn released 15,000 Confederates from the Gulf states to join General Joseph E. Johnston in north Georgia. These changes in combat strength probably substantially postponed southern defeat in Georgia and may have lengthened the war by weeks or months. The Red River campaign is, however, most significant to history as an illustration of the way political and economic considerations shape military strategy.

MANSFIELD AND PLEASANT HILL

8–9 April 1864

Arthur W. Bergeron, Jr.

Confederate Major General Richard Taylor decided that his army had retreated far enough when it reached the little town of Mansfield, Louisiana. The Union army, commanded by Major General Nathaniel Prentiss Banks, had left the protection of Rear Admiral David Dixon Porter's fleet on the Red River. The Federals had marched away from the river at Natchitoches and moved into northwestern Louisiana along the Old Stage Road (now Louisiana Highway 175), a narrow track through dense pine forests and rolling hills. Once past Mansfield, Banks could put his men on any of three roads leading to Shreveport, and one of those roads would place the Federals back under the protection of their fleet. Taylor saw the strategic advantage in striking the Federals while the terrain forced them into a long line strung out along the Old Stage Road.

Taylor positioned his army about three miles southeast of Mansfield on the Moss plantation, along a road that intersected the Old Stage Road. This road led east toward Blair's Landing and the Red River and west toward the Sabine River. The 8,800 Confederates established their line just inside the woods between a cleared field and the crossroads, with the infantry division of Brigadier General Jean Jacques Alfred Alexander Mouton to the east of the main road and the infantry division of

Major General John George Walker to the west of it. Cavalrymen under the command of Brigadier General Thomas Green covered both flanks. Because of the dense forest, Taylor kept most of his artillery in reserve.

Shortly after noon on April 8, 1864, Union cavalrymen under Brigadier General Albert Lindley Lee, supported by one brigade of Colonel William Jennings Landrum's Fourth Division, Thirteenth Corps, emerged in the clearing across from the Confederate positions. The Federal soldiers slowly crossed the field and drove the skirmishers stationed along the crest of Honeycutt Hill back to their main line. As the Union cavalrymen neared the hidden line of General Mouton's infantry, they were hit by a heavy volley of musketry. Falling back to the crest of Honeycutt Hill east of the main road, the Federals took a position protected by a rail fence.

At about 3:30 P.M., Landrum's second brigade arrived on the field. The Union line soon formed a ninety-degree angle, one arm stretching south of the Old Stage Road and the other to the east. Lee placed one cavalry brigade on each flank of the infantry forces. Federal artillery batteries were interspersed at various points along the line. In all, about 5,700 Union soldiers were on the battlefield. Brigadier General Thomas Edward Greenfield Ransom, who led the detachment of the Thirteenth Corps in

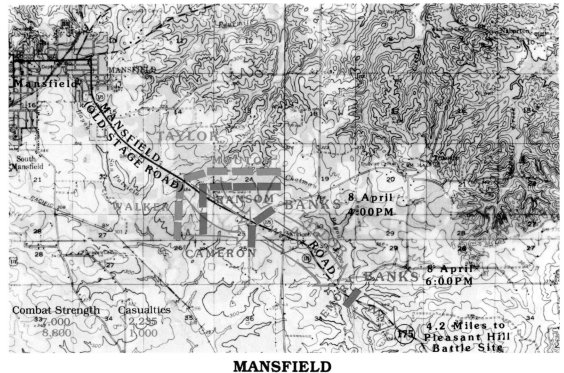

MANSFIELD

Combat Strength 37,000 / 8,800

Casualties 2,235 / 1,000

8 April 4:00PM

8 April 6:00PM

4.2 Miles to Pleasant Hill Battle Site

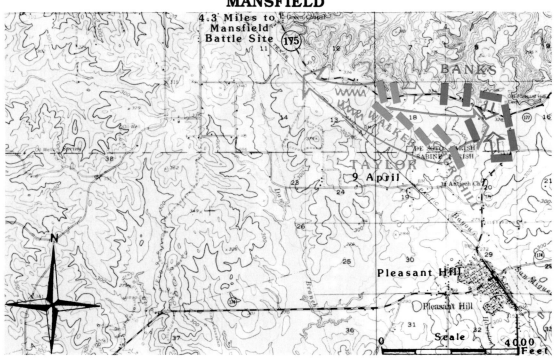

4.3 Miles to Mansfield Battle Site

9 April

Pleasant Hill

N

0   Scale   4000 Feet

Combat Strength
12,100
12,500

PLEASANT HILL

8–9 April 1864

Casualties
1,369
1,626

Banks's army, held command on the field during this first phase of action.

After the two sides had skirmished for a while, Taylor decided to attack the Federals before daylight ended. Mouton's division opened the assault at about 4:00 P.M. The Confederates suffered heavy casualties, particularly in officers, as they crossed the open space under a heavy fire of musketry and artillery. Soon Walker's men and the cavalry joined in the attack and helped Mouton's depleted ranks rout the Federals. Brigadier General Robert Alexander Cameron's Third Division of the Thirteenth Corps had formed a second Union line about a half mile behind Ransom's force near Sabine Crossroads. Placing his 1,300 men on either side of the Old Stage Road, Cameron ordered them forward. Some of the men from the first Union line joined Cameron's. This force held the Confederates back for about an hour but, outflanked on both sides, they were soon routed. The Confederates overran the Union cavalry wagon train, which was stranded along the narrow road.

About three miles from the first Union line, Brigadier General William Hemsley Emory's First Division of the Nineteenth Corps formed a third line at Pleasant Grove along the edge of a clearing overlooking Chatman's Bayou and a small creek. Taylor's Confederates struck this position at about 6:00 P.M. and pushed the Federals back slightly from the two streams. During the night Emory's men retreated to Pleasant Hill.

In the battle of Mansfield the Confederates captured twenty artillery pieces, hundreds of small arms, around 150 wagons loaded with supplies, and nearly 1,000 horses and mules. The price was about 1,000 men killed and wounded. Included among the dead was Mouton, who fell just as his men were throwing back the first Union line. Federal casualties numbered 113 men killed, 581 wounded, and 1,541 missing.

At Pleasant Hill, Banks ordered the supply train, the remnants of two cavalry brigades, and the men of the Thirteenth Corps back to

Natchitoches. On the field he had about 12,000 men in the two divisions of Brigadier General Andrew Jackson Smith's Sixteenth Corps, Emory's division of the Nineteenth Corps, and two cavalry brigades. On the morning of April 9 they took up positions near their camps, which were widely dispersed on a cleared plateau near the town of Pleasant Hill. There were wide gaps between the various Federal brigades. Banks, shaken by the defeat at Mansfield, failed to correct the faulty placement of his troops and failed to exercise command of his army during the battle.

In contrast, Taylor planned a masterful strategy on April 9 to keep the Federals demoralized and to force them to continue their retreat from Shreveport. With the addition of two infantry divisions of nearly 4,000 men from Arkansas and Missouri under Brigadier General Thomas James Churchill, Taylor had about 12,100 men, a very slight numerical superiority over the Yankees. Taking advantage of the Federals' scattered positions, Taylor planned a flanking movement. Churchill's troops would march south of the road that ran from Pleasant Hill to the Sabine River, turn toward the northeast, and crush the Union left flank. Walker's division would move between the Mansfield and Sabine River roads, charge the enemy when it heard Churchill's men making their attack, and connect their lines with Churchill's. Two cavalry brigades would attack the town once the Union flank was crushed, and two other cavalry brigades would then ride toward the north around the Federals' right to cut off their retreat toward Blair's Landing on the Red River.

The Confederates took most of the day to march the nearly twenty miles from Mansfield to Pleasant Hill. Churchill's men had marched about forty-five miles in the past two days, and the remainder of the army was still tired from the battle the afternoon before. Although the advance elements of Taylor's cavalry reached the vicinity of Pleasant Hill about 9:00 A.M., the head of Churchill's column did not arrive at a point about two miles west of the town until 1:00 P.M. Taylor allowed his men to rest for two hours before moving forward. Things began to go wrong from the first. Confused by the heavily wooded and hilly terrain, Churchill's men did not march far enough past the Sabine River Road and thus could not outflank the Union left. Their attack began about 5:00 P.M. When Churchill's troops came out of the pine forest, they found themselves facing enemy troops in a deep ravine. The Arkansans and Missourians charged and drove the Federals back up the hill and almost into the town. Another Union force counterattacked. Soon this portion of the Confederate assault was repulsed with heavy losses. Once Churchill's flank movement failed, the other elements of Taylor's plan could not succeed. All of the Confederate assaults bogged down after some initial successes, and a number of the men fell back in confusion. Eventually night put an end to the fighting, and Taylor's men withdrew to look for water. The Federals did not attempt to follow them.

Controversy exists over the winner of the battle of Pleasant Hill. Most historians concede a tactical victory to Banks's men, while a few call the engagement a draw. The Union commander decided to order his army back toward Natchitoches during the night, and this retreat gave Taylor's men a strategic victory. Had Churchill's flank attack succeeded, Taylor would have won a second smashing victory on the battlefield. The Confederate army lost about 1,200 men killed and wounded and 426 captured. Casualties in Banks's army amounted to 150 men killed, 844 wounded, and 375 missing, a total of 1,369.

These two battles blunted Banks's Red River campaign; Mansfield was one of the last major field victories by a Confederate army. Though the Union army outnumbered his force, Taylor had succeeded in striking three enemy detachments and defeating them in detail. He aggressively pursued the Federals, and the Confederate attack at Pleasant Hill caused the Yankees to continue their retreat. Taylor demonstrated generalship of a high order in these battles.

Lieutenant General Ulysses S. Grant ordered Banks to send Smith's men to assist in the Atlanta campaign and to move his other troops against Mobile, Alabama, ending Banks's march toward Shreveport and, once his army had reached the safety of the Mississippi River, ending his career as a field commander.

Mansfield Battle Park is 4 miles south of Mansfield, Louisiana, on State Route 175, 35 miles south of Shreveport on U.S. Route 171. There are 44 acres of the historic battlefield within its authorized boundaries.

Pleasant Hill battlefield is 20 miles south of Mansfield on State Route 175 near Pleasant Hill, Louisiana, 50 miles south of Shreveport. The entire battlefield is privately owned.

HALLOWED GROUND

Sam Nunn

The American Civil War, the most violent and traumatic chapter in our nation's history, shaped the course of American history more than any other event since the War of Independence. The war had its greatest impact on the American South in large part because it was waged almost entirely on southern soil. This may explain why southerners even today retain a depth of fascination with the conflict rarely found among their fellow citizens in other parts of the country.

The loss of life in the Civil War marred future generations. Some 365,000 Union and 260,000 Confederate soldiers and sailors lost their lives from 1861 to 1865, numbers all the more staggering when one considers that they were drawn from a population of only 31 million Americans. For every U.S. serviceman who died in Vietnam, almost eleven died in the Civil War.

Yet those who died at such places as Chancellorsville, Shiloh, Brandy Station, Cedar Creek, Vicksburg, Gettysburg, Fredericksburg, Antietam, Chickamauga, and the Wilderness did not sacrifice their lives in vain. The Civil War resolved forever two great issues that had sapped the health of the American Republic from Yorktown to Fort Sumter: the future of a cruel institution, slavery, and the political relationship of individual states to the Union. Though the Union did not enter

the Civil War seeking to abolish slavery where it legally existed, the circumstances of the war itself made slavery's elimination possible and necessary. President Abraham Lincoln did not fail to take advantage of the war as an engine of fundamental social change.

Of equal importance for the future of our nation was the final defeat of a theory of constitutional government that threatened to produce a Disunited States of America — the claim that individual states, having voluntarily joined the Union, had a right to leave it. The surrender of the Confederate armies in the spring of 1865 put an end to the threat of weakness and division, of America's political balkanization.

The Civil War was also important from a military standpoint. It was the first truly modern war, for it saw the first widespread use of railroads for military movements and of the telegraph for strategic communications, the first mass employment of rifled firearms, the first use of machine guns, the first appearance of tinned rations, the first combat between ironclad warships, and the first use of railmounted artillery.

The war also produced American military leaders whose place in the lists of great captains is forever secure. Few armies in history have operated under military genius equal to that of the Army of Northern Virginia's

The Resaca battlefield. Drawing by Walton Taber

General Robert E. Lee, Lieutenant General Thomas J. "Stonewall" Jackson, and Lieutenant General James Longstreet.

Though the Civil War was a human tragedy, we are a far better and more powerful country today because of the changes the war brought about. The war had a tremendous impact on what we stand for as Americans today.

For these reasons and many others, we must not allow the battlefields where so much American blood was so heroically spilled over such fundamental issues to become disposable property subject to commercial development.

Civil War battlefields are a historical legacy belonging to all Americans, a resource as precious as our national parks and forests and worthy of the same protection. To sell off bits and pieces of them is to sell off pieces of American history and to break faith with the hundreds of thousands of Americans who died on those battlefields.

THE ATLANTA CAMPAIGN

7 May–2 September 1864

Jay Luvaas

Major General William T. Sherman's Atlanta campaign was a vital part of the strategic plan devised by Lieutenant General Ulysses S. Grant in the spring of 1864. Sherman, the commander of the Military Division of the Mississippi, was to break up Confederate General Joseph E. Johnston's army in north Georgia and, according to Grant's orders, "get into the interior of the enemy's country as far as you can, inflicting all the damage you can against their War resources."

Sherman led the army group that included Major General George H. Thomas's Army of the Cumberland (60,733 men), Major General James B. McPherson's Army of the Tennessee (24,465), and Major General John M. Schofield's Army of the Ohio (13,559), in all nearly 100,000 troops and 254 pieces of artillery. The estimated strength of the Confederate forces under Johnston was 65,000, including Lieutenant General Leonidas Polk's corps from the Army of Mississippi, which joined Johnston's Army of Tennessee about one week after active operations began.

Johnston had taken command of the Army of Tennessee after the Confederate defeat at Chattanooga late the previous November. His problems included the condition of the army's horses, his infantry's lack of shoes, blankets, and small arms, and the morale and discipline of his troops. Sherman's overriding concern

was logistics: he had sufficient men and equipment, but he had to accumulate vast quantities of food and forage in the Nashville and Chattanooga storehouses and make sure they reached his armies.

The campaign began on May 7 when Sherman directed Thomas's Army of the Cumberland and Schofield's Army of the Ohio to move against the Confederate defenses north and west of Dalton, Georgia. Ordering Thomas and Schofield to press strongly at all points, Sherman sent McPherson's Army of the Tennessee on a secret march fifteen miles south through Snake Creek Gap to attack the railroad near Resaca and "fall on the enemy's flank when he retreated." McPherson neither seized Resaca, which was held by several Confederate brigades behind strong earthworks, nor managed to cut the railroad, missing, as Sherman later told him, the opportunity of his life. On the thirteenth, the Confederates withdrew from Dalton to Resaca, followed by the Union armies.

On May 14 and 15 there was heavy fighting along the line at Camp Creek near Resaca. A Confederate counterattack against the Union left flank nearly succeeded. On the night of the fifteenth, Johnston slipped away, his line of communications threatened by Union artillery occupying high ground within range of the railroad bridge across the Oos-

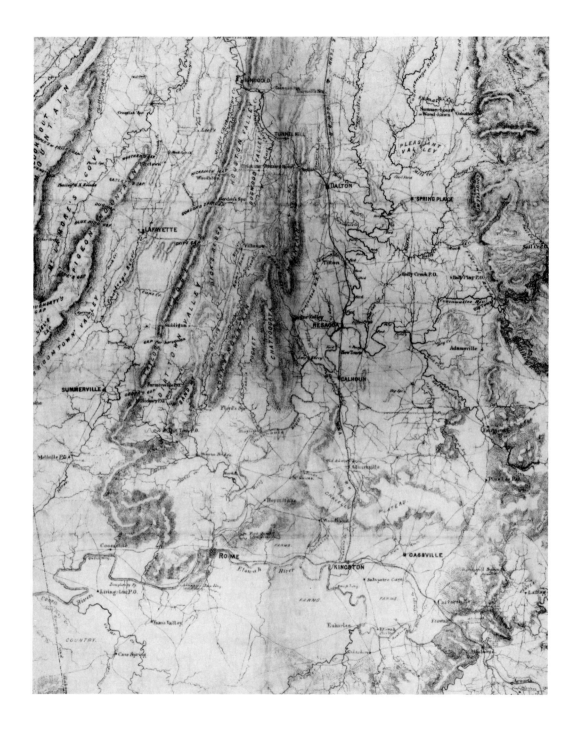

tanaula River as well as by a Union division that had crossed the river downstream at Lay's Ferry.

Elements from the two armies met again at Adairsville two days later. After stubborn skirmishing, the Confederates fell back from one line of breastworks to another, gaining time for the army to retreat to Cassville. There Johnston occupied "an excellent position" from which he intended to assault Sherman's converging columns on May 19. He called off his attack, however, when reports suggested that Lieutenant General John B. Hood's corps on the right was threatened. The Confederates withdrew to high ridges south and east of Cassville. Although it was a formidable position, their lines on the right could be enfiladed by Union artillery, causing Johnston once again to abandon his position. Johnston's next stronghold was in the Allatoona Mountains, but Sherman surprised him by leaving his railroad supply line and striking out cross-country. He bridged the Etowah River downstream from Johnston and continued marching south, with Thomas, McPherson, and Schofield in separate columns converging on Dallas, an important road junction from which he could threaten Marietta and Atlanta. This move forced Johnston to abandon Allatoona Pass and move toward Dallas.

On May 24 and 25 Johnston's forces marched south to intercept the Federals near New Hope Church. Both sides quickly threw up breastworks, and for the next five days there was constant firing and sporadic heavy fighting in the thickly wooded hills and rav-

Before beginning his campaign to capture Atlanta in 1864, General William T. Sherman ordered the compilation and publication of a detailed map of the field of operations. In addition to the standard edition lithographed on paper, the map was printed in three parts on cotton muslin, mainly for the convenience of cavalry officers. Depicted here is the first of three sheets. (Sherman map collection no. 31, Geography and Map Division, Library of Congress)

ines from Dallas to northeast of New Hope Church — an area the soldiers called the "hellhole." On both sides the men were almost constantly under fire and were engaged each night in fatigue duty, building breastworks and digging rifle pits. They had little opportunity for rest and poor facilities for cooking. "It is useless to look for the flank of the enemy," Sherman concluded, "as he makes temporary breastworks as fast as we travel. We must break his line without scattering our troops too much, and then break through."

He was not successful. On May 27 Sherman marched two divisions behind his lines to the left to get around Johnston's entrenchments. After a difficult flank march "through dense forests and the thickest jungle," Brigadier General Thomas J. Wood's division of Major General Oliver O. Howard's Fourth Corps attacked the Confederates near Pickett's Mill. Struggling through thick undergrowth and rough ravines, they encountered Major General Patrick R. Cleburne's troops, who had extended the Confederate line to meet the threat. During the next several hours Wood suffered about 1,400 casualties and Cleburne, 450. On May 28 Major General William B. Bate's Confederate division attacked McPherson's Army of the Tennessee but suffered a bloody repulse.

Sherman decided to shift to the left and reestablish his line of communications on the railroad. He continued edging left to gain possession of the roads leading to Allatoona and Acworth. On June 2 Union cavalry under Major General George Stoneman and Brigadier General Kenner Garrard occupied Allatoona Pass, forcing Johnston to evacuate his lines at Dallas, New Hope Church, and Pickett's Mill. Johnston fell back to a new position, about ten miles long, in which three prominent hills — Lost Mountain, Pine Mountain, and Brush Mountain — served as imposing redoubts.

Even these natural barriers, however, were useless against troops who could maneuver, and on June 10, having shifted McPherson's army to his extreme left, Sherman moved his columns forward — McPherson along the railroad, Thomas obliquing toward the right at Pine Mountain, and Schofield to the vicinity of Lost Mountain. The railroad bridge over the Etowah had been completed the day before, and supplies and reinforcements had arrived. Sherman's superior numbers enabled him to keep working around the flanks, and when Thomas's Army of the Cumberland threatened to extend the Union line beyond Lost Mountain, Johnston abandoned Pine Mountain and fell back by stages to a new line in which Kennesaw Mountain served as a salient. The Confederate flanks were refused, and the line was heavily fortified. By this time, to quote Sherman, the whole area was "one vast fort. . . . Johnston must have fifty miles of connected trenches," with Kennesaw "the key to the whole country." On June 22 Hood's corps made a sudden but unsuccessful attack on two divisions, one from Major General Joseph Hooker's corps of Thomas's army and one from Schofield's, at Kolb's farm. This fight halted Sherman's initial attempt to bypass the Confederates' mountain stronghold.

Faced with the alternative of continuing his turning movements or assaulting the Confederate earthworks, Sherman decided on a frontal attack. "An army to be efficient must not settle down to a single mode of offensive," he explained (or perhaps rationalized), and by changing his pattern he hoped to surprise the enemy. Orders specified that "each attacking column will endeavor to break a single point of the enemy's line, make a secure lodgment beyond, and be prepared for following it up toward Marietta and the railroad in case of success." On June 27 two Union columns advanced upon the center of the Confederate lines, and in two hours the assaults had failed, with Union losses three times those of the Confederates.

On the extreme Union right, however, a portion of Schofield's Army of the Ohio crossed Olley's Creek, which protected the Confederate left, and entrenched. This prompted Sherman

to shift McPherson's army from the left to his extreme right. To counter this new threat to his line of retreat, Johnston abandoned the lines at Kennesaw on the night of July 2 and fell back to a position at Smyrna Station, blocking the road to Atlanta. Two nights later the Confederates withdrew to a previously fortified bridgehead covering the railroad bridge and ferry crossings over the Chattahoochee River. From the nearby hills Sherman could see Atlanta.

The military situation had changed significantly in Sherman's favor. He was now out of the mountains with his army united and his line of communications secure. There had been 17,000 or more Federal casualties thus far in the campaign, but Sherman had more troops on hand or within supporting distance than when the campaign began. His effective system of bringing men forward from furloughs and hospitals and calling up fresh divisions reinforced his armies in the field. Johnston's losses were about 14,000.

The day after Sherman was repulsed at Kennesaw, Grant authorized him to make movements "entirely independent of any desire to retain Johnston's forces where they are," changing significantly his original mission to break up the opposing army *and* to capture and destroy Confederate war resources in Atlanta. He now had greater flexibility.

When Johnston was replaced by Hood on July 18, Sherman and his staff agreed that they "ought to be unusually cautious and prepared at all times for sallies and for hard fighting." Hood delivered a series of blows to Sherman's army as it tightened its grip around Atlanta, but Sherman had more troops, better subordinate commanders, and an army of seasoned veterans. There were more important battles before the end of the campaign: Peachtree Creek on July 20, Hood's first battle as commander; Atlanta on July 22, where McPherson was killed; Ezra Church on July 28; and, finally, Jonesboro on August 31–September 1, after which Atlanta fell. (Today most of these battlefields are under asphalt and concrete.) On September 3 Sherman wired the Washington authorities: "So Atlanta is ours, and fairly won. . . . Since May 5, we have been in one constant battle or skirmish, and need rest."

The Atlanta campaign was a masterpiece of *both* offensive and defensive maneuver. With greater numbers and mobility, Sherman managed to outflank or threaten the lines of communication of every position occupied by his opponent. Johnston succeeded against formidable odds in keeping his army intact and always between Sherman and Atlanta, although he seems to have understood little of Atlanta's political, diplomatic, economic, and psychological importance.

The most significant aspect of the campaign was Sherman's special genius for logistics. He moved reinforcements and supplies forward over immense and hostile territory against a skilled opponent, even though his general objective was known and his line of advance was dependent upon a single railroad. Greater industrial and manpower resources were among the reasons the North won the war. Sherman's concepts, organization, and efficiency brought those resources together before Atlanta.

While Federal soldiers near Jonesboro were making "Sherman neckties" out of the rails of the last railroad into Atlanta, the Democrats meeting in convention in Chicago were opposing the war and nominating Major General George B. McClellan for the presidency. After Atlanta fell, McClellan moved to distance himself from the Peace Democrats and called for union as "the one condition of peace." Sherman suddenly became a national hero, and gloom descended over the South. The opposition to Lincoln subsided, in large part as a result of the Union victory at Atlanta.

ROCKY FACE RIDGE AND RESACA

7–15 May 1864

Jay Luvaas

Confederate earthworks and gun positions lined the precipitous Rocky Face Ridge near Dalton. At Mill Creek Gap, known locally as Buzzard's Roost, there were more formidable earthworks. According to Union Major General William T. Sherman, batteries extended the "whole length from the spurs on either side, and more especially from a ridge at the farther end like a traverse directly across its debouch." Confederate General Joseph E. Johnston had fortified all approaches to Dalton from the north and west to protect the junction there of the East Tennessee and Georgia Railroad with the Western and Atlantic. He had also been working since December to raise his troops' morale and increase their strength.

By May 7 Sherman's army group was in motion. He ordered Major General James B. McPherson's Army of the Tennessee (24,465 men) on a turning movement through Snake Creek Gap to sever the railroad near Resaca. To keep Johnston distracted at Dalton, Sherman sent the Army of the Cumberland (60,733 men), commanded by Major General George H. Thomas, to move in force against Tunnel Hill, a lesser ridge west of Rocky Face. By late afternoon the Confederate outposts had fallen back to prepared positions on the slopes of Rocky Face. Major General John M. Schofield's Army of the Ohio (13,559 men) approached Dalton from the north.

On May 8 a regiment of the Union Fourteenth Corps seized Blue Mountain, southeast of Tunnel Hill, and used it as a lookout and signal station. A brigade from Major General Oliver O. Howard's Fourth Corps ascended the northern end of Rocky Face and moved south along the narrow crest. Thomas was ordered to seize Dug Gap, four miles farther to the south, and to attack Confederate works along the northern half of Rocky Face Ridge. Schofield was to make a strong demonstration against the Confederate right flank in Crow Valley, north of Dalton. In the afternoon two brigades from Major General John W. Geary's division of the Twentieth Corps assaulted the Confederate position at Dug Gap but were thrown back by the troops of Brigadier General Daniel H. Reynolds and Colonel J. Warren Grigsby, later supported by Brigadier General Hiram B. Granbury's infantry brigade.

On May 9 Union infantry moved forward to probe for other possible weak points in the five-hundred-foot-high Rocky Face barrier. Brigadier General Charles G. Harker's brigade reached the crest, but the terrain was so rough and narrow that in places the men could advance only in single file. Harker hit the angle where the right of Confederate Major General Benjamin F. Cheatham's division joined the left of Major General Carter L. Stevenson's division. Here the fight "was obstinate and

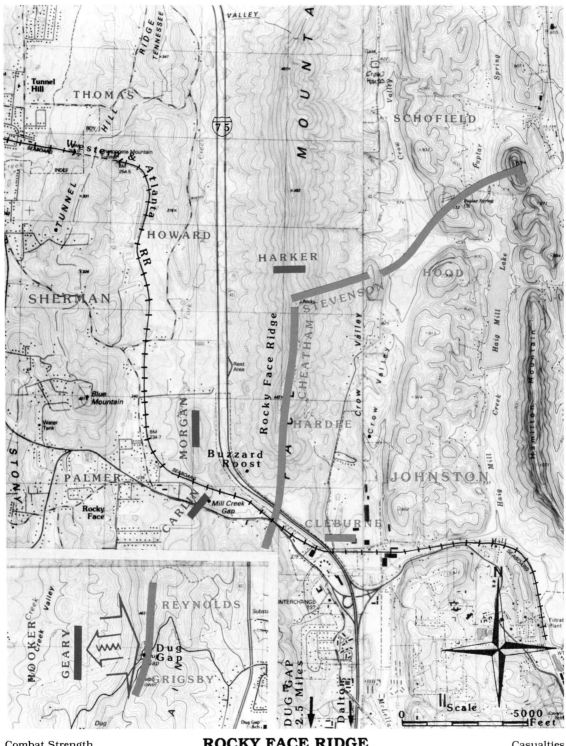

ROCKY FACE RIDGE

7–15 May 1864

Combat Strength
62,227
42,858–52,992

Casualties
837
600

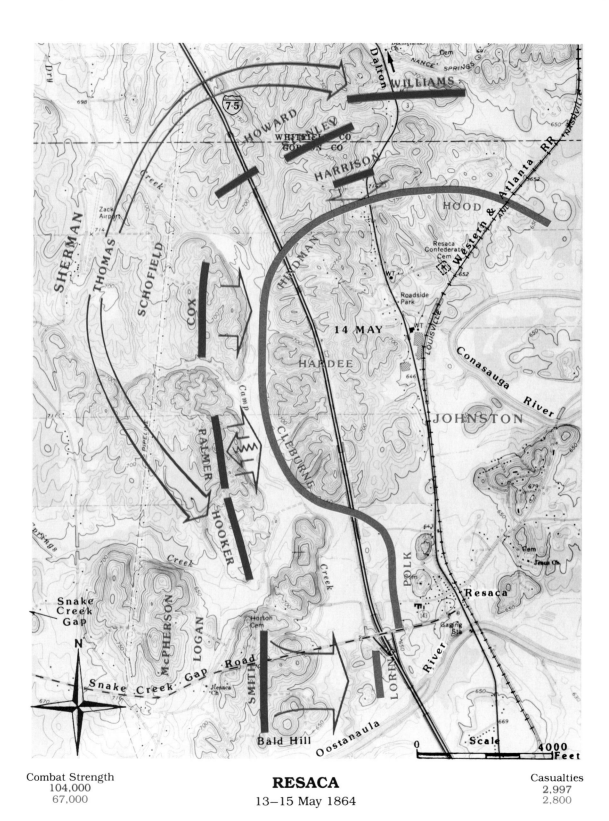

Combat Strength
104,000
67,000

RESACA

13–15 May 1864

Casualties
2,997
2,800

bloody," Stevenson reported. The main Confederate position on the slope and crest of Rocky Face Ridge could not be carried. The Union suffered 837 casualties, the Confederates 600.

Sherman concluded that his troops could not take Rocky Face Ridge and that any attempt to insert columns "into the jaws of Buzzard Roost would be fatal." Sherman called the gap "the door of death." On May 11 he left Howard's Fourth Corps and two cavalry divisions to "keep up the feint of a direct attack on Dalton" and marched with the rest of his forces to join McPherson at Snake Creek Gap. The following afternoon Major General Joseph Wheeler's Confederate cavalry division followed the trail of Schofield's Army of the Ohio around the north end of Rocky Face. He learned from prisoners that Sherman was headed for Resaca. By 1:00 A.M. on May 13 the Confederates had withdrawn from their positions near Buzzard's Roost and marched to Resaca, pursued by Howard's Fourth Corps.

On May 9, while Sherman was probing Johnston's position at Rocky Face Ridge, McPherson marched the Army of the Tennessee through Snake Creek Gap and advanced toward Resaca, with Major General G. M. Dodge's Sixteenth Corps and Major General John A. Logan's Fifteenth Corps. The Confederates had about 4,000 troops at the Oostanaula River bridges near Resaca, composed of Brigadier General James Cantey's brigade, part of Lieutenant General Leonidas Polk's corps, and a brigade from the vicinity of Dalton.

Dodge first encountered Confederate cavalry and then pressed forward to the old Calhoun and Dalton crossroads. While his Fourth Division secured the crossroads, Brigadier General Thomas W. Sweeny's Second Division captured Bald Hill from Cantey's brigade of infantry. (This hill, which today is heavily forested, overlooks the Oostanaula River and is not to be confused with the cleared hill about four tenths of a mile to the north, where State Road 136 crosses before descending into the Camp Creek Valley.) The Confederates fell back across Camp Creek to the Resaca defenses.

McPherson was cautious and missed his opportunity for a major victory. He recalled Dodge to the mouth of Snake Creek Gap to entrench and bring forward supplies. McPherson later explained, "If I could have had a division of good cavalry, I could have broken the railroad at some point." For the next two days McPherson remained in his defensive stance on the Resaca side of Snake Creek Gap. On May 10 Major General Joseph Hooker's corps was ordered to reinforce McPherson, to be followed the next day by the rest of the Army of the Cumberland except for Howard's Fourth Corps, which continued to hold the Union position at Buzzard's Roost. On the thirteenth, Schofield's Army of the Ohio also moved into Snake Creek Gap.

Johnston used the time given him by McPherson to concentrate his forces at Resaca and to prepare the battlefield. Polk's corps occupied the Confederate left, its flank anchored on the Oostanaula River. Lieutenant General William J. Hardee's corps held the center along the high ridge overlooking Camp Creek. Lieutenant General John B. Hood's corps was posted on the right, his line running east to a hill near the Conasauga River.

On May 14 Sherman's army closed in, enveloping the Confederate lines from the north and west. Hooker's Twentieth Corps marched out the Resaca Road to support McPherson's troops, while Major General John M. Palmer's Fourteenth Corps advanced along a parallel route two miles to the north with orders to fight its way to the railroad. Palmer attacked at about noon, supported on his left by Schofield's troops and later by Howard's Fourth Corps on Schofield's left.

The fighting was severe as Schofield and Howard drove the Confederates back into their prepared positions. Palmer's subordinates were unaware of these breastworks and took heavy losses in front of Major General Patrick R. Cleburne's position at the center of Hardee's line.

The heaviest fighting was near the headwaters of Camp Creek, where late in the afternoon Major General Jacob D. Cox's division of Schofield's Army of the Ohio drove the Confederate outposts over rough and wooded ground into their works. Two divisions of Howard's Fourth Corps later moved up to secure the position, opposite Major General Thomas C. Hindman's division on the left of Hood's line.

At 6:00 P.M. Johnston launched a fierce counterattack from the Confederate right with two of Hood's divisions, supported by two brigades from Major General William H. T. Walker's division of Hardee's corps. Holding with his left, Hood executed a swing movement that enabled his right to advance about two miles, overrunning a round-topped hill just east of the Dalton Road that anchored the Union flank. The lead division of the Twentieth Corps under Brigadier General A. S. Williams was rushed to the vicinity of Nance Springs at dusk, just in time to repel Hood's assault.

The Union attacks succeeded on the right, led by a brigade of Major General Morgan L. Smith's division of the Fifteenth Corps, which stormed across Camp Creek. The fighting continued until dark, but McPherson's men held. Throughout the night the Union troops dug entrenchments.

The attack on May 15 did not materialize as Sherman had planned. The rough, unknown terrain on the Union left slowed the deployment of the divisions of major generals Daniel Butterfield and John W. Geary. The configuration of the terrain gave the Confederates "unusual facilities for cross firing and enfilading," and the Union brigades were forced to attack in columns without adequate artillery support. The brunt of the Union attacks was borne by Stevenson's division. In places the Federals advanced to within thirty paces of Stevenson's defenses and captured a Georgia artillery battery, but the Confederate line held.

The Confederates were not driven back into Resaca, and an assault upon the town was in fact not necessary, because Sherman already had two pontoon bridges laid across the Oostanaula River at Lay's Ferry, about three miles below Resaca. During the day, Brigadier General T. W. Sweeny's Second Division of the Sixteenth Corps crossed the river. With the aid of two batteries on the northern bank, his troops beat back an attack by a portion of General Walker's division. Once Sweeny's men had fortified the bridgehead, Johnston's position was turned. He crossed the river that night, burned the bridges, and headed for Calhoun. At Resaca the Confederates had lost about 2,800 of their 67,000 men; the Federals, 2,997 of their 104,000.

Rocky Face Ridge battlefield is near Dalton, Georgia, on U.S. Route 41 and and Interstate 75, 19 miles southeast of Chattanooga, Tennessee. The battlefield is privately owned.

Dug Gap Battle Park is located southwest of Dalton, Georgia, on Dug Gap Battle Road, 1.7 miles off Interstate 75. Three acres of the historic battlefield are owned by the Whitfield-Murray Historical Society and are open to the public with prior permission (Chattanooga Avenue, Dalton, Georgia).

Resaca battlefield is near Resaca, Georgia, on Interstate 75 and U.S. Route 41, 33 miles southeast of Chattanooga, Tennessee. The battlefield is privately owned except for a state of Georgia commemorative plaque near the entrance of Resaca Confederate cemetery on U.S. 41, 6 miles north of Calhoun.

NEW HOPE CHURCH, PICKETT'S MILL, AND DALLAS

25–29 May 1864

Jay Luvaas

When Union Major General William T. Sherman's army crossed the Etowah River on May 23, the Atlanta campaign entered a new phase. Sherman's purpose had been to turn or outflank General Joseph E. Johnston's army by threatening the railroad in his rear. Sherman knew from a visit to the area twenty years earlier that Allatoona Pass was very strong. Instead of attacking Johnston there at the pass, where he was guarding the railroad, Sherman surprised the Confederates by leaving the railroad supply line and striking out cross-country toward Marietta via Dallas with 100,000 fighting men and twenty days' supplies in his wagons.

Sherman's army advanced in separate columns: Major General James B. McPherson's Army of the Tennessee in the west near Van Wert, Major General George H. Thomas's Army of the Cumberland in the center along the main road to Dallas, and Major General John M. Schofield's Army of the Ohio to the left rear. Major General Joseph Hooker's Twentieth Corps of the Army of the Cumberland took the lead. On May 25 his three divisions advanced on roughly parallel roads: Major General Daniel Butterfield's division on the left, Major General John W. Geary's in the center, and Brigadier General A. S. Williams's on the right.

Geary's division encountered Confederate cavalry near Owen's Mill on Pumpkin Vine Creek. The lead brigade pushed ahead for three more miles and encountered Confederates, who fought a delaying action for about a mile back to Lieutenant General John B. Hood's main line centering on New Hope Church. Lieutenant General Leonidas Polk's corps was not far away in the direction of Dallas. The total Confederate strength was about 75,000. Geary halted on a ridge in the woods, entrenched, and waited for Butterfield and Williams to arrive.

The terrain was crisscrossed by small ravines and covered by dense woods with considerable underbrush, and as Williams's division advanced in three lines, the troops could scarcely see the main Confederate rifle pits. The massed Union formations were exposed to a continuous fire of canister and shrapnel. Hooker's troops were repulsed at all points, although the leading line penetrated to within twenty-five or thirty paces of the Confederate defenses before a thunderstorm washed out the attack, forcing them to fall back and entrench. The Confederates lost 350 men, while Hooker reported losses of 1,665.

Major General Oliver O. Howard's Fourth Corps then moved into position on Hooker's left during the dark, rainy night, prolonging

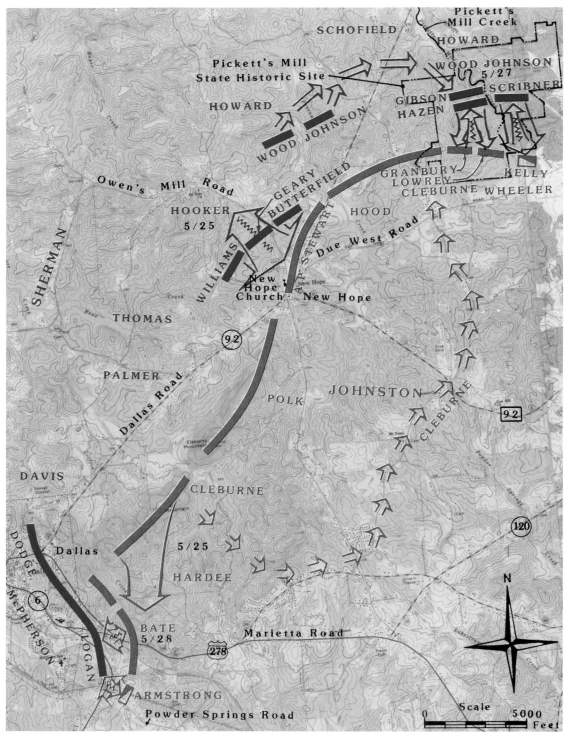

NEW HOPE CHURCH, PICKETT'S MILL, AND DALLAS

25–29 May 1864

Combat Strength
93,600–102,000
75,000

Casualties
4,500
3,000

the line beyond Brown's Mills. The next morning the leading division of Major General John M. Palmer's Fourteenth Corps arrived and entrenched on Hooker's right. On May 26 Schofield's Army of the Ohio came up to extend Howard's line to the left. To meet this threat, Hood moved Major General Thomas C. Hindman's division to the right of his line. For four days the fighting in the area near New Hope Church was incessant. Visibility was poor in the dense woods, and the lines were so close that the troops were constantly under fire. The Confederates had the advantage of position, being entrenched on higher ground. Sherman's superior artillery and ability to maneuver were generally negated by the terrain. "We have been here now five days," a Union general wrote his wife, "and have not advanced an inch. . . . On some points the troops sent to relieve us did not hold, and some of our dead lie there unburied. . . . It is a very tedious and worrying life."

At first Sherman assumed that he had only Hood's corps in his front. He ordered McPherson to move into Dallas, link up with Brigadier General Jefferson C. Davis's division of Palmer's Fourteenth Corps, and then advance toward New Hope Church to hit Hood's left flank. On May 26 Union Major General John A. Logan's Fifteenth Corps entered and moved south through Dallas on the Powder Springs Road. It ran into Confederate Lieutenant General William J. Hardee's corps behind strong fieldworks that extended across the Powder Springs and Marietta roads. McPherson's men threw up a line of works during the night. The next morning Sherman ordered McPherson to use the Marietta Road and close in toward Hooker. McPherson would then be able to move his army to the left around Johnston's right flank and place it between the Confederates and the railroad.

On May 27 Howard led 14,000 Federals to the Union left to attack the Confederates on Hood's right, initiating the battle of Pickett's Mill. This was the bloodiest thus far in the campaign. After struggling through dense forests and deep ravines and over difficult ridges, Brigadier General Thomas J. Wood's division of Howard's corps attacked the Confederate right flank at 4:30 P.M. The Confederate line had just been extended by Major General Patrick R. Cleburne's division. The next fifty minutes were terrible for Brigadier General William B. Hazen's brigade, which began the assault. Everything went wrong. Colonel William H. Gibson's brigade suffered heavier losses than Hazen's and was unable to provide support. Hazen's first line advanced a quarter mile and was hit by Brigadier General Hiram B. Granbury's heavy fire. Hazen's men exhausted their ammunition supply, and Brigadier General Mark P. Lowrey's Confederate brigade edged into a position from which it attacked Hazen's second line.

Several hundred yards to the east, Colonel Benjamin F. Scribner's brigade of Brigadier General Richard W. Johnson's division of the Fourteenth Corps found its way blocked by Confederate Brigadier General John H. Kelly's dismounted cavalry, sheltered behind rude breastworks. Scribner was not close enough to align with Hazen, so Lowrey's brigade was able to fire into Hazen's left rear.

The fighting lasted well into the night, but the Confederate flank held firm. The Union troops withdrew in the dark and entrenched on a ridge farther to the north. Wood's division alone suffered about 1,400 casualties in what one Union officer described as "the crime at Pickett's Mill." The Union forces, Cleburne reported, "displayed a courage worthy of an honorable cause. . . . The piles of his dead on this front [were] pronounced by the officers . . . who have seen most service to be greater than they had ever seen before." Cleburne lost about 450 men killed and wounded.

The final act in this phase of the campaign occurred at Dallas on May 28, when, because of faulty communications, Confederate Major General William B. Bate's division, on the left of Hardee's corps, mistakenly stormed out of its trenches late in the afternoon to assault McPherson's force in his front. "Fortunately,"

Sherman noted, "our men had erected good breast-works, and gave the enemy a terrible and bloody repulse." The Union troops held, and in about two hours Bate's men fell back, leaving more than 300 dead on the field. On June 1 all three Union armies slid a few miles to the left. By June 4 Union cavalry occupied Allatoona Pass. With the great railroad bridge over the Etowah rebuilt, Sherman could sidestep Johnston, link up with the railroad, and push on toward Marietta and the Chattahoochee.

The fighting along the Dallas–New Hope Church–Pickett's Mill line represented a new phase in Civil War tactics, at least for the western armies. Although some units at Chickamauga and Chattanooga the previous fall had resorted to earthworks and log breastworks, not until the Atlanta campaign did both armies habitually entrench, and even then one side usually had to advance from its own lines to attack an enemy position. In the fighting around New Hope Church, however, both armies fought from behind breastworks in the near presence of the enemy and often under intense fire. According to Sherman, even the skirmishers "were in the habit of rolling logs together, or of making a lunette of rails, with dirt in front, to cover their bodies." This was characteristic of a siege but a new experience for armies in the field.

At New Hope Church, Johnston either an-ticipated Sherman's moves or reacted quickly enough to utilize the terrain and the defensive power of earthworks to offset Sherman's advantage in numbers. He used his cavalry effectively not only to provide timely information but also as mobile firepower. Without Wheeler's dismounted troops to hold the right of the line at Pickett's Mill, Sherman's effort to turn Johnston's right flank might well have succeeded. Eventually the fighting along the Dallas–New Hope Church–Pickett's Mill line convinced Sherman that the best way out of the impasse was to discontinue his efforts to outflank Johnston. He decided instead to shift to the east around Johnston's lines to the railroad, regain his line of communications, resupply his armies, and then advance upon Marietta and the Chattahoochee. The total losses for the three battles were Union, 4,500; Confederate, about 3,000.

New Hope Church battlefield is at New Hope, Georgia, 25 miles northwest of Atlanta on Interstate 75 and south on State Route 92. The entire battlefield is privately owned.

Pickett's Mill Historic Site is northeast of New Hope, Georgia, 25 miles northwest of Atlanta on Interstate 75 off State Route 92. There are 765 acres of the historic battlefield within its authorized boundaries.

Dallas battlefield is east of Dallas, Georgia, on state routes 6 and 120 and U.S. Route 278. The entire battlefield is privately owned.

KENNESAW MOUNTAIN

27 June 1864

Jay Luvaas

In the first week of June, following the battles of New Hope Church, Pickett's Mill, and Dallas, Union Major General William T. Sherman moved eastward to Acworth to reconnect with his vital rail supply line from Chattanooga. Confederate General Joseph E. Johnston, failing to block Sherman from reaching the railroad, ordered his 65,000 troops to fall back to a ten-mile-long line from Lost Mountain on the left to a line of cavalry on the right extending behind Noonday Creek. On June 9, after receiving reinforcements and supplies and securing his communication lines, Sherman advanced his armies. The men could see the new Confederate position that ran from Brush Mountain to Pine Mountain and on to Lost Mountain, forming a triangle that, from the Federal position, covered Marietta and the railroad to Atlanta. "On each of these peaks," Sherman reported, "the enemy had his signal station, the summits were crowned with batteries, and the spurs were alive with men busy in felling trees, digging pits, and preparing for the grand struggle impending. The scene was enchanting; too beautiful to be disturbed by the harsh clamor of war; but the Chattahoochee lay beyond, and I had to reach it."

On June 11 Union Major General George H. Thomas's Army of the Cumberland was slowed by hard rains, which continued for more than two weeks. The rains did not, however, halt long-range artillery fire, and on June 14 Federal gunners killed Confederate Lieutenant General Leonidas Polk on Pine Mountain. Sherman wheeled his army toward his left, skirmishing aggressively and extending his right.

On the eighteenth, Johnston pulled back his left, then fell back to a new line along the crest of Kennesaw Mountain and extending southward to high ground overlooking Olley's Creek. Lieutenant General John B. Hood's corps was on the right covering Marietta; Polk's corps, now commanded by Major General William W. Loring, stretched along the crests of Big and Little Kennesaw; and Lieutenant General William J. Hardee's corps blocked the roads to Marietta from the west. On the left, Union Major General James B. McPherson's Army of the Tennessee bombarded the twin-peaked mountain. Thomas extended the Federal lines to the right, and Major General John M. Schofield worked the columns of his Army of the Ohio to the south and east along the Powder Springs Road.

To counter this move, Johnston on June 21 switched Hood's 11,000 men from the right to the left of his line, leaving Major General Joseph Wheeler's cavalry to hold the vacated entrenchments confronting McPherson's infantry and Brigadier General Kenner E. Garrard's cavalry. The next day two of Hood's

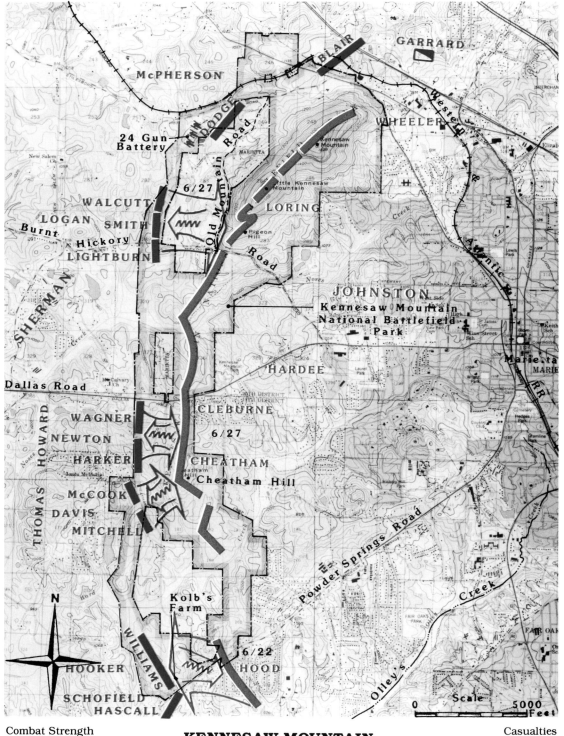

KENNESAW MOUNTAIN

27 June 1864

Combat Strength
110,000
65,000

Casualties
3,000
1,000

divisions struck Brigadier General A. S. Williams's division of Major General Joseph E. Hooker's Twentieth Corps and Major General Milo S. Hascall's division of Schofield's army near Kolb's farm, on the Powder Springs Road southwest of Marietta. Although Hood lost about 1,000 men in his impetuous assault, compared to a Union loss of fewer than 300, he stopped Sherman's flanking movement.

Sherman reported to Washington that he was reduced to siege tactics: "The whole country is one vast fort, and Johnston must have at least fifty miles of connected trenches with abatis and finished batteries. We gain ground daily, fighting all the time. . . . Our lines are now in close contact and the fighting incessant, with a good deal of artillery. As fast as we gain one position the enemy has another all ready. . . . Kennesaw . . . is the key to the whole country."

From the top of Kennesaw Mountain, the Confederates could easily observe Sherman's movements. Wagon trains, hospital encampments, quartermaster and commissary depots, and long lines of infantry were visible as far as the eye could see.

Sherman decided to break the stalemate with an attack on June 27 intended to destroy the Confederate army. He had ordered Schofield to extend his right in order to force Johnston to lengthen his lines. McPherson would make a feint on his extreme left with his cavalry and a division of infantry, but his attack would be aimed at a point southwest of Kennesaw. Thomas was to assault the Confederate works near the center. Schofield would exploit the toehold his troops had gained south of Olley's Creek on June 20. The exact points of assault would be determined by each commander. Preparations were to be carried out as secretly as possible. Each attacking column would try to break a single point in the enemy's line, make a secure lodgment beyond, and then be prepared to advance toward Marietta and the Western and Atlantic Railroad.

At 8:00 A.M., after a "furious cannonade"

by about two hundred guns, the 5,500 Federal soldiers advanced. At Pigeon Hill, near the Burnt Hickory Road, three brigades of Major General John A. Logan's Fifteenth Corps moved forward. The officers knew nothing of the terrain and very little of the Confederate position, and they struggled through a dense thicket and a swampy creek. On the right Brigadier General Joseph A. J. Lightburn's brigade attacked south of the hill and was stopped short of the Confederate breastworks by enfilading fire. Brigadier General Giles A. Smith, commanding the center brigade, moved in two lines against Pigeon Hill. The terrain was rugged and the works were formidable. Farther to the left, Colonel Charles C. Walcutt's brigade worked its way into a deep gorge between Little Kennesaw and Pigeon Hill. Although the attacking troops overran the rifle pits, they failed to dent the main Confederate line. Before the men could get within thirty feet of the Confederates' principal defenses, they were driven to cover.

An hour later, behind schedule, and two miles to the south, two divisions from the Army of the Cumberland (8,000 men) assaulted entrenchments held by the divisions of major generals Benjamin Franklin Cheatham and Patrick R. Cleburne. At the report of two signal guns, Major General John Newton's division of the Fourth Corps and Brigadier General Jefferson C. Davis's division of the Fourteenth Corps advanced. Newton's division charged in two columns of "division closed in mass" — one regiment following another, each with a front of two companies, making a formation ten ranks deep and perhaps forty files across, preceded by a strong line of skirmishers. On the left Brigadier General George D. Wagner's brigade penetrated the dense undergrowth, timber slashing, and abatis to the foot of the Confederate works but was unable to break through. To its right Brigadier General Charles D. Harker's brigade suffered a similar fate. Repulsed once, Harker was shot in an effort to lead his men forward in a second charge.

Davis's division on Newton's right suffered a similar experience. Here the ground sloped down toward the marshy bed of a creek, beyond which the ground rose abruptly to the crest, where it jutted outward to form an angle on Cheatham Hill. At 9:00 A.M., when the Union bombardment ceased, Colonel Daniel McCook's brigade, in columns of regiments at intervals of ten paces, swept down the slope to the creek with orders to make the assault in silence, capture the works at Cheatham Hill, "and then *cheer*, as a signal for the reserves to go forward and beyond us, to secure the railroad and to cut Johnston's army in two." Crossing the stream and the wheat field

beyond, they advanced to the top of the hill. "The air seemed filled with bullets," one survivor recorded, "giving the sensation of moving swiftly against a heavy wind and sleet storm." When McCook's men came to within ten or fifteen feet of the Confederate works, "with one accord the line halted, crouched, and began firing." The brigade lost its momentum, as well as two commanders, nearly all of its field officers, and one third of its men. Colonel John G. Mitchell's brigade, advancing on McCook's right, suffered a similar fate. After brutal hand-to-hand fighting, the Federals dug in. Both sides recalled this place as the "Dead Angle."

The assaults of June 27 cost Sherman about 3,000 casualties; the Confederates lost at most one third of that number. Although the sur-

Kennesaw Mountain National Battlefield Park
© David Muench, 1990

Kennesaw Mountain

vivors of the assaulting columns at Cheatham Hill spent the next five days in advanced works only thirty yards from the Confederate position, there was no more heavy fighting at Kennesaw. On July 2, when Sherman sent McPherson's Army of the Tennessee and Major General George Stoneman's cavalry around the Confederate left, Johnston once again fell back to a previously prepared position at Smyrna, where he could again block the railroad to Atlanta.

At Kennesaw Sherman learned again the cost of assaulting an enemy behind earthworks. For Johnston the lesson learned had been evident since the beginning of the campaign: earthworks can delay but not defeat a determined enemy who can maneuver.

Kennesaw Mountain National Battlefield Park is near Marietta, Georgia, northwest of Atlanta. There are 2,882 acres of the historic battlefield within its authorized boundaries.

BRICES CROSS ROADS

10 June 1864

Edwin C. Bearss

In March 1864, President Abraham Lincoln placed Lieutenant General Ulysses S. Grant, the victor at Vicksburg and Chattanooga, in command of all Union armies. Grant concluded that the only way to win the war was to employ the North's superior resources to destroy the two major Confederate armies. Grant maintained his headquarters with the Army of the Potomac and oversaw the campaign against General Robert E. Lee's Army of Northern Virginia. Major General William T. Sherman, on his return from the Meridian expedition, took charge of the armies massed near Chattanooga. Sherman's mission was the destruction of General Joseph E. Johnston's Army of Tennessee, which was camped in and around Dalton, Georgia, and the capture of Atlanta. The Union armies began their advance in the first week of May. Johnston, a masterful defensive fighter, withdrew to Resaca, where he was reinforced by Lieutenant General Leonidas Polk's two infantry divisions. Major General Stephen Dill Lee commanded the Confederate forces in Mississippi and Alabama.

As Sherman drove toward Atlanta, he was concerned about the security of the single-track railroad over which he supplied his 100,000 men. Major General Nathan Bedford Forrest, the great Confederate cavalry leader, was then based in northeast Mississippi. To

keep Forrest occupied and away from his supply line, Sherman proposed to employ the Union forces based at Memphis and Vicksburg. Early in May Brigadier General Samuel D. Sturgis advanced from Memphis to Ripley and returned without seriously engaging Forrest, who was recruiting for his corps at Tupelo following his raid into western Tennessee and Kentucky.

In late May, while Sherman was facing Johnston in front of New Hope Church, he ordered Sturgis to undertake another expedition to seek out and destroy Forrest's corps. Sturgis left Memphis on June 2 with 8,100 infantry and cavalry and twenty-two cannon manned by 400 artillerists. One cavalry regiment was armed with seven-shot Spencer carbines. The march was methodical, and by June 7 the Union troops were at Ripley. Sturgis's advance came at an inopportune moment for the South because Forrest, in accordance with instructions from General S. D. Lee, had left Tupelo en route to middle Tennessee to raid the Nashville and Chattanooga Railroad, Sherman's lifeline. On June 3, before he crossed the Tennessee River, Forrest was recalled to meet Sturgis.

To counter Sturgis, Forrest deployed his brigades at Rienzi, Booneville, and Baldwyn on the Mobile and Ohio Railroad, with patrols thrown out toward New Albany. On June 9

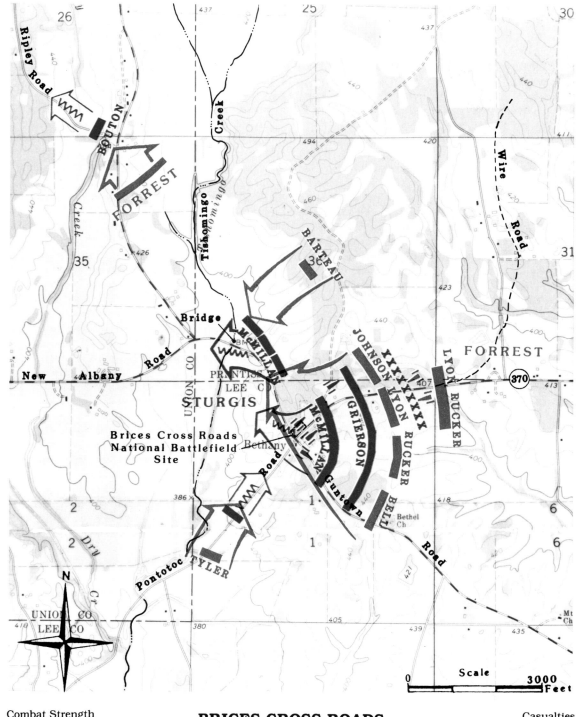

BRICES CROSS ROADS

10 June 1864

Combat Strength
8,100
3,500

Casualties
2,612
493

Scale
0   3000
Feet

Sturgis advanced from Ripley and massed his army on the Stubbs plantation, nine miles northwest of Brices Cross Roads. Lee's plan was for Forrest to engage the Federals near Okolona. Forrest, however, ordered his three columns to meet the Union forces at Brices Cross Roads.

On June 10 Sturgis's 3,300 cavalry, led by Brigadier General Benjamin H. Grierson, broke camp at 6:00 A.M. and started toward Brices. Sturgis's infantry and artillery followed an hour later. It had been raining for days and the roads were muddy. At daybreak the clouds cleared, and the day became hot and humid. Grierson's cavalry put to flight the Confederate patrol sent by Forrest to pinpoint the Union column, and the Federals reached Brices Cross Roads by 9:45. The Union vanguard hounded the Confederates down the Baldwyn Road for about a mile until they encountered one of Forrest's brigades fighting dismounted. Although outnumbered by more than three to one, the Confederates held their own until Forrest arrived from Booneville with Colonel Edward Rucker's brigade. Forrest boldly seized the initiative in slashing attacks in the wooded area, with each of his men armed with two six-shot Colt revolvers. His plan, to beat Grierson's cavalry before Sturgis could bring up his infantry, was successful.

By 1:00 P.M. Forrest, still outnumbered three to one, had beaten Grierson. Sturgis marched the infantry forward on the double, and his men's energy was sapped by the time they reached the crossroads. Colonel Tyree H. Bell's brigade joined Forrest in a frontal attack, which, in conjunction with a dash at the Union force's left and right, compelled Sturgis's army to give ground, grudgingly at first. In bitter fighting the Union soldiers were driven from the crossroads and, with their flanks threatened, fell back into the Tishomingo Creek bottoms. A wagon driven by a frightened teamster overturned and blocked the bridge. Most of the Federals broke and crossed the creek at fords upstream and downstream from the bridge. Forrest led his hard-hitting cavalry up the Ripley Road in an all-out pursuit of Sturgis's battered army. Roadblocks manned by black soldiers were broken as Forrest kept the "skeer" (scare) on Sturgis. As the Union troops straggled across the Hatchie Bottom on the night of June 10, what had been a disorganized retreat became a rout. Fourteen cannon and more than one hundred wagons were abandoned. Sturgis declared, "For God's sake, if Mr. Forrest will let me alone, I will let him alone."

The Confederates continued the relentless pursuit throughout the daylight hours on June 11 and captured hundreds of fleeing Federals. On the morning of the thirteenth, Sturgis and the disorganized and dismayed survivors of his once-proud army were back in Memphis. Union casualties in the battle of Brices Cross Roads were 2,612 killed, wounded, or missing, while Forrest's command had only 493 killed and wounded in the fight. Forrest captured 250 wagons and ambulances, 18 cannon, and 5,000 stands of small arms.

The battle of Brices Cross Roads was a bitter defeat for the Union troops. It is of national significance because of the leadership exhibited by General Forrest, one of the few geniuses of the Civil War, and because of the repercussions it had for the Union's grand strategy. The key to the victory was Forrest's use of cavalry as mounted infantry. Horses and mules gave his men mobility, which, combined with their ability to dismount and fight as infantry, meant victory. Although the concept of mounted infantry did not originate with Forrest, British Field Marshal Viscount Garnet J. Wolseley wrote, "Forrest was the first general who in modern days taught us what Truenne and Montecuculli knew so well, namely the use of the true dragoon, the rifleman on horseback, who from being mounted, has all the mobility of the horse soldier." Forrest's men, along with Major General Philip H. Sheridan's corps in the Army of the Potomac, were the precursors of World War II's panzer grenadiers and armored infantry.

Forrest's tactical employment of his heavily armed escort was well in advance of his day. Always at or near the point of danger, he employed his escort as a strategic reserve to exploit successes or to reinforce units struggling to contain an enemy breakthrough.

On June 15, 1864, General Sherman, having learned of the Brices Cross Roads disaster, wrote to Secretary of War Edwin M. Stanton: "But Forrest is the very devil, and I think he has some of our troops under cower. I have two officers at Memphis that will fight all the time — A. J. Smith and Mower. . . . I will order them to make up a force and go out and follow Forrest to the death, if it cost 10,000 lives and breaks the Treasury. There never will be peace in Tennessee till Forrest is dead."

Brices Cross Roads National Battlefield Site is 17 miles north of Tupelo on U.S. Route 45 and 6 miles west of Baldwyn on State Route 370 in Mississippi. It is administered by the Natchez Trace Parkway. One acre of the historic battlefield is within its authorized boundaries.

Major General Nathan Bedford Forrest

TUPELO

14–15 July 1864

Frank Allen Dennis

Confederate Major General Nathan Bedford Forrest openly broke with General Braxton Bragg in October 1863 and obtained an essentially independent command from President Jefferson Davis. From late 1863 until the Franklin-Nashville campaign of November–December 1864, Forrest and his gray riders operated throughout western Tennessee and northern Mississippi, with a foray in the spring of 1864 north as far as Paducah, Kentucky, on the Ohio River. At Tupelo, Mississippi, Forrest made one of his attempts to interdict the long supply line to Major General William T. Sherman's armies in Georgia. The Confederate forces were led by Lieutenant General Stephen Dill Lee, commander of the Department of Mississippi, Alabama, and East Louisiana. Lee and Forrest were friends, and their relationship appears to have been cordial, even though the uneducated Tennessee cavalry genius, who had grown rich as a slave trader and planter, had little in common with his commander, a West Point artillery officer from South Carolina. As large as Forrest loomed in Confederate mythology, he was larger still in the fears of the Federals. They knew of his flinty courage at Fort Donelson and of his daring and his swift recovery from a severe wound at Shiloh.

Major General Cadwallader Colden Washburn, commander of the Federal District of West Tennessee, was ordered to "get" Forrest even if, in Sherman's words, "it cost 10,000 lives and breaks the Treasury." Washburn ordered Major General Andrew Jackson Smith, a veteran of the Vicksburg and Red River campaigns, to move his 14,000 troops from Memphis fifty miles due east to La Grange, Tennessee. The Federals then left La Grange on July 5, headed toward a rendezvous with Forrest. It strains definition to call this movement a march; it was more like a tiptoe. Roll was called three times daily, allegedly to prevent stragglers, but more likely to prevent desertion. Memphis and La Grange were friendly places compared to Forrest's haunts in northeast Mississippi.

Sherman had authorized Smith to punish the area and its people. His forces burned much of Ripley, Mississippi, eighteen miles south of the Tennessee line, and then headed due south. They crossed the Tallahatchie River at New Albany and moved toward Pontotoc, seventeen miles west of Tupelo. Smith had two infantry divisions from his Sixteenth Corps, commanded by Brigadier General James Anthony Mower and Colonel David Moore. Brigadier General Benjamin H. Grierson commanded a Sixteenth Corps cavalry division, and Colonel Edward Bouton led the First Brigade of U.S. Colored Troops (USCT). During the march most of Smith's cavalry cov-

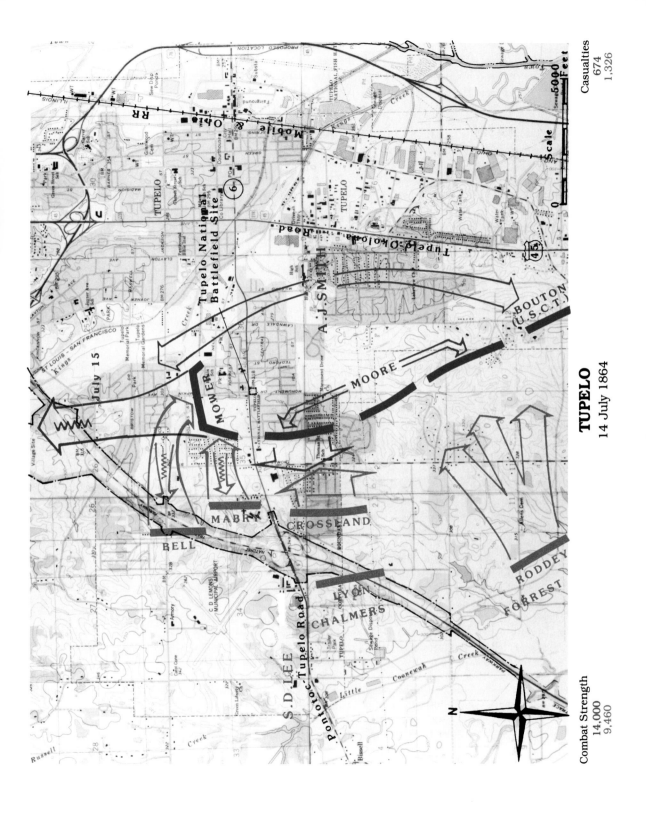

TUPELO

14 July 1864

Combat Strength
14,000
9,460

Casualties
674
1,326

ered the march to the left (east) side, frequently fighting running skirmishes with Confederate scouts.

Meanwhile Forrest and Lee were responding to Smith's movements by hastily gathering their scattered forces. By the time the battle was joined at Tupelo on July 14, three cavalry divisions and one of infantry were on or near the field. Brigadier generals James R. Chalmers, Abraham Buford, and Philip D. Roddey commanded the cavalry divisions, while Brigadier General Hylan B. Lyon directed a loose assortment of infantry, dismounted cavalry, and artillery. Total Confederate strength was 9,460.

Intelligence gathered by Confederate scouts during the Federal thrust was accurate. Forrest and Lee knew that the enemy strength was between 12,000 and 15,000; they knew the number of Union artillery pieces; and they even knew about the unusually tight control regarding roll calls and stragglers. What they did not know was exactly where the Federals were headed. For that matter, neither did Smith. Lee and Forrest knew that Smith's main assignment was to keep the Confederate cavalry away from Sherman's supply line, and they knew that Smith would do whatever damage he could to the Confederates' vital Mobile and Ohio Railroad, which ran through Tupelo and Okolona.

Lee's objective was to fight Smith quickly and whip him decisively so he could send reinforcements to Major General Dabney Maury to help him protect Mobile. Lee had an additional problem: Forrest was suffering intense pain from boils.

If Forrest could have picked his spot to fight, it would have been near Okolona, eighteen miles due south of Tupelo. Forrest knew the area well, and the route of Smith's march seemed to indicate that the Federals would head in that direction. Okolona was twenty-two miles southeast of Pontotoc, where Smith camped on the night of July 11–12. Anticipating that Smith would march toward Okolona, Lee and Forrest had positioned most of the Confederate troops closer to Okolona than to Tupelo. But when Smith abruptly turned east toward Tupelo on July 13, a race began. Grierson's cavalry, leading the Federal column, occupied Tupelo by noon and tore up portions of the Mobile and Ohio Railroad. The remainder of Smith's forces followed, tailed and flanked by Confederates.

Forrest termed Smith's movement toward Tupelo a "retreat." Smith, on the other hand, reported that he had found too many of the enemy along the Pontotoc-Okolona Road and had decided to move on Tupelo to damage the Confederates' railroad. By nightfall the main body of Smith's force had reached Harrisburg, a virtual ghost town one mile west of Tupelo. During the night the Federals constructed fortifications, which Forrest later called "impregnable," from rail fences, cotton bales, and pieces of buildings that had been destroyed at Harrisburg.

On the morning of July 14 the Federal battle line stretched almost two miles in a shallow arc along a low ridge from northwest to southwest of Tupelo, facing open territory dotted by a few cornfields. King's Creek was in the rear, Moore's division was on the left facing southwest, and Mower's division was on the right facing west and north. Bouton's USCT and Grierson's cavalry backed up Moore and guarded the Union left and rear. The Confederate line was in a similar arc, with Roddey's division on the right, Colonel Edward Crossland's Kentucky Brigade in the center, backed by Chalmers and Lyon, and colonels Tyree H. Bell's and Hinchie P. Mabry's brigades on the left. Roddey's wing was recessed behind Crossland, Bell, and Mabry.

The Confederates attacked at about 7:00 A.M. Crossland slid toward Roddey to compensate for the ill-formed line and made a disastrous frontal attack. Mabry moved farther left, while Bell moved toward the center. A series of uncoordinated attacks, uncharacteristic of either Forrest or Lee, spent themselves against the well-defended Federal lines. By 1:00 P.M. the fighting had eased. That night, as the Federals burned what was left of Harrisburg, the flames silhouetted their positions, making them easy marks for Confederate artillery. Forrest even led a night attack against Moore's wing and Bouton's black troops, but he pulled back when the Federals, instead of panicking, opened well-aimed and heavy fire.

On July 15 Smith's forces began moving north toward La Grange from Harrisburg, harried closely by the undaunted Confederates. On a fork of Old Town Creek another confrontation occurred when Bell and Crossland attacked the Federal rear. While coordinating another assault against this position, Forrest was shot in the right foot. Despite his painful wound, he commandeered a buggy and rode among his men to dispel the rumor that he had been killed.

By July 21 Smith's men were back in La Grange. Although the Confederates held the field at Tupelo, the statistics reflect a decisive Federal victory. Estimates vary, but the most reliable figures are 1,326 Confederate casualties and 674 Union. The Confederate force was about two thirds that of the Federals.

The battle of Tupelo was over, and Smith had kept Forrest away from Sherman's supply line. But Forrest still lived.

Tupelo National Battlefield is in Tupelo, Mississippi, on State Route 6. It is administered by the Natchez Trace Parkway. One acre of the historic battlefield is within its authorized boundaries.

CLOYD'S MOUNTAIN

9 May 1864

James I. Robertson, Jr.

Cloyd's Mountain was the largest Civil War battle fought in southwestern Virginia. A future president of the United States was conspicuous on the field, and the engagement produced some of the most violent combat of the entire war. As a result of the action, the Confederacy lost its only rail connection to eastern Tennessee.

The battle resulted from Lieutenant General Ulysses S. Grant's 1864 grand offensive into Virginia. While two Union armies drove toward Richmond and a third advanced into the Shenandoah Valley, another Federal column began creeping through the gaps of the Appalachian Mountains. Its aim was to destroy the Virginia and Tennessee Railroad connecting Richmond with Tennessee. This Union force, under Brigadier General George R. Crook, numbered 6,500 infantry and twelve artillery pieces. For ten days in late April and the beginning of May, Crook's troops struggled through rough country and foul weather to reach the New River railroad bridge and the nearby town of Dublin.

On May 5 Brigadier General Albert G. Jenkins received orders to take command of the meager and scattered Confederate forces in the southwestern part of the state. Jenkins, a heavily bearded cavalry brigadier then recovering from a serious wound received at Gettysburg, had been at his new duties less than a day when he learned of Crook's approach. The Confederate general frantically called in an infantry brigade about to embark by train for the Shenandoah Valley. He also rounded up an artillery battery plus several companies of home guards. Although woefully outnumbered, Jenkins was determined to make a contest of it.

Jenkins and his second-in-command, Brigadier General John McCausland, resolved to make a stand at the parallel wooded bluffs to the east of Cloyd's Mountain, long and imposing, running north to south. Between the two ridges lay a 500-yard-wide open valley, with Back Creek meandering through its center. Bolstered by the last-minute arrival of 700 additional troops, Jenkins had 2,400 Confederates and ten guns stretched along a half-mile front.

The sun had barely risen on May 9, a clear day, when Crook's brigades arrived at Cloyd's Mountain. A quick survey of the Confederate position across the way convinced Crook that a frontal attack would be suicidal. He ordered his brigades to swerve around through underbrush and drive for the Confederate right flank.

Shortly before noon, following a brisk artillery duel, Federal infantry assailed the Confederate works. The West Virginia division, in its first battle, drove to within twenty yards of

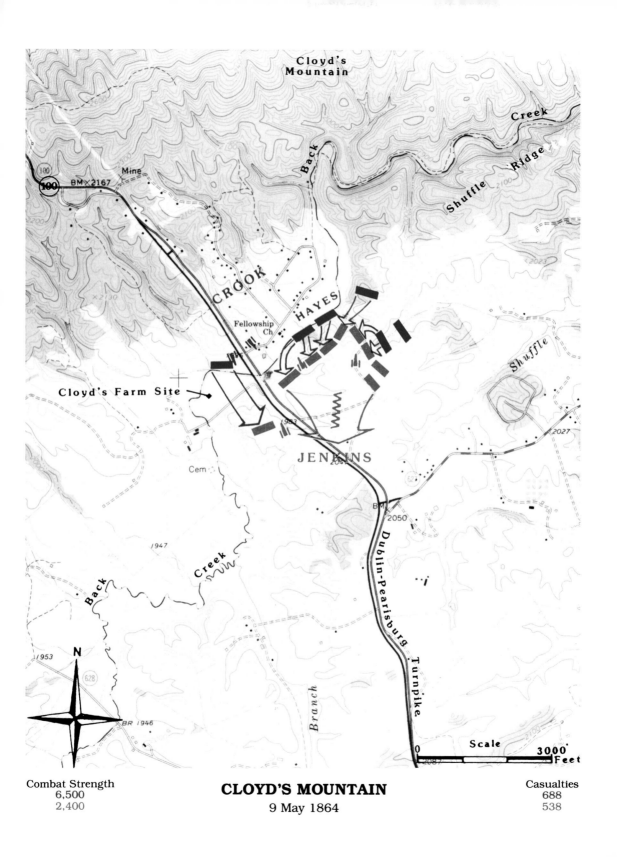

Cloyd's
Mountain

Creek

Back

Shuffle Ridge

BM×2167

Mine

100

CROOK

HAYES

Fellowship
Ch.

Shuffle

Cloyd's Farm Site →

JENKINS

Cem

BM
2050

1947

Creek

Back

Branch

Dublin-Pearisburg Turnpike

1953

628

BR 1946

N

Scale

0   3000
Feet

Combat Strength
6,500
2,400

CLOYD'S MOUNTAIN

9 May 1864

Casualties
688
538

the Confederate line. The West Virginians could go no farther and, in an exposed position, steadily took casualties. On their left the Ohio division likewise became pinned down by musketry. Meanwhile the gunfire caused a thick carpet of leaves to burst into flames. Many wounded and helpless soldiers were cremated.

Jenkins was still desperately shifting troops to his endangered right flank when Colonel Rutherford B. Hayes led his Ohio brigade in a concerted attack against the Confederate right center. Hand-to-hand combat raged in and around the crude earthworks. The battle area became what an Ohioan called "one living, flashing sheet of flame."

As the Union troops began falling back through the smoke and heat, Crook sent two fresh regiments into the action. Other Federals overran the Confederate cannon that had checked their advance. Jenkins fell wounded, his arm shattered. McCausland took command and maintained a spirited rear-guard action for a quarter hour before ordering his outflanked and outmanned soldiers from the field.

The battle lasted little more than an hour, yet the ferocity of the fighting was evident from the casualty lists. Union losses were 688, roughly 10 percent of those engaged. Confederate losses were 538, about 3 percent of their numbers. General Jenkins was captured by the Federals and later died of complications following the amputation of his arm. Crook continued his advance and severed the Virginia and Tennessee Railroad, one of the Confederacy's last vital lifelines, at Dublin.

Cloyd's Mountain battlefield is 43 miles southwest of Roanoke, Virginia, on Interstate 81 and north of Dublin, Virginia, on State Route 100. The entire battlefield is privately owned.

THE WILDERNESS

5–6 May 1864

Noah Andre Trudeau

Though they made few efforts to memorialize it after the war, the soldiers who fought there never forgot the Wilderness. "Imagine," wrote a North Carolina officer named W. A. Smith, "a great, dismal forest containing . . . the worst kind of thicket of second-growth trees . . . so thick with small pines and scrub oak, cedar, dogwood and other growth common to the country . . . [that] one could see barely ten paces." It was, according to the Bostonian Charles Francis Adams, Jr., a "fearfully discouraging place." Civil War correspondent William Swinton argued that it was "impossible to conceive a field worse adapted to the movements of a grand army." Yet two grand armies not only moved through but fought across this area for two bloody days in early May 1864.

The region, which was known as the Wilderness long before the Civil War, lay ten miles west of Fredericksburg, Virginia, a patch of natural entanglement some twelve miles wide and six miles deep along the south bank of the Rapidan River. German colonists brought over in the early eighteenth century by Virginia governor Alexander Spotswood had tried to tame the Wilderness and failed. Spotswood's attempt to establish mining in the area resulted in heavy cutting of timber to shore up the mine tunnels, plank the roads, and fuel small iron-smelting operations, such as the one at Catharine Furnace. When the would-be

industry was abandoned, the forest returned with a vengeance; by 1860 it had produced an almost impenetrable second-growth woodland.

The land shaped the strategies of the opposing forces that met there. For Union planners the Wilderness was something to be crossed with the least possible delay. For General Robert E. Lee the Wilderness was an ally that would negate the enemy's numerical advantage in artillery and men. From the moment on May 4 when Lee learned that the massive Union army was heading into the Wilderness, he planned to stop it there.

The Federal movement was one part of Lieutenant General Ulysses S. Grant's grand strategy to squeeze the pressure points of the Confederacy. Simultaneously with this move, other Union forces were advancing aggressively against Atlanta and Petersburg and into the fertile Shenandoah Valley. The role given to the Army of the Potomac and its commander, Major General George Gordon Meade, seemed simple: engage the Army of Northern Virginia in battle, defeat it if possible, and under no circumstances allow it enough freedom of action to upset Union plans. To make certain Meade carried out this role, Grant made his headquarters in the field with the Army of the Potomac.

The Union army entered the Wilderness in

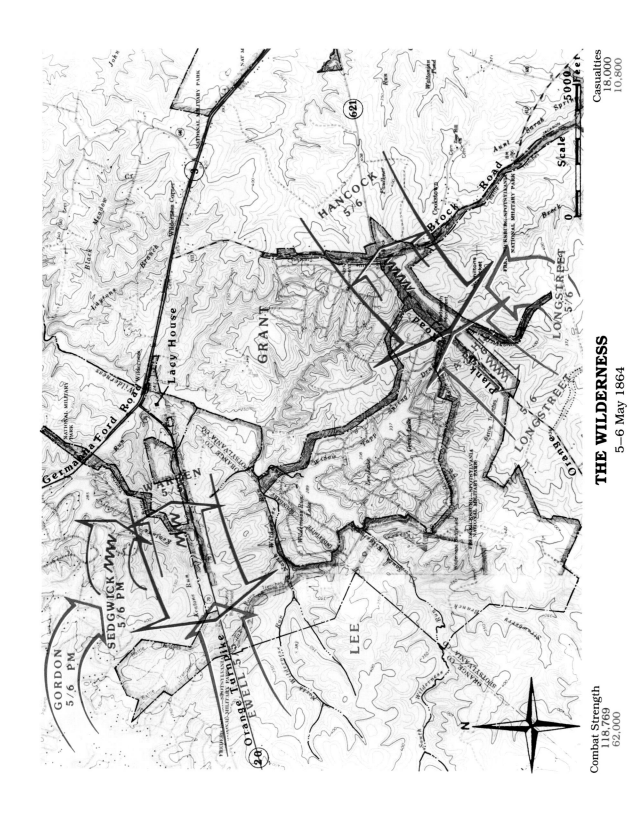

THE WILDERNESS

5–6 May 1864

Combat Strength
118,769
62,000

Casualties
18,000
10,800

two dusty, spiky columns totaling 118,769 men. The Union Fifth, Sixth, and Ninth corps marched in from the northwest via the Germanna Ford Road. Farther east the Union Second Corps, most of the Yankee cavalry, and the long army supply train crossed the Rapidan at Ely's Ford to camp for the night on another Wilderness battlefield of unpleasant memory — Chancellorsville. Lee's 62,000-man army moved from its winter quarters west and south of the Wilderness. Lieutenant General Richard S. "Baldy" Ewell's Second Corps marched eastward along the Orange Turnpike (now State Route 20), while Lieutenant General A. P. Hill's Third Corps moved on a parallel course farther south, on the Orange Plank Road (now State Route 621). These two corps were a day closer to the Union army than Lieutenant General James Longstreet's.

Union plans to clear the Wilderness on May 5 were upset shortly after dawn when some of Major General Gouverneur Warren's Fifth Corps, screening the area to the east, spotted Ewell's men moving toward them. Soon afterward reports came to Union headquarters near the Lacy house of Hill's movement farther south, which threatened to sever connections between the two-pronged Union advance.

Fighting began early in the afternoon alongside the Orange Turnpike and raged across a small clearing known as Saunders Field. The combat spread slowly southward as more units came into line. Initial Union gains were rolled back by savage Confederate counterattacks. Even the late-afternoon arrival of portions of Major General John Sedgwick's Sixth Corps was unable to break the stalemate.

Farther south, Hill's corps was less successful. A small Union cavalry force managed to delay Hill's eastward advance long enough for a Union division to seize and hold the vital intersection of the Plank and Brock roads. Later that afternoon troops from Major General Winfield S. Hancock's Second Corps arrived on the scene and launched a poorly coordinated but fierce attack that was finally stopped through the use of every available Confederate reserve. By nightfall the northern half of the Confederate line was bloodied but solid. Its southern half, however, was scattered, exhausted, and ill prepared for what the morning would surely bring. Robert E. Lee, who had not wanted to fight a major battle with only two thirds of his army, downplayed the problem. Around midnight he refused a request from Hill to regroup, with the excuse that Longstreet's corps would arrive from Gordonsville in time to take the burden of battle off Hill's men.

Dawn came, but not Longstreet. At Grant's urging, Union forces attacked at first light. The assaults along the axis of the Orange Turnpike stalled before effective Confederate defenses. To the south, attacking westward in a direction marked out by the Orange Plank Road, Union forces met significant success. Just when it seemed that Lee's right flank would be destroyed, Longstreet's men did arrive. Their vicious counterattack stunned the Federals, who came to a standstill. The drama of Longstreet's arrival was heightened when an exuberant Lee tried personally to lead the first counterattacking units across the open fields of the Tapp farm. Brigadier General John Gregg's Texans politely but firmly sent him back. The cries of "Lee to the rear" capped one of the most memorable episodes of the battle. Longstreet's men later went on an offensive of their own, flanked the advancing Union line, and sent it whirling back to a line of entrenchments thrown up earlier along the north-south Brock Road.

The confusing tangles of the Wilderness knew no allegiance. At the high point of the Confederate success that day, Longstreet, Lee's ablest corps commander, was seriously wounded by his own men. Early that evening an all-out Confederate offensive surged against both flanks of the Union line. The assault across the bloody ground along the Plank Road was stopped at the Brock Road line. To the north, Confederate Brigadier General

John B. Gordon led his men on a flanking swing against the Union right, which succeeded for a brief, intoxicating moment, but any substantial gains were nullified by darkness and the unwillingness of the field commander, Major General Jubal Early, to press the matter.

In the May 5–6 fighting in the Wilderness nearly the full force of both armies was engaged. Union casualties tallied nearly 18,000, and the Confederate toll was estimated at 10,800. To the claustrophobic nature of the combat was added the terror of numerous flash fires that raged through the dry underbrush, incinerating soldiers too badly wounded to escape. A northern private wrote that "it was a blind and bloody hunt to the death, in bewildering thickets, rather than a battle." A southern officer declared, "I do not think I have ever seen a battlefield where there was more destruction and more horrors than that of the Wilderness."

Despite his heavy losses, General Grant ordered the Army of the Potomac to continue its campaign by sliding past Lee's flank and moving south. For the first time in his Civil War experience, Robert E. Lee faced an adversary who had the determination to press on despite the cost. Grant's overland campaign moved along to other bloody battlefields, ending in the slow strangulation of Lee's army at Petersburg. The moment of truth came in the Wilderness. Once Grant decided to move forward and not retreat, it was just a question of time. The battle of the Wilderness marked the beginning of the end for the Army of Northern Virginia and for the Confederacy itself.

The Wilderness Battlefield, a unit of Fredericksburg and Spotsylvania National Military Park, is on State Route 3, west of Fredericksburg, Virginia. There are 1,981 acres of the historic battlefield within the authorized boundaries of this unit; 212 of these are privately owned.

The Wilderness

SPOTSYLVANIA COURT HOUSE

8–21 May 1864

William D. Matter

As darkness settled over northern Virginia on the evening of May 6, 1864, the two-day series of military engagements that would become known as the battle of the Wilderness came to a close. The first encounter between the war's most prominent military leaders — Lieutenant General Ulysses S. Grant, commanding all United States armies from a headquarters in the field with the Army of the Potomac, and General Robert E. Lee, commanding the Army of Northern Virginia — had ended. At 6:30 A.M. on May 7 Grant issued a directive to the Army of the Potomac commander, Major General George Gordon Meade. The order, one of the most important of Grant's military career, began, "General: Make all preparations during the day for a night march to take position at Spotsylvania Court-House."

On the night of May 7–8 the Union Fifth Corps and the Confederate First Corps, moving independently and unknown to each other, led the marches of their respective armies toward Spotsylvania Court House. In the morning the lead elements met on the Spindle farm along the Brock Road (today State Route 613), and the fighting lasted throughout the day as more units from each army arrived. Elements of the Federal Sixth Corps joined in the attack around midday, but the Union troops were unable to force their way through, and nightfall found two sets of parallel fieldworks

across the Brock Road. What the Federals had thought would be a rapid march into open country had stalled behind these works. The battle of Spotsylvania Court House was under way.

More units of each army continued to arrive on May 9. The Confederate Third Corps marched along the Shady Grove Church Road (today State Route 608) to the village of Spotsylvania Court House. The Federal Second Corps, commanded by Major General Winfield S. Hancock, moved from Todd's Tavern along the Brock Road, then moved off the road to take position to the right of the Fifth Corps, overlooking the Po River. Late in the afternoon troops from the Second Corps crossed the river and moved east on the Shady Grove Church Road as far as the Block House bridge over the Po before darkness halted them.

During the night Lee sent one brigade, commanded by Brigadier General William Mahone, to block and one division, led by Major General Henry Heth, to attack the Federal force the following day. On the morning of May 10 the three divisions of the Federal Second Corps south of the Po River were directed to return north of that stream to assault another segment of the Confederate line. Two divisions recrossed successfully, but the third crossed under Confederate fire.

Elsewhere that day, the Federal command-

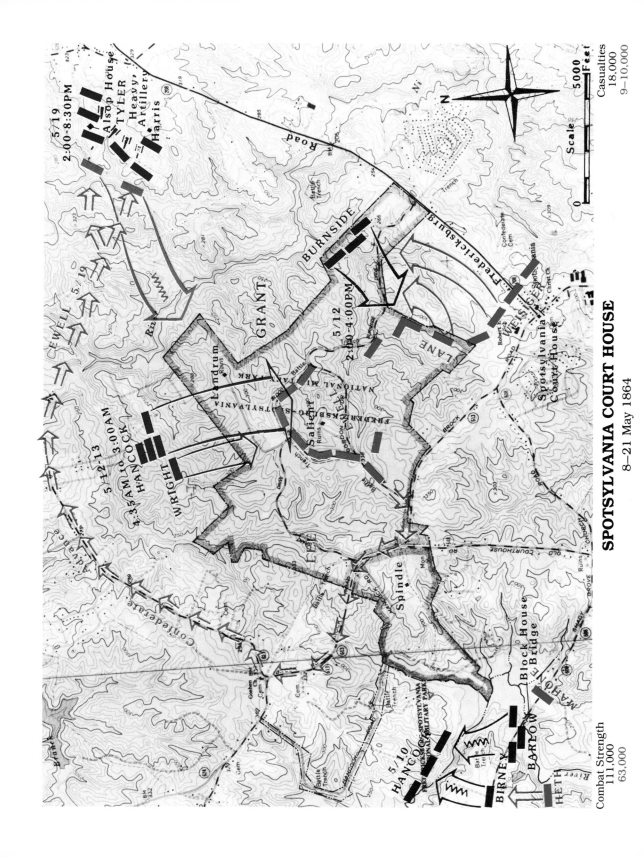

SPOTSYLVANIA COURT HOUSE

8–21 May 1864

Combat Strength
111,000
63,000

Casualties
18,000
9–10,000

Scale

0 ___ 5,000
Feet

ers attempted to execute a combined attack all along the lines. A series of piecemeal assaults by elements of the Fifth and Second corps at Laurel Hill proved unsuccessful. A bit farther east a charge by twelve Union regiments against the western face of a great salient in the Confederate line was far more carefully arranged. The British military historian C. F. Atkinson, writing in 1908 in *Grant's Campaigns of 1864 and 1865*, labeled the charge "one of the classic infantry attacks of military history." This dramatic action also failed, because of the failure of a supporting assault and because of strong Confederate counterstrokes.

Grant decided to attack the apex of the Confederate salient with the entire Federal Second Corps on May 12. Two divisions of Major General Ambrose Burnside's Ninth Corps were to attack the east face of the Confederate position simultaneously. The Second Corps moved into position after dark.

At 4:35 A.M. on May 12 the Federal Second Corps moved forward from its position near the Brown house, advanced across the Landrum farm clearing, and struck the apex of the salient. Continuing forward for about half a mile, the Federals captured approximately 3,000 prisoners from Major General Richard S. Ewell's Second Corps before being driven back to the outside of the works by Confederate reserve forces. Both sides forwarded reinforcements (the Federals added units of Major General Horatio Wright's Sixth Corps to the assault), and the northern face of the salient became the focus of close firing and fighting that lasted for twenty-three hours. In midafternoon a division of the Ninth Corps advanced, and a portion of it was struck by an advancing pair of Confederate brigades, James H. Lane's and David A. Weisiger's, in an area approximately three quarters of a mile north of the village of Spotsylvania Court House. The resulting engagement was a wild melee in dark woods, with every soldier trying to fight his way back to his own lines.

A Federal Second Corps soldier, viewing the churned landscape around the "bloody angle" on the morning of May 13, wrote: "The trench on the Rebel side of the works was filled with their dead piled together in every way with their wounded. The sight was terrible and ghastly." Sometime before 2:00 A.M. on May 13 a large oak tree just behind the west face of the salient crashed to the ground. Its trunk, twenty inches in diameter, had been severed by musket balls.

The Confederates successfully withdrew to a newly constructed line along the base of the salient at 3:00 A.M. On the night of May 13–14 the Federal Fifth and Sixth corps marched around to the Fredericksburg Road (today State Route 208) and went into position south of that road on the left of the Ninth Corps. On May 15 the Second Corps joined the other three Union corps so that the Federal lines, east of the village, now faced west and ran north and south. Three days later two Union corps returned to the salient and attacked the Confederates' final line but were unsuccessful.

On May 19 Ewell's Confederate Second Corps made a forced reconnaissance around to the Fredericksburg Road to attempt to locate the right flank of the Union line. There they ran into some newly arrived Federal troops that had formerly manned the forts surrounding Washington, D.C. These heavy artillerymen, most of whom were serving under Brigadier General Robert O. Tyler, were acting as infantry for the first time. The resulting engagement on the Harris farm exacted a heavy toll on both sides: it cost the Confederates 900 casualties and the Federals slightly more than 1,500.

The battle of Spotsylvania Court House was over. If Grant's intention had been to defeat or even destroy the Army of Northern Virginia, he was unsuccessful at Spotsylvania. Assuming that Lee's primary objective was to hold the line of the Rapidan River and keep the enemy out of central Virginia, the battles of the Wilderness and Spotsylvania can be considered strategic defeats. However, by delaying

**Fredericksburg and Spotsylvania
National Military Park**
Spotsylvania, the Bloody Angle. © David Muench,
1990

Grant for two weeks at Spotsylvania, Lee permitted other Confederate forces to resist Union efforts in the vicinity of Richmond and in the Shenandoah Valley, unmolested by the Army of the Potomac.

Confederate casualties for the two-week-long battle were estimated at 9,000–10,000 (combat strength: 63,000). Federal casualties were reported as slightly less than 18,000 (combat strength: 111,000). Perhaps the most notable death was that of Sixth Corps commander Major General John Sedgwick, killed by a sharpshooter's bullet as he prowled the front lines on May 9. Shortly before, Sedgwick had chided some infantrymen trying to dodge the occasional minié balls whistling past with the comment that the Confederates "couldn't hit an elephant at this distance."

Both armies departed Spotsylvania on May 20 and 21. Lee rode south, aware that he had to avoid a siege of Richmond or the Confederacy would be doomed. He would next meet Grant at the North Anna River.

Grant had sent a dispatch on May 11 declaring, "I propose to fight it out on this line if it takes all summer." It would take that long and more.

Spotsylvania Court House Battlefield, a unit of Fredericksburg and Spotsylvania National Military Park, is on state routes 613 and 208, southwest of Fredericksburg, Virginia, and north of Spotsylvania Court House, 45 miles south of Washington, D.C. There are 1,448 acres of the historic battlefield within the authorized boundaries of this unit; 105 of these are privately owned.

NORTH ANNA RIVER

23–26 May 1864

J. Michael Miller

The battle of North Anna River was the culmination of the 1864 overland campaign, which began with the battle of the Wilderness and continued at Spotsylvania Court House. General Robert E. Lee knew Lieutenant General Ulysses S. Grant had an overwhelming superiority in numbers. He also knew that Grant could not be defeated in open battle. Lee's plan after Spotsylvania was to continue to fight Grant behind earthworks until the Confederates had an opportunity to crush the Union army. At some point during the campaign of May 1864, Grant would make an error and leave himself open to attack. Until that time Lee would conserve his army and wait.

The opportunity came near the North Anna River. On May 21 Grant lured Lee from behind his earthworks at Spotsylvania by sending an entire army corps to Milford Station to threaten Hanover Junction, the intersection of two Confederate supply lines to Richmond. The separation of the Union infantry from the main body of the Army of the Potomac invited Lee to attack. The Army of Northern Virginia marched down the Telegraph Road and other back roads to protect the junction, its vanguard arriving at the North Anna River on the morning of May 22. The Confederate troops relaxed in the shade and bathed off the grime of two long weeks of fighting.

Lee was confident that Grant would do as all his previous opponents had done: hold his army in check for several weeks to recuperate from the heavy fighting of the Wilderness and Spotsylvania and then continue to advance. Grant had no such intention. He knew that both armies had suffered heavy losses, and he concluded that since Lee had not attacked the exposed men at Milford Station on May 21, the Confederate army was too damaged for offensive operations. Early on the morning of May 23 the Union army marched south to the North Anna River, expecting easy progress.

The lead Union column reached the river along the Telegraph Road, surprising the Confederates, who had not entrenched. Faulty maps confused Grant's columns, but they deployed to cross the river and open the road to Richmond. Union Major General Winfield S. Hancock's Second Corps moved against the Telegraph Road bridge, while the Fifth Corps, commanded by Major General Gouverneur K. Warren, marched upstream to cross the North Anna at a ford at Jericho Mill. Lee, believing the Union forces were only a reinforced scouting party, kept most of his men in camp. He left a single brigade on the north bank of the river to cover the Telegraph Road bridge and awaited further Union movements.

In the late afternoon of May 23, Union artillery signaled an assault on the Confederate brigade on the Telegraph Road. Lee, now

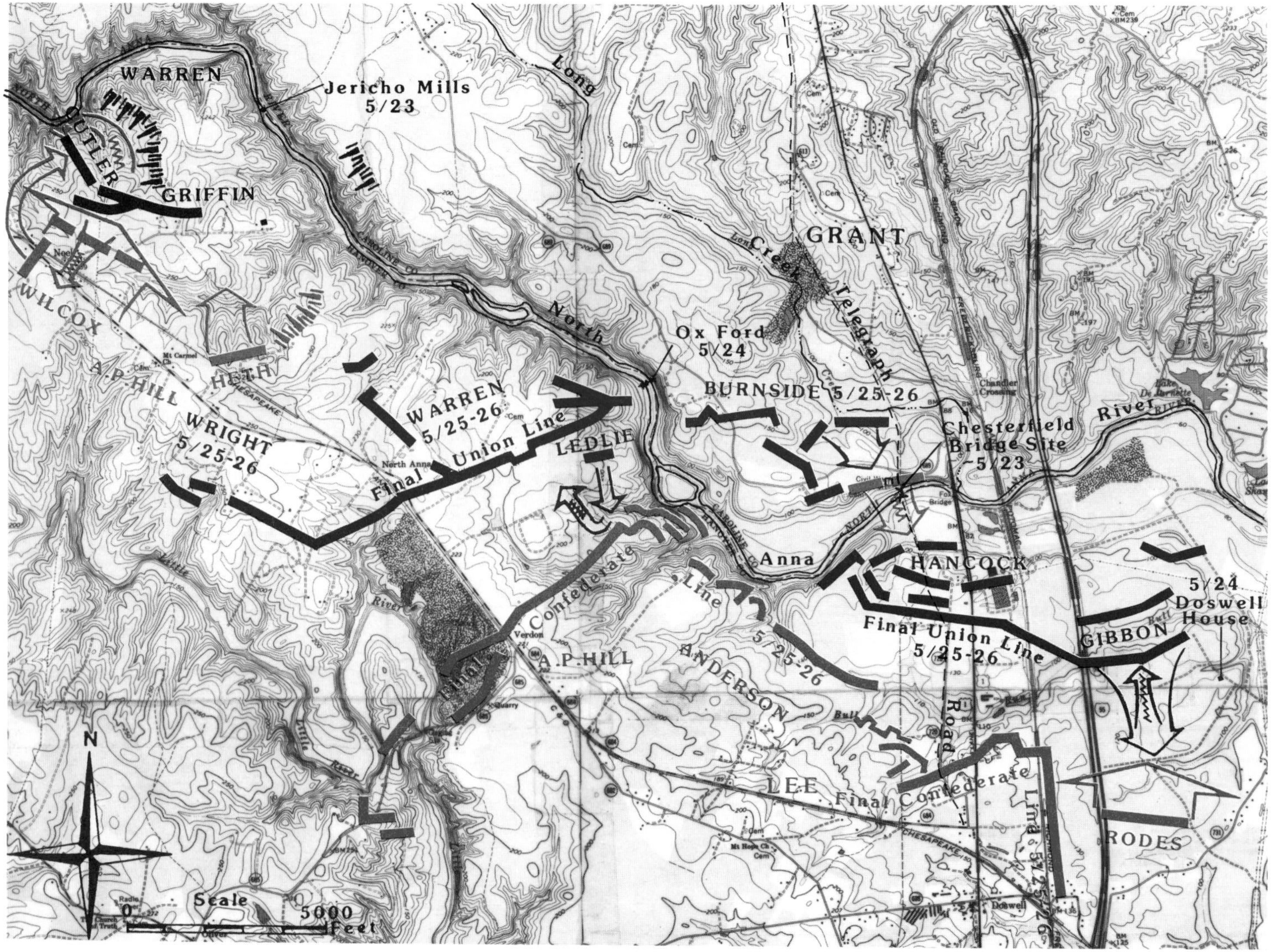

NORTH ANNA RIVER

23–26 May 1864

Combat Strength
68,000
53,000

Casualties
2,623
2,517

alerted to the Union intention to attack, still believed the thrust to be a small one, so he left the single brigade on the north bank. At 6:00 P.M. two Union brigades attacked, charging across Long Creek into an open plain, where they were slowed by Confederate artillery fire. They continued their advance and drove the Confederates back across the river in confusion, capturing the bridge intact. The bridge provided Grant with the necessary access to the south side of the river for his advance on May 24. Lee's men tried to burn the bridge during the night but were unsuccessful. The Confederates did destroy a railway bridge downstream.

At Jericho Mill the Union Fifth Corps crossed the river with little trouble and camped on the south bank. The supposedly formidable Confederate defense line on the North Anna River had been easily breached. The Federals met so little opposition that most began to cook their evening meal without entrenching. However, the Union crossing had been reported to Confederate Lieutenant General A. P. Hill, who ordered an attack before dark. He took the Union line by surprise, but the Federal forces rallied behind three batteries of artillery, which slowed the Confederate attack. Infantry reinforcements drove Hill's men back at nightfall. Additional Confederate troops arrived on the field in time to join in the fighting, but they were committed to the opposite side of the battlefield instead of bolstering the attack.

Under the cover of darkness Lee pondered his army's awkward position. Grant had pierced his defenses in two separate places, making a river defense line impossible. If Lee retreated any closer to Richmond, he would lose his most valuable tool, maneuverability. If Grant got too close to Richmond, Lee could prevent its capture only by keeping his army between Grant and the city. Lee had to defeat Grant on the North Anna River or lead the defense of Richmond.

Lee held a conference of his officers at Hanover Junction and devised a remarkable plan.

He decided to form his army into an inverted V with the point on the North Anna River at Ox Ford, a crossing that the Confederates still held. The end of one arm of the V rested on the Little River, the other on a bend of the North Anna as it flowed to the Pamunkey River. Hill's Third Corps held the left arm of the V, while Major General Richard H. Anderson's First Corps and Lieutenant General Richard S. Ewell's Second Corps held the right arm. The formation was intended to draw Grant over the river in two places separated by the V: Jericho Mill and the Telegraph Road bridge. Grant's army would be split into three pieces, one at Jericho Mill on the south bank of the North Anna, one on the north bank (unable to cross at Ox Ford), and one on the south bank on the Telegraph Road. Lee could hold one side of his V with a small force and then concentrate his army against one of the three Federal sections and crush it.

Grant fell into the trap on May 24. Finding the Confederates gone from in front of his Jericho Mill and Telegraph Road bridgeheads, he assumed that Lee had given up the fight and retreated to the defense of Richmond. He ordered his army to pursue. Major General Horatio G. Wright's Sixth Corps and Warren's Fifth Corps faced the V on the Union right, while Major General Ambrose E. Burnside's Ninth Corps held the center. Hancock's Second Corps completed the concentration, facing the V on the Union left. Advancing formations of Federal infantry met bloody repulses in a driving rainstorm at Ox Ford and the Doswell house on the evening of May 24. A Union Ninth Corps brigade, led into hopeless combat by its drunken commander at Ox Ford, was butchered by the Confederates, who called out to their enemy, "Come on to Richmond." A Second Corps division was mauled at the Doswell house by a mere reinforced Confederate skirmish line, often in hand-to-hand combat.

Not until evening did Grant realize that Lee had constructed overnight the strongest field fortification the Union general had ever faced. Grant ordered his army to entrench, and by dawn of the following day the Union army was safely under cover of heavy earthworks. The two armies skirmished that day and on May 26. The battle involved 68,000 Union soldiers and 53,000 Confederates. Losses were about equal: Union 2,623, Confederate 2,517.

Grant withdrew, then moved to within a day's march of the Confederate capital. Why did Lee allow Grant to pass out of his trap? The Confederate leader became so ill on May 24 that he was confined to his tent and unable to lead his men. He repeated over and over, "We must strike them a blow, we must never allow them to pass us again." But he had no trusted lieutenant to lead the attack.

Grant and his army escaped, and it was on to Richmond.

North Anna River battlefield is on U.S. Route 1 near Doswell, Virginia, 15 miles north of Richmond, on Interstate 95. The entire battlefield is privately owned.

Jericho Mill on the North Anna River

COLD HARBOR

31 May–3 June 1864

Richard J. Sommers

Lieutenant General Ulysses S. Grant's Federals and General Robert E. Lee's Confederates had fought almost incessantly from May 5 to May 24 at the Wilderness, Spotsylvania, and the North Anna River. Checked at the battle of the North Anna, Grant withdrew to the north bank overnight on May 26–27, then resumed his characteristic strategic advance around the Confederate right. Such advances assured him of uninterrupted supplies up Virginia's tidal rivers and, more important, allowed him to preserve the strategic initiative and forge farther into Virginia.

Major General Philip H. Sheridan's one infantry and two cavalry divisions led the way down the North Anna and its parent stream, the Pamunkey, crossing into Hanover County at Hanovertown on May 27. The following day the four Federal infantry corps crossed both there and upstream at Nelson's Ferry. The Union army was now safely south of the Pamunkey and east of the Confederates guarding the two vital railroads running north from Richmond.

While the infantry was crossing the river, Sheridan struck south, overcame heavy Confederate cavalry resistance at Enon Church on May 28, and secured the crucial Haw's Shop intersection. Behind Sheridan's cavalry screen, Major General George G. Meade's Army of the Potomac turned northwest and west toward the railroads on May 29. To meet this threat, Lee skillfully maneuvered his ten infantry divisions onto the low ridge along the headwaters of Totopotomoy Creek. For three days heavy skirmishing flared near Polly Hundley's Corner, Pole Green Church, the Whitlock house, and Sydnor's Mill. Meade overran some outer works but could not — and did not really attempt to — crack Lee's main position.

The efforts of the Union Sixth Corps to turn Lee's left were mired along the swampy Crump's Creek. The ground at Bethesda Church was more favorable, but when the ever-aggressive Lee struck the Federal left there on May 30, the results were not favorable. Major General Jubal A. Early's Second Corps drove an advance Union brigade from Bethesda Church but was repulsed by Major General Gouverneur K. Warren's main Fifth Corps.

Lee and Early were not the only commanders seeking strategic advantage in the unoccupied country south from Totopotomoy Creek to the Chickahominy River. On May 30 Sheridan forced Confederate cavalry from the Old Church Road crossing of Matadequin Creek. He continued southwestward on May 31 and drove the cavalry, as well as a feeble foot brigade, from the crucial Old Cold Harbor crossroads.

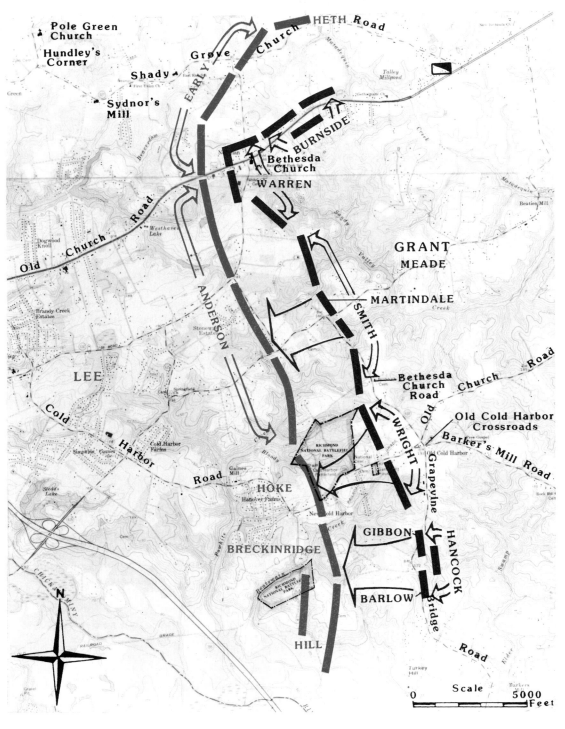

Pole Green
Church

Hundley's
Corner

Sydnor's
Mill

Shady

Grove

Church

HETH Road

EARLY

BURNSIDE

Bethesda
Church

WARREN

GRANT
MEADE

MARTINDALE

SMITH

ANDERSON

Old Church Road

LEE

Cold

Harbor

Road

Bethesda
Church
Road

Old Church Road

Old Cold Harbor
Crossroads

Barker's Mill Road

WRIGHT

Grapevine

HOKE

BRECKINRIDGE

GIBBON

HANCOCK

BARLOW

Bridge

HILL

Road

N

Scale
0   5000
Feet

Combat Strength
114,000
59,000

COLD HARBOR
3 June 1864   4:30 A.M.

Casualties
10,000
4,000

On the roads radiating from that point, Grant could threaten not only the Confederate army to the northwest but Richmond itself, just ten miles to the southwest beyond the Chickahominy. He could also cover his new depot at White House on the Pamunkey and prevent the interception of his reinforcements.

Those reinforcements, nine Army of the James brigades under Major General William F. Smith of the Eighteenth Corps, sailed down the James from Bermuda Hundred, then up the York and Pamunkey to White House, where they landed on May 30 and 31. One brigade remained there, and the others, 10,000 strong, marched toward Grant. Misworded orders led them astray up the Pamunkey instead of directly to Sheridan. On discovering the error, they trudged south over narrow, dusty roads into Old Cold Harbor, exhausted by ten extra miles of marching. Still, by 3:00 P.M. on June 1 they began reaching the front.

Throughout May, Lee too had requested reinforcements. Seven of his own brigades and Major General John C. Breckinridge's two Shenandoah Valley brigades joined him in the middle of May. Now that he was near Richmond, he asked for more troops from General P. G. T. Beauregard's army blocking the Army of the James at Bermuda Hundred. Lee's appeals, initially unproductive, turned to demands as he learned of Smith's approach. Minutes before he was ordered by Richmond to act, Beauregard dispatched Major General Robert F. Hoke's division to Lee.

Hoke's van reached Old Cold Harbor on May 31 but could not save it from the subsequent Federal attack. By the next day his whole division was massed to the west. Early's small corps to the northwest exchanged places with Lieutenant General Richard H. Anderson's larger First Corps in the center. Once on the right, Anderson advanced southeastward and eastward against Old Cold Harbor with Major General Joseph B. Kershaw's and Hoke's divisions on June 1.

Intelligence reports of the danger led Sheridan to withdraw from Old Cold Harbor. Meade, however, ordered him to return and hold the intersection at all costs. Sheridan's dismounted cavalry poured devastating fire from their repeating carbines into the Confederate attackers. Kershaw's inexperienced van broke and fled, sweeping his veterans off, too. Even worse, the typically uncooperative Hoke remained inactive. Anderson's great counterattack failed totally, and he then withdrew onto a north-south ridge between Old and New Cold Harbor and hastily began fortifying.

The tactical initiative reverted to the Federals. About 10:00 A.M. Major General Horatio G. Wright's Sixth Corps from the Union far right replaced Sheridan's troopers at Old Cold Harbor. Six hours later Smith's arriving Eighteenth Corps deployed to Wright's right.

Although the hour was late, Meade attacked. Two divisions each from Wright's and Smith's corps struck west from Old Cold Harbor at 6:00 P.M. They drove skirmishers from a wood line, then continued over the broad open slope up to Anderson's breastworks. Heavy fire stopped the outer two divisions, but the two center divisions poured up a ravine and penetrated the line between Hoke's left and Kershaw's right, routing two Confederate brigades. Before the Federals could exploit the breakthrough, however, Anderson brought up three brigades and sealed the penetration.

On June 1 Grant thus secured Old Cold Harbor, bowed in Anderson's right, and captured 750 prisoners. But he lost 2,800 men and failed to turn or overrun Lee's right. Achieving those larger objectives would require further fighting.

Both commanders deemed it necessary to continue fighting. Lee might have retired across the Chickahominy, but with characteristic audacity he risked battle with that deep, swampy river behind him in order to cover his railroads. Accordingly, on June 2 he moved Breckinridge and two divisions of Lieutenant General A. P. Hill's Third Corps to connect Hoke's right to the Chickahominy Swamp. In taking this position, Breckinridge drove Union outposts off Turkey Hill, part of the 1862 battlefield of Gaines' Mill.

Those outposts belonged to Major General

Winfield Scott Hancock's Second Corps, which had marched from Meade's right to the left overnight on June 1–2. Grant believed that massing three corps at Old Cold Harbor would provide enough punch to break Anderson's line. Once broken, the Confederates might well be driven into the Chickahominy.

However, Hancock's night march, like so many in the Civil War, went astray. The Second Corps took ten hours to march twelve miles, and when it finally reached Old Cold Harbor, Hancock concluded that his men were too exhausted to attack. Meade and Grant reluctantly acquiesced.

Except for skirmishing at Turkey Hill, the only action on June 2 occurred to the north at Bethesda Church, where Early had failed to turn the Federal left on May 30. The armies sidled southward, and by June 2 the Union right was resting there. It too withstood Early's assault. After initially overrunning part of Major General Ambrose E. Burnside's Ninth Corps, Early was repulsed by Burnside's and Warren's main line.

Throughout that day and into the night the armies prepared to renew the battle. The Confederates continued to improve their field fortifications, which ran from Turkey Hill northwest along a low ridge, whose gentle, open, east-facing slope offered excellent fields of fire. The Federals also prepared: the generals deployed troops, and the soldiers pinned on name tags for identification if they were killed.

Many of the Union soldiers were killed when fighting resumed at 4:30 A.M. on June 3. Hancock, Wright, and Smith attacked simultaneously, but their advance was soon fragmented. From Hancock's left, Brigadier General Fran-

Richmond National Battlefield Park
Cold Harbor, Union trenches. © David Muench, 1990

cis C. Barlow's division drove the Confederate pickets from a wood line and penetrated a swampy, poorly defended portion of Breckinridge's sector. Barlow, however, lacked support, and Hill soon repelled him.

No other Federals fared even that well. To Barlow's right Brigadier General John Gibbon's division became mired in a swamp and was bloodily repulsed. In the center Wright found that his June 1 penetration now exposed him to shattering crossfire. Farther north most of Smith's troops, under Brigadier General John H. Martindale, were massed in a ravine leading into Anderson's line. The ravine proved a slaughter pen, raked by devastating crossfire.

Within barely half an hour all three Union corps were repulsed, with the staggering loss of 7,000 men. The survivors entrenched as near the front as they dared, often fifty yards or less from Lee's lines. Throughout the day sharpshooting and shelling took their toll.

However, the charge and the battle of Cold Harbor were over. For another nine days the armies remained in place, and many of the wounded remained between the lines unattended, suffering in the sweltering heat. When Grant, usually a humane commander, finally brought himself to request a truce on June 7, most of those wounded had died. In mid-June both armies departed: the cavalry to Trevilian Station, Breckinridge and Early to Lynchburg and the Shenandoah Valley, and the main bodies to Petersburg.

Approximately 117,000 Federals and 60,000 Confederates participated in operations from May 28 to June 3. Some 13,000 Union troops and perhaps 5,000 southerners were casualties. Half the Union losses (versus 1,200 Confederates) occurred that final morning. However, thousands more soldiers fought and fell from Haw's Shop to Bethesda Church. The final onslaught was just one part of the overall operation in Hanover County, but it was not characteristic of those operations or of Grant's generalship. Even after the war he reflected, "I have always regretted that the last assault at Cold Harbor was ever made."

In a broader sense, the overall operations at this time carried the Federals more deeply into Virginia. When their southward strategic drive from Culpeper to the Chickahominy was finally checked at Cold Harbor, Grant, undaunted, sought a new route to Richmond: from the south via its rail center, Petersburg. By late June the mobile war of spring would change to the stagnant siege of summer as Grant, who characteristically learned from experience, evolved new tactics to match his new strategy.

These Federal operations denied Lee the initiative and burdened him with the constricting strategic imperative of closely defending Richmond and Petersburg. Yet in this defense the masterful Virginian remained dangerous, as he had clearly demonstrated at Cold Harbor, his last great victory in the field.

Cold Harbor Battlefield, a unit of the Richmond National Battlefield Park, is southeast of Richmond, Virginia, on State Route 156 south of State Route 249. There are 149 acres of the historic battlefield within the authorized boundaries of this unit.

THE STAFF RIDE AND CIVIL WAR BATTLEFIELDS

William A. Stofft

If history is the memory of mankind, then military history is the memory of the profession of arms. First-rate armies have consistently required their leaders to undertake the systematic study of military history. This has been true, with brief exceptions, throughout the history of the U.S. Army. As the success of our deterrent strategy lengthens the period of peace and broadens the gap between training and battle experience, military history plays a greater role in the training and education of army leaders as a legitimate and necessary experience in preparation for national defense.

As Dwight David Eisenhower, general of the army and president of the United States, stated in his foreword to *The West Point Atlas of American Wars:*

> Through a careful and objective study of the significant campaigns of the world, a professional officer acquires a knowledge of military experience which he himself could not otherwise accumulate. The facts of a given battle may no longer serve any practical purpose except as a framework on which to base an analysis; but when the serious student of the military art delves into the reasons for the failure of a specific attack — or soberly analyzes the professional qualities of one of the responsible commanders of the past — he is, by this very activity, preparing for a day in which he, under different circumstances, may be facing decisions of vital consequence to his country.

The staff ride is a long-standing tradition in our army. Revisiting battlefields in a thoughtful and structured way helps connect today's officers to military history. In 1906 the assistant commander of the Staff College at Fort Leavenworth, Kansas, took twelve student officers to the Civil War battlefields in Georgia. Up through the 1930s these staff rides played an important role in the Leavenworth curriculum. They were begun again in the late 1960s and early 1970s by the Army War College at Carlisle, Pennsylvania, the Command and General Staff College at Leavenworth, and the United States Military Academy at West Point.

Today the U.S. Army tramps battlefields around the world wherever American soldiers are stationed. In 1987 army organizations reported well over 300 staff rides, an average of nearly one per day, illustrating the importance of the ride as a teaching technique.

There are three basic phases of the staff ride. The preliminary study phase may take various forms, depending upon the available time. Through formal classroom instruction, individual study, or a combination of both, students learn the purpose of the exercise and acquire a basic knowledge of the campaign and battle by studying memoirs, after-action reports, and secondary sources.

In the field study phase, having read extensively about the battle, the students follow the course of the action on the field. At various places the leader stops to make significant points. Some individuals may play out the roles of the actual staff officers and commanders. Discussion of both facts and interpretation is encouraged. What happened? How did it happen? Why did it happen that way?

The final phase, integration, takes place on the battlefield immediately after the field study. The staff ride leader moderates the discussion, placing the battlefield just visited in the context of today's army and its problems.

The lessons learned on former battlefields are endless. At Gettysburg, for example, the student officers, including lieutenants and four-star generals, learn to appreciate the importance of terrain and understand the influence of technology on warfare, the functioning of the military staff, the role of logistics, and the necessity for good intelligence and communications. Leadership examples abound; one of the most moving is that of Colonel Joshua Lawrence Chamberlain, the professor from Maine, whose leadership at Little Round Top during the battle of Gettysburg provides inspiration even today.

The use today by the U.S. Army of our national battlefield parks underscores the foresight of those who in the 1890s campaigned successfully to have Congress enact legislation to establish the nation's first five battlefield parks. The legislated mission of these parks was to preserve and protect the hallowed ground on which these great battles were fought, to commemorate the battle participants, and to provide field classrooms for the United States military officer corps.

THE 1864 SHENANDOAH VALLEY CAMPAIGN

15 May 1864–2 March 1865

Joseph W. A. Whitehorne

The Union viewed control of the Shenandoah Valley of Virginia as vital for two reasons. First, the Valley's southwest-northeast alignment and its excellent road system, including the hard-surface Valley Pike, could allow the Confederates to move rapidly into the vulnerable Union areas of Maryland, Pennsylvania, and Washington, D.C. Second, since the Valley had seen little warfare since Lieutenant General Thomas J. "Stonewall" Jackson's brilliant 1862 campaign, farmers there continued to raise produce for the Confederacy.

The 1864 Valley campaign was part of the strategic plan initiated by Lieutenant General Ulysses S. Grant when he assumed command of all Union forces. Grant concluded that the Union's greatest failing was not taking full advantage of its preponderance of men and matériel over the smaller Confederate resources. Accordingly, he developed a scheme to impose pressure everywhere along the line from Richmond to Mobile. One element in that plan was a renewed Union offensive in the Shenandoah Valley, commanded by Major General Franz Sigel.

That offensive began with the defeat of Sigel's 8,940 troops on May 15 at New Market by a Confederate force skillfully led by Major General John C. Breckinridge, whose 5,335

troops included 247 cadets from the Virginia Military Institute. Sigel withdrew down the Valley, and General Robert E. Lee called Breckinridge and his men to the North Anna River to help him against Grant's grinding attacks. This gave Sigel's replacement, Major General David Hunter, the opportunity to make another thrust up the Valley. Hunter defeated a Confederate force at Piedmont on June 5, pressed on to Lexington, where he burned the Virginia Military Institute, then moved against Lynchburg. This forced Lee to hurry Breckinridge and his command back to the Valley. In addition, Lee sent Lieutenant General Jubal A. Early with Jackson's old corps, the Second Corps of the Army of Northern Virginia, to Lynchburg. (Early referred to his reinforced Second Corps as the Army of the Valley.) The arrival of Early's larger force caused Hunter to break contact and withdraw across West Virginia to the Kanawha Valley. His force eventually reappeared at Harpers Ferry after a roundabout trek. However, its prolonged absence gave Early the opportunity to carry out Lee's orders to engage the Federal forces in the Valley so that Grant would have to reinforce them with men from the Richmond-Petersburg area.

Once he was certain that Hunter was out of

the way, Early moved his 14,000-man army down the Valley. He made short work of a Union force of 5,800 in Winchester under Major General Robert Milroy and was in Frederick, Maryland, by July 9. On that day Major General Lewis Wallace fought a stubborn delaying action at Monocacy against the Confederate invaders. Early pressed on and arrived at Silver Spring, on the outskirts of Washington, on July 11, stirring panic in the capital. President Lincoln pressed Grant to send reinforcements to augment the militia and the convalescents who were being rushed to the city's defense. Grant quickly sent the Sixth and Nineteenth corps to man the strong fortifications around the capital.

Early saw that he was outnumbered, and by July 14 he had pulled his force across the Potomac into Loudoun County, Virginia, and on to Berryville. The Sixth and Nineteenth corps did not pursue him aggressively. At Snicker's Gap these Federals were joined by elements of Hunter's old command, now back in the Valley and redesignated the Eighth Corps under the leadership of Brigadier General George R. Crook. Early pulled back to the Strasburg area after a sharp encounter on July 18 at Cool Springs near Snicker's Gap. The Union command then assumed that Early had been driven away, so they left the care of the Valley to Crook's little force and went to rejoin Grant at Richmond and Petersburg. Early again lashed out and defeated Crook on July 24 at the second battle of Kernstown. He then advanced to destroy the Martinsburg rail yards while dispatching brigadier generals John McCausland and Bradley T. Johnson to burn Chambersburg, Pennsylvania.

This was the final straw for Grant. He sent the Sixth and Nineteenth corps back to the Valley, and on August 5 he created the Middle Military Division under the command of one of his most trusted subordinates, Major General Philip H. Sheridan. Grant told Sheridan to lock onto Early, wreck his army, and destroy everything in the Valley that he could not carry away. The opposing forces maneuvered warily

across Jefferson and Clarke counties for nearly a month. Then Early made a mistake. He spread his elements too far apart, and Sheridan battered him at the third battle of Winchester on September 19, then again at Fisher's Hill on the twenty-second. In each case Sheridan's aggressively led cavalry played a decisive role.

Early was forced to withdraw southward to Rockfish Gap. Sheridan pressed him as far as Staunton. He then presumed that Early was no longer a factor and embarked upon the burning of the Valley. From the Blue Ridge to the Alleghenies the sky was dark with smoke as the slowly withdrawing Union forces destroyed barns, mills, crops, and anything else that could help the Confederate war effort. Sheridan's 32,000 men finally went into camp along Cedar Creek between Middletown and Strasburg. There, to their great surprise, on October 19 Early's 21,000 troops attacked. The skillful Confederate assault nearly overwhelmed the Union side. However, Sheridan rallied his men, counterattacked, and turned the day into a disaster for Early. The shattered Confederates retreated to New Market. From there Early launched a few probes northward, which led to some indecisive skirmishing during November before the two armies went into winter camp.

While the infantry units were in camp the Union cavalry continued to campaign, despite the increasingly grim winter weather. On December 19 Sheridan's horse commander, Major General Alfred T. A. Torbert, led two of his divisions on a raid toward Gordonsville that accomplished little. Union Brigadier General George A. Custer's division, which had been sent up the Valley as a diversion, was surprised at Lacy's Springs by the brigades of Major General Lunsford L. Lomax and Brigadier General William H. F. Payne. Although he repulsed the Confederate attack, Custer was nearly captured. He quickly pulled back to Winchester, where he joined the rest of the cavalry in winter camp.

Meanwhile Sheridan's infantry strength

gradually declined as General Grant ordered parts of his army to other theaters. The Sixth Corps left for Richmond in December. The Eighth Corps and Brigadier General William H. Powell's cavalry division were scattered throughout the lower Valley and West Virginia as garrison and security forces. Part of the Nineteenth Corps was sent to Georgia in January, while the remainder was committed to garrison missions. By mid-January Sheridan's mobile force was limited to the veteran First Cavalry Division, led by Brigadier General Thomas C. Devin, and Custer's equally seasoned Third Cavalry Division. They were considered a sufficient force to counter any threat from Early.

In fact Early's forces had gradually withered away during the winter. Supply problems forced him to disperse his cavalry over a wide area, and Lee's increasingly desperate situation siphoned most of the Valley's infantry away to the defense of Richmond and Petersburg. Thus, when Sheridan emerged from Winchester on February 27 with two full cavalry divisions, it was no contest. He brushed aside Early's cavalry at Mount Crawford on March 1 and brought Old Jube's small infantry force to bay at Waynesboro the next day. There on a cold wintry afternoon Custer demolished the last sizable Confederate force in the Valley.

Sheridan and his forces went on to the Appomattox campaign. Having destroyed Confederate military power and control in the Valley, he had completed the task assigned by Grant and attempted by Sigel and Hunter, but delayed so well and so long by Early.

Laying waste to the Shenandoah Valley. Drawing by Theodore R. Davis

NEW MARKET

15 May 1864

Joseph W. A. Whitehorne

The first battle of the Valley campaign of 1864 occurred at New Market, Shenandoah County, on May 15. The opposing forces had begun marching slowly toward the town on about May 1. The situation was so critical on the southern side that General Robert E. Lee had authorized Major General John C. Breckinridge, the local commander, to order out the Virginia Military Institute corps of cadets in his support. The participation of the 247 young men gives the battle an added interest and poignancy. Breckinridge had massed his forces effectively at Staunton by May 12, while his Union opponent, Major General Franz Sigel, allowed his units to become badly strung out between New Market and Woodstock as he moved south toward Mount Jackson to gain control over the terminus of the Manassas Gap Railroad and to New Market to control the only road across Massanutten Mountain.

Skirmishing between the two sides began in earnest on May 13 at the Mount Jackson bridge eight miles north of New Market. Growing Union forces pressed the Confederate cavalry screen south along the Valley Pike throughout May 14. By nightfall the Federals had established a line on the north side of the village and on the high ground to its west. The Confederate screen broke contact late in the night, and its commander, Brigadier General John D. Imboden, briefed Breckinridge, who

was with his main force at Lacy's Springs, twelve miles to the south.

Breckinridge immediately decided to move north and confront the Union troops. His force of 5,335 men left Lacy's Springs at about 1:00 A.M. on May 15 and reached the Shenandoah–Rockingham County line (old Fairfax survey line) at about 6:00 A.M. Breckinridge moved his artillery forward to Shirley's Hill, just southwest of New Market, and deployed the rest of his force on the high ground farther south. In the meantime more Union units continued to arrive on the line established during the night. However, confusion persisted, and the Union command realized that the force of 8,940 men was too spread out. When Sigel arrived at about noon, he directed a new line to be formed on the high ground north of the Bushong farm, two miles below the village. By pulling farther north he hoped to combine his dispersed forces sufficiently to give battle.

When Breckinridge realized that the Union troops would not attack him, he decided to go on the offensive. By 11:00 A.M. he had deployed his infantry, under the command of Brigadier General Gabriel C. Wharton and Brigadier General John Echols, on Shirley's Hill and eastward in a line to Smith Creek. Shortly thereafter the Confederates swept over Shirley's Hill into the New Market Valley. One

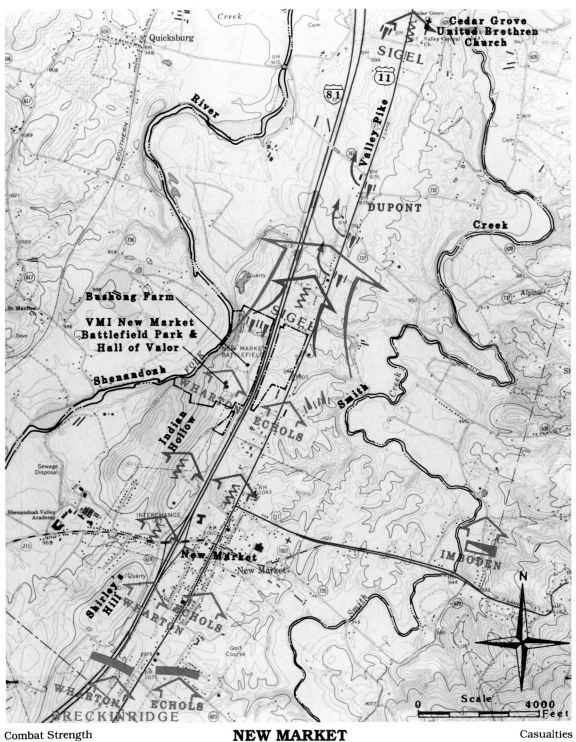

Quicksburg

Creek

Cem

Cedar Grove

**Cedar Grove
United Brethren
Church**

Valley Central
Ch

SIGEL

11

81

River

Valley Pike

DUPONT

Creek

Alpine

St Martins
Ch

Bushong Farm

**VMI New Market
Battlefield Park &
Hall of Valor**

SIGEL

Quarry

NEW MARKET
BATTLEFIELD

Dove

Shenandoah

WHARTON

FORK

Smith

ECHOLS

Creek

Indian Hollow

Sewage
Disposal

**Shenandoah Valley
Academy**

INTERCHANGE

New Market

New Market

IMBODEN

N

Shirley's Hill

WHARTON

ECHOLS

Quarry

Smith

Golf
Course

WHARTON

ECHOLS

BRECKINRIDGE

Scale

0   4000
                    Feet

Combat Strength
8,940
5,335

NEW MARKET

15 May 1864

Casualties
841
520

New Market Battlefield Park
Above: From Shirley's Hill, circa 1880. Courtesy of
D. Coiner Rosen

Below: From Shirley's Hill, 1986. © Joseph W. A.
Whitehorne

Virginia Military Institute cadet Thomas Garland Jefferson was killed in action at the battle of New Market. He was a collateral descendant of President Thomas Jefferson. Courtesy of Virginia Military Institute

unit moved up Indian Hollow, a small valley running to the north-northwest, while the rest pressed northward onto the ridge leading to the Bushong farm and beyond. The Union rear guard resisted briefly in the positions established the night before, then was forced back. The Federals held again briefly midway back to the line north of the farm, but soon were shattered by the Confederate advance. By 12:30 P.M. the village was cleared of Federal soldiers, and the Confederates were pressing toward the final Union position. Thunderstorms occurred throughout the battle and became increasingly violent.

Sigel had established a line on the ridge that now bears his name, about three hundred yards north of the Bushong farm. Its flanks were anchored on the west by the bluffs of the Shenandoah River and on the east by Smith Creek. The western part of the line was manned by three batteries of artillery and was then extended eastward by three infantry regiments with one more in reserve. It was a strong position, and the artillery fire was increasingly effective as the Confederates approached. By the time Breckinridge's advance reached the line of the Bushong farm, his units around the farm had suffered all they could take. When they began to waver, he put in the corps of Virginia Military Institute cadets to restore his line.

Sigel tried to direct a charge against the weakened Confederate lines, but it was not well managed and soon sputtered to a halt. Sigel had been minister of war for the revolutionary forces in Germany during the unsuccessful revolution of 1848 and had come to America in 1852. According to his chief of staff, Sigel gave his orders in German during the New Market battle, which caused considerable confusion. As the Union faltered, Breckinridge saw his chance and directed a charge call along his line. Sigel ordered his artillery to

withdraw and regroup around a church visible at the base of Rude's Hill, two miles to the north (now the Cedar Grove United Brethren Church). The loss of this firepower doomed the Union infantry line, and it was soon forced back in disorder by the charging Confederates. They swept on for about a quarter mile until confronted by a Union battery commanded by Captain Henry A. du Pont, at which point Breckinridge ordered a halt to reorganize. By the time he was ready to go again, Sigel had pulled all of his forces north of the river, and at 7:00 P.M. he destroyed the Mount Jackson bridge across the North Fork of the Shenandoah to prevent close pursuit. By the night of May 16, Union troops were back at Cedar Creek, having suffered 841 casualties. Confederate losses were about 520, including 61 of the cadets.

Breckinridge's victory temporarily unhinged Union plans for the Valley, preserving its resources longer for the faltering Confederate war effort. The Union loss resulted in Sigel's replacement and an intensification of the Union war effort in the Valley.

New Market Battlefield Park is 20 miles north of Harrisonburg on Interstate 81 and U.S. Route 11 at New Market, Virginia. There are 260 acres of the historic battlefield within the authorized boundaries of the Virginia Military Institute New Market Battlefield Park and Hall of Valor.

PIEDMONT

5 June 1864

Joseph W. A. Whitehorne

The defeat of Union Major General Franz Sigel at New Market on May 15 led General Robert E. Lee and Major General John C. Breckinridge to assume that once more the Union forces had been neutralized as a threat in the Shenandoah Valley. They did not take into account the persistence of the new Union leadership. Sigel was replaced by Major General David Hunter, who made preparations for a move up the Valley with a larger, better-organized force than that of his predecessor. Brigadier General Jeremiah C. Sullivan commanded the two brigades of infantry, while Major General Julius Stahel led the two brigades of cavalry. Hunter also began a much harsher policy toward Confederate sympathizers, destroying enemy property and assets. Many of his units had been with Sigel and wanted to avenge their defeat at New Market.

On May 26 the 12,000-man Union army began moving from its base at Belle Grove on Cedar Creek and headed south to Fisher's Hill and then on to Woodstock, where Hunter paused for a few days to resupply and to complete his planning. He arranged to rendezvous with the forces of Brigadier General George R. Crook and Brigadier General William Averill in the Staunton area. Crook was to bring his command from Meadow Bluff, West Virginia, having cut the Virginia and Tennessee Railroad at Dublin, Virginia, on May 9. Lieutenant

General Ulysses S. Grant directed both commanders to travel light and to live off the land. The advancing armies foraged and pillaged vigorously, motivated in part by the effects of partisan operations against their own supply lines.

Hunter's column moved to New Market on May 29, pausing to rest and rebury properly those who had fallen during the previous battle. Hunter pushed on south of Harrisonburg on June 2, where he encountered the first significant Confederate defense, Brigadier General John G. Imboden's cavalry deployed at Mount Crawford. Imboden resisted desperately while requesting reinforcements from Richmond. Virtually every able-bodied Confederate was called into service in the emergency, including supply soldiers, miners, and elderly militia reserves. Even more important, Brigadier General William E. "Grumble" Jones's brigade of infantry was rushed by rail from Bristol, Virginia, bringing the Confederate strength to about 5,600 men.

The Confederate position at Mount Crawford blocked the Valley Pike at a point where it crossed the North Fork of the Shenandoah. Imboden's preparations promised a hard fight. Consequently Hunter decided to sidestep the prepared Confederate defenses with a move east to Port Republic, then south on the East Road toward Staunton. His move surprised Imboden and Jones, who were in the

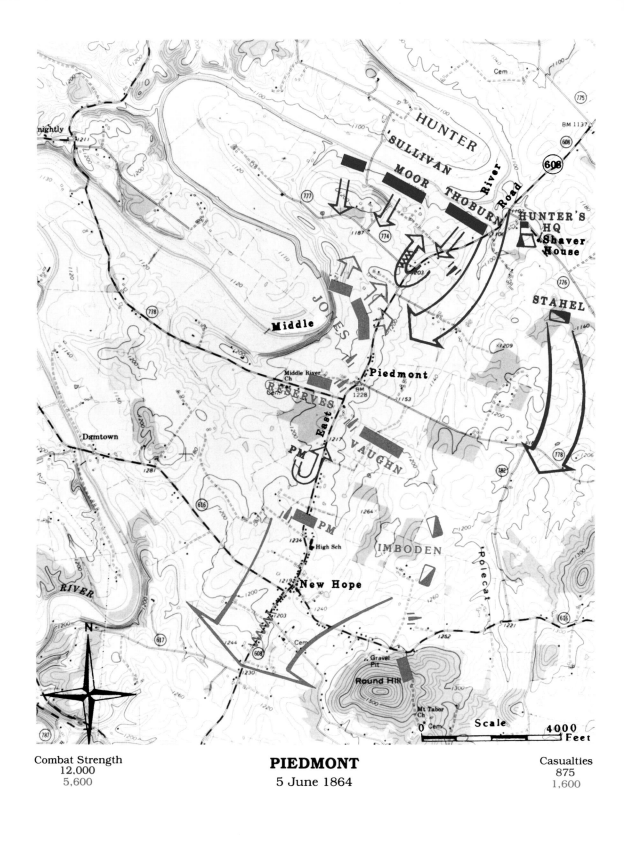

HUNTER

SULLIVAN

MOOR

THOBURN

River Road

HUNTER'S HQ

Shaver House

STAHEL

JONES

Middle

Middle River Ch

Piedmont

RESERVES

East

PM

VAUGHN

Damtown

PM

High Sch

IMBODEN

Polecat

New Hope

RIVER

N

Round Hill

Gravel Pit

Mt Tabor Ch

Scale

0   4000
                Feet

Combat Strength
12,000
5,600

PIEDMONT

5 June 1864

Casualties
875
1,600

process of organizing and integrating their commands at Mount Crawford. But Hunter was delayed crossing the river near Port Republic because of the inefficiency of his engineers, and this gave Imboden time to hustle his cavalry eastward to confront the Union threat. Jones followed with the infantry and more cavalry under Brigadier General John C. Vaughn, and these troops took up positions in the vicinity of Piedmont, located about seven miles south of Port Republic and one mile north of New Hope on the East Road to Staunton.

In 1864 the hamlet of Piedmont consisted of about ten houses nestled in rolling farmland interspersed with woods southeast of the steep banks of a looping curve of the Middle River. Jones deployed most of his infantry northwest of the town, with its flank anchored on the river. Jones concentrated his cavalry southeast of the intersection of the road west from the pike and the East Road and gave specific orders to hold and block a Union move around the east flank. This placement inadvertently created a gap between the two wings of his force near the village.

Early on the morning of June 5 Hunter's cavalry, across the river near Port Republic, ran into some cavalry outposts set up by Imboden at the crossroads near Mount Meridian. A swirling cavalry "pile on" took place, soon joined by horse artillery, as the greater Union numbers pressed Imboden's men south a mile to the Crawford farmhouse, Bonnie Doon. The Confederates held there until Union artillery massed on the road to the north and forced them farther south to another delaying position at Crawford Run near the Shaver farm, later Hunter's headquarters. Again the preponderant Union artillery forced the Confederates back to the main positions around Piedmont that Jones had selected.

Jones positioned two infantry brigades behind barricades of rails and trees to form a large arc along the woods northwest of Piedmont, while less reliable infantry reserves were positioned along the crossroads in town. Most of the Confederate artillery supported the infantry. When Imboden's horsemen clattered back from delaying the Union advance, they joined Vaughn's cavalry southeast of the village. No one noted the large gap between the infantry and the cavalry.

At about noon the Union forces came up to this line just as the sun emerged after the morning rains. Hunter decided to concentrate on the Confederate infantry. Sullivan's two brigades, led by Colonel Joseph Thoburn and Colonel Augustus Moor, advanced in an attempt to flank the Confederate positions. One brigade made at least three desperate frontal attacks to fix Confederate attention, while the other took advantage of low ground to move around the right flank of Jones's infantry. This force was resisted fiercely by Confederate artillery. However, the Union attacks did reveal the gap in the Confederate lines. The flanking Union brigade tried another attack into this gap with heavy artillery support just as the Confederates were shifting some units. In the meantime the Union cavalry under Stahel rode eastward en masse, forcing the Confederate cavalry to remain southeast of the town to protect Jones's eastern flank.

The violent Union attack into the gap presaged thirty minutes of hand-to-hand struggle in the woods. Jones rushed from one imperiled point to another, encouraging the troops, until he was killed instantly by a bullet to the head. His death marked the collapse of his line and the precipitous withdrawal of the Confederate infantry, making the position of the cavalry untenable. Vaughn and Imboden withdrew southward down the East Road to Fishersville. The Confederate rear guard on the East Road between New Hope and Piedmont discouraged any Union pursuit.

The battle was a disaster for the Confederates. Hunter shattered their military force in the Valley (casualties: Confederates, 1,600; Union, 875) and exposed the well-established depots and logistical facilities in Staunton and elsewhere. The upper Valley was opened to invasion for the first time in the war, with serious psychological and economic implications for the Confederacy. In the North the victory solidified President Lincoln's position at the Republican convention then in progress in Baltimore.

Piedmont battlefield is one mile north of New Hope and seven miles south of Port Republic on State Route 608, approximately 13 miles northeast of Staunton, Virginia, on Interstate 81. The entire battlefield is privately owned.

MONOCACY

9 July 1864

Gary W. Gallagher

Confederate Lieutenant General Jubal A. Early and the 14,000 soldiers of his Army of the Valley (Early's name for the Second Corps of the Army of Northern Virginia plus other attached units) were on the move in the second week of July 1864. Early had received orders from General Robert E. Lee to clear the Shenandoah Valley of Union forces, menace Washington and Baltimore, and compel Lieutenant General Ulysses S. Grant to counter his movements, thereby weakening the Army of the Potomac. Early drove Union troops from the Valley and then crossed the Potomac, swinging north and east from Shepherdstown to approach Washington from the rear. On the morning of July 9 his army was in the vicinity of Frederick, Maryland. Major General Stephen Ramseur's division was in the lead, edging southward on the Georgetown Pike from Frederick to Washington. Within easy supporting distance of Ramseur were the divisions of major generals Robert E. Rodes, John B. Gordon, and John C. Breckinridge, the cavalry of Brigadier General John McCausland, and three battalions of artillery.

A Union force of about 5,800 soldiers under Major General Lewis Wallace awaited the Confederates on the east bank of the Monocacy River just below Frederick. Uncertain whether Early's goal was Washington or Baltimore, Wallace had selected a position from which he could dispute Confederate crossings of the Monocacy on both the National Road to Baltimore and the Georgetown Pike. Northern estimates placed Early's force at between 20,000 and 30,000 men — far too many for Wallace to defeat in a stand-up fight. The Union commander did hope to determine Early's destination, secure an accurate count of Confederate numbers, and detain the army long enough for Grant to "get a corps or two into Washington and make it safe." Wallace's command included home guards and other second-line troops consolidated as a brigade under Brigadier General Erastus B. Tyler, as well as Brigadier General James B. Ricketts's veteran division from the Army of the Potomac. Sent away from the Petersburg lines in response to Early's campaign in Maryland, Ricketts's two brigades had joined Wallace at about 1:00 A.M. on July 9.

Wallace expected the Confederates to attack in the vicinity of Monocacy Junction — where the Georgetown Pike and the Baltimore and Ohio Railroad cross the river — or to seize fords farther downstream. Watching both of these critical points on the line were Ricketts's brigades, positioned on high ground running southwest from a covered wooden bridge that carried the Georgetown Pike across the river. Tyler's brigade held the Union right, guarding fords and bridges from the Baltimore and

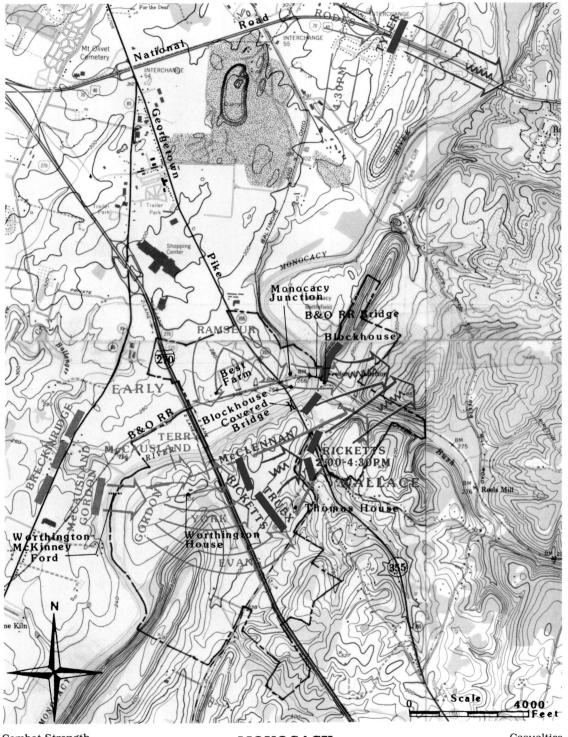

MONOCACY

9 July 1864

Combat Strength
5,800
14,000

Casualties
1,968
700–900

Ohio's iron bridge upstream to the National Road. Union defenders at the junction made use of two blockhouses, one on each side of the Monocacy, and rifle pits on the east bank of the river. A line of Union skirmishers crouched behind the railroad embankment west of the river. Six three-inch rifled guns and a twenty-four-pounder howitzer, the latter in an emplacement overlooking the bridges near the junction, supported the Union infantry.

The morning of July 9 was bright and warm, with a cooling breeze sweeping over the lush countryside south of Frederick. Skirmishing erupted at about 6:30 A.M. between Ramseur's division and Union soldiers positioned astride the Georgetown Pike west of the river. The Confederates pushed the Union pickets back and moved into position in the fields of the Best farm, west of the railroad and the pike. Soon three Confederate batteries were dueling with the Federal guns across the river. Convinced by the volume of Union fire that it would be costly to storm the covered bridge on the Georgetown Road, Ramseur asked Early if there were some other route across the Monocacy. To the north, meanwhile, Rodes's division had engaged Tyler's troops in fitful fighting along the National Road.

The focus of the battle shifted to the southwest when McCausland's Confederate cavalry forced its way across the Monocacy a mile and a quarter below the junction at the Worthington-McKinney Ford. Ricketts reacted swiftly by moving across the Thomas farm toward the Worthington farm and placing some of his soldiers behind a fence that divided the two properties. Late in the morning McCausland's dismounted cavalrymen advanced through waist-high corn between the Worthington house and the river. Union infantry, partially hidden by the fence, easily stopped the surprised Confederate troopers. McCausland reformed his men and renewed the attack at about 2:00 P.M., this time striking the Union force farther to the right. After gaining ground

in the direction of the Thomas farm, the Confederates fell back a second time in the face of superior Union firepower.

Both Wallace and Early realized the importance of McCausland's movements. Wallace sensed potential disaster on his left and decided to commit all of Ricketts's veterans on that end of the line. He ordered the covered bridge burned, thus releasing its defenders from their stations, and deployed all but one piece of artillery on Ricketts's front. As smoke billowed skyward from the blazing span shortly after noon, Early was at work on the west side of the Monocacy. Orders went to Breckinridge "to move rapidly with Gordon's and Wharton's division to McCausland's assistance . . . and strike the enemy on his left flank, and drive him from the position commanding the crossings in Ramseur's front, so as to enable the latter to cross."

The climactic phase of the battle began at about 3:30 P.M. Rodes and Ramseur continued to apply pressure at Monocacy Junction and the National Road, while Gordon's three brigades prepared to assault the Union left from positions on the Worthington farm. The Confederate attacks began with Brigadier General Clement A. Evans's brigade of Georgians, which moved over Brooks Hill to strike Colonel W. S. Truex's brigade of Ricketts's division. Bitter fighting in the wheatfield on the Thomas farm brought a bloody stalemate. Evans received a serious wound, and a Georgia private wrote later that "it made our hearts ache to look over the battle field and see so many of our dear friends, comrades and beloved officers, killed and wounded."

Gordon's two other brigades rapidly added their power to the Confederate attacks. Brigadier General Zebulon York's regiments engaged Truex just to Evans's left, followed closely by Brigadier General William Terry's men, who collided with Colonel Matthew R. McClennan's Union brigade near the river. Union defenders fought valiantly in the fields and among the buildings of the Thomas farm, yielding slowly to pressure from Gordon's infantry and the enfilading fire from Confederate artillery across the Monocacy. A final Union line took advantage of fences and cuts in the Georgetown Pike on the west side of the Thomas farm. Sheltered by that natural breastwork, men from New York, Pennsylvania, Vermont, and New Jersey sent a crippling fire into Confederates struggling up from a small creek bottom in their front. "In this ravine the fighting was desperate and at close quarters," General Gordon recalled after the war. "Nearly one half of my men and large numbers of the Federals fell there."

It soon became clear that Union courage must give way to Confederate numbers. Wallace, fearing that prolonged resistance might bring the destruction of his small force, ordered a withdrawal to the National Road. At about 4:30 P.M. the Union army abandoned its position in front of Ramseur, enabling the Confederates to cross the railroad bridge. Gordon's exhausted troops watched as Ramseur's soldiers harried the retreating Union soldiers. Rodes subsequently joined Ramseur, but Early called off the pursuit and allowed Wallace to escape. Early's somewhat puzzling explanation after the war was that he did not wish to be encumbered by a large number of prisoners.

The battle of the Monocacy was a clear tactical victory for Jubal Early. At a cost of between 700 and 900 men killed and wounded, the Army of the Valley drove Wallace's troops from the field and inflicted heavy casualties. In Ricketts's division, which bore the brunt of the fighting on the northern side, 595 were killed and wounded and 1,054 listed as missing. Tyler's brigade lost 83 killed and wounded and 236 missing. Union losses totaled 1,968 of the 5,800 present for duty.

Despite suffering a clear tactical defeat, Wallace achieved his larger strategic goal. Early expended a precious twenty-four hours, which permitted reinforcements from the Army of the Potomac to reach Washington ahead of the Confederates. Had Wallace failed to intercept Early south of Frederick, the Army of the Valley might have fought its way into Washington on July 10. The political implications of such a victory for the Confederacy are interesting to contemplate but impossible to gauge with any certainty. It can be said with confidence that Wallace's troops spared the Lincoln government a potential disaster, and for that reason the battle of the Monocacy must be considered one of the more significant actions of the Civil War.

Monocacy National Battlefield is three miles south of Frederick, Maryland, on Interstate 270. There are 1,647 acres of the historic battlefield within its authorized boundaries; 580 of these are privately owned.

Lieutenant General Jubal A. Early recrossing the Potomac River

SECOND KERNSTOWN

24 July 1864

Joseph W. A. Whitehorne

Lieutenant General Jubal A. Early quickly withdrew his forces from in front of Washington when he learned that the Union defenders had been reinforced with substantial elements of the Sixth and Nineteenth corps. He crossed the Potomac on July 14 near Leesburg, then moved west of the Blue Ridge to the vicinity of Berryville. The Union corps followed him slowly and were joined near Snicker's Gap by Brigadier General George R. Crook with a portion of the newly designated Eighth Corps. This force had been part of Major General David Hunter's column, which had traversed much of West Virginia in the retreat from Lynchburg the previous month.

Union Major General Horatio G. Wright, in command of the pursuit, put a portion of Crook's force across the Shenandoah River at Cool Spring, about two miles north of Snicker's Ferry. On July 19 part of Early's force turned and dealt it a sharp blow. However, the next day at Stephenson's Depot, north of Winchester, Confederate Major General Stephen Ramseur's division was routed by Hunter's cavalry. Early decided to withdraw to Fisher's Hill, south of Strasburg, to reorganize his men and determine Union intentions. Wright, assuming that Early had broken contact in order to move up the Valley to rejoin Lee near Richmond, immediately ordered the Sixth and Nineteenth corps to return to Washington and

then prepare for their move to Petersburg. Wright left Crook with his three small, tired infantry divisions and some cavalry to secure the Valley.

On July 22 Crook moved his force to Winchester, where he learned that Early was in the vicinity of Strasburg. The Union cavalry was in contact with Confederate cavalry, and their skirmishing intensified throughout the day. Crook intended to remain in Winchester only a day or two to rest his troops before continuing north. However, on July 23 the fighting became so intense that he ordered the infantry divisions to march from Winchester and form a support line just north of Kernstown. When the cavalry was pressed north late in the afternoon, Colonel Isaac H. Duval's infantry division, including a brigade commanded by Colonel Rutherford B. Hayes (who became president of the United States in 1877), advanced and cleared Kernstown of Confederates. Crook then left a cavalry brigade to picket Kernstown and pulled the rest of his force back to Winchester.

Early learned from his cavalry that the Union pursuit was over and that his forces outnumbered the Union's, 14,000 to 9,500. At first light on July 24, Confederate forces headed by Major General John C. Breckinridge began to advance down the Valley Pike to attack Crook. The divisions of Major General

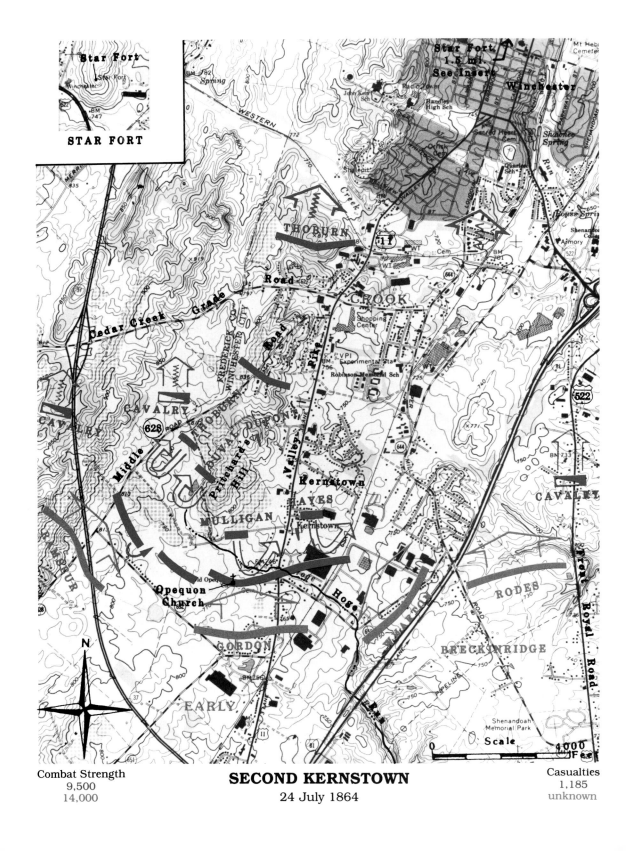

STAR FORT

STAR FORT

SECOND KERNSTOWN

24 July 1864

Combat Strength
9,500
14,000

Casualties
1,185
unknown

John B. Gordon and Brigadier General Gabriel C. Wharton were to press the Union line in its center at Kernstown. Ramseur's division left the pike at Bartonsville and headed west to the Middle Road to turn the Federals' right flank. Major General Robert E. Rodes's division was ordered over to the Front Royal Road to make a similar move on the east. Confederate cavalry was placed on each flank to exploit the expected infantry victory.

The cavalry skirmishing intensified. When Crook learned from his scouts that a large infantry force was on the way, he moved his infantry back into position at Kernstown. Colonel James A. Mulligan's division set up behind some stone walls north of Hoge Run, west of the Valley Pike. Mulligan immediately sent out skirmishers to Opequon Church and southward to relieve the cavalry, which then deployed to the west to guard the Union flank. At midmorning Duval's two brigades each moved to one of Mulligan's flanks, and Hayes's brigade set up east of the pike. Crook's Third Division, led by Colonel Joseph Thoburn, moved into trenches in the woods on Pritchard's Hill, northwest of the main line. Captain Henry A. du Pont unlimbered Crook's artillery on the hill.

The infantry battle began at noon as elements of Gordon's division chased back the Union skirmish line. Mulligan immediately ordered a counterattack supported by Hayes's brigade. The Union right advanced to the protection of the walls of Opequon Church and its cemetery; the Federals farther east fought in an open orchard next to the pike. Within half an hour they were compelled to fall back under the intense fire of Gordon's men, many of whom had fought in the same place under Lieutenant General Thomas J. "Stonewall" Jackson two years before. The Union soldiers in the churchyard were forced back as well, and the Confederates then pressed into the area.

The Union line underwent some changes during this adjustment. Duval's brigade on Mulligan's right (west) moved farther west, near the cavalry on Middle Road. The gap created was filled by Thoburn's division. The Confederate line was extended westward by another of Gordon's brigades, which arrived and swept across the open ground west of Opequon Church, forcing Thoburn's units from the protection of one stone wall to a second stone wall farther north. They were soon dislodged from this position and forced back to their original places on the northwest slope of Pritchard's Hill. By that time Thoburn was aware of Ramseur's approach on the west. This shift exposed Mulligan's division to vicious fire on its west flank as it desperately held on to the Hoge Run line.

A new Confederate threat then appeared on the east. Breckinridge had moved Wharton's division to a ridge southeast of Kernstown, where it formed close to the Union left flank. Hayes had noted the movement as he tried to support Mulligan's increasingly desperate defense north of the church. Hayes's left flank, unprotected, began to crumple as soon as Wharton's men began their advance. Hayes rallied his men briefly behind a stone wall just east of the pike but soon was forced to pull back farther. Wharton's charge was a signal for Gordon's men to advance as well. This placed Confederate forces on both of Mulligan's flanks. Soon his line began to yield. Mulligan tried to rally his men but was mortally wounded. The collapse of the Union center forced Crook to withdraw his entire force.

The remnants of Hayes's brigade held the north part of Pritchard's Hill to enable du Pont's artillery to withdraw. The Union cavalry on the west charged into the advancing Confederates to buy time for Thoburn's division and the remainder of Duval's to pull back in good order. The Union cavalry on the Front Royal Road withdrew without making any contribution to the battle. One brigade of Thoburn's division blocked the Valley Pike briefly on the high ground at Cedar Creek Grade north of Pritchard's Hill, then retreated under pressure.

The Union troops quickly retreated through

Second Kernstown battlefield
Opequon Church. © David E. Roth, *Blue & Gray Magazine*, Columbus, Ohio

Winchester, in some disorder, to Bunker Hill, having suffered 1,185 casualties. On July 25 they continued their retrograde movement to the Potomac, eventually reaching Harpers Ferry on July 27. The victorious Confederates (casualties unknown) remained in the Winchester area and held Union prisoners at Star Fort, north of the town. (Star Fort had been lost one other time by the Federals in June 1863, when Major General Robert H. Milroy was defeated at the second battle of Winchester.) Once more the Valley was cleared of Union troops, and Jubal Early soon had his cavalry on the march. They destroyed the rail yards at

Martinsburg and burned Chambersburg, Pennsylvania, a few days later.

News of the defeat and Early's actions once again raised concerns for the security of Washington. More significant, it was the final straw for Lieutenant General Ulysses S. Grant. He fired a number of inept Union commanders, returned the Sixth and Nineteenth corps to the Valley, and put his friend Major General Philip Sheridan in command. Sheridan had orders to neutralize the Valley once and for all and to end its economic value to the Confederacy. Second Kernstown marks the beginning of the Valley's most tragic wartime period.

Second Kernstown battlefield is on U.S. Route 11 and Interstate 81, south of Winchester, Virginia. The entire battlefield is privately owned.

FISHER'S HILL

22 September 1864

Joseph W. A. Whitehorne

Union Major General Philip H. Sheridan's victory at the third battle of Winchester on September 19 was incomplete. Lieutenant General Jubal Early's force, battered as it was, remained intact, and Early retreated twenty miles south to a strong position at Fisher's Hill, two miles from Strasburg. Massanutten Mountain rises just east of Fisher's Hill, narrowing the Shenandoah Valley to about five miles. Fisher's Hill itself is a high, rocky ridge fronted by a small stream, Tumbling Run. The hill and the stream block the Valley, creating a formidable barrier that stretches from the Shenandoah River near the base of Massanutten westward to Little North Mountain in the foothills of the Alleghenies. Early's position was enhanced further by prepared trenches, some of which still may be seen. The Valley Pike emerged from Strasburg and penetrated the ridge somewhat farther west than it does today.

Early placed Major General Gabriel C. Wharton's division on his right, east of the pike. His remaining infantry divisions, commanded by major generals John B. Gordon, John Pegram, and Stephen D. Ramseur, extended his line farther westward. Unfortunately, he had insufficient manpower to occupy his whole line in strength, and the last mile of his front continued to Little North Mountain with a thin line of dismounted cavalry. Anticipating that the greatest threat to his line was in the eastern part, he concentrated the bulk of his artillery there with Wharton's and Gordon's men. He sent the remainder of his cavalry into the Luray Valley to prevent any Union attack against his line of retreat through the more southerly Massanutten gaps.

The 20,000-man Union force reached the area on the afternoon of September 20. The Sixth Corps deployed midway between Strasburg and the Back Road, which runs along the base of Little North Mountain. The Nineteenth Corps occupied a position closer to Strasburg on the high ground overlooking the pike and the Shenandoah. Brigadier General George Crook's Eighth Corps was positioned miles to the rear in the woods north of Cedar Creek near Belle Grove. Sheridan, very much aware of the Confederate lookout station at Signal Knob on the Massanutten, wanted the Eighth Corps to remain concealed to deceive his opponent about his strength and intentions. Sheridan sent most of his cavalry into the Luray Valley with orders to cut Early's line of retreat at New Market.

Late on the afternoon of September 20 a division of the Union Sixth Corps seized part of the high ground north of Tumbling Run within 700 yards of the Confederate positions. This provided a good view of a large part of the Confederate defenses and gave the Union artillery good firing positions. The Sixth Corps

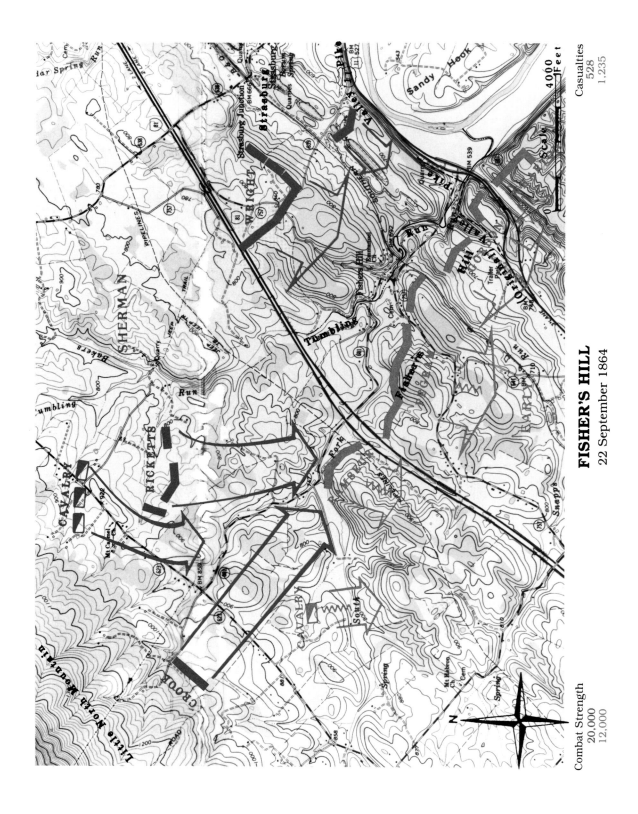

FISHER'S HILL
22 September 1864

Combat Strength
20,000
12,000

Casualties
528
1,235

was also in a better position to support the main element of Sheridan's attack. Sheridan recognized that Early's strength on the east precluded any successful frontal assault straight up the pike, while his thin line to the west invited a movement against that flank. Sheridan placed his remaining cavalry on the Back Road in a position to exploit any infantry success on that side and directed the Eighth Corps to execute a flanking move to the west. The other two corps were to create as much distraction as possible.

Crook moved his Eighth Corps, carefully screened from the Confederate observers on Signal Knob, from Cedar Creek to the north side of Hupp's Hill below Strasburg and on to the Back Road. Once he had his force in the protection of the forest along Little North Mountain, he hurried them southward to a point opposite Early's western flank. He was in position by 4:00 P.M. on September 22 and immediately threw both of his divisions into the attack. The Confederate line buckled, and the weak resistance from the 12,000 startled Confederates was the signal for the western-most Sixth Corps division to attack, while its artillery provided support.

The Confederate line began to unravel from west to east as the triumphant Union troops advanced. The Sixth and Nineteenth corps joined in as the resistance diminished. Soon the entire Confederate line was in retreat, "at first stubborn and slow, then rapid, then — rout," in Gordon's words. The Confederate stampede was hastened by the Union cavalry coming in from the west behind Crook.

In the Luray Valley, Confederate cavalry stymied Sheridan's horsemen in a series of sharp delaying engagements and kept Early's line of retreat open. Early pulled back to Narrow Passage north of Edinburg the day of the battle, to New Market the next day, and then, under Union pressure, all the way back to Rockfish Gap near Waynesboro. Although his force was relatively intact, Early had lost large amounts of equipment, and 240 of his men had been killed or wounded. Most of the 995 missing straggled in over the next few weeks. Union losses totaled 528. Sheridan assumed that the Confederate forces were no longer a threat after their second defeat in less than a week. The victory was acclaimed throughout the north as vindication of Grant's strategy and Lincoln's policy. Locally it presaged the other phase of that policy, the economic destruction of the Valley. Fisher's Hill marks the beginning of "Red October," the burning of the Valley, which was to leave its mark on the people, the terrain, and the economy for generations.

Fisher's Hill battlefield is on U.S. Route 11 near Strasburg, Virginia. The entire battlefield is privately owned.

CEDAR CREEK

19 October 1864

Joseph W. A. Whitehorne

The last major battle of the 1864 Shenandoah Valley campaign took place at Cedar Creek on October 19. The battle area extended from Fisher's Hill, just south of Strasburg, north to a point about three miles below Middletown. A few days earlier, after burning the Valley as far south as Staunton, Union Major General Philip Sheridan had established his lines along the high ground north of Cedar Creek. Sheridan and his men were confident that Lieutenant General Jubal Early's Army of the Valley was no longer a threat, even though there had been a sharp cavalry engagement on October 9 at Tom's Brook near Round Hill, south of Strasburg. As a result, at Cedar Creek the Union troops focused more on rest and recuperation than on a possible renewal of the struggle.

The aggressive Early, reinforced with Major General Joseph B. Kershaw's division to offset his September losses, quickly pressed his 21,000 men northward. He occupied Fisher's Hill and probed the Union positions for weak points. A sharp fight at Hupp's Hill on October 13 signaled the cautious Sheridan that Early was on more than a scouting mission. The 32,000 Union soldiers were deployed in echelon from southeast to northwest, conforming to the flow of Cedar Creek. The Eighth Corps was east of the Valley Pike, its two divisions almost a mile apart. The Nineteenth Corps was just west of the pike, occupying strong positions along Cedar Creek, where its trenches still may be seen. The Sixth Corps was farther north and west. This corps, en route to Washington after the Hupp's Hill fight, was recalled by Sheridan and returned just in time to set up camp, but without any fortifications. On October 16 Sheridan went to a conference in Washington, leaving Major General Horatio G. Wright in command. Wright placed the large cavalry corps to the west of the Sixth Corps.

The strong Union positions seemed to stymie Early, who, because of a shortage of supplies, would soon be forced to pull back unless he acted quickly. One of his division commanders, Major General John B. Gordon, and his corps cartographer, Captain Jedediah Hotchkiss, gave him a plan. The two men had climbed up to Signal Knob on Massanutten Mountain, where they had a full view of the Union positions. They noted the dispersal of the Eighth Corps and the apparent reliance on the rough terrain along Cedar Creek and the North Fork of the Shenandoah to secure its eastern flank. A local resident told them of a trail that infantry could use to cross the tongue of Massanutten to reach fords on the river. They could then get to the Union flank east of the Eighth Corps.

Early then approved a plan of great daring. It was in essence a three-column, converging night attack with cavalry support on each flank. Gordon took his division, along with Major General Stephen Ramseur's and Major General John Pegram's, over the trail to McInturff's and Bowman's fords on the North Fork. From there they hustled northward until Ramseur's division in the lead reached the Cooley mansion. At this point all they had to do was stop and face west; they were a half mile east of Brigadier General Rutherford B. Hayes's division of the Eighth Corps. Meanwhile Kershaw's division marched from the Fisher's Hill assembly area up the pike through Strasburg to Bowman's Mill Ford across Cedar Creek. From there he confronted the other division of the Union Nineteenth Corps. Brigadier General Gabriel C. Wharton's division moved farther north up the pike to Hupp's Hill, from which it prepared to cross Cedar Creek at the Valley Pike bridge when conditions allowed.

The Confederate approach on October 19 was aided first by moonlight and then by an early morning fog. Kershaw's men opened the fight as scheduled at 5 A.M., quickly shattering the First Division, Eighth Corps, commanded by Colonel Joseph Thoburn. A few minutes later Gordon's men smashed into Hayes's division, forcing it westward into the confused Nineteenth Corps. That corps put up greater resistance, especially around the Belle Grove mansion, which was serving as corps and army headquarters. Finally, however, the Nineteenth was pressed westward through a line established by the Sixth Corps. The time bought by the Eighth and Nineteenth corps had allowed the Sixth Corps to get well established on the high ground just west of Belle Grove. Each of its three divisions fought fiercely, although all were slowly pressed back. Finally most of the Union forces broke contact and retreated to the north, eventually setting up a line perpendicular to the pike about three quarters of a mile north of today's Lord Fairfax Community College.

The Second Division of the Sixth Corps held on alone in a position around the Middletown Cemetery just northwest of the village. For more than one hour the Second resisted everything the Confederates threw at it, halting the Confederate momentum while buying time for the main Union force to reorganize. Early lost full vision of the battlefield and was unable to control all of his forces. Despite the entreaties of his senior commanders to bypass the problem, he decided to concentrate on this one division, which was finally forced back to the new Union position. The Confederates then established a line westward from the north edge of town. Later they edged half a mile farther north, waiting for the next Union move.

In the meantime Sheridan had returned to Winchester from Washington on October 18. On the morning of the nineteenth he was two miles south of town when he began to encounter numerous stragglers, each with his own tale of disaster. Sheridan rode quickly up the Valley Pike, inspiring the retreating ranks of men to turn and join him in saving the army. At Newtown (now Stephens City) he directed a young Eighth Corps staff officer, Captain William McKinley, to set up a straggler line to halt and channel the men southward to reinforce the Federal lines set up by Wright. Sheridan then rode along the new line, waving and bowing to the cheers of the Union soldiers. His presence, in the words of one, was like an "electric shock." Sheridan later said he had resolved to give his men a success or to suffer defeat with them.

The fiery army commander quickly reestablished control and restored morale, then spent the afternoon carefully planning an assault on Early's lines. At about 4:00 P.M. he led his massed cavalry in a counterattack that sent the Confederates into a retreat that turned into a rout. A bridge broke on the south side of Strasburg, forcing Early's troops to abandon all their rolling stock and all that they had captured. The infantry survivors rallied at Fisher's Hill and withdrew southward the next morning. The Confederate casualties totaled 2,910; the Union casualties, 5,672.

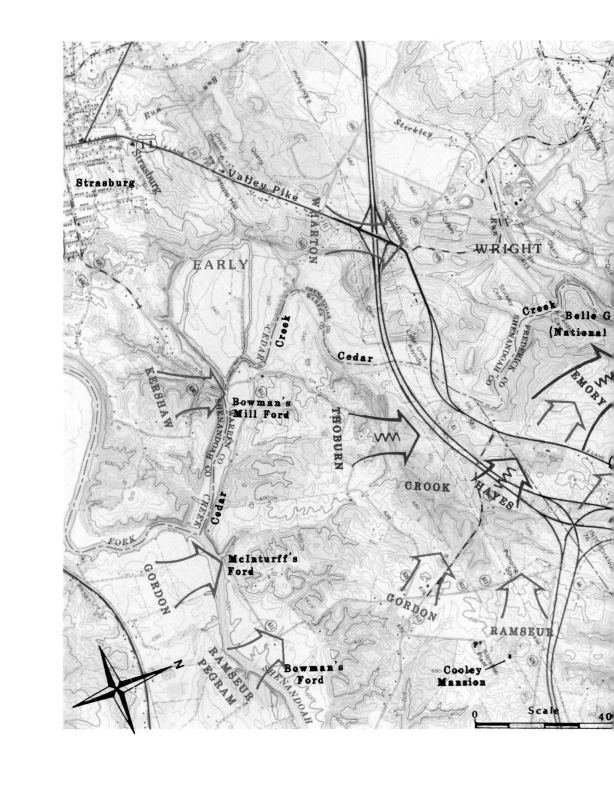

Strasburg

Valley Pike

WHARTON

EARLY

Spring Run

Cripple Creek

Hupp Hill

Cripple Creek

PIPELINES

Stickley

Run

WRIGHT

INTERCHANGE

Cem

Shenandoah River

WARREN CO

Cedar

CEDAR Creek

Cripple Creek Waysid

Creek

Belle G
(National

SHENANDOAH CO
FREDERICK CO

KERSHAW

Bowman's
Mill Ford

THOBURN

CROOK

EMORY

Cedar

CREEK

Cedar

SHENANDOAH CO
WARREN CO

FORK

McInturff's
Ford

GORDON

HAYES

INTERCHANGE

GORDON

RAMSEUR
PEGRAM

Bowman's
Ford

SHENANDOAH

Cooley
Mansion

RAMSEUR

N

Scale

0   40

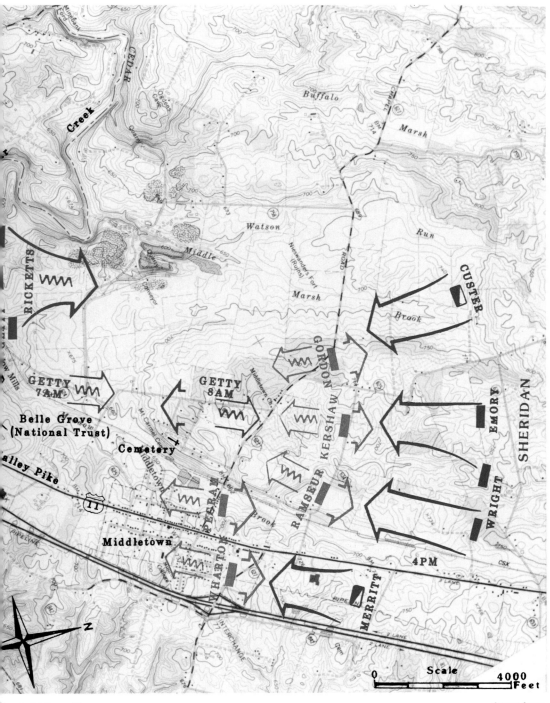

RICKETTS

Buffalo

Marsh

CUSTER

CEDAR Creek

Middle

GORDON

Watson

Marsh

Run

Brook

GETTY
7AM

GETTY
8AM

RAMSEUR

KERSHAW

EMORY

SHERIDAN

Belle Grove
(National Trust)

Cemetery

WRIGHT

Valley Pike

Middletown

PEGRAM

Brook

11

4PM

WHARTON

Middletown

MERRITT

N

Scale

0   4000
Feet

Combat Strength
32,000
21,000

CEDAR CREEK
19 October 1864

Casualties
5,672
2,910

Cedar Creek battlefield
Belle Grove. © Jack Kotz, 1990

Early had helped Lee's defense of Richmond by tying down a large Union force for several months. However, at a moment of great opportunity, he made the fatal decision to pull back, allowing Sheridan to smash the Confederate military power in the Valley forever. The news of Sheridan's triumph assured a Repub-lican victory in the upcoming November elections and the prosecution of the war to its end on President Abraham Lincoln's and Lieutenant General Ulysses S. Grant's terms.

Cedar Creek battlefield is on U.S. Route 11 and Interstate 81 at Middletown, Virginia, north of Strasburg. The battlefield is privately owned except for a 100-acre historic property, Belle Grove, owned by the National Trust for Historic Preservation, and 101 state-owned acres occupied by Lord Fairfax Community College.

THE PETERSBURG CAMPAIGN AND SIEGE

15 June 1864–1 April 1865

Christopher M. Calkins

In early June 1864, General Robert E. Lee told Lieutenant General Jubal A. Early, "We must destroy this army of Grant's before he gets to the James River. If he gets there, it will become a siege, and then it will be a mere question of time."

Lieutenant General Ulysses S. Grant's objectives that spring were to capture Richmond and destroy Lee's army. After his attempt to take Richmond by direct force failed at the battle of Cold Harbor in early June, Grant concluded that "the key to taking Richmond is Petersburg." Most of the major supply lines into the capital converged at Petersburg and were funneled into one line, the Richmond and Petersburg Railroad. If Petersburg could be captured, then only the Richmond and Danville Railroad would be left to supply the city of Richmond.

In 1860 the population of Petersburg was around 18,000; by 1864 it had increased to about 22,000 because of refugees and military personnel. Located on the south bank of the Appomattox River at the fall line, Petersburg was a shipping port as well as a rail center. It was protected by defensive earthworks constructed by Captain Charles H. Dimmock with slave labor. The earthworks were in the shape of a flattened horseshoe, with both ends rest-ing on the south bank of the Appomattox. The Dimmock Line, as it was called, was ten miles in length and contained fifty-five batteries for artillery. When Grant first attacked, a skeleton force of troops under General P. G. T. Beauregard held the eastern front, two and a half miles from the center of the city.

Major General William F. "Baldy" Smith's Eighteenth Corps attacked Confederate batteries 5–11 on June 15. Troops commanded by brigadier generals John H. Martindale, William T. H. Brooks, and Edward N. Hinks captured a section of the Dimmock Line, held by Brigadier General Henry A. Wise. They did not take advantage of their success and press on into the city, so the Confederates were able to build a secondary line closer in. For the next two days, as more of Grant's men arrived, they attempted, unsuccessfully, to breach this temporary defensive position. On the night of June 17 the Confederates withdrew to a third, stronger line just outside the city limits. Grant assaulted these lines with his entire army on June 18 but was thrown back. His attack was uncoordinated, and Lee arrived with reinforcements. The next day Grant began the prolonged siege.

The Petersburg campaign lasted nine and a half months, was spread over 176 square

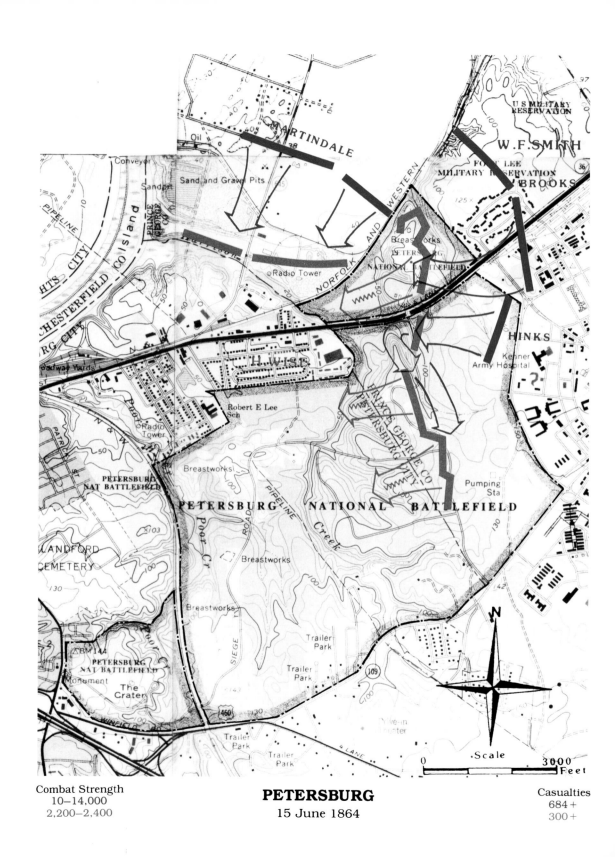

Combat Strength
10–14,000
2,200–2,400

PETERSBURG

15 June 1864

Casualties
684+
300+

miles, and involved six major battles, eleven engagements, forty-four skirmishes, six assaults, nine actions, and three expeditions. The Federal army suffered 42,000 casualties; the Confederate, 28,000. Grant's forces averaged 109,000 men, while Lee's numbered 59,000. The Confederate defense line not only protected Petersburg but ran the distance of the Bermuda Hundred peninsula, then crossed the James River to terminate northeast of Richmond. Lee had to spread his force over a thirty-five-mile front.

On June 19 Grant ordered the Union position fortified with rifle pits, trenches, and forts, and he sent a force to block the Weldon Railroad, Lee's supply line connecting him to Weldon and Wilmington, North Carolina. A bold move by Confederate forces on June 22 quickly sent the Union forces reeling back to the safety of their lines with the loss of many prisoners. The Federals did, however, succeed in extending their trenches west across the Jerusalem Plank Road, where they dug in closer to the Weldon Railroad.

Another Union effort involved a group of Pennsylvania soldiers, former coal miners, who dug a tunnel under a Confederate salient southeast of the city. Their plan was to explode a mine at the end of the tunnel and, in the ensuing chaos, press through the gap in the fortifications and on into Petersburg. Major General Ambrose E. Burnside had given an untested division of black soldiers special training to lead the assault that would follow the explosion. Major General George G. Meade changed the battle plan and ordered Burnside to send in white troops first. The mechanical operation itself was a success, with the detonation going off early on the morning of July 30. Burnside's unprepared white division went forward, but the men crowded into the crater instead of fanning out to continue the assault, making the Federals easy targets for Confederate artillery and mortars. The blacks, the final division to be sent in, were hit by the southern counterattack. When it was over, the Union had suffered 4,000 casualties and the Confederacy less than 1,300. Grant reported to Halleck, "It was the saddest affair I have witnessed in the war. Such opportunity for carrying fortifications I have never seen and do not expect again to have."

Within a few weeks Union troops led by Major General Gouverneur K. Warren were once again on the move to seize the Weldon Railroad. On August 18 they were successful, withstanding a three-day counterattack at Globe Tavern by Lee's men, vainly attempting to regain the supply route. On August 25 Federal soldiers led by Major General Winfield S. Hancock were defeated by Lieutenant General A. P. Hill's columns at Reams Station, twelve miles south of Petersburg. Even with the victory of Reams Station, Lee was unable to use the Weldon Railroad farther north than Stony Creek Depot, sixteen miles south of Petersburg. At that point he had to load his supplies into wagons for the cross-country journey to Dinwiddie Court House via the Flat Foot Road. From this county seat village the wagons followed the Boydton Plank Road into the city. Consequently, this roadway and newly developed supply route became an intermediate objective for Grant's army.

Grant continued his alternating blows first north, then south of the James River. In late September he authorized Major General Benjamin F. Butler to pressure Lee at Fort Harrison and at New Market Heights. At the same time Grant ordered two offensive movements to gain the Boydton Plank Road and then capture the last remaining rail connection into Petersburg, the South Side Railroad. There was fighting in the final days of September and the first of October in the Peebles farm area, just west of Warren's position on the Weldon Railroad. Although Grant was unable to reach his goal, he gained more ground for his army so it could extend its trenches westward. On October 27 another force was sent out that briefly held the Boydton Plank Road near Burgess Mill on Hatcher's Run. A combined attack by Confederate infantry and cavalry sent the Federals back to their lines.

There was little battle action during the winter. Rain, snow, and sleet made the sandy Virginia byways too sloppy for any major movement of forces. The men built small cities of log huts to protect themselves from the weather. However, in three days of fighting near Armstrong's Mill on February 5–7, Grant was able to extend the Union lines all the way to Hatcher's Run, less than three miles from the Boydton Plank Road.

As spring came and the muddy roads began to harden, Lee knew that the Federals would soon start their major thrust for the South Side Railroad. He decided to attack the Union lines on the eastern front at Fort Stedman to force Grant to move men from the lines west of Petersburg. Lee had concluded that he would soon have to move out of Petersburg to save his army, and he needed an escape route toward General Joseph E. Johnston in North Carolina. The southern offensive began early on the morning of March 25, and the Confederates were initially successful in capturing the fort and the adjoining lines. However, by noon a Union counterattack had regained the lost ground, and the Confederates were forced back to their lines. The stage was now set for Grant's final spring campaign.

The Union columns began their march from the entrenchments on the morning of March 29, and by evening they held the Boydton Plank Road near its intersection with Quaker Road. On the thirty-first, as the Federals closed in, there was fighting both south of the White Oak Road and at nearby Dinwiddie Court House. Lee's men made a desperate attempt to keep the Federals away from the

A portion of the map "Central Virginia showing Lieut. Gen'l. U.S. Grant's Campaign and Marches of the Armies under his Command in 1864–65," published by the Engineer Bureau of the U.S. War Department. Many maps such as this were produced during and after the war to illustrate campaigns and events of special significance. (Civil War map no. 516, Geography and Map Division, Library of Congress)

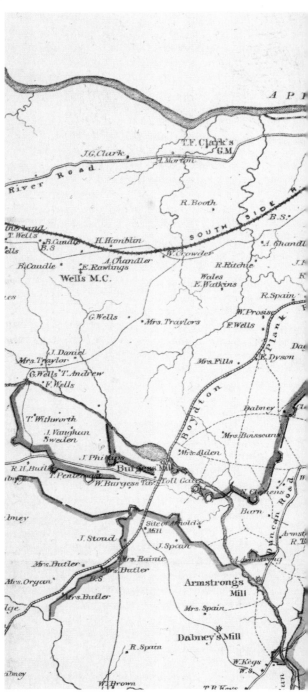

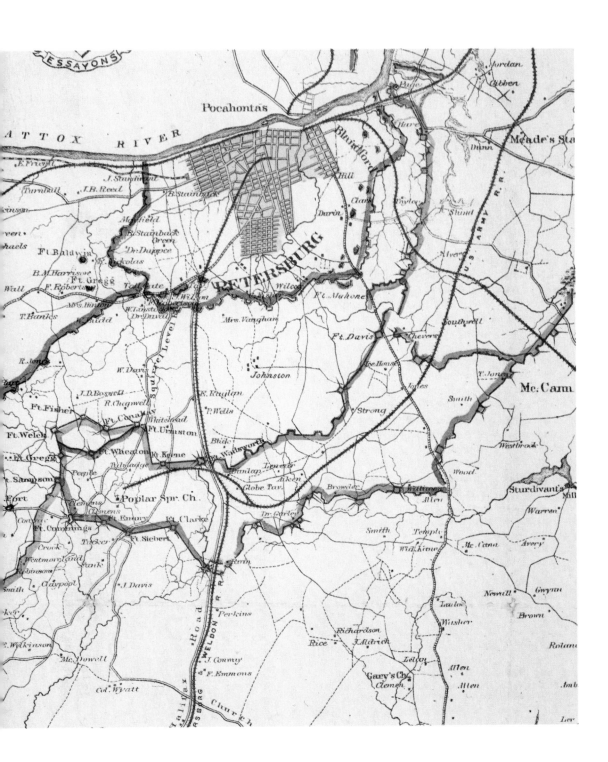

South Side Railroad by holding the important road junction at Five Forks. On the evening of April 1 a combined Union force of infantry and cavalry defeated Major General George E. Pickett at Five Forks. The path was now open to grab the last Confederate supply line into Petersburg.

Grant quickly sent orders for an all-out assault. On the morning of April 2 two Federal corps made attacks at different points along the Confederate defenses. One corps forced a breakthrough that isolated a section of Lee's army near Hatcher's Run. Confederate Lieutenant General A. P. Hill was killed while riding forward to close this breach. Major General Edward O. C. Ord's Army of the James attacked a Confederate outpost west of the city, Fort Gregg, eventually overwhelming its defenders. In a final fight at Sutherland Station, the South Side Railroad was officially cut by Federal forces. That night Lee began withdrawing his forces from the city to the north side of the Appomattox River, where they would begin their westward trek.

The morning of April 3 General Grant and President Lincoln met briefly in Petersburg. They discussed the president's plans for a lenient policy toward the South after the anticipated surrender. With this policy in mind, Grant rode off to catch up with his army, now on the road to Appomattox.

Petersburg National Battlefield is at Petersburg, Virginia, 25 miles south of Richmond on Interstate 85. There are 2,761 acres of the historic battlefield within its authorized boundaries; 1,206 of these are privately owned.

Part of a map produced in 1865 by the U.S. Army Corps of Engineers of the "Region embraced in the Operations of the Armies against Richmond and Petersburg." It has been hand-colored to indicate "Union Works" in red and "Rebel Works" in blue. (Civil War map no. 644, Geography and Map Division, Library of Congress)

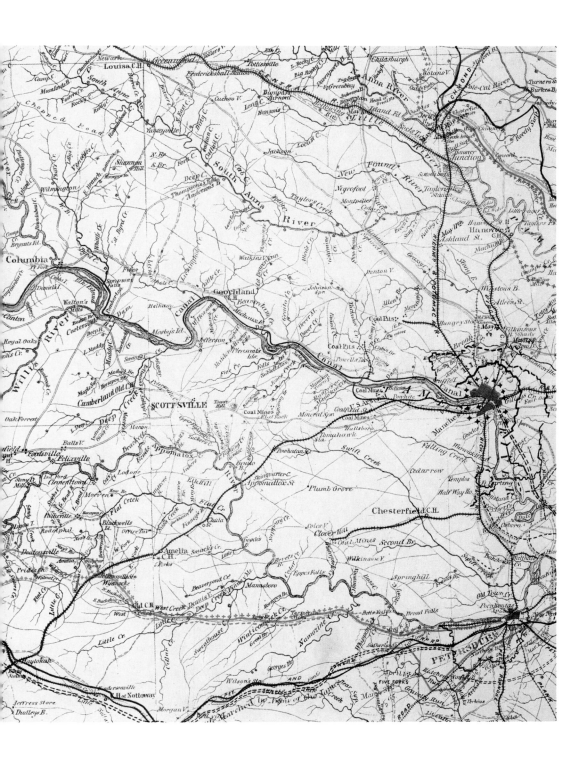

REAMS STATION

25 August 1864

Christopher M. Calkins

The Weldon Railroad, one of General Robert E. Lee's lifelines, connected Petersburg, Virginia, and the Confederacy's last major port at Wilmington, North Carolina, via Weldon. The Union effort to cut that connection began on August 18 near Globe Tavern, six miles south of Petersburg. Federal Major General Gouverneur K. Warren's forces took control of the railroad and fought Confederate General P. G. T. Beauregard's forces to a standstill. The next day a Confederate flank attack on Warren's troops took nearly 2,700 prisoners, including Brigadier General Joseph Hayes, but did not push the Federals away from the railroad. Major General William Mahone's attempt on August 21 was also unsuccessful. This four-day conflict, known as the battle of Weldon Railroad, gave the Union control over the railroad from Reams Station to Petersburg, twelve miles north. In September the Federals built Fort Wadsworth on the site of that battle to protect their gain. (The fort is on the Halifax Road and is preserved in the Petersburg National Battlefield Park.)

On August 24 Federal Major General Winfield S. Hancock's 7,000-man Second Corps was ordered to destroy the fourteen miles of Weldon Railroad track from Globe Tavern through Reams Station, which had been burned by Union cavalry raiders in late June, to Rowanty Creek. Hancock took two of his

divisions and Brigadier General David M. Gregg's 2,000-man cavalry division, and by that evening, his men had destroyed the track to a point about three miles beyond Reams Station.

On August 25 the Federals were five miles short of Rowanty Creek when Lieutenant General A. P. Hill approached rapidly with 8,000–10,000 Confederate troops. Hancock's men moved quickly back to Reams Station into an elliptical line of breastworks with an opening in the rear that provided inadequate protection for the soldiers. These poorly built works had been thrown up by the Union soldiers who had burned the station buildings two months earlier. Only about 700 yards of low parapet faced the enemy, with the returns extending approximately 800–1,000 yards and curving inward. The returns were so close together that the troops holding them were exposed to enfilading and rear fire. This parapet paralleled the railroad twenty to thirty yards behind the track, which ran through a cut, then up on an embankment. If the Union troops needed supplies or had to retreat along the rail line, they would be exposed to enemy view and fire. Adjacent to the railroad was the Halifax Road. At the north end of the parapet was the Oak Grove Methodist Church, later to serve as a hospital.

The battle of Reams Station began when

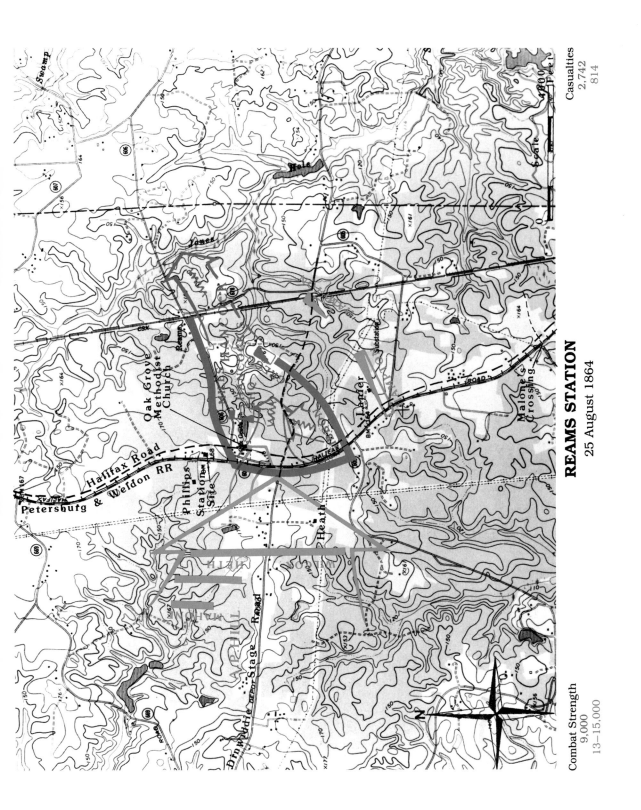

REAMS STATION

25 August 1864

Casualties

2,742

814

Combat Strength

9,000

13–15,000

Gregg's cavalry was pushed in from its post at Malone's Crossing by Confederate Major General Wade Hampton's 5,000-man cavalry. At the same time Hancock's pickets were pressed from the west by the van of Major General Henry Heth's columns (Heth was in command because Hill reported himself sick) advancing on the Dinwiddie Stage Road. At 2:00 P.M. Hancock's two divisions, under Major General John Gibbon and Brigadier General Nelson Miles, readied themselves behind the breastworks for the enemy assault.

Three brigades under Major General Cadmus Wilcox arrived first, followed by two divisions of horsemen under Hampton. Wilcox's soldiers quickly made two stabs from the west, coming within yards of the parapet before being forced back. They were reinforced by Heth's and Mahone's divisions. At about 5:30 P.M., after Confederate artillery under Lieutenant Colonel William Pegram had peppered the Union troops, the final attack began. This time the Confederates were able to break through at the northwest angle of the Union line and carry the fighting into the nearby railroad cut. Simultaneously, Hampton's troopers assailed the lower return from the south. Miles held his line along the northern return, but Gibbon's men broke or were captured. Hancock tried to rally his fleeing troops and was partially successful in keeping the battle from turning into a rout. Nightfall and a heavy rainstorm brought an end to the inglorious defeat of Hancock's Second Corps. The poor performance of the corps has been attributed to numerous factors, but especially to the men's exhaustion after their recent expedition north of the James River and to the large number of new draftees.

The Union army withdrew to the Petersburg entrenchments along the Jerusalem Plank Road after suffering 2,742 casualties, mostly prisoners. The Confederates lost 814. The destruction of the railroad was stopped for a time, and Lee was able to use the line as far north as Stony Creek Depot, sixteen miles south of Petersburg and nine miles south of Reams Station. From that point, supplies had to be unloaded and carried by wagon train to Dinwiddie Court House, then via the Boydton Plank Road into the besieged city.

Even with the victory at Reams Station, the prospects for Lee's army and Petersburg were dimming.

Reams Station battlefield is on State Route 604 between interstates 85 and 95, 10 miles south of Petersburg, Virginia. The entire battlefield is privately owned.

"MAKING FREE": AFRICAN AMERICANS AND THE CIVIL WAR

James O. Horton

The cause of antislavery, for which black Americans worked and prayed so long, entered the political arena in the late 1830s with the formation of the Liberty party. In the 1840s the Free Soil party diluted the abolitionist message with the politically popular appeal to "keep the western territories free of slavery and open for the settlement of free labor." The aim of isolating slavery in the South attracted many white workers who were anxious to exclude African Americans from the frontier lands. In 1854 the Republican party, an amalgamation of the politically disaffected, entered the field with the motto "Free Labor, Free Soil, Free Men."

The Republican candidate in 1860, Abraham Lincoln, had long refused to advocate federal action to abolish slavery and would not publicly condemn Illinois laws forbidding blacks to testify in state and local court cases involving whites. "If a white man happens to owe me anything," one black leader explained, "unless I can prove it by testimony of [another] white man, I cannot collect the debt." Nor did Lincoln oppose Illinois regulations that barred the children of tax-paying black property owners from attending public schools. Lincoln's record led many blacks to join antislavery whites in forming the Radical Abolitionist

party, backing Gerrit Smith, a white abolitionist from New York State, who stood no chance to win but whose candidacy would raise the antislavery issue. "Ten thousand votes for Gerrit Smith . . . ," Frederick Douglass contended, "would do more for the ultimate abolition of slavery in this country than two million for Abraham Lincoln."

Although Lincoln's inaugural address made clear his intention not to interfere with slavery where it existed, the blacks of Philadelphia, for example, took consolation in the election of "if not an Abolitionist, at least an antislavery reputation to the Presidency." As the South declared itself separated from the United States, many blacks welcomed the secession. "Go at once," urged one black spokesman from Illinois. "There can be no union between freedom and slavery." With slavery isolated in the South and no longer protected by the military might of the United States, many abolitionists believed successful slave uprisings were inevitable.

Although abolition was not yet official U.S. policy, an *Anglo-African* editorial expressed the common belief: "The colored Americans cannot be indifferent. . . . Out of this strife will come freedom." All over the North blacks organized military units and offered their services to the Union. New York City units drilled in hired halls, African Americans in Boston petitioned their state for permission to serve, Pittsburgh blacks sent a letter to the state militia declaring their readiness, blacks in Washington, D.C., petitioned the War Department directly. In all cases they were turned down. The War Department's position was clear: "This Department has no intention at present to call into service of the Government any colored soldiers."

The long bloody war, however, forced a rethinking of this policy. In July 1862 Congress provided for the enlistment of black troops into segregated units under white officers. The successes of these troops in combat created a more positive northern public opinion of black soldiers. The *New York Tribune* asserted, "Facts are beginning to dispel prejudices." Lincoln, quick to grasp the impact of Confederate defeats at the hands of black troops, urged white commanders to take advantage of every opportunity to use them.

By the summer of 1863 the Bureau of Colored Troops was in operation within the War Department. As the war droned on, the growing reluctance of white men to join the military increased the need for African American troops, but discriminatory policies made it more difficult to recruit black soldiers; they were paid less than whites and received inferior equipment and food. Another deterrent to serving in the military was the Confederates' announcement, in the spring of 1863, that captured black soldiers would be executed or enslaved and their white officers executed. Later that year reports confirmed that the Confederates had slaughtered several dozen black prisoners at Fort Pillow, Tennessee, after they had surrendered. At Memphis black troops took an oath on their knees to avenge this barbarism. "Remember Fort Pillow" became a rallying cry for black soldiers for the duration of the war.

The booming northern economy also made military service less attractive to blacks. At the same time, white resentment of the blacks newly employed in industry was aggravated by whites' perception of the war as being for the benefit of blacks. Whites protesting the military draft attacked black communities, destroying property and killing black men, women, and children. African Americans had always been vulnerable to insults and sporadic violence, but during the war they were especially targeted. Black soldiers were attacked on the streets of Washington, New York, Boston, and other cities, sometimes in the presence of the police, who provided no protection. In spite of these deterrents, the recruitment efforts of black leaders such as Frederick Douglass, Williams Wells Brown, and John Mercer Langston maintained a steady enlistment.

At the same time abolition was gradually becoming a northern war aim. Congress passed a series of confiscation acts to deprive the Confederacy of its human property, and Lincoln issued the dramatic Emancipation Proclamation. A military measure, the proclamation applied only to slaves who remained under Confederate control, but blacks and many white abolitionists treated it as a proclamation of general abolition. For them, New Year's Day, 1863, began the "Year of Jubilee."

Almost 180,000 blacks served officially in the Union army, and countless others served unofficially as scouts, spies, and laborers building military fortifications. Blacks were sometimes employed as shock troops in the most dangerous missions and were provided with insufficient supplies and inferior weapons. Black troops made up less than 10 percent of the Union army, but their casualty rate was disproportionately high. More than 30,000 were killed or died during the war, nearly 3,000 in combat. Sixteen black soldiers and four black sailors received the Medal of Honor. By the war's end just under 100 blacks had been promoted to officer ranks, the highest-ranking being a surgeon, Lieutenant Colonel Alexander T. Augustana.

The bravery of blacks in the war was the subject of many news reports. Although such reports did not eradicate prejudice, they did have some short-term effect on racial attitudes in the North. One black Philadelphian stated that "public sentiment has undergone a great change in the past month or two, and more especially since the brilliant exploits of several colored regiments."

This change in sentiment had legislative effect when the U.S. Congress repealed the prohibition against blacks carrying the U.S. mail, struck down the exclusion of blacks as witnesses in federal courts, and included African American males as eligible voters in the District of Columbia. In Illinois blacks successfully lobbied against laws prohibiting their immigration to the state; in Illinois and California they won the right to testify in trials involving whites.

By the end of the war most restrictive laws had been abolished in the North, but racially restrictive traditions and customs continued. Job discrimination ensured the perpetuation of black poverty. Although formal policies discriminating against blacks on public conveyances and in public schools were abolished in some northern cities after the war, discrimination in public accommodations continued. The fourteenth and fifteenth constitutional amendments, ratified in 1868 and 1870, granted citizenship to blacks and encouraged (but did not ensure) black suffrage.

In the South after the war ended, new forms of racial control were asserted through restrictive legislation and political terrorism. Most southern African Americans remained economically dependent and politically mute. Although the freedom that the Emancipation Proclamation symbolized was generations away, progress toward racial equality through the next century was built on the foundation laid by black and white abolitionists and soldiers.

Black Medal of Honor winners

NEW MARKET HEIGHTS

29 September 1864

William W. Gwaltney

In September 1864 Lieutenant General Ulysses S. Grant ordered Major General Benjamin F. Butler to prepare his Army of the James for an advance against Confederate defenses southeast of Richmond. The attack would include infantry, cavalry, and artillery and would have two objectives: first, to force Lee to weaken his Petersburg defenses by drawing troops from there to repel Butler's attacks (Lee was also shuttling troops back and forth between Richmond/Petersburg and the Shenandoah Valley) and, second, to capture Richmond. Butler directed a two-pronged attack. He ordered Major General Edward O. C. Ord to cross the James River with two Eighteenth Corps divisions. They crossed at Aiken's Landing, upstream from Jones Neck, and advanced up the Varina Road to assault Fort Harrison, the bulwark of Richmond's eastern exterior defenses. At the same time Butler sent Major General David Bell Birney's Tenth Corps across the James to join Brigadier General Charles J. Paine's black division from the Eighteenth Corps at Deep Bottom. From that bridgehead Birney and Paine's combined force was to strike north on farm roads against the formidable Confederate line that stretched west to east along the New Market Road.

Butler was an advocate of enlisting black soldiers, and his attacking columns included fourteen regiments of blacks, primarily United States Colored Troops. The USCT were rested and reasonably well trained. For many of these soldiers the army was more than merely a job or a chance to show their gratitude for emancipation. They saw it as an opportunity to strike a blow against slavery and to demonstrate their willingness to fight and die. Some of these men were free blacks and others were escaped slaves, or "contrabands."

On the foggy morning of September 29 the 13,000 Union troops left the staging area at Deep Bottom Landing in three columns. Brigadier General Alfred H. Terry, on the right, marched his Tenth Corps division north to take a position along Four Mile Creek, south of the New Market Road. In the middle a black brigade headed north and then filed in behind Terry. Birney's other two divisions advanced along a road west of Terry's line of march and parallel to it. Paine's USCT took the lead, followed by Brigadier General Robert S. Foster's division. Paine's column turned east as it approached Four Mile Creek and formed the Union line of battle facing the Confederate right. Dismounted black cavalry linked Paine's right to Terry's left. West of those troopers Colonel Samuel A. Duncan's brigade of USCT formed Paine's spearhead. Foster's division halted along the Grover House Road, ready to serve as a reserve force.

North of Paine and Terry loomed the Con-

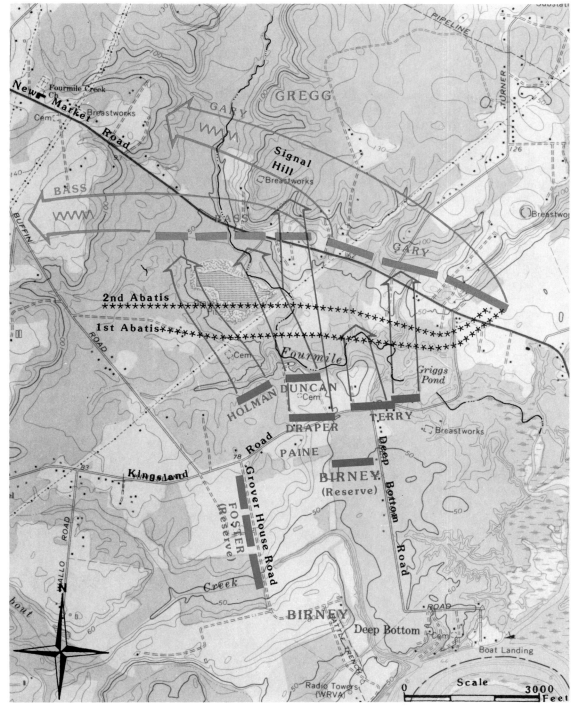

Combat Strength
13,000
1,800

NEW MARKET HEIGHTS
29 September 1864

Casualties
850
50

federate position at New Market Heights. Emplacements atop the towering heights protecting artillery were sited to command the approaches to the Confederate works. On the western end of the heights, Signal Hill, a well-prepared earthen fortification with cannon that commanded much of the ground below, became a focus of the battle. Confederate infantry entrenchments along the southern foot of the heights swept the gentle slopes descending from the New Market Road to Four Mile Creek. In addition to making rifle pits, the Confederate soldiers had covered their front with a double line of abatis to delay and entangle the attacking soldiers. One abatis was constructed of felled trees with the branches facing the enemy, tops lopped off to snag the Union soldiers' clothing and expose them to gunfire. Closer to the entrenchments was a second abatis, parallel to the first. Much of it was a *chevaux-de-frise*, a dangerous-looking impediment made by boring holes in logs and embedding rows of sharpened timbers.

Lieutenant Colonel Frederick S. Bass commanded the troops confronting Duncan's black brigade. Bass's troops were General Robert E. Lee's "grenadier guards" — the First, Fourth, and Fifth Texas and the Third Arkansas regiments of infantry. To their left was Brigadier General Martin W. Gary's veteran cavalry brigade, prepared to fight dismounted. These soldiers, in the trenches at the foot of the heights, along with artillery units of the Third Richmond Howitzers and the First Rockbridge Artillery, were led by Brigadier General John Gregg, the senior Confederate officer on the field. The total southern force numbered less than 1,800 men.

At about 5:30 A.M. Duncan's infantry, having forded Four Mile Creek, attacked the Confederate positions to their front. Bass's infantry waited until the black soldiers reached the first line of abatis and struggled to move over, under, and around the obstructions. The long line of Confederate riflemen, supported by the artillery on the heights, sent a crashing volley into the USCT.

Gary's Twenty-fourth Virginia Cavalry, fighting dismounted, enfiladed the Union right. The seasoned Confederates poured well-aimed volleys into the ranks of the black soldiers. After two color bearers were shot down, Sergeant Major Christian Fleetwood of the Fourth USCT seized the national colors. Duncan was wounded, and Colonel John W. Ames, the senior regimental commander, called a retreat. Many blacks were killed or wounded, and some surrendered, only to be killed or imprisoned by the enraged Confederates. During this attack another of Paine's brigades under Colonel Alonzo Draper moved forward; however, before Draper was able to reach the Confederate lines, he was forced to cover Ames's retreat.

Stubbornly, Birney held to the initial plan for storming the Confederate works. The USCT under Draper moved forward again in a line six companies wide and ten ranks deep, while Terry's three brigades demonstrated on the USCT's right toward the Confederate works. Draper's soldiers of the Fifth, Thirty-sixth, and Thirty-eighth USCT were supported on the left by the Twenty-second USCT deployed as skirmishers.

Draper moved out of the Four Mile Creek ravine and over the field of Duncan's attack. With the fog lifting, the Federals were easy targets. Draper's men broke into a charge but, being too far west, were slowed at the marshy creek. They then became tangled in the abatis, where Bass's Texans blasted them with deadly volleys. Unable to hear or unwilling to heed Draper's efforts to resume the charge, the USCTs halted to fire back in self-defense, unwittingly assisting the Confederates. For nearly a half hour the soldiers fought a desperate, inconclusive battle. When the Confederate fire slackened, Draper's orders to continue the charge were finally obeyed. Penetrating the first abatis, then the *chevaux-de-frise*, the troops stormed the Confederate rifle pits, drove off the few remaining defenders in hand-to-hand fighting, and took the summit. After the officers of Company G, Fifth USCT

Regiment, had been killed, First Sergeant Powhatan Beaty took command of his company and led it into combat. To Draper's left, west of Four Mile Creek, the Twenty-second USCT consolidated into battle line and reached New Market Road. A charge by the Third New Hampshire and the Twenty-fourth Massachusetts of Terry's division against the Confederate left, held by the First Rockbridge Artillery, sent the battery into retreat. When the fighting was over and the smoke cleared, it was only about 8:00 A.M.

The fighting at New Market had turned when word of Ord's forces, striking up the Varina Road against Fort Harrison, had compelled Gregg to withdraw troops from New Market Heights to strengthen the Confederate forces there. This redeployment so weakened the forces opposing Birney that his men were able to overpower the few who remained and seize the heights. The Confederates, with 1,800 soldiers engaged, lost perhaps 50 men. The Federals lost 850 of their 13,000 men.

The men of the USCT proved themselves worthy soldiers in those hours of battle. Numerous soldiers were cited for gallantry in the assault, but none of the citations speaks more eloquently than the one granted for bravery to Corporal James Miles of Company B, Thirty-sixth USCT. "Having had his arm mutilated, making immediate amputation necessary, he loaded and discharged his piece with one hand and urged his men forward; this within thirty yards of the enemy's works." Miles was one of fourteen black soldiers and two white officers at the battle of New Market Heights who were later awarded the nation's highest military accolade, the Medal of Honor.

New Market Heights battlefield is on State Route 5 and Kingsland Road, 4 miles south of the Byrd International Airport at Richmond, Virginia. Part of the battlefield is owned by Henrico County.

Black Medal of Honor winners

BENTONVILLE

19–21 March 1865

John G. Barrett

In January 1865 Union Major General William Tecumseh Sherman's 60,000 veterans began crossing the Savannah River into South Carolina. As he had done on the march to the sea, Sherman divided his army into two parts, each following a different line of advance. Major General Oliver O. Howard commanded the right wing, composed of the Fifteenth and Seventeenth corps. The left wing, under Major General Henry W. Slocum, consisted of the Fourteenth and Twentieth corps. Brigadier General H. Judson Kilpatrick was in charge of the cavalry. By March 3 Sherman's army had reached Cheraw, its last stop in South Carolina. Here the general learned that General Joseph E. Johnston had replaced General P. G. T. Beauregard as commander of the Confederate forces in the Carolinas. Sherman correctly surmised that his able opponent would somehow unite his various commands, which were scattered from Mississippi to North Carolina, and choose a place to give battle.

Five days later Sherman's entire army was in North Carolina, and by the fifteenth it had crossed the Cape Fear River at Fayetteville. The final phase of the great march that had begun in November 1864 at Atlanta was now unfolding. From Savannah to Fayetteville, Sherman had moved his army almost flawlessly, but he committed a major error in failing to recognize the importance of a Confederate delaying action on March 16 at Averasboro, east of Fayetteville. Howard's wing, moving on the extreme right, continued its march on Goldsboro, but the stout defense put up at Averasboro by Lieutenant General W. J. Hardee stopped the advance of the Union Twentieth Corps. As a result, the columns of Slocum's left wing became strung out, and the distance between the wings of the army increased.

It was almost daylight on March 18 when the Confederate chief of cavalry, Lieutenant General Wade Hampton, notified Johnston that the Union army was marching on Goldsboro, not Raleigh, and that Sherman's right wing was approximately half a day's march in advance of the left wing. Johnston saw an opportunity to crush one of the Union columns while it was separated from the others. In order to strike the head of Sherman's left wing the next morning, Johnston ordered his troops at Smithfield and Elevation to march immediately to Bentonville, a village approximately twenty miles west of Goldsboro. At Smithfield, Confederate General Braxton Bragg had Major General Robert F. Hoke's division of North Carolinians as well as remnants of the once-proud Army of Tennessee, the survivors of Franklin and Nashville, now under the command of Lieutenant General A. P. Stewart. Hardee was encamped at Elevation with the divisions of Major General La-

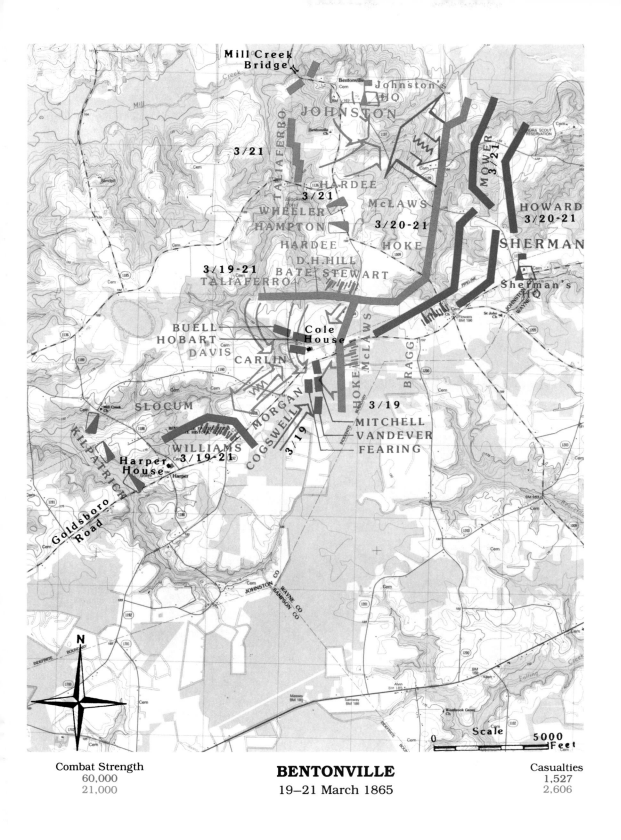

Mill Creek
Bridge

Johnston's
HQ

JOHNSTON

3/21

TALIAFERRO

HARDEE
3/21

WHEELER
HAMPTON

McLAWS
3/20-21

HARDEE   HOKE
D.H.HILL
3/19-21   BATE STEWART
TALIAFERRO

MOWER
3/21

HOWARD
3/20-21

SHERMAN

Sherman's
HQ

BUELL
HOBART
DAVIS

Cole
House

CARLIN

McLAWS

BRAGG

SLOCUM

MORGAN
COGSWELL

3/19

HOKE

3/19

MITCHELL
VANDEVER
FEARING

KILPATRICK

WILLIAMS
3/19-21

Harper
House

Goldsboro
Road

N

Scale

0   5000
                      Feet

Combat Strength
60,000
21,000

BENTONVILLE
19–21 March 1865

Casualties
1,527
2,606

fayette McLaws and Brigadier General W. B. Taliaferro. When Bragg and Stewart reached Bentonville on the eighteenth, Hardee was still six miles away.

Johnston's combat strength was about 21,000, considerably fewer than the 40,000 Sherman thought opposed him. This paucity in manpower was offset, at least in part, by the large number of able Confederate commanders present. Besides Johnston and Bragg, who were full generals, three officers — Hampton, Hardee, and Stewart — carried the rank of lieutenant general. Also on the field were many seasoned officers of lesser rank, including major generals D. H. Hill, Joseph Wheeler, Robert F. Hoke, Lafayette McLaws, and William W. Loring. Bentonville was singular among Civil War battles for having so few men led in combat by so many veteran officers of high rank.

During the evening of the eighteenth, Hampton informed Johnston that Union troops — Slocum's column with the Fourteenth Corps in the lead, Major General Jefferson C. Davis commanding — were moving down the Goldsboro Road. He recommended a surprise attack at the eastern end of the Cole plantation, about two miles south of Bentonville near the Goldsboro Road. The land there was marshy and covered with dense thickets of blackjack pine.

Sunday morning, March 19, dawned clear and beautiful, and the unsuspecting Union soldiers expected a day of peace and quiet. They thought little of the fact that the Confederate cavalry was giving ground grudgingly and even revived an expression of the Atlanta campaign, "They don't drive worth a damn." Slocum, who had no idea that Johnston's entire army was gathering only a few miles down the road, sent a dispatch to Sherman, who was with Howard, that only Confederate horsemen and a few pieces of artillery were in his front. Sherman did not anticipate an attack because he could not imagine that Johnston would risk a fight with the Neuse River in his rear.

The deployment of the Confederate troops was slow because only one road led through the dense woods and thickets between Bentonville and the battlefield. First Hoke's division was placed on the Confederate left with its line crossing the Goldsboro Road almost at right angles. Stewart's Army of Tennessee was to the right of Hoke, with its right strongly thrown forward to conform to the edge of an open field. The center of Johnston's position was at a corner of the Cole plantation approximately a mile north of the Goldsboro Road. The two wings went forward from the center, the left blocking the advance of Union Brigadier General W. P. Carlin's division of the Fourteenth Corps. The right was partially hidden in a thicket, ready to stop any flanking movements by the enemy. However, Hardee, who was to hold the ground between Hoke and Stewart, had not reached the field when the two commands went into position, so Johnston had to change the deposition of his troops. Hardee did not arrive until around 2:45 P.M., long after Hoke's artillery had opened fire on Carlin's advance troops, the brigades of brigadier generals H. C. Hobart and G. P. Buell, as they approached the Cole house.

As the morning advanced, Slocum, still convinced that he faced only cavalry, sent word to Sherman that help was not needed. At the same time he ordered a general advance. The Confederate right responded fiercely to the assault, and in the words of a Union officer, "I tell you it was a tight spot . . . [we] stood as long as man could stand . . . [then] we run like the devil." Carlin's men fell back to the vicinity of the Cole house, where they deployed carelessly into a weak defensive line. Soon they were joined by Brigadier General J. S. Robinson's brigade of the Twentieth Corps. By this time Brigadier General J. D. Morgan's division of the Fourteenth Corps and Lieutenant Colonel David Miles's brigade of Carlin's division had moved into position south of the Goldsboro Road opposite Hoke and on Carlin's right. Log breastworks, thrown up in great haste by Morgan's brigade commanders, brigadier generals John G. Mitchell, W. Vandever, and B. D. Fearing, contributed to the Union success late in the day when the Confederates went on the offensive. One Federal officer said that those logs "saved Sherman's reputation." It wasn't until 1:30 P.M. that Slocum realized that he was in trouble. He decided to go on the defensive and to contact Sherman immediately for reinforcements. He also ordered reserves from his column to hasten forward.

The initiative at this point passed to Johnston, who at about 3:00 P.M. ordered his right wing under Hardee to take the offensive. As the men of Major General William B. Bate and those of Taliaferro, Hill, and Stewart moved out, Rebel yells pierced the air. The Army of Tennessee, determined to redeem itself on the battlefield, saw this as an opportunity to meet its old antagonist of the Atlanta campaign. Hardee, Stewart, and Hill led the charge on horseback (described by a teenage member of Hoke's command, Walter Clark) "across an open field . . . with colors flying and line of battle in . . . perfect order. . . . It was gallantly done but for those watching from Hoke's trenches it was . . . painful to see how close their battleflags were together, regiments being scarcely larger than companies and divisions not much larger than a regiment should be." The Union left was crushed by this stirring, well-executed move and driven back in confusion upon the Twentieth Corps under Brigadier General A. S. Williams, a mile to the rear.

Bragg's troops did not participate in the charge. The general failed to put Hoke's division into action until the Confederate right halted to reform its lines. McLaws's division, sent to reinforce Bragg, also remained in reserve. However, the rout of Carlin's troops had exposed the Union right, enabling Hill to break through and strike Morgan's division in the rear while Hoke attacked from the front. The result was the bitterest fighting of the day, the crucial period of the battle. Veterans of the Army of Northern Virginia thought "it was the hottest infantry fight they had been in except Cold Harbor." Only the timely arrival of Brigadier General William Cogswell's brigade of the Twentieth Corps saved Morgan from defeat. This was the turning point of the battle of Bentonville.

The third and final phase of the fighting on the nineteenth involved a Confederate move against the Twentieth Corps on the Union left, which had dug in effectively. Five times between 5:00 P.M. and sundown, McLaws's division and the exhausted troops of Taliaferro and Bate tried without success to carry the formidable Union works. A North Carolina sergeant was certain that there was no spot "in the battle of Gettysburg as hot as that place."

As dusk faded into darkness, the weary combatants gradually ceased their firing. Nightfall brought an end to the day's bloody fighting, but the smoke of battle and hundreds of smoldering pine stumps and trees added to the dark gloom of the evening. After burying their dead, the Confederate soldiers withdrew to the position they had occupied earlier in the day.

The Union wounded were taken to the home of John and Amy Harper, which had been converted into a field hospital. "A dozen surgeons and attendants in their shirt sleeves stood at rude benches cutting off arms and legs and throwing them out of the window where they lay scattered on the grass," observed an eyewitness. "The legs of the infantrymen could be distinguished from those of the cavalry by the size of their calves."

The next morning Johnston, anticipating the arrival of Sherman's right wing, changed his position. He bent his left back to form a bridgehead, with the only bridge to his rear on Mill Creek. This put the Confederate line, in the shape of a large irregular V, entirely north of the Goldsboro Road.

On the late afternoon of March 20, Sherman's army of 60,000 was again united. Howard's troops, the last to arrive on the battlefield, dug in on the right. The Union left was held by the Fourteenth and Twentieth corps. There was no heavy fighting this day, only brisk skirmishing up and down the line, some of it involving the three regiments of North Carolina Junior Reserves in Hoke's command. These youths, none over eighteen years of age and affectionately referred to as "the seed corn of the Confederacy," fought well, and Hoke praised them for repulsing "every charge that was made upon them."

Johnston, now firmly entrenched, hoped the enemy would launch a major attack, but Sherman, his well-fortified line conforming roughly to the Confederate position, had other ideas. His first priority was to open communications with major generals John M. Schofield and Alfred Terry, who were awaiting him at Goldsboro with their troops.

On the twenty-first the only important action occurred on the Union right when Brigadier General J. A. Mower, without consulting his superiors, managed to push two brigades around the Confederate left flank. He reached a point less than a mile from the strategically important Mill Creek bridge before being halted. Among the Confederate units helping to blunt this offensive was the skeletal Eighth Texas Cavalry under Hardee's immediate command. In a gallant charge by the cavalrymen against the Union left, Hardee's sixteen-year-old son, Willie, was killed. A few hours earlier the father had reluctantly given his teenage son permission to join the Texans. Mower retreated but was in the process of reforming his lines for a renewal of the attack when orders arrived from Sherman instructing him to remain where he was and dig in. This dispatch brought to an end all offensive action for the day.

During the night of the twenty-first, Johnston ordered his army to cross Mill Creek and to move on Smithfield, beginning a withdrawal that could have "but one end." The next day Sherman, after burying the dead and removing the wounded, put his troops in motion for Goldsboro rather than in pursuit of his long-time antagonist.

Bentonville was neither a large battle (Federal losses, 1,527; Confederate, 2,606) nor a decisive engagement compared with, say, Gettysburg or Chancellorsville. Yet it was a major contest, involving 80,000 troops, and, most important, was the climax of Sherman's highly successful Carolinas campaign. At Goldsboro he joined his army with those of Schofield and Terry and gained rail connections to the large supply bases on the North Carolina coast. Sherman's campaign had laid waste a forty-five-mile-wide swath of countryside from Savannah to Goldsboro.

Even though his men had fought bravely at Bentonville and his army was still intact, Johnston had no illusions about the future. He knew his small force could do little more than annoy Sherman; it certainly could not stop him. And when morale among his troops began to wane badly with the rumors of Richmond's fall, he directed that all executions for desertion be suspended. The time was almost at hand to end all killing.

Bentonville State Battleground is west of Goldsboro on State Road 1008 near Newton Grove, North Carolina, 45 miles southwest of Raleigh on U.S. Route 70. There are 90 acres of the historic battlefield within its authorized boundaries.

FIVE FORKS

1 April 1865

Christopher M. Calkins

Lieutenant General Ulysses S. Grant began his spring offensive at Petersburg on the overcast morning of March 29, ordering the Federals to move around the Confederate right to force General Robert E. Lee's army out of the Petersburg fortifications. Major General Philip Sheridan's cavalry headed for Dinwiddie Court House. If the Confederates pulled out of their fortifications to attack him, he was to send his entire force against them. If they did not, he was authorized to wreck the Richmond and Danville Railroad and the South Side Railroad. Union Major General Gouverneur K. Warren's 12,000 troops were ordered to leave their winter camps south of Petersburg and march southwest up Quaker Road toward the Boydton Plank Road. The vanguard of Warren's column, under Brigadier General Joshua L. Chamberlain, ran into Confederate resistance around the Lewis farmhouse. They pushed the Confederates back into their lines along the White Oak Road, and the long-sought Boydton Plank Road was firmly in Union hands.

On March 30 Warren's soldiers continued fortifying their position on the Boydton Plank Road in a driving rainstorm. In front of them Confederate Lieutenant General Richard H. Anderson's small corps was well entrenched along the White Oak Road. Anderson's left flank rested on Hatcher's Run near Burgess Mill, and the right angled back along the Claiborne Road to Hatcher's Run. To the west of Warren, 6,400 Confederate infantrymen commanded by Major General George E. Pickett and 4,200 cavalrymen under Major General William H. Fitzhugh "Rooney" Lee, the commanding general's son, were moving to a rendezvous at Five Forks.

Five Forks was the intersection of the White Oak Road, Scott's Road, Ford's — or Church — Road, and the Dinwiddie Court House Road. Located five miles northwest of the Dinwiddie county seat, Five Forks was crucial to Lee's last supply line into Petersburg, the South Side Railroad. Southeast of the junction stood a little white frame building called Gravelly Run Methodist Episcopal Church; nearby were the Barnes and Sydnor farmhouses. There were a few large plantations in the area, including those of the Gilliam and Boisseau families. Tangled thickets and pine woods were interspersed with swampy bogs, open spaces, and woods dotted with large outcroppings of granite boulders.

On March 31 Warren's forces were resting behind their new lines south of the White Oak Road when they were pounced upon by a detachment of Major General Bushrod Johnson's force. The Confederates pushed Warren's men to a branch of Gravelly Run, where the retreating Union force held its ground. Warren received reinforcements,

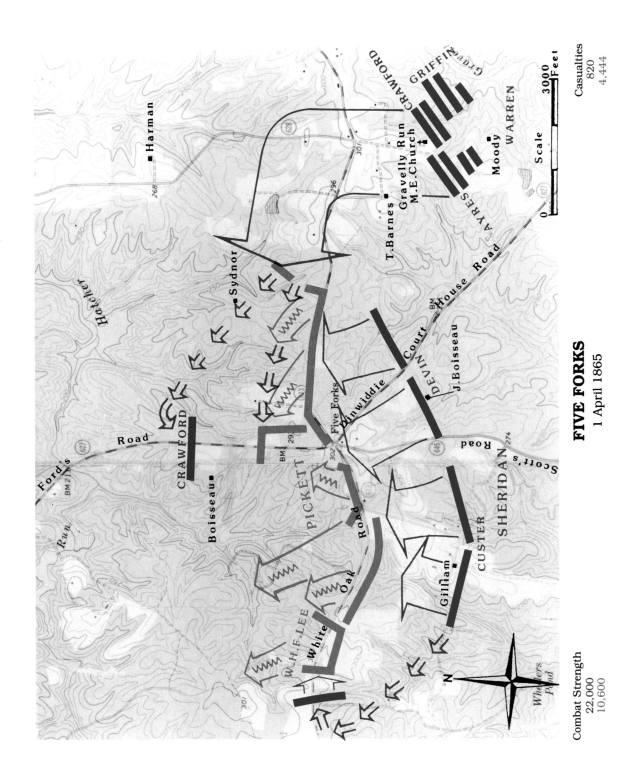

FIVE FORKS

1 April 1865

Combat Strength
22,000
10,600

Casualties
820
4,444

Scale

0   3000

Feet

counterattacked, and sent the Confederates back to their works along the Claiborne Road, cutting off the White Oak Road to the west. This battle at the White Oak Road effectively penned Johnson's men in their lines and severed their direct route of communication to Pickett's force.

Pickett's cavalry left its position at Five Forks, forced a passage over the swampy bottomlands of Chamberlain's Bed, a branch of Stony Creek, and pushed Sheridan's troopers back to Dinwiddie Court House. That night Sheridan's forces entrenched a mile north of the village, with Pickett's force interposed between them and Five Forks. Grant responded to Sheridan's request for infantry to reinforce his 10,000 cavalrymen by ordering Warren's Fifth Corps to move quickly on March 31— April 1 by night march along the Boydton Plank Road to Dinwiddie Court House. The soldiers' arrival was delayed because they had to build a forty-foot bridge to get across Gravelly Run.

Earlier on March 31, after gaining a foothold on the White Oak Road, Warren had dispatched a brigade to a position behind Pickett's left flank, facing Sheridan. Realizing that now the Union army had him in check, the Confederate commander decided to withdraw his men to Five Forks. Soon the lead elements of Warren's Fifth Corps column began arriving on the Dinwiddie Court House Road following Sheridan's troopers, who were pressing Pickett to the strategic crossroads.

When the Confederates arrived at Five Forks, Pickett set the men to strengthening their log and dirt fortifications. This line covered a two-mile front, with a return on the left flank about 150 yards long. The cavalry guarded each flank, and artillery was placed at key points along the works. Pickett received instructions from General Robert E. Lee: "Hold Five Forks at all hazards. Protect road to Ford's Depot and prevent Union forces from striking the Southside Railroad. Regret exceedingly your forces' withdrawal, and your inability to hold the advantage you had gained."

While Sheridan impatiently awaited the arrival of the remainder of Warren's forces, he received a dispatch: "General Grant directs me to say to you, that if in your judgment the Fifth Corps would do better under one of the division commanders, you are authorized to relieve General Warren, and order him to report to General Grant, at headquarters." Warren's fate as a corps commander was now in Sheridan's hands. Later that night, after the battle had ended, he replaced Warren with Brigadier General Charles Griffin.

It was nearly 4:00 P.M. by the time Warren finally had his force of 12,000 men readied for the attack. He formed his battle lines in a bottom near Gravelly Run Church and instructed his three division commanders to advance until they intersected with the White Oak Road. Sheridan's dismounted troopers were to press the Confederate line all along its front. Brigadier General Romeyn B. Ayres formed the left of Warren's line, and Brigadier General Samuel W. Crawford the right, with Griffin in his rear. Because of faulty reconnaissance and the map Sheridan had provided him, Warren thought that Pickett's left flank extended to the intersection of Gravelly Run Church Road and the White Oak Road. When his advancing columns reached that area and began to wheel, they found the return was still three quarters of a mile to the west. This error caused the three columns to diverge from the original intended alignment. Nonetheless, they overwhelmed the angle and the Confederate line. One of Warren's divisions swung around to the north of Pickett's position and attacked the Confederates in their rear at Five Forks. On the Confederate right flank, Union Brigadier General George A. Custer's troops battled with cavalry led by Rooney Lee. Brigadier General Thomas C. Devin's dismounted troopers pushed forward between Custer and Warren.

Groups of Pickett's men formed pockets of resistance along the line, but to no avail. Their commander did not arrive on the scene until the fighting was well under way, having spent most of the afternoon at a shad bake two miles in the rear with some of his officers. By the time he addressed the situation, it was too late. Those who were not taken prisoner scattered into the pine forests and escaped the best way they could. Darkness brought an end to the fighting, and Union campfires were lit held the key to the South Side Railroad.

On April 2 a division of the Second Corps under Brigadier General Nelson Miles pushed up the Claiborne Road to Sutherland Station on the South Side Railroad. After a savage fight, Miles's troops physically gained control of the railroad by overwhelming the Confederate force defending it. Lee's final supply route was closed. Union losses were about 820; Confederate, about 4,444.

Five Forks battlefield is southwest of Petersburg, Virginia, at the intersection of routes 613 and 627 between U.S. Route 460 and Interstate 85. The entire battlefield is privately owned.

Five Forks battlefield
By Bruce Dale, © 1965, National Geographic Society

SAILOR'S CREEK

6 April 1865

Christopher M. Calkins

On April 5 General Robert E. Lee and his army left Amelia Court House and continued the march toward Danville, Virginia, following the line of the Richmond and Danville Railroad. They were heading toward North Carolina, where Lee could combine his force with that of General Joseph E. Johnston. When Major General William H. Fitzhugh "Rooney" Lee (General Lee's son) reported Union cavalry entrenched across the road, Lee had to change his plans. Because the hour was late and his column was spread out, he decided to make a night march, passing to the north of the Union left flank and heading west for Farmville, twenty-three miles away on the South Side Railroad. There he could obtain supplies for his army, then march south, intersecting the Danville line near Keysville. His success depended once again upon outdistancing Grant's army.

The Confederates' route would take them across the ford at Flat Creek, past the resort of Amelia Springs, through the crossroads called Deatonsville, and then through the bottomlands traversed by Little Sayler's Creek, which joins Big Sayler's Creek at Double Bridge. They would continue west, reaching the South Side Railroad at Rice's Depot and from there go directly to Farmville. The rolling terrain is slashed by various watercourses: Flat Creek, Big and Little Sayler's creeks, and

Sandy and Bush rivers. On the north is the Appomattox River, which had crossings only at Farmville and three miles northeast at the High Bridge — the South Side Railroad trestle.

In the van of Lee's column was Lieutenant General James Longstreet's combined First and Third corps, followed by Lieutenant General Richard Anderson's small corps, then Lieutenant General Richard S. Ewell's reserve corps, made up of Richmond garrison troops, the main wagon train, and, finally, Lieutenant General John B. Gordon's Second Corps acting as rear guard.

Longstreet was ordered to march fast for Rice's Depot, three miles short of the Appomattox River. He sent the cavalry, commanded by Major General Fitzhugh Lee, to stop a Union bridge-burning party of 900 cavalry and infantry heading for the High Bridge. The Confederates defeated the Federals, took prisoners, and protected this important crossing of the Appomattox River, but the cost was high. Brigadier General James Dearing was killed, the last Confederate general to die in Virginia in the war.

The rear of Longstreet's column became separated from the head of Anderson's corps. On the morning of April 6, observant Union cavalry led by Brigadier General George A. Custer charged into the gap and established

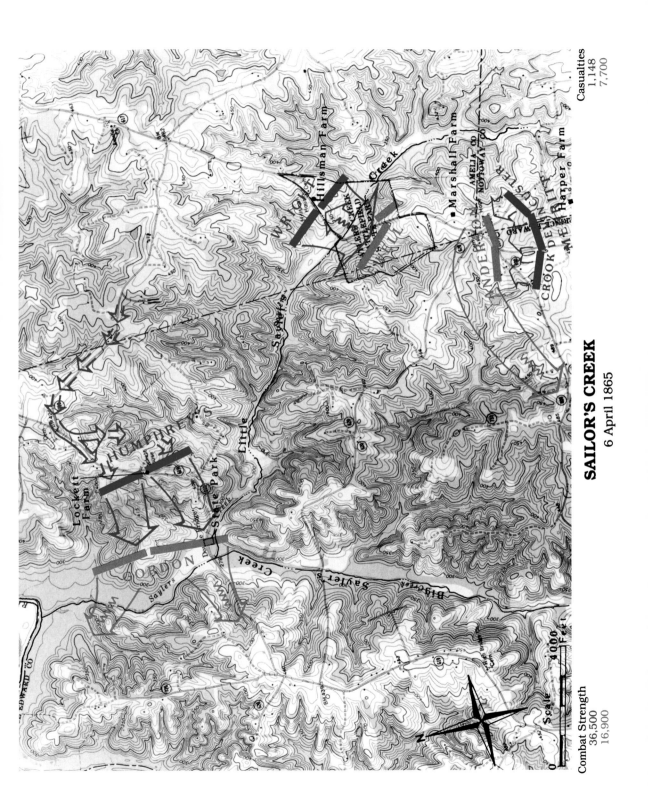

SAILOR'S CREEK

6 April 1865

Combat Strength
36,500
16,900

Casualties
1,148
7,700

Brigadier General George A. Custer at the battle of Sailor's Creek. Drawing by Alfred Waud

a roadblock in front of Anderson, cutting him off from Longstreet. Close behind Major General Philip H. Sheridan's fast-riding Union cavalry was Major General Horatio G. Wright's Sixth Corps. Ewell realized that further attacks were imminent and decided to send the wagon train on a more northerly route. Gordon, who was heavily pressed by Union Major General Andrew A. Humphreys's Second Corps, followed the train. The stage was set for the battle of Sailor's Creek. (The spelling of the battle and the state park has been changed by the state of Virginia from Sayler's to Sailor's; the spelling of the creeks remains the same.) The battle included three separate engagements: one between Wright and Ewell at the Hillsman farm, another between Humphreys and Gordon at the Lockett farm, and the third between Brigadier General Wesley Merritt and Anderson at a crossroads bounded by the Harper and Marshall farms.

Ewell took his 3,600-man force to the southwest side of the creek, where he formed a battle line on a ridge parallel to the creek facing northeast, overlooking the Hillsman farm. The 10,000 Union soldiers occupied the high ground on the opposite side of the creek. Wright emplaced his artillery and, at about 5:00 P.M., opened fire on Ewell's line. After bombarding the Confederates for a half hour, Wright's men formed their battle line and advanced to the creek. Because of spring rains, Little Sayler's Creek was out of its banks and was two to four feet deep. The men crossed it with difficulty, reformed their lines, and began the assault upon the Confederates. When the Union troops came within easy range, Ewell's men rose and fired a volley into them, causing them to break and fall back. A group of Confederates made a counterattack, only to be thrown back themselves with great loss. The Federals regrouped and again charged Ewell's line, this time overwhelming it. They captured more than 3,000 soldiers, including six generals. Confederate losses totaled 3,400; Union, 440.

When the wagons Gordon was following became bogged down at Double Bridge, the crossing over the confluence of Big and Little Sayler's creeks, his men were forced to protect them. Making a stand just before dusk on the high ground of the Lockett farm, the 7,000 Confederates awaited the arrival of Humphreys's 16,500-man corps. With the sound of fighting echoing from the south, the Union infantry gradually pushed the Confederates back into the low ground near the creek. Using the wagons as protection, Gordon's men fought desperately. When they saw a Union flanking column crossing farther to the north at Perkinson's Sawmill, they were forced to retreat up the opposite slope. At nightfall, when the fighting ended, the Confederate losses were 1,700; the Union, 536. Humphreys's men had taken more than two hundred wagons.

The third fight was farther to the south, at a crossroads bounded by the Harper and Marshall farms, about a mile southwest of the road crossing Little Sayler's Creek. Merritt's cavalry, commanded by brigadier generals Custer and Thomas Devin and Major General George Crook, overcame Anderson's stubborn resistance, led by major generals George E. Pickett and Bushrod Johnson. They captured two more Confederate generals, although many of Anderson's men managed to escape through the woods. Anderson lost 2,600 of his 6,300 men. The Federals lost 172 of their 10,000 cavalrymen.

As the Confederate refugees fled the battlefield and headed west toward Rice's Depot, they had to scramble through the valley of Big Sayler's Creek. General Lee had ridden to a knoll overlooking the creek and, seeing this disorganized mob, exclaimed, "My God! Has the army been dissolved?" The total casualties for the battle of Sailor's Creek were 7,700 Confederates and 1,148 Federals.

That night Lee's soldiers marched again. Gordon's men trudged on to the High Bridge, crossed the Appomattox, and headed for Farmville. The others who had escaped the debacle were assembled under the command of Major General William Mahone and also crossed on the gigantic railroad bridge. Lee took Longstreet's troops and Fitzhugh Lee's cavalry along the road running south of the river into Farmville, arriving there in the early morning hours. Awaiting them were seven trainloads of supplies containing more than 80,000 rations. As the men began to receive their rations and prepare their meals, the popping of carbine fire was heard to the east: Union cavalry was approaching the outskirts of town. The Confederates quickly closed up the boxcars and sent the trains westward down the rail line. They intended to get the rest of their rations later, probably at Appomattox Station, thirty miles away.

Sailor's Creek Battlefield State Park is on State Route 617 in Amelia County, Virginia, 56 miles west of Petersburg near U.S. Route 460. There are 217 acres of the historic battlefield within its authorized boundaries.

APPOMATTOX COURT HOUSE

9 April 1865

William C. Davis

As the spring of 1865 blossomed, it was certain that the Civil War would end soon and that the Confederacy would fall. With armies spread over half the continent, the war could hardly cease all at once everywhere. The question was where the end would begin.

It started in Virginia. For ten months, since June 1864, Lieutenant General Ulysses S. Grant's forces, chiefly the Army of the Potomac commanded by Major General George G. Meade, had besieged General Robert E. Lee's Army of Northern Virginia in and around Petersburg and Richmond. Steadily the blue noose drew tighter until, by April 1, 1865, all but one of the supply routes into Petersburg were cut off. On that day the Confederate defeat at Five Forks, on the far right of Lee's line, threatened the South Side Railroad, the last lifeline. There was no choice for Lee but to abandon Petersburg and Richmond to Grant and retreat to the southwest.

On April 2 Lee pulled out of Petersburg one step ahead of his foes. President Jefferson Davis and his cabinet fled Richmond, and the Confederacy became a government truly on the run. Lee headed west to Amelia Court House on April 4, to Jetersville on April 5, then toward Farmville and the Appomattox River the following day. In the rolling hills east and west of Sayler's Creek, Lee's army inadvertently split in two, and the Federals swarmed

in on the rear position. About a quarter of Lee's army, some 8,000 men, were captured, including most of Lieutenant General Richard S. Ewell's Richmond Defense Corps and much of Lieutenant General Richard Anderson's corps.

In spite of the disaster Lee pushed on, pursued relentlessly by Meade's infantry and the Union cavalry, commanded by Major General Philip H. Sheridan. On April 7 Lee repulsed the foe near Farmville and continued his retreat on the north side of the Appomattox, heading toward Appomattox Court House. Lee neared the small town at about 9:00 P.M. on April 8, only to see the glow of Sheridan's campfires to the west, his route of retreat. Sheridan was ahead of him, and Meade and Grant were behind him.

Lee and the remnant of his once-mighty army bivouacked for the last time at the village clustered around the Appomattox County courthouse. The village was important to Lee because it was on the road to Appomattox Station, where he had hoped to find supplies. But now that hope was fading. Lee's Second Corps, commanded by Major General John B. Gordon, occupied the town itself, assisted by the cavalry of Major General Fitzhugh Lee. To the southwest they faced portions of Major General Charles Griffin's Fifth Corps and, due west of them, more elements of Major General

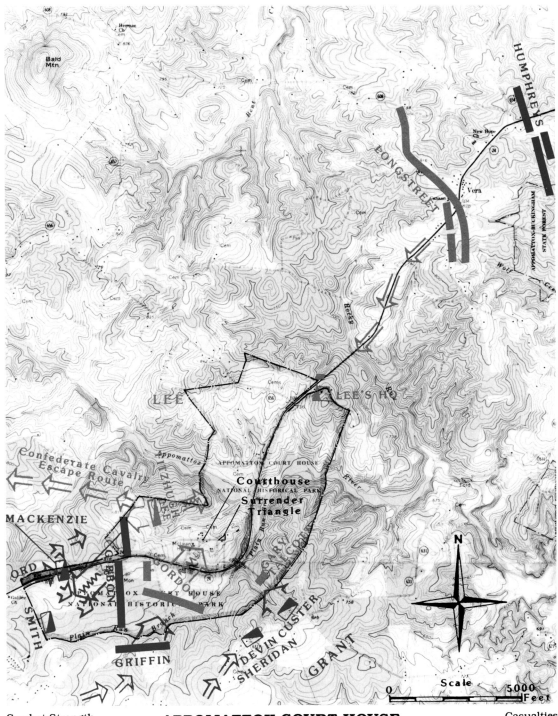

APPOMATTOX COURT HOUSE

9 April 1865

Combat Strength
63,285
31,900

Casualties
164
500
(Surrendered and
paroled: 28,231)

John Gibbon's Twenty-fourth Corps of the Army of the James, commanded by Major General E. O. C. Ord. At the same time Sheridan's cavalry had nearly encircled Lee. Two divisions under Major General George A. Custer and Brigadier General Thomas C. Devin cut off any escape to the southeast, where only a small Confederate cavalry brigade led by Brigadier General Martin Gary and the engineer battalions of Colonel T. M. R. Talcott could oppose them. Off to Gibbon's left the cavalry division of Brigadier General Ranald S. Mackenzie stood poised to meet any attempt to move around Gibbon. About three miles away to the northeast, Lee and Lieutenant General James Longstreet, commanding what was left of the First and Third corps, faced Federal Major General Andrew A. Humphreys's Second Corps of the Army of the Potomac. Lee made his headquarters to the rear of Longstreet, about a mile northeast of the village.

Grant had sent Lee a note on April 7 stating that the events of the past few days must have shown the futility of further resistance and suggesting surrender. Lee declined but kept the door open by asking what terms Grant would request. Grant responded on April 8 that peace was his "great desire." He asked the Confederates to give up their arms, give their parole not to fight again, and go home. In response, Lee suggested that they meet to talk. Grant declined to talk unless it was to discuss surrender.

Grant's refusal did not reach Lee until the morning of April 9, and by then something had happened to change Lee's mind about surrender. The evening before, when Lee learned that the Federals were ahead of him and were at Appomattox Station, he called together his few remaining commanders, Fitzhugh Lee, Longstreet, and Gordon, to discuss what could be done. Gordon and the younger Lee argued that if only cavalry was in their front, they could attack and perhaps break through, opening a route to continue the retreat. Should Sheridan have infantry with him, however, they would be trapped, with sur-

render the only alternative. Lee, with an ill-concealed lack of confidence, agreed and set the hour for attack at 5:00 A.M. He dressed in his finest uniform, commenting to a friend that "I have probably to be General Grant's prisoner. I must make my best appearance."

On Palm Sunday, April 9, the Confederates followed their battle flags into the Army of Northern Virginia's last assault. Gordon initially realized — or so he thought — some success as he pushed Sheridan's cavalry back before him, not knowing that Sheridan was pulling his troopers back to allow Gibbon's infantry to come into the fight. On Gordon's right Fitzhugh Lee seemed to make progress until they both came face to face with the infantry of the Twenty-fourth Corps. Lee and his cavalry fell back. Gordon, forced to withdraw, sent the commanding general a message: "I have fought my corps to a frazzle." Longstreet could not send reinforcements because he was engaged in holding off Humphreys. General Lee called off the engagement. "There is nothing left for me to do but to go and see General Grant," said the proud Virginian, "and I would rather die a thousand deaths."

At about 8:30 A.M. Lee rode for the meeting with Grant that he had proposed the previous day. Soon after, he received Grant's reply refusing the meeting. Lee wrote again, specifically requesting a meeting to discuss surrender. Word then came that Fitzhugh Lee's cavalry had succeeded in breaking out after all but that Gordon was trapped. Lee ordered a cease-fire and awaited Grant's reply.

It came just after noon; Grant agreed to the meeting. Lee sent a staff officer ahead to Appomattox Court House to find a suitable place, and the man chose the home of Wilmer McLean, about sixty yards down the road from the courthouse. It was ironic that McLean had lived near Manassas in 1861 at the time of the first major battle of the war. He had moved to the modest brick house in Appomattox Court House after the battle.

Lee arrived at the McLean home first and

The McLean house

went into a side parlor, where he sat at a table to await Grant, who came half an hour later. Grant had had a terrible headache that morning, but it disappeared when he received Lee's note. The two generals presented quite a contrast: Lee in full formal uniform, Grant in a private's dress with only the general's stars to denote his rank. They spoke briefly of mutual service in the Mexican War. Then Grant proposed the same terms he had mentioned in his note the day before. When Lee said that many of the Confederates owned the horses they rode, Grant allowed them to take the animals home with them. "This will have the best possible effect upon the men," said Lee. Grant also authorized 25,000 rations to feed Lee's men. The two generals signed the surrender documents, shook hands, and left.

A committee of officers from both armies was appointed to work out the actual details of the surrender, including the formal turning over of arms and flags and the signing of paroles. The committee set the ceremonies for April 12. Brigadier General Joshua L. Chamberlain of Maine was given the honor of formally receiving the surrender.

On April 12 Chamberlain formed his command on either side of the Richmond Stage Road leading out of town toward the Confederate camps. At the appointed hour the Confederates formed ranks as if on parade and marched off for the last time, Gordon's corps in the lead. There were so few men and so many flags that when Chamberlain saw them approach, he thought that "the whole column seemed crowned with red." Chamberlain ordered a bugler to sound a marching salute. The Federals snapped to "carry arms." Gordon, astride his horse, caught the spirit of the event, rose erect in his stirrups, wheeled his horse magnificently, and brought the point of his sword to his boot toe, at the same time ordering his men to the same position at arms, "honor answering honor."

And so the Confederates passed, only 22,000 infantry, to lay down their arms, furl their flags, and say their farewells. On the road to Richmond behind them another 13,800 had been captured and 6,300 killed or wounded. Only Fitzhugh Lee's 2,400 troopers escaped. Grant had a total available Federal force of 63,285 in the area, though only a portion was actually engaged. Fewer still were privileged to stand along the road to see the last moments of Lee's army. Chamberlain later wrote of "memories that bound us together as no other bond." Among the Union soldiers, he observed, "not a sound of trumpet more, nor roll of drum; not a cheer, nor whisper of vain-glorying, nor motion of man standing again at the order, but an awed stillness rather, and breath-holding, as if it were the passing of the dead!"

Although the men in gray went home, Lee's surrender did not end the war. Other Confederate armies were still in the field, and it was more than two months before all had capitulated. But Appomattox would always symbolize the end for the South. For four years the indomitable Army of Northern Virginia had been the fighting standard by which all other armies, blue or gray, were measured. For most of that time Robert E. Lee stood as the unrivaled general of the war. When he and his army surrendered, the hopes of the Confederacy were over.

It had been a terrible ordeal for North and South. The structure of the old Union and the nature of the constitutional compact had been shaken to their core. The young men of the continent, nearly three million of them, had gone off to war, and more than 620,000 would never go home again. The questions of slavery and secession had been settled forever, but the old sectional feelings continued as the reunited nation began Reconstruction.

Still, out of that war experience came the ties that Chamberlain sensed as his old enemies filed past him at Appomattox. All that the men on both sides had endured bound them together. As the passions subsided, their common experiences helped to rebind the nation. In the terrible storm of fire and blood, millions of farm boys and clerks had participated in the greatest event of their century. It gave them a brotherhood that transcended even the ties of blood.

They are all gone now; the last of them died in the 1950s. Yet some participants in that conflict can still be seen today. Although Johnny Reb and Billy Yank now rest beneath the sod, the ground for which they fought yet endures. Alas, much of it has been altered or built over to the point that little remains to link it with the events of the 1860s, as is the case in Atlanta. Other hallowed places live in daily peril, unprotected from private exploitation. Many of the battlefields in this book are privately owned, including Brandy Station, Champion Hill, and Glorieta. So long as they remain in private hands, there is no surety that they will endure for future generations. Happily, however, grateful and committed citizens have preserved some of the great battlefields — Manassas, Antietam, Gettysburg, Shiloh, Vicksburg, Chickamauga, and others — so that today they are much as they were when the guns echoed across their hills and fields. Appomattox Court House, too, is set aside as a special place where blue met gray and created something greater than themselves. As long as these mute yet eloquent reminders remain to show us where men fought and for what, we cannot forget. So long as we preserve these fields and seek to save even more, we shall preserve ourselves.

Appomattox Court House National Historical Park is on State Route 24 at Appomattox, Virginia, 21 miles east of Lynchburg. There are 1,325 acres of the historic battlefield and village within its authorized boundaries.

General James S. Wadsworth Monument, Gettysburg
© David E. Roth, *Blue & Gray Magazine*, Columbus, Ohio

In great deeds something abides. On great fields something stays.
Forms change and pass; bodies disappear; but spirits linger, to consecrate ground for the vision-place of souls. And reverent men and
women from afar, and generations that know us not and that we
know not of, heart-drawn to see where and by whom great things
were suffered and done for them, shall come to this deathless field, to
ponder and dream; and lo! the shadow of a mighty presence shall
wrap them in its bosom, and the power of the vision pass into their
souls.

— General Joshua Lawrence Chamberlain, Gettysburg, October 3, 1889

COMPREHENSIVE LIST OF
CIVIL WAR BATTLES

Site	State	Current Management	National Register/NHL
Fort Sumter	South Carolina	NP	NR
First Manassas	Virginia	NP	NR
Wilson's Creek	Missouri	NP	NR
Lexington	Missouri		NR
Rich Mountain	West Virginia		
Balls' Bluff	Virginia		NHL
Belmont	Missouri		
Mill Springs	Kentucky	VA	
Fort Henry	Tennessee	TVA	NR
Fort Donelson	Tennessee	NP	NR
Columbus	Kentucky	SP	NR
Roanoke Island	North Carolina		
Valverde	New Mexico		
Pea Ridge	Arkansas	NP	NR
Glorieta	New Mexico		NHL
Shiloh	Tennessee	NP	NR
Yorktown Siege	Virginia	NP	NR
Island #10	Tennessee		
Williamsburg	Virginia		NR
Corinth Siege	Mississippi		NR
Fort Jackson	Louisiana	CP	NHL
Fort St. Philip	Louisiana		NHL
Fort Pulaski	Georgia	NP	NR
Seven Pines	Virginia		
First Kernstown	Virginia		
McDowell	Virginia		
Front Royal	Virginia		

NP = National Park; SP = state park; CP = city park; TVA = Tennessee Valley Authority; VA = Veterans Administration; VMI = Virginia Military Institute; NR = listed in the National Register of Historic Places; NHL = National Historic Landmark

Site	State	Current Management	National Register/NHL
First Winchester	Virginia		
Cross Keys	Virginia		
Port Republic	Virginia		
Seven Days Battles	Virginia	NP	NR
Gaines' Mill	Virginia	NP	NR
Glendale	Virginia	VA	
Malvern Hill	Virginia	NP	NR
Cedar Mountain	Virginia		
Second Manassas	Virginia	NP	NR
Chantilly	Virginia		
South Mountain	Maryland		
Harpers Ferry	West Virginia, Maryland, Virginia	NP	NR
Antietam	Maryland	NP	NR
Baton Rouge	Louisiana		NR
Richmond	Kentucky		
Corinth	Mississippi	CP	NR
Perryville	Kentucky	SP	NHL
Iuka	Mississippi		
Fredericksburg	Virginia	NP	NR
Stones River	Tennessee	NP	NR
Chickasaw Bayou	Mississippi		NR
Prairie Grove	Arkansas	SP	NR
Arkansas Post	Arkansas	NP	NR
Vicksburg Campaign and Siege	Mississippi	NP	NR
Grand Gulf	Mississippi	SP	NR
Port Gibson	Mississippi		NR
Raymond	Mississippi		NR
Champion Hill	Mississippi		NHL
Helena	Arkansas		NR
Chancellorsville	Virginia	NP	NR
Brandy Station	Virginia		
Second Winchester	Virginia		
Gettysburg	Pennsylvania	NP	NR
Droop Mountain	West Virginia	SP	NR
Bristoe Station	Virginia		
Mine Run	Virginia		
Chickamauga	Georgia	NP	NR
Chattanooga	Tennessee	NP	NR
Knoxville	Tennessee		
Port Hudson	Louisiana	SP	NHL
Sabine Pass	Louisiana, Texas		
Honey Springs	Oklahoma		NR
Battery Wagner	South Carolina		

NP = National Park; SP = state park; CP = city park; TVA = Tennessee Valley Authority; VA = Veterans Administration; VMI = Virginia Military Institute; NR = listed in the National Register of Historic Places; NHL = National Historic Landmark

Site	State	Current Management	National Register/NHL
Mansfield	Louisiana	SP	NR
Pleasant Hill	Louisiana		
Jenkins' Ferry	Arkansas	SP	NR
Westport	Missouri	CP	
Fort Pillow	Tennessee	SP	NHL
Brices Cross Roads	Mississippi	NP	NR
Tupelo	Mississippi	NP	NR
Fort Morgan	Alabama	SP	NHL
Rocky Face Ridge	Georgia		
Resaca	Georgia		
Dug Gap	Georgia		
New Hope Church	Georgia		
Dallas	Georgia		
Pickett's Mill	Georgia	SP	NR
Kennesaw Mountain	Georgia	NP	NR
Peachtree Creek	Georgia		NR
Atlanta	Georgia		
Ezra Church	Georgia		
Jonesboro	Georgia		
Franklin	Tennessee		NHL
Nashville	Tennessee		
Fort McAllister	Georgia	SP	
Olustee	Florida		NR
Cloyd's Mountain	Virginia		
The Wilderness	Virginia	NP	NR
Spotsylvania Court House	Virginia	NP	NR
Yellow Tavern	Virginia		
North Anna River	Virginia		
Bethesda Church	Virginia		
Cold Harbor	Virginia	NP	NR
Drewry's Bluff	Virginia	NP	NR
Petersburg	Virginia	NP	NR
Trevilian Station	Virginia		
Reams Station	Virginia		
New Market Heights	Virginia		
Fort Harrison	Virginia	NP	NR
New Market	Virginia	VM1	NR
Lynchburg	Virginia		
Piedmont	Virginia		
Monocacy	Maryland	NP	NHL
Fort Stevens	District of Columbia	NP	NR
Second Kernstown	Virginia		
Cool Springs	Virginia		

NP = National Park; SP = state park; CP = city park; TVA = Tennessee Valley Authority; VA = Veterans Administration; VMI = Virginia Military Institute; NR = listed in the National Register of Historic Places; NHL = National Historic Landmark

Site	State	Current Management	National Register/NHL
Opequon Creek (Third Winchester)	Virginia		
Fisher's Hill	Virginia		
Tom's Brook	Virginia		
Cedar Creek	Virginia		NHL
Waynesboro	Virginia		
Fort Fisher	North Carolina	SP	NHL
Averasboro	North Carolina		
Bentonville	North Carolina	SP	NR
Surrender of Johnston's Army (near Durham)	North Carolina	SP	NR
Five Forks	Virginia		NHL
Sailor's Creek	Virginia	SP	NHL
Appomattox Court House	Virginia	NP	NR
Selma	Alabama		
Fort Blakely–Spanish Fort	Alabama		NR
Citronelle (site of surrender by Taylor to Canby)	Alabama		

NP = National Park; SP = state park; CP = city park; TVA = Tennessee Valley Authority; VA = Veterans Administration; VMI = Virginia Military Institute; NR = listed in the National Register of Historic Places; NHL = National Historic Landmark

LOST CIVIL WAR BATTLEFIELDS

Portions of some of these battlefields can still provide some understanding of the military actions; others are completely lost.

Alabama
Selma
Spanish Fort

Georgia
Peachtree Creek
Ezra Church
Atlanta
Jonesboro

Louisiana
Baton Rouge
Fort St. Philip

Mississippi
Iuka

South Carolina
Battery Wagner

Tennessee
Fort Henry
Franklin
Island #10
Knoxville
Nashville

Virginia
Bethesda Church
Chantilly
Front Royal
Seven Pines/Fair Oaks
Waynesboro
Yellow Tavern

West Virginia
Rich Mountain

Chantilly battlefield, Virginia

Above: In October 1915, veterans of the New Jersey Brigade dedicated monuments to Generals Philip Kearny and Isaac Stevens, who died in the battle of Chantilly. Today the monuments and the surrounding two acres of land are the only protected areas of the battlefield. © David E. Roth, *Blue & Gray Magazine*, Columbus, Ohio

Below: View from the Kearny and Stevens monuments across the new Monument Road (site of the Confederate line of defense) toward the townhouses on the site of the cornfield where Kearny was killed. © Clark B. Hall

Petersburg National Battlefield, Virginia

Left: On April 2, 1865, Colonel George W. Gowen died leading the Forty-eighth Pennsylvania Regiment in a charge against Confederate fortifications. In 1907 Union and Confederate veterans gathered near the site to dedicate this monument to the colonel and the regiment. During his address the adjutant general of Pennsylvania, Thomas J. Stewart, spoke of the importance of commemorating that place:

"Round about us are heroic fields. Round about us the dead of both armies sleep, while the living survivors of the war-worn and veteran legions of Grant and Lee are gathered here fraternally, recalling the incidents of that great struggle. These men gaze again upon the unforgettable pictures that have hung these many years upon the chamber walls of their memory; and today, they and we thank God that the sword has been sheathed, the cannon silenced, the muskets stacked, the war flags furled, and that once again, in glorious Virginia, Pennsylvania is welcome."

Below: The monument in 1989, at the intersection of Sycamore Street and Crater Road on the south side of Petersburg.

Fredericksburg and Spotsylvania
National Military Park, Virginia
Salem Church. On May 3, 1863, Union and Confederate forces battled in the fields and woods surrounding Salem Church. During the battle the Confederates used the church as a makeshift fortress. Today only the church and its grounds are preserved. © Patricia Lanza

COMBAT STRENGTHS AND CASUALTIES

Battle	Combat Strength		Casualties	
	U	C	U	C
Fort Sumter	84	5,000	11	4
First Manassas	39,000	32,000	2,896	1,982
Wilson's Creek	7,000	12–13,000	1,317	1,222
Fort Donelson	27,000	21,000	2,832	17,000
Pea Ridge	10,250	16,500	1,384	1,500
Glorieta	1,340	1,200	108	108
Shiloh	62,000	44,000	13,047	11,694
Fort Pulaski	1,000	385	1	1
McDowell	6,000	9,000	256	500
Cross Keys	10,500	5,000	684	288
Port Republic	3,000	6,000	500	800
Gaines' Mill	35,000	56,000	6,837	8,750
Malvern Hill	80,000	80,000	3,000	5,355
Cedar Mountain	12,000	22,000	2,500	1,400
Second Manassas	63,000	55,000	13,826	8,353
Harpers Ferry	14,000	24,000	12,719	286
Antietam	75,000	38,000	12,401	10,318
Corinth	23,000	22,000	2,350	4,800
Perryville	36,940	16,000	3,696	3,145
Fredericksburg	120,000	78,000	12,600	5,300
Stones River	44,000	34,000	13,000	13,000
Chancellorsville	130,000	60,000	17,000	12,800
Brandy Station	11,000	9,500	868	515
Gettysburg	95,000	75,000	23,000	28,000
Vicksburg Campaign and Siege	77,000	62,000	10,000	38,600
Port Gibson	24,000	8,000	875	787

Note: Combat strengths and casualties for each battle are not known exactly because many reports were incomplete, and some records were lost. These figures are reasonable approximations from the evidence available.

Battle	Combat Strength		Casualties	
	U	C	U	C
Raymond	12,000	4,000	442	514
Champion Hill	32,000	22,000	2,441	3,840
Port Hudson	40,000	7,500	10,000	7,500
Chickamauga	62,000	65,000	16,170	18,454
Chattanooga	70,000	50,000	5.815	6,667
Mansfield	7,000	8,800	2,235	1,000
Pleasant Hill	12,100	12,500	1,369	1,626
Rocky Face Ridge	62,227	42,858–52,992	837	600
Resaca	104,000	67,000	2,997	2,800
New Hope Church ⎫ Pickett's Mill ⎬ Dallas ⎭	93,600–102,000	75,000	4,500	3,000
Kennesaw Mountain	110,000	65,000	3,000	1,000
Brices Cross Roads	8,100	3,500	2,612	493
Tupelo	14,000	9,460	674	1,326
Cloyd's Mountain	6,500	2,400	688	538
The Wilderness	118,769	62,000	18,000	10,800
Spotsylvania Court House	111,000	63,000	18,000	9–10,000
North Anna River	68,000	53,000	2,623	2,517
Cold Harbor	114,000	59,000	10,000	4,000
New Market	8,940	5,335	841	520
Piedmont	12,000	5,600	875	1,600
Monocacy	5,800	14,000	1,968	700–900
Second Kernstown	9,500	14,000	1,185	unknown
Fisher's Hill	20,000	12,000	528	1,235
Cedar Creek	32,000	21,000	5,672	2,910
Petersburg Campaign and Siege	109,000	59,000	42,000	28,000
Petersburg	10–14,000	2,200–2,400	684+	300+
Reams Station	9,000	13–15,000	2,742	814
New Market Heights	13,000	1,800	850	50
Bentonville	60,000	21,000	1,527	2,606
Five Forks	22,000	10,600	820	4,444
Sailor's Creek	36,500	16,900	1,148	7,700
Appomattox Court House	63,285	31,900	164	500

(surrendered and paroled: 28,231)

WAR STATISTICS

Robert W. Meinhard

Dead and wounded in the Civil War, 1861–1865*

	Dead	Wounded	Total
Federal	364,511	281,881	646,392
Confederate	260,000	194,000	454,000
Total	624,511	475,881	1,100,392

*The number of dead and wounded, especially for the Confederates, is not known exactly because many reports were incomplete or inaccurate, and records were lost. These figures are estimates from the evidence available. Sources include the Department of Defense; E. B. Long, *The Civil War Day by Day: An Almanac;* Thomas L. Livermore, *Numbers and Losses in the Civil War in America, 1861–1865;* and James M. McPherson, *Battle Cry of Freedom.*

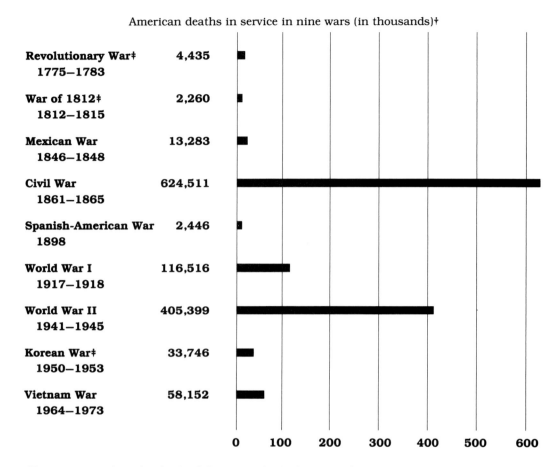

American deaths in service in nine wars (in thousands)†

Revolutionary War‡ 1775–1783	4,435
War of 1812‡ 1812–1815	2,260
Mexican War 1846–1848	13,283
Civil War 1861–1865	624,511
Spanish-American War 1898	2,446
World War I 1917–1918	116,516
World War II 1941–1945	405,399
Korean War‡ 1950–1953	33,746
Vietnam War 1964–1973	58,152

†Figures, except those for the Confederates in the Civil War, are from the Department of Defense, 1989. Another source for the Revolutionary War, *The Toll of Independence*, ed. Howard Peckham, gives the number of battle deaths as 7,174, and the number of probable deaths in service as 25,674. The number of deaths in service but not in battle during the Korean War was not available from the Department of Defense in 1989. The number given by the Department of Defense in 1957 was 20,617.
‡Battle deaths only.

GLOSSARY

Abatis. A network of felled trees in front of an entrenched position, with branches interlaced and facing the enemy's position to form an obstacle to attacking troops.

Angle and return. A turn made in a fortified line to provide covering fire for other parts of the line or to protect the line from enfilading fire and flank attack.

Army. The armies were composed of corps, which controlled divisions, composed of brigades, consisting of regiments. Two to ten (usually three to five) regiments were assigned to a brigade, two to six (usually three or four) brigades to a division, and two to five (usually two or three) divisions to a corps. In 1863, for example, the average Federal brigade contained about 2,000 men and the Confederate about 1,800.

Artillery. Field artillery maneuvered with troops, while heavy artillery was used to defend or attack fixed positions. Guns were either smoothbore or rifled; rifled guns had greater range and accuracy, while the smoothbore were more effective as close-range antipersonnel weapons. Types of artillery included:

Napoleon — a smoothbore twelve-pounder with a range of about 1,600 yards.

Parrott — a rifled gun invented by R. P. Parrott in calibers for both field and heavy artillery. One such caliber, the twenty-pounder, had a maximum range of about 3,500 yards. Ten- and twenty-pounders were used by the field artillery, while Parrotts ranging from thirty- to three hundred–pounders were used in fortifications and to bombard cities.

Ordnance (three-inch) — a rifled ten-pounder. The maximum effective range of rifled artillery was about 2,500 yards.

Columbiad — a large, smoothbore cannon (eight, ten, and fifteen inches) used in inland as well as coastal fortifications. Columbiads were occasionally rifled.

Break contact. To move away from the enemy intentionally for tactical or strategic reasons.

Breastworks. A barricade of logs, fence rails, stones, sandbags, or other material to protect troops fighting on the defensive. When erected in front of trenches, breastworks are covered with the dirt excavated from the trenches.

Cashier. To dismiss an officer from the service for disciplinary reasons.

Contraband. Technically, enemy property or goods subject to seizure by a belligerent power in war. During the Civil War "contrabands" became the popular name for freed slaves.

Note: The definitions for abatis, breastworks, cashier, contraband, countermarch, demonstrate, earthworks, enfilade, envelop, feint, flank, flotilla, forage, forced march, parole, picket, quartermaster, redan, regular, repeating firearm, salient, screen, solid shot, transport, trooper, volley, and works are reprinted by permission of McGraw-Hill Publishing Company from *Ordeal by Fire*, pages 651–53, by James M. McPherson (New York: Alfred A. Knopf, 1982).

Countermarch. To reverse the direction of marching troops and return to or near the starting point.

Demonstrate. In military operations, to make a show of force on a given front without actually attacking in order to distract enemy attention from the actual point of attack. A demonstration is similar to a feint.

Earthworks. Military fortifications constructed of earth, sand, gravel, etc.

Echelon. To deploy troops in echelon is to arrange them in parallel lines to the side and rear of the front line, presenting the appearance of steps. To attack in echelon is to have each unit advance as soon as the unit next to it moves forward; such attacks were successive rather than simultaneous and often broke down if just one unit in the sequence failed to advance.

Enfilade. To bring an enemy position under fire from the side or end instead of directly or obliquely from the front. The advantage of enfilading fire is twofold: shots that miss the initial target may hit men farther down the line, and the enemy has difficulty returning the fire effectively without risk of hitting their own men.

Envelop. To undertake an attack on one or both flanks or the rear of an enemy position; to encircle or surround.

Face. Either of the two outer sides that form the foremost angle of a fort or breastworks.

Feint. A limited attack or movement of troops against one objective to mislead the enemy and cause him to weaken his defenses at the intended point of real attack. Similar to but more aggressive than a demonstration.

Flank. The side or end of a moving or stationary column or line of troops. To "flank" an enemy position is to get around to its side or rear in order to enfilade the position. A "flanking march" is the movement of troops to get on the enemy's flank or rear.

Flotilla. A group of warships and transports acting in concert for a specific purpose. A flotilla generally contains a smaller number of ships than a fleet.

Forage. As a noun, grass, hay, or grain for horses and mules. Forage was as necessary for a Civil War army as petroleum is for a modern army. The verb "to forage" means to seek food for humans as well as for animals.

Forced march. A long march of troops at a fast pace made necessary by an impending battle or other emergency.

Garrison. A force stationed at a fortified place. It can also mean the place where troops are stationed, usually a permanent facility. As a verb, garrison means to provide a fort with a force.

General officers. The Union army had three grades of general officer: lieutenant general (Ulysses S. Grant), major general, and brigadier general. The Confederate army grades included general (Samuel Cooper, Robert E. Lee, and six others), lieutenant general, major general, and brigadier general. Brevet rank, a higher rank, usually without an increase in pay and with a limited exercise of the higher rank, was granted as an honor when there was no vacancy for promotion to a higher substantive grade.

Lunette. A work consisting of a salient angle with two flanks open to the rear.

Parole. An oath by a captured soldier, given in return for release from captivity, not to bear arms against the captors until formally exchanged for one of the captor's soldiers. To parole a captured soldier is to exact such an oath as a condition of his release.

Picket. A soldier assigned to the perimeter of an army encampment or position to give warning of enemy movements.

Quartermaster. An officer responsible for supplying army units with uniforms, shoes, equipment (exclusive of ordnance), transportation, and forage. The Quartermaster Bureau or Quartermaster Corps is the army administrative department in charge of this function.

Redan. Earthworks or breastworks thrown up in front of a cannon in the form of an inverted V to protect the gun and its crew from enemy fire.

Refused. Describes a flank that is protected from enemy attack by being angled toward the rear or anchored on a difficult or impenetrable natural or manmade obstacle; also refers to troops deployed in echelon.

Regular. An officer or soldier in the peacetime army, or "regular army," as distinguished from a "volunteer" in the "volunteer army," who enlisted for the specific purpose of fighting in the Civil War.

Repeating firearm. A gun that can be fired two or more times before reloading.

Retrograde. A backward movement or retreat.

Return. The portion of a fortification (including trenches) that connects a salient (angle) with the main axis of the defenses.

Salient. A portion of a defensive line or trench that juts out toward the enemy.

Screen (cavalry). A patrol of the front and flanks of an army to prevent enemy cavalry or scouts from getting close enough to the main army for observation.

Solid shot. Round cannonballs that do not explode.

Stand of arms. A soldier's rifle musket and cartridge belt or his complete set of equipment: rifle musket, bayonet, cartridge belt, and box.

Transport. An unarmed ship carrying troops or supplies.

Trooper. A cavalryman.

Unlimber. To detach the artillery piece from the limber (a two-wheeled cart pulled by six horses or mules) and prepare it for use.

Van. The troops who march at the front of an army; the advance guard.

Volley. The simultaneous firing of guns by an entire unit of soldiers.

Works. A general term to describe defensive military fortifications of all kinds.

ABOUT THE AUTHORS

Don E. Alberts is president of Historical Research Consultants of Albuquerque and president of the Glorieta Battlefield Preservation Society. He was chief historian for Kirtland Air Force Base. He is the author of *Brandy Station to Manila Bay: The Biography of General Wesley Merritt*, *Rebels on the Rio Grande: The Civil War in New Mexico*, and *Balloons to Bombers: Albuquerque Aviation 1928–1982*.

Michael J. Andrus was a park ranger at Manassas National Battlefield Park and at Fredericksburg and Spotsylvania National Military Park, and is currently a park ranger at Richmond National Battlefield Park. He is writing a history of northern Virginia artillery units for the Virginia Regimental History Series.

John G. Barrett, professor of history emeritus, Virginia Military Institute, is the author of *Sherman's March Through the Carolinas* and *The Civil War in North Carolina*.

Edwin C. Bearss is the chief historian for the National Park Service. He is the author and editor of fourteen books on the Civil War and western expansion and more than two hundred historical monographs, including *Forrest at Brice's Cross Roads and in North Mississippi in 1864*, *Hardluck Ironclad: The Sinking and Salvage of the Cairo*, and *The Vicksburg Campaign*.

Arthur W. Bergeron, Jr., is the historian for the Louisiana Office of State Parks in Baton Rouge. He is the author of *Guide to Louisiana Confederate Military Units, 1861–1865*, coauthor with Lawrence L. Hewitt of *Miles' Louisiana Legion:*

A History and Roster and *Boone's Louisiana Battery: A History and Roster*, and editor of *Reminiscences of Uncle Silas: A History of the Eighteenth Louisiana Infantry*.

Daniel A. Brown began his work with the National Park Service at Fort Pulaski National Monument. He was the historian at Kennesaw Mountain National Battlefield, and is now at Cumberland Gap National Historical Park.

Christopher M. Calkins is a historian with the National Park Service at Petersburg National Battlefield, his third Civil War battlefield. He has written numerous articles and five books on the Civil War, most recently *The Battles at Appomattox* and *The Final Bivouac: The Surrender at Appomattox and the Disbanding of the Armies*.

William C. Davis was the editor of the *Civil War Times Illustrated* magazine and is now a book developer and marketer. He has published more than twenty works of Civil War history, including *Fighting Men of the Civil War*, an illustrated history of the common soldier North and South.

Frank Allen Dennis is professor of history at Delta State University and assistant editor of the *Journal of Mississippi History*. He is the editor of *Kemper County Rebel: The Civil War Diary of Robert Masten Holmes, C.S.A.*, *Southern Miscellany: Essays in History in Honor of Glover Moore*, and *Recollections of the 4th Missouri Cavalry*.

Dennis E. Frye is the historian with the National Park Service at Harpers Ferry National Historical

Park. He has written *2nd Virginia Infantry* and *12th Virginia Cavalry* as well as two dozen articles on Civil War topics relating to the Harpers Ferry area. He is presently writing a book on Stonewall Jackson's siege and capture of Harpers Ferry.

Gary W. Gallagher is a member of the Department of History at Pennsylvania State University. He is the author of *Stephen Dodson Ramseur: Lee's Gallant General* and *Fighting for the Confederacy: The Personal Recollections of General Edward Porter Alexander*, and he is writing a biography of Jubal A. Early. He is president of the Association for the Preservation of Civil War Sites.

A. Wilson Greene is the staff historian with the National Park Service at Fredericksburg and Spotsylvania National Military Park. His writings include *J. Horace Lacy: The Most Dangerous Rebel of the County.*

William W. Gwaltney is a National Park Service ranger specializing in nineteenth-century American history. He was in a re-enactment group for the film *Glory*, about the 54th Massachusetts, one of the first black units to be officially recruited during the Civil War.

Clark B. Hall is president of the Chantilly Battlefield Association and serves on the board of the Association for the Preservation of Civil War Sites and on the Fairfax County History Commission. He is writing a book on the battle of Brandy Station. He is supervisory special agent in the Office of Special Investigation of the U.S. General Accounting Office.

Richard W. Hatcher III is a historian with the National Park Service at Wilson's Creek National Battlefield. He is the author of the article "Scotsman in Gray: William Watson" for the *Journal of the Confederate Historical Society of Great Britain.*

Herman Hattaway is professor of history at the University of Missouri–Kansas City. He is the author of *General Stephen D. Lee* and coauthor of *How the North Won: A Military History of the Civil War* and *Why the South Lost the Civil War* (also available in revised, updated, and synopsized form as *The Elements of Confederate Defeat*).

Paul Hawke is a historian with the National Park

Service in the Southeast Regional Office in Atlanta, Georgia. He has worked at Petersburg National Battlefield, at Fredericksburg and Spotsylvania National Military Park, at Independence National Historical Park, and at Pea Ridge National Military Park.

John Heinz is the senior United States senator from Pennsylvania. He is coauthor of "Project 88: Harnessing Market Forces to Protect Our Environment: Initiatives for the New President," an analysis of major conservation issues recommending new natural resources policies.

John Hennessy was a historian at Manassas National Battlefield Park and is now with the New York State Office of Parks, Recreation and Historic Preservation. He is the author of *The First Battle of Manassas: An End to Innocence* and *Vortex of Hell: Second Manassas Campaign*, scheduled for completion in 1990.

Earl J. Hess is assistant professor of history at Lincoln Memorial University. He recently published *Liberty, Virtue, and Progress: Northerners and Their War for the Union*, and he is collaborating with William L. Shea on a forthcoming history of the Pea Ridge campaign and a guide to the battlefield.

Lawrence Lee Hewitt is associate professor of history at Southeastern Louisiana University. He was historic site manager of the Port Hudson State Commemorative Area. He is the author of *Port Hudson, Confederate Bastion on the Mississippi* and coauthor of *Miles Legion: A History & Roster, Boone's Louisiana Battery: A History & Roster*, and *The Battle of Fort Bisland: Historical Research and Development of an Archeological Research Design.*

James O. Horton is associate professor of American history and civilization at George Washington University and director of the Afro-American Communities Project at the National Museum of American History, Smithsonian Institution. He is a 1988–89 recipient of a Fulbright senior professorship at the University of Munich. He is coauthor of *Black Bostonians: Family Life and Community Struggle in the Antebellum North* and coeditor of the pilot series for *City of Magnificent Intentions: A Social History of Washington, D.C.*

Ludwell H. Johnson is professor of history at

the College of William and Mary and the author of *Red River Campaign: Politics and Cotton in the Civil War* and *Division and Reunion: America, 1848–1877*.

Robert K. Krick is a historian with the National Park Service at Fredericksburg and Spotsylvania National Military Park and the author of nine books, including *Lee's Colonels* and *Stonewall Jackson at Cedar Mountain*.

Michael D. Litterst was a National Park Service park ranger at Gettysburg National Military Park and is currently a park ranger at Richmond National Battlefield Park.

Jay Luvaas is professor of military history at the U.S. Army War College. He is coauthor of the U.S. Army War College series *Guide to Civil War Battlefields and Campaigns*, author of *The Military Legacy of the Civil War: The European Inheritance*, and editor of *The Civil War: A Soldier's View*, by G. R. Henderson.

William D. Matter is a retired United States Air Force pilot and the author of *If It Takes All Summer: The Battle of Spotsylvania*.

James M. McPherson is Edwards Professor of American History at Princeton University. His books include *The Struggle for Equality*, *The Abolitionist Legacy*, *Ordeal by Fire*, and *Battle Cry of Freedom*.

Grady McWhiney, Lyndon Baines Johnson Professor of History at Texas Christian University, is the author of *Cracker Culture*, *Attack and Die*, and *Braxton Bragg and Confederate Defeat*.

Robert W. Meinhard is professor of history emeritus at Winona State University and has been national chairman of the Battlefield Preservation Civil War Round Table Associates. His next book will be *My Dear Companion: The Civil War Letters of Albion O. Gross*.

J. Michael Miller is the curator of personal papers for the Marine Corps museum system at the Marine Corps Historical Center in Washington, D.C. He has published articles on Civil War and Marine Corps history, is the author of *Even to Hell Itself: The North Anna River Campaign*, and is writing a detailed tactical study of the 1862 Shenandoah Valley campaign.

Sam Nunn is the senior United States senator from Georgia. He is chairman of the Senate Armed Services Committee.

Donald C. Pfanz is a historian with the National Park Service at Fort Sumter National Monument in South Carolina and has worked at two Civil War sites in Virginia. He has written *Abraham Lincoln at City Point* and is currently working on a biography of General Richard S. Ewell.

Harry W. Pfanz was the historian at Gettysburg National Military Park for ten years and was the chief historian of the National Park Service at the time of his retirement in 1981. He is the author of *Gettysburg: The Second Day*.

George A. Reaves III is the National Park Service supervisor ranger at Shiloh National Military Park and has worked in six other National Park Service military parks. He has written publications for Shiloh National Military Park, Manassas National Military Park, and Horseshoe Bend National Military Park.

James I. Robertson, Jr., is C. P. Miles Professor of History at Virginia Polytechnic Institute and State University. He is the author or editor of twenty-two books on the Civil War, including *Soldiers Blue and Gray*, *General A. P. Hill*, and *Civil War Sites in Virginia*.

William Glenn Robertson is an associate professor at the U.S. Army Command and General Staff College, Fort Leavenworth, Kansas. He is the author of *Back Door to Richmond: The Bermuda Hundred Campaign, April–June, 1864* and *The Petersburg Campaign: The Battle of Old Men and Young Boys, June 9, 1864*. Forthcoming works include *River of Death: The Chickamauga Campaign* and *A Walking Guide to Chickamauga*.

Charles P. Roland is alumni professor emeritus at the University of Kentucky. He has been president of the Southern Historical Association and has served as the visiting professor of military history at the U.S. Army War College and the U.S. Military Academy. He is the author of *The Confederacy* and *Albert Sidney Johnston: Soldier of Three Republics*.

Stephen W. Sears is the author of *Landscape Turned Red: The Battle of Antietam* and *George B. McClellan: The Young Napoleon*, and the editor of *The Civil War Papers of George B. McClellan*.

William L. Shea is professor of history at the University of Arkansas at Monticello. He is collaborating with Earl J. Hess on a forthcoming history of the Pea Ridge campaign and a guide to the battlefield.

John Y. Simon is professor of history at Southern Illinois University at Carbondale, executive director of the Ulysses S. Grant Association, and editor of sixteen volumes of *The Papers of Ulysses S. Grant.*

Richard J. Sommers is chief archivist-historian of the U.S. Army Military History Institute and author of *Richmond Redeemed: The Siege at Petersburg,* which was awarded the National Historical Society's Bell I. Wiley Prize. He is on the board of the Society of Civil War Historians and of the Jefferson Davis Association.

Richard W. Stephenson is the specialist in American cartographic history in the Geography and Map Division of the Library of Congress. He is the compiler of several Library of Congress bibliographies, including the recently published second edition of *Civil War Maps: An Annotated List of Maps and Atlases in the Library of Congress.* He also compiled the facsimile atlas *The Cartography of Northern Virginia.*

William A. Stofft is director of management at Headquarters, Department of the Army. He was formerly the chief of military history for the U.S. Army and supervised the staff ride program for the army leadership. He is also coeditor of *America's First Battles, 1776–1965.*

Robert G. Tanner practices law in the Atlanta area and is the author of *Stonewall in the Valley.*

Noah Andre Trudeau is a broadcast producer for National Public Radio. He writes on American musical subjects as well as the Civil War. He is the author of *Bloody Roads South: The Wilderness to Cold Harbor, May–June, 1864.*

William H. Webster is director of Central Intelligence. He has served as a judge of the United States Court of Appeals for the Eighth Circuit and as director of the Federal Bureau of Investigation.

Joseph W. A. Whitehorne was staff historian for the inspector general of the army. He is now professor of history at Lord Fairfax Community College. He has written books and articles on military subjects, including two guidebooks, *The Battle of Cedar Creek* and *The Battle of New Market,* and is currently working on the fourth volume of a five-volume study on the army inspector general.

INDEX

THE CONSERVATION FUND

Partners in Land Conservation

The Conservation Fund works in partnership with other organizations and agencies to acquire land for conservation. As a national nonprofit organization, the Fund is committed not only to helping preserve land — wildlife habitat, open space, historic sites — but also to advancing conservation in the United States with creative ideas and new resources. Fund projects and programs include the:

Civil War Battlefield Campaign — preserving critical areas on sites from Gettysburg to the Gulf, from Glorieta to the Atlantic.

Greenways for America — helping establish open space corridors to link natural, cultural, and recreation areas.

Spring and Groundwater Resources Institute — using new techniques to protect vital groundwater reserves.

Conservation Leadership Project — increasing the effectiveness of America's nonprofit conservation organizations.

Conservation Partners — providing specialized skills in land planning and acquisition.

Conservation Enterprise Program — demonstrating how land conservation can be "good business" for individuals and corporations.

Donations from individuals, corporations, and foundations support the conservation activities of The Conservation Fund, a 501(c) (3) organization. All contributions are tax deductible to the limit permitted by law.

Proceeds to The Conservation Fund from the sale of this book are dedicated to protecting Civil War battlefields. Please join the Civil War Battlefield Campaign to preserve our nation's hallowed ground.

THE CONSERVATION FUND
CIVIL WAR BATTLEFIELD CAMPAIGN
1800 North Kent Street, Suite 1120
Arlington, Virginia 22209